MATH

ADVANTAGE

TEST COPYING MASTERS

- **Multiple-Choice (Standardized) Format Tests**
- **Free-Response Format Tests**
- **Answer Keys**
- **Management Forms**

Harcourt Brace & Company

Orlando • Atlanta • Austin • Boston • San Francisco • Chicago • Dallas • New York • Toronto • London

http://www.hbschool.com

CONTENTS

▶ Formal Assessment

Tests • Multiple-Choice Format..A1-118
Multiple-Choice Test Answers...119-148
Tests • Free-Response Format...B151-268
Free-Response Test Answers...269-298

▶ Management Forms

Test Answer Sheet...301
Grading Made Easy..303
Individual Record Form...305-314
Formal Assessment Class Record Form...315-318

Multiple-Choice Format Tests (Standardized)

The multiple-choice format is provided to assess mastery of the learning goals of the program. These tests assess concepts, skills, and problem solving. The use of these tests helps prepare students for standardized achievement tests.

There is an Inventory Test which tests the learning goals from the previous grade level. This can be used at the beginning of the year or as a placement test when a new student enters your class.

There is a Chapter Test for each chapter and a Multi-Chapter Test to be used as review after several chapters in a content cluster. Also, there are Cumulative Tests at the same point as the Multi-Chapter Tests. Each Cumulative Test reviews content from Chapter 1 through the current chapter.

Math Advantage also provides free-response format tests that parallel the multiple-choice tests. You may wish to use one form as a pretest and one form as a posttest.

Harcourt Brace School Publishers

Choose the letter of the correct answer.

1. What is the value of the digit 5 in the number 150,987,432?

    A. 5 thousands
    B. 5 ten thousands
    C. 5 millions
    D. 5 ten millions

2. Which shows the three numbers ordered from least to greatest?

    A. 20,084; 20,408; 20,480
    B. 20,480; 20,084; 20,408
    C. 20,408; 20,480; 20,084
    D. not here

3. Joel has 1,200 baseball cards. His sister has 725 baseball cards. How many more cards does Joel have than his sister?

    A. 475 more   **B.** 1,525 more
    C. 1,925 more   **D.** not here

4. What is $5,000 + 300 + 0 + 4 + 0 + 0.08 + 0.002$ in standard form?

    A. 534.082   **B.** 5,304.082
    C. 5,304.82   **D.** not here

5. $5.6 - 0.246 = n$

    A. 5.354   **B.** 5.364
    C. 5.446   **D.** not here

6. Estimate the sum to the nearest tenth.

    $\begin{array}{r} 3.12 \\ +2.78 \\ \hline \end{array}$

    A. about 5.8   **B.** about 5.9
    C. about 6.0   **D.** about 6.1

7. Find the area of the rectangle.

    8 ft

    24 ft

    A. 162 sq ft   **B.** 182 sq ft
    C. 192 sq ft   **D.** not here

8. $\begin{array}{r} 205 \\ \times\ 24 \\ \hline \end{array}$

    A. 4,820   **B.** 4,920
    C. 4,924   **D.** 5,920

9. Estimate the product by rounding each factor to its greatest place-value position.

    $29 \times 537 = n$

    A. 10,000   **B.** 12,000
    C. 15,000   **D.** not here

10. Estimate the quotient.

    $4\overline{)174}$

    A. about 30   **B.** about 40
    C. about 50   **D.** about 60

11. $45\overline{)374}$

    A. 7 r14   **B.** 7 r16
    C. 8 r16   **D.** not here

12. Choose the number sentence that can be used to solve the word problem.

Mel bought a new stereo that cost $1,380. She paid for it in 12 monthly payments. How much was each payment?

A. $1,380 + 12 = n
B. $1,380 − 12 = n
C. $1,380 × 12 = n
D. $1,380 ÷ 12 = n

13. What is the mean for the set of data?

24, 13, 12, 14, 12

A. 12   **B.** 13
C. 14   **D.** 15

14. Use the graph.

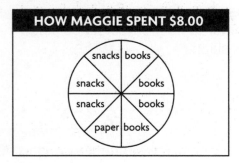

| HOW MAGGIE SPENT $8.00 |
| snacks books |
| snacks books |
| snacks books |
| paper books |

What fraction of her money did Maggie spend on snacks?

A. $\frac{1}{8}$ **B.** $\frac{2}{8}$

C. $\frac{3}{8}$ **D.** $\frac{4}{8}$

15. From a bag that has 7 red marbles and 2 blue marbles, pulling a red marble is __?__ .

A. certain   **B.** impossible
C. likely   **D.** unlikely

16. Use the spinner.

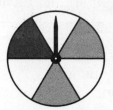

What is the probability the pointer will stop on the darker shaded section?

A. $\frac{1}{6}$ **B.** $\frac{2}{6}$

C. $\frac{3}{6}$ **D.** $\frac{4}{6}$

17.   3.46
       × 2.8
       ‾‾‾‾‾

A. 0.9688   **B.** 9.688
C. 96.88   **D.** 968.8

18. 2)‾17.42

A. 0.871   **B.** 8.71
C. 87.1   **D.** not here

19. Which is the most reasonable unit for finding the length of a piece of notebook paper?

A. millimeter   **B.** centimeter
C. meter   **D.** kilometer

20. In a 5-person relay race, each person on the relay team must run 600 m. How many kilometers long is the whole race?

A. 0.3 km   **B.** 3 km
C. 30 km   **D.** not here

Harcourt Brace School Publishers

21. Choose the fraction shown by the shaded area on the fraction strip.

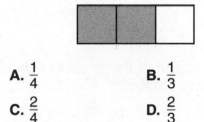

  A. $\frac{1}{4}$ **B.** $\frac{1}{3}$

  C. $\frac{2}{4}$ **D.** $\frac{2}{3}$

22. Compare the fractions using the LCM.

$$\frac{3}{4} \bigcirc \frac{2}{3}$$

  A. $\frac{6}{8} > \frac{5}{8}$ **B.** $\frac{3}{6} < \frac{4}{6}$

  C. $\frac{30}{40} > \frac{20}{40}$ **D.** $\frac{9}{12} > \frac{8}{12}$

23. Use division to find an equivalent fraction for $\frac{8}{24}$.

  A. $\frac{1}{3}$ **B.** $\frac{1}{2}$

  C. $\frac{4}{8}$ **D.** $\frac{2}{3}$

24. Mike made some bread. He used 2 cups of whole wheat flour. He used 8 cups of flour in all. In simplest terms, what fraction of the flour was whole wheat flour?

  A. $\frac{1}{8}$ **B.** $\frac{1}{4}$

  C. $\frac{1}{3}$ **D.** $\frac{1}{2}$

For questions 25–26, use fraction strips to find the sum or difference expressed in simplest form.

25. $\frac{1}{2} + \frac{3}{10} = \underline{\ ?\ }$

  A. $\frac{3}{8}$ **B.** $\frac{3}{4}$ **C.** $\frac{4}{5}$ **D.** $\frac{5}{10}$

26. $\frac{3}{4} - \frac{1}{3} = \underline{\ ?\ }$

  A. $\frac{1}{6}$ **B.** $\frac{5}{12}$

  C. $\frac{7}{12}$ **D.** $\frac{5}{8}$

27. Estimate the sum. $\frac{8}{9} + \frac{1}{6}$

  A. about $\frac{1}{2}$ **B.** about 1

  C. about $1\frac{1}{2}$ **D.** about 2

28. Find the answer in simplest form.

$$2\frac{1}{3}$$
$$+3\frac{5}{6}$$

  A. $5\frac{1}{6}$ **B.** $5\frac{2}{3}$

  C. $6\frac{1}{6}$ **D.** $6\frac{2}{3}$

29. Book reports are due on May 15. Jen will work on her report for 1 week. When should she begin working on the report?

  A. April 15   **B.** May 1

  C. May 8   **D.** May 16

30. Find the product in simplest form.

$$\frac{3}{4} \times 2\frac{1}{2} = n$$

  A. $n = \frac{3}{4}$ **B.** $n = \frac{7}{8}$

  C. $n = 1\frac{3}{4}$ **D.** $n = 1\frac{7}{8}$

Name _____

31. Use this figure.

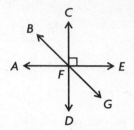

Which of these angles is not a right angle?

A. ∠AFB **B.** ∠AFD
C. ∠CFE **D.** ∠DFE

32. Which quadrilateral has 4 congruent sides and 4 right angles?

A. rhombus **B.** parallelogram
C. rectangle **D.** square

33. A cake platter has a diameter of 12 in. What is the radius of the platter?

A. 1 in. **B.** 4 in.
C. 6 in. **D.** 12 in.

34. Identify the solid figure.

A. rectangular prism
B. pentagonal pyramid
C. rectangular pyramid
D. triangular pyramid

35. Which ratio is equivalent to 4:24?

A. 1:4 **B.** 6:1
C. 2:12 **D.** not here

36. Find the length of the missing side in the similar triangles.

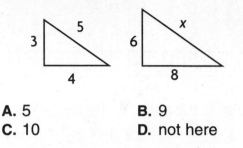

A. 5 **B.** 9
C. 10 **D.** not here

37. What is 25% written as a decimal?

A. 0.025 **B.** 0.25
C. 2.5 **D.** 25

38. What is $\frac{3}{10}$ written as a percent?

A. 3% **B.** 10%
C. 30% **D.** 100%

Form A • Multiple-Choice   A4   ▶ **Stop!**

Name _____

Choose the letter of the correct answer.

For questions 1–2, use the place-value chart below.

PLACE VALUE									
Millions	Hundred Thousands	Ten Thousands	Thousands	Hundreds	Tens	Ones	Tenths	Hundredths	Thousandths
1	4	2	6	3	2	1	.0	7	9

1. What is the value of the digit 4?

  A. 4 tens
  B. 4 thousands
  C. 4 ten thousands
  D. 4 hundred thousands

2. What is the value of the digit 7 in the place-value chart?

  A. 7 tenths
  B. 7 hundredths
  C. 7 thousandths
  D. 7 ten-thousandths

3. What is the value of the digit 8 in the number 407,836.21?

  A. 8 hundreds
  B. 8 thousands
  C. 8 ten thousands
  D. 8 hundred thousands

4. What is the value of the digit 5 in the number 1.275?

  A. 5 tens   B. 5 hundreds
  C. 5 hundredths   D. 5 thousandths

5. What is the standard form of four million, sixty thousand, one hundred two?

  A. 4,060,102   B. 460,102
  C. 46,000,102   D. 4,006,102,000

6. Which shows six hundredths written in standard form?

  A. 0.006
  B. 0.06
  C. 0.60
  D. 600.0

7. Which is greater than 10.25?

  A. 10.4
  B. 1.40
  C. 0.14
  D. 10.04

8. Which shows the numbers written in order from least to greatest?

  A. 2.2, 2.02, 2.12
  B. 2.2, 2.12, 2.02
  C. 2.12, 2.02, 2.2
  D. 2.02, 2.12, 2.2

9. The batting averages of three players are 0.240, 0.229, and 0.252. Which shows these averages written in order from greatest to least?

  A. 0.229, 0.240, 0.252
  B. 0.252, 0.229, 0.240
  C. 0.252, 0.240, 0.229
  D. 0.240, 0.252, 0.229

10. A rabbit can run 56.3 km per hour, a coyote 69.2 km per hour, a giraffe 51.3 km per hour, and a greyhound 63.3 km per hour. Which of the four animals runs the fastest?

  A. rabbit
  B. coyote
  C. giraffe
  D. greyhound

Form A • Multiple-Choice   A5   **Go on. ▶**

11. How can you change the fraction $\frac{1}{6}$ to a decimal?

   A. Multiply 10 by $\frac{1}{6}$.
   B. Divide 10 by $\frac{1}{6}$.
   C. Divide 6 by 1.
   D. Divide 1 by 6.

12. What is 0.07 written as a fraction?

   A. $\frac{7}{10}$ **B.** $\frac{1}{7}$

   C. $\frac{7}{100}$ **D.** $\frac{1}{70}$

13. What is $\frac{2}{5}$ written as a decimal?

   A. 0.10   **B.** 0.20
   C. 0.25   **D.** 0.40

14. What decimal makes the following inequality true?

$$\frac{15}{25} < \underline{\ ?\ }$$

   A. 0.20   **B.** 0.45
   C. 0.50   **D.** 0.8

15. The lake was 1 mi away. Terry rode his bike 0.25 of the way. What is the distance Terry rode, expressed as a fraction?

   A. $\frac{1}{8}$ mi   **B.** $\frac{1}{5}$ mi

   C. $\frac{1}{4}$ mi   **D.** $\frac{1}{3}$ mi

16. Katie walked $\frac{3}{5}$ mi. What is the distance she walked, expressed as a decimal?

   A. 0.006 mi
   B. 0.06 mi
   C. 0.6 mi
   D. 6.0 mi

17. How many zeros are in the standard form of 10^6?

   A. 4   **B.** 5
   C. 6   **D.** 7

18. Which expression represents 5^2?

   A. $5 + 2$
   B. 5×2
   C. 5×5
   D. $2 \times 2 \times 2 \times 2 \times 2$

19. What is $4 \times 4 \times 4 \times 4 \times 4$ written in exponent form?

   A. 4^3 **B.** 3^4
   C. 4^5 **D.** 5^4

20. What is the value of 6^3?

   A. 18   **B.** 36
   C. 42   **D.** 216

21. Which is less than 0?

   A. $^-2$ **B.** 0
   C. 4   **D.** 6

22. Which of these shows the integers written in order from least to greatest?

   A. 0, $^-4$, 2, 4
   B. 0, 2, $^-2$, 4
   C. $^-4$, 0, 2, 4
   D. $^-2$, 2, 0, $^-4$

23. Which of these shows the integers written in order from least to greatest?

   A. 1, $^-3$, $^-5$, 0
   B. 1, $^-5$, $^-3$, 0
   C. $^-3$, $^-5$, 1, 0
   D. $^-5$, $^-3$, 0, 1

24. What is the opposite of $^-4$?

   A. $-\frac{1}{4}$ **B.** $^+\frac{1}{4}$

   C. $^+4$ **D.** $^+4^2$

Choose the letter of the correct answer.

For questions 1–4, use mental math.

1. $7 + 18 + 13$

   A. 28   B. 31
   C. 35   D. 38

2. $29 + 41 + 31 + 9$

   A. 99   B. 100
   C. 110   D. 113

3. $53 - 29$

   A. 21   B. 22
   C. 23   D. 24

4. $62 - 17$

   A. 27   B. 38
   C. 40   D. 45

5. A rectangular box has a perimeter of 50 ft. The box is 5 ft longer than it is wide. What is the width of the box?

   A. 10 ft   B. 15 ft
   C. 20 ft   D. 40 ft

6. Barry sold a total of 42 green or red banners. He sold 10 more green banners than red banners. How many green banners did he sell?

   A. 16 banners
   B. 22 banners
   C. 26 banners
   D. 32 banners

7. The Rogers hockey team played a total of 20 games. They tied in 3 games and lost 1 more game than they won. How many games did they win?

   A. 7 games
   B. 8 games
   C. 9 games
   D. 10 games

8. Ms. Lee baked a total of 60 pies. She baked a dozen more apple pies than lemon pies. How many apple pies did she bake?

   A. 18 pies   B. 24 pies
   C. 36 pies   D. 48 pies

9. Which property of multiplication is being used below?

   $7 \times 25 = (7 \times 20) + (7 \times 5)$

   A. Distributive Property
   B. Property of One
   C. Commutative Property
   D. Associative Property

For questions 10–11, use mental math to find the product.

10. 4×44

   A. 156   B. 160   C. 176   D. 180

11. $4 \times 10 \times 6$

   A. 240   B. 260   C. 360   D. 400

12. Find the missing factor:

   $27 \times 43 = (27 \times \blacksquare) + (27 \times 3)$

   A. 34   B. 40   C. 43   D. 74

13. Rob is solving the multiplication problem below. What mistake, if any, has Rob made?

$$
\begin{array}{r}
126 \\
\times\ 23 \\
\hline
378 \\
252
\end{array}
$$

   A. His work has no mistake.
   B. The product 3×126 is 370.
   C. The products are lined up incorrectly.
   D. He did not multiply by the hundreds.

Form A • Multiple-Choice   A7   **Go on.** ▶

14. In this division problem, where would you put the first digit of the quotient?

$17\overline{)1,840}$

A. in the ones place
B. in the tens place
C. in the hundreds place
D. in the thousands place

15. 120
$\times\ 35$

A. 960
B. 3,200
C. 4,100
D. not here

16. 437
$\times 226$

A. 97,862
B. 98,762
C. 106,662
D. 107,662

17. $6\overline{)324}$

A. 50 r4   B. 52 r2
C. 53   D. 54

18. $20\overline{)4,060}$

A. 203   B. 213
C. 230   D. 233

19. Clea's parents bought a computer for $1,530.00. They are paying for it in 18 monthly payments. How much is each payment?

A. $77.50
B. $85.00
C. $95.00
D. $127.50

20. The Stone family spends $125 on groceries each week. How much does the family spend on groceries in one year? (HINT: 1 yr = 52 wk.)

A. $650   B. $2,500
C. $5,250   D. $6,500

21. Choose the best estimate of the sum.

5,199
4,206
$+3,749$

A. 11,000   B. 12,000
C. 13,000   D. 15,000

22. Choose the best estimate of the quotient.

$1,765 \div 28$

A. 0.6   B. 60
C. 600   D. 6,000

23. The music store sold 589 CDs of waterfall sounds and 209 audiotapes of the sounds. About how many more CDs were sold than audiotapes?

A. about 200 more CDs
B. about 300 more CDs
C. about 400 more CDs
D. about 500 more CDs

24. The movie theater at the waterfall park had 213 shows this summer. The theater, which holds 480 people, was full for every show. About how many people attended the shows?

A. about 10,000 people
B. about 10,200 people
C. about 80,000 people
D. about 100,000 people

Choose the letter of the correct answer.

For questions 1–2, estimate the sum.

1. 0.85 + 2.25 + 12.95

A. 6   **B.** 14
C. 16   **D.** 18

2. 5.42 + 0.76 + 4.06

A. 7   **B.** 9
C. 10   **D.** 15

For questions 3–4, find the sum.

3. 0.26 + 0.04

A. 0.03   **B.** 0.3
C. 0.36   **D.** 0.66

4. 3.2 + 10.07 + 0.64

A. 4.84   **B.** 9.6
C. 13.91   **D.** 19.6

5. A hiking trail has four sections. The lengths of the sections are 1.8 mi, 2.5 mi, 1.05 mi, and 0.75 mi. How many miles long is the hiking trail?

A. 5.6 mi
B. 6.1 mi
C. 7.05 mi
D. 7.5 mi

6. Rhonda spent $4.50 for a movie ticket. Her bus fare to the movie was $0.85 each way. At the movie, she bought popcorn for $1.60. How much did she spend in all?

A. $6.10
B. $6.80
C. $6.95
D. $7.80

7. 5.5 − 0.7

A. 2.2   **B.** 2.8
C. 3.2   **D.** 4.8

8. $7.63 − $1.58

A. $5.05   **B.** $5.15
C. $5.95   **D.** $6.05

9. 42.09 − 11.6

A. 30.49   **B.** 31.03
C. 31.3   **D.** 31.49

10. 18 − 10.005

A. 7.995
B. 8.995
C. 16.995
D. 16.095

11. Mrs. Ruiz drove 127.8 mi on Tuesday and 204.3 mi on Wednesday. How much farther did she drive on Wednesday?

A. 72.5 mi
B. 76.5 mi
C. 77.5 mi
D. 78.5 mi

12. The winning time in a swimming race was 91.26 sec. The second-place finisher had a time of 92.08 sec. What was the difference between the two times?

A. 0.66 sec
B. 0.72 sec
C. 0.82 sec
D. 1.14 sec

Name _____

13. Use the decimal square to find 3 × 0.12.

0.12 0.12 0.12

A. 0.036 B. 0.36
C. 3.6 D. 36.0

14. How many decimal places are there in the product 0.055 × 0.07?

A. 2 decimal places
B. 3 decimal places
C. 4 decimal places
D. 5 decimal places

15. 5 × 0.7

A. 0.035 B. 0.35
C. 35 D. not here

16. $2.75 × 8

A. $16.60 B. $22.00
C. $22.50 D. not here

17. 0.3 × 0.4

A. 0.12 B. 1.12
C. 1.2 D. not here

18. 0.27 × 4.2

A. 0.1134 B. 1.134
C. 1.34 D. not here

19. Brittany charges $3.50 per hour for baby-sitting. If she baby-sits for 4.5 hr, how much will she earn?

A. $14.00 B. $14.75
C. $15.25 D. $15.75

20. Craig is planning a cookout for 27 students. He needs 0.25 lb of hamburger for each student. How many pounds of hamburger does he need in all?

A. 6.75 lb B. 12.5 lb
C. 16.5 lb D. 67.5 lb

21. Which of these numbers should you multiply by to make the divisor in the division problem a whole number?

$0.65)\overline{2.145}$

A. 1 B. 10
C. 100 D. not here

22. 15.3 ÷ 9

A. 0.17 B. 1.7
C. 1.77 D. 17

23. $0.18)\overline{3.96}$

A. 0.022 B. 0.22
C. 2.2 D. 22

24. 13.44 ÷ 0.24

A. 0.56 B. 5.06
C. 5.6 D. 56

Form A • Multiple-Choice A10 ▶ **Stop!**

Harcourt Brace School Publishers

Choose the letter of the correct answer.

1. Which of these numbers is a prime number?

A. 27	**B.** 29
C. 33	**D.** 39

2. What is the next multiple of 12?

12, 24, 36, __?__

A. 40	**B.** 42
C. 44	**D.** not here

3. What are the factors of 49?

A. 1, 7
B. 1, 3, 7, 13, 49
C. 1, 7, 49
D. 3, 7, 13

4. Which of these numbers is a composite number?

A. 2	**B.** 17
C. 51	**D.** 47

5. Herbert has a game every seventh day during November. His first game is on November 7. How many games does he have in November?

A. 3 games
B. 4 games
C. 5 games
D. 7 games

6. In February Dorothy runs 2 mi every third day. She begins on February 3. How many miles does she run in February?

A. 9 mi	**B.** 12 mi
C. 18 mi	**D.** 24 mi

7. What is the missing factor?

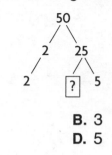

A. 2	**B.** 3
C. 4	**D.** 5

8. What is the missing factor?

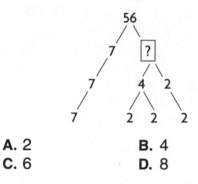

A. 2	**B.** 4
C. 6	**D.** 8

9. What is the prime factorization of 39?

A. 3×13	**B.** $3 \times 3 \times 7$
C. $3^2 \times 2$	**D.** $3 \times 6 \times 3$

10. Solve for n to complete the prime factorization.

$2^n = 16$

A. 2	**B.** 4
C. 6	**D.** 8

11. What is the least common multiple of 3 and 4?

3:   3   6   9   12   15   18   21   24

4:   4   8   12   16   20   24   28   31

A. 7	**B.** 8
C. 12	**D.** 24

Form A • Multiple-Choice   A17   **Go on.** ▶

Name _____

12. Use the factor trees to find the greatest common factor of 16 and 12.

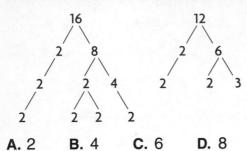

A. 2   **B.** 4   **C.** 6   **D.** 8

13. What is the LCM of 6 and 10?

A. 6   **B.** 10   **C.** 30   **D.** 60

14. Which pair of numbers has 24 as the LCM?

A. 3, 4   **B.** 3, 6
C. 8, 12   **D.** 24, 48

15. What is the GCF of 24 and 40?

A. 2   **B.** 4   **C.** 8   **D.** 12

16. Harry has 40 erasers and 60 pencils to put in packages. All the packages will contain the same number of erasers and the same number of pencils. What is the greatest number of packages he can make?

A. 10   **B.** 12   **C.** 15   **D.** 20

17. Which fraction is the simplest form of $\frac{8}{12}$?

A. $\frac{2}{3}$ **B.** $\frac{3}{4}$

C. $\frac{4}{6}$ **D.** not here

18. Which fraction is the simplest form of $\frac{35}{40}$?

A. $\frac{4}{5}$ **B.** $\frac{5}{7}$

C. $\frac{7}{8}$ **D.** not here

19. Which fraction is the simplest form of $\frac{36}{48}$?

A. $\frac{2}{3}$ **B.** $\frac{3}{4}$

C. $\frac{12}{16}$ **D.** not here

20. The model shows 3 whole pizzas and $\frac{1}{4}$ of another pizza. What fraction could you use to show this?

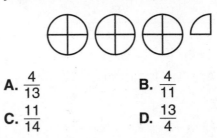

A. $\frac{4}{13}$ **B.** $\frac{4}{11}$

C. $\frac{11}{14}$ **D.** $\frac{13}{4}$

21. What is $2\frac{1}{2}$ written as a fraction?

A. $\frac{2}{5}$ **B.** $\frac{3}{2}$

C. $\frac{5}{2}$ **D.** $\frac{12}{4}$

22. What is $\frac{22}{7}$ written as a mixed number?

A. $5\frac{5}{7}$ **B.** 3

C. $3\frac{1}{7}$ **D.** $3\frac{3}{7}$

23. What is the missing number?

$$5\frac{3}{12} = \frac{\blacksquare}{12}$$

A. 36   **B.** 48
C. 63   **D.** not here

24. What is the missing number?

$$\frac{\blacksquare}{4} = 4\frac{3}{4}$$

A. 11   **B.** 15
C. 16   **D.** 19

Harcourt Brace School Publishers

Name _____

Choose the letter of the correct answer.

1. Use the model to find the sum.

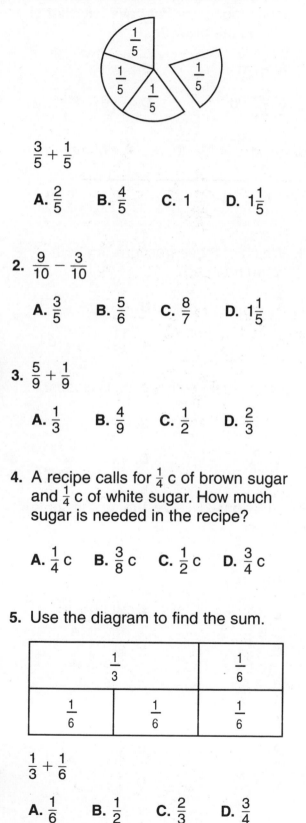

$$\frac{3}{5} + \frac{1}{5}$$

A. $\frac{2}{5}$ B. $\frac{4}{5}$ C. 1   D. $1\frac{1}{5}$

2. $\frac{9}{10} - \frac{3}{10}$

A. $\frac{3}{5}$ B. $\frac{5}{6}$ C. $\frac{8}{7}$ D. $1\frac{1}{5}$

3. $\frac{5}{9} + \frac{1}{9}$

A. $\frac{1}{3}$ B. $\frac{4}{9}$ C. $\frac{1}{2}$ D. $\frac{2}{3}$

4. A recipe calls for $\frac{1}{4}$ c of brown sugar and $\frac{1}{4}$ c of white sugar. How much sugar is needed in the recipe?

A. $\frac{1}{4}$ c   B. $\frac{3}{8}$ c   C. $\frac{1}{2}$ c   D. $\frac{3}{4}$ c

5. Use the diagram to find the sum.

$\frac{1}{3}$		$\frac{1}{6}$
$\frac{1}{6}$	$\frac{1}{6}$	$\frac{1}{6}$

$$\frac{1}{3} + \frac{1}{6}$$

A. $\frac{1}{6}$ B. $\frac{1}{2}$ C. $\frac{2}{3}$ D. $\frac{3}{4}$

6. Use the diagram to find the difference.

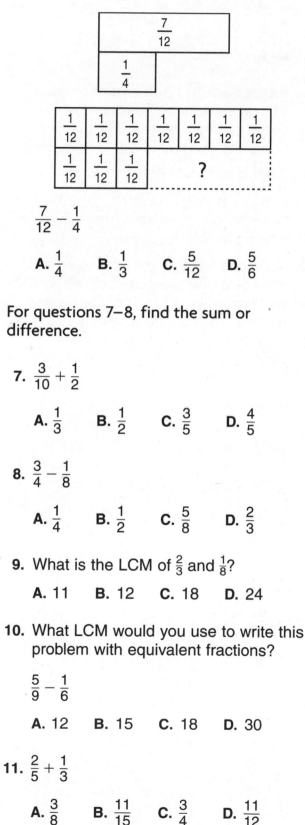

$$\frac{7}{12} - \frac{1}{4}$$

A. $\frac{1}{4}$ B. $\frac{1}{3}$ C. $\frac{5}{12}$ D. $\frac{5}{6}$

For questions 7–8, find the sum or difference.

7. $\frac{3}{10} + \frac{1}{2}$

A. $\frac{1}{3}$ B. $\frac{1}{2}$ C. $\frac{3}{5}$ D. $\frac{4}{5}$

8. $\frac{3}{4} - \frac{1}{8}$

A. $\frac{1}{4}$ B. $\frac{1}{2}$ C. $\frac{5}{8}$ D. $\frac{2}{3}$

9. What is the LCM of $\frac{2}{3}$ and $\frac{1}{8}$?

A. 11   B. 12   C. 18   D. 24

10. What LCM would you use to write this problem with equivalent fractions?

$$\frac{5}{9} - \frac{1}{6}$$

A. 12   B. 15   C. 18   D. 30

11. $\frac{2}{5} + \frac{1}{3}$

A. $\frac{3}{8}$ B. $\frac{11}{15}$ C. $\frac{3}{4}$ D. $\frac{11}{12}$

Form A • Multiple-Choice   **Go on.** ▶

12. $\frac{3}{4} + \frac{3}{8}$

A. $\frac{2}{3}$
B. $\frac{7}{8}$
C. $1\frac{1}{8}$
D. 1

13. Renee spent $\frac{1}{2}$ hr on math homework, $\frac{1}{4}$ hr on spelling homework, and $\frac{3}{4}$ hr on social studies homework. How many hours did she spend doing homework?

A. 1 hr
B. $1\frac{1}{4}$ hr
C. $1\frac{1}{2}$ hr
D. $1\frac{3}{4}$ hr

14. Katie planted $\frac{2}{5}$ of her garden on Saturday. She planted $\frac{3}{10}$ of the garden on Sunday. How much of the garden did she plant on the weekend?

A. $\frac{1}{3}$
B. $\frac{1}{2}$
C. $\frac{3}{5}$
D. $\frac{7}{10}$

15. $\frac{5}{6} - \frac{1}{2}$

A. $\frac{1}{3}$
B. $\frac{3}{8}$
C. $\frac{5}{12}$
D. $\frac{1}{2}$

16. $\frac{2}{3} - \frac{3}{8}$

A. $\frac{5}{24}$
B. $\frac{7}{24}$
C. $\frac{1}{3}$
D. $\frac{5}{12}$

17. Terri walks $\frac{9}{10}$ mi to school. Louisa walks $\frac{3}{5}$ mi to school. How much farther does Terri walk than Louisa?

A. $\frac{1}{10}$ mi
B. $\frac{1}{5}$ mi
C. $\frac{3}{10}$ mi
D. $\frac{3}{5}$ mi

18. Pat needed $\frac{1}{2}$ yd of fabric to make a pillow. She bought $\frac{7}{8}$ yd of fabric. How much fabric will Pat have left after she makes the pillow?

A. $\frac{1}{4}$ yd
B. $\frac{3}{8}$ yd
C. $\frac{7}{16}$ yd
D. $\frac{1}{2}$ yd

For questions 19–20, use the number line.

$$\overset{\displaystyle 0 \quad \frac{1}{12} \quad \frac{2}{12} \quad \frac{3}{12} \quad \frac{4}{12} \quad \frac{5}{12} \quad \frac{1}{2} \quad \frac{7}{12} \quad \frac{8}{12} \quad \frac{9}{12} \quad \frac{10}{12} \quad \frac{11}{12} \quad 1}{\longleftarrow\!\!\mid\!\mid\!\mid\!\mid\!\mid\!\mid\!\mid\!\mid\!\mid\!\mid\!\mid\!\mid\!\mid\!\!\longrightarrow}$$

19. Which of these fractions is about $\frac{1}{2}$ when rounded?

A. $\frac{1}{12}$
B. $\frac{3}{12}$
C. $\frac{7}{12}$
D. $\frac{11}{12}$

20. Which of these fractions is closest to 1?

A. $\frac{2}{12}$
B. $\frac{3}{12}$
C. $\frac{8}{12}$
D. $\frac{11}{12}$

For questions 21–22, estimate the sum or difference.

21. $\frac{1}{16} + \frac{2}{6}$

A. $\frac{1}{2}$
B. 1
C. $1\frac{1}{2}$
D. 2

22. $\frac{7}{8} - \frac{1}{12}$

A. 0
B. $\frac{1}{2}$
C. 1
D. $1\frac{1}{2}$

Name _____

Choose the letter of the correct answer.

1. Which is the standard form of two million, four hundred six thousand, five hundred thirty?

   A. 246,530 **B.** 2,406,530
   C. 2,406,503 **D.** 2,460,530

2. What is the value of the digit 5 in the number 8.952?

   A. 5 tens **B.** 5 hundreds
   C. 5 hundredths **D.** 5 thousandths

3. What is $\frac{3}{4}$ written as a decimal?

   A. 0.30 **B.** 0.40
   C. 0.70 **D.** 0.75

4. What is $4 \times 4 \times 4 \times 4 \times 4$ written in exponent form?

   A. 4^4 **B.** 4^5
   C. 5^4 **D.** 5^5

5. Which of these shows the integers written in order from least to greatest?

   A. 0, ⁻2, 9, 2
   B. 0, 2, ⁻2, 9
   C. ⁻9, 0, 2, 9
   D. ⁻2, 2, 0, ⁻9

6. Use mental math to find the sum.

   $25 + 18 + 15 + 22$

   A. 70 **B.** 80
   C. 90 **D.** 100

7. Jeff has a total of 26 model cars and trucks. He has 4 more cars than trucks. How many trucks does Jeff have?

   A. 9 trucks **B.** 11 trucks
   C. 13 trucks **D.** not here

8. 240
    $\times$ 57

   A. 12,680 **B.** 13,580
   C. 13,680 **D.** not here

9. $7\overline{)3,654}$

   A. 520 **B.** 520 r2
   C. 522 **D.** 522 r2

10. Choose the best estimate of the product.

     58
    $\times$39

    A. 1,500 **B.** 1,800
    C. 2,400 **D.** 3,000

11. The water-skiing show was held once a day for 11 days. There were 5,103 people who attended the shows. About how many people attended each of the shows?

    A. about 5 people
    B. about 50 people
    C. about 500 people
    D. about 5,000 people

12. 73.52 − 15.7

A. 57.22 B. 57.82
C. 62.22 D. 67.82

13. Brian bought 5.5 lb of apples at $0.80 a pound. How much did the apples cost?

A. $4.00 B. $4.40
C. $4.80 D. $5.00

14. 26.88 ÷ 0.42

A. 0.064 B. 0.64
C. 6.4 D. 64

15. Which of these numbers is a composite number?

A. 13 B. 17
C. 18 D. 23

16. What is the prime factorization of 54?

A. $2^2 \times 3$ B. $2^3 \times 3$
C. 2×3^2 D. 2×3^3

17. What is the GCF of 12 and 20?

A. 2 B. 4
C. 6 D. 10

18. Which fraction is the simplest form of $\frac{12}{20}$?

A. $\frac{2}{3}$ B. $\frac{3}{5}$
C. $\frac{4}{10}$ D. not here

19. What is $\frac{20}{7}$ written as a mixed number?

A. $1\frac{4}{5}$ B. $1\frac{6}{7}$
C. $2\frac{4}{5}$ D. $2\frac{6}{7}$

20. What is the missing number?

$4\frac{2}{3} = \frac{?}{3}$

A. 10 B. 12
C. 14 D. 15

For questions 21–22, find the sum or difference. Answers are in simplest form.

21. $\frac{8}{9} - \frac{5}{9}$

A. $\frac{1}{9}$ B. $\frac{1}{3}$
C. $\frac{1}{2}$ D. $1\frac{5}{9}$

22. $\frac{3}{4} + \frac{5}{8}$

A. $\frac{3}{8}$ B. $1\frac{1}{8}$
C. $1\frac{1}{4}$ D. $1\frac{3}{8}$

23. Estimate the difference.

$\frac{11}{12} - \frac{4}{7}$

A. 0 B. $\frac{1}{2}$
C. 1 D. $1\frac{1}{2}$

For questions 24–25, find the sum or difference. Answers are in simplest form.

24. $2\frac{1}{4} + 3\frac{7}{12}$

   A. $5\frac{5}{12}$ **B.** $5\frac{5}{6}$

   C. $6\frac{5}{12}$ **D.** $6\frac{5}{6}$

25. $6\frac{3}{4} - 1\frac{1}{10}$

   A. $4\frac{7}{20}$ **B.** $4\frac{7}{10}$

   C. $5\frac{7}{10}$ **D.** not here

26. Choose the best estimate for the word problem.

Josh bought $4\frac{9}{10}$ lb of potatoes on Monday and $2\frac{1}{2}$ lb of potatoes on Tuesday. About how many pounds of potatoes did he buy?

   A. about 6   **B.** about $6\frac{1}{2}$

   C. about 7   **D.** about $7\frac{1}{2}$

For questions 27–28, find the product or quotient. Answers are in simplest form.

27. $2\frac{2}{7} \times \frac{7}{8}$

   A. $1\frac{1}{8}$ **B.** $1\frac{5}{8}$

   C. 2   **D.** $2\frac{1}{8}$

28. $\frac{7}{12} \div \frac{1}{3}$

   A. $\frac{1}{4}$ **B.** $\frac{3}{4}$

   C. $1\frac{1}{4}$ **D.** $1\frac{3}{4}$

29. Jean wants to make a rectangular pen for her dog with an area of $48\frac{1}{2}$ sq ft. The length of the pen will be 5 ft. How wide should the pen be?

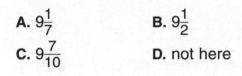

   A. $9\frac{1}{7}$ **B.** $9\frac{1}{2}$

   C. $9\frac{7}{10}$ **D.** not here

30. An angle that measures 120° is classified as a(n) __?__ .

   A. obtuse angle   **B.** right angle

   C. acute angle   **D.** straight angle

31. Which could be the measure of the angle shown below?

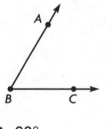

   A. 60°   **B.** 90°

   C. 135°   **D.** 180°

32. What construction do the figures below represent?

   A. congruent line segments
   B. bisected line segments
   C. congruent angles
   D. perpendicular line segments

Harcourt Brace School Publishers

Name _____

33. How many angles does a hexagon have?

A. 5   **B.** 6

C. 8   **D.** 10

34. This figure has rotational symmetry. What is the angle measure of each turn?

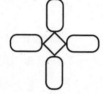

A. 45°   **B.** 90°

C. 120°   **D.** 180°

35. Choose the figure that is a reflection of the original figure.

Original   Figure 1   Figure 2   Figure 3

A. Figure 1   **B.** Figure 2

C. Figure 3   **D.** not here

36. Bryon is planning a design that will tessellate a plane. Which shape could he *not* use?

A. octagon   **B.** triangle

C. square   **D.** hexagon

37. Jen built a rectangular pyramid, using toothpicks for edges and miniature marshmallows for vertices. How many toothpicks did she use?

A. 6 toothpicks   **B.** 8 toothpicks

C. 10 toothpicks   **D.** 12 toothpicks

38. What solid figure has these views?

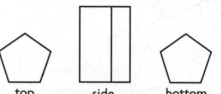

top   side   bottom

A. pentagonal pyramid

B. pentagonal prism

C. hexagonal pyramid

D. hexagonal prism

39. The top and bottom views of a solid figure are circles. The front view is a rectangle. What kind of figure is it?

A. cube   **B.** cone

C. cylinder   **D.** rectangular prism

40. Blair wants to make a paperweight by covering each face of a hexagonal pyramid with a separate piece of paper. How many pieces of paper will she use?

A. 6   **B.** 7

C. 8   **D.** 9

Choose the letter of the correct answer.

1. Which of the following is a numerical expression?

   A. $r^2 - 3$ B. $x + 4$

   C. $2\frac{1}{2} + \frac{3}{5}$ D. $3a - 1$

2. Choose the algebraic expression that matches the word expression.

   18 more than x

   A. $x - 18$ B. $18 - x$
   C. $x > 18$ D. $x + 18$

3. A baseball team with 20 players ate pizza after a game. The players were given equal amounts of pizza. If y represents the total number of pizza slices, which algebraic expression represents how many pizza slices each player got?

   A. $y \div 20$ B. $y - 20$
   C. $y + 20$ D. $20 \times y$

4. Evaluate this numerical expression.

   $15 \div 3 + 15$

   A. 5   B. 20
   C. 33   D. 75

5. Evaluate this algebraic expression for $t = 3$.

   $20 - t$

   A. 17   B. $3 - t$
   C. 20   D. 23

For questions 6–7, use the input-output table.

Input	Algebraic Expression	Output
v	$v - 8$	
8	$8 - 8$	0
9	?	?
?	$10 - 8$	?

6. What is the output when the input is 9?

   A. 0   B. 1   C. 2   D. 8

7. When the output is 2, what is the input?

   A. 8   B. 9   C. 10   D. 12

8. $x + 11 = 40$

   A. $x = 11$ B. $x = 29$
   C. $x = 31$ D. $x = 51$

9. $22 = b - 5$

   A. 5   B. 17   C. 27   D. 32

For questions 10–11, choose the equation that represents each statement.

10. Twelve more than a number, n, is 43.

   A. $n + 12 = 43$ B. $n - 12 = 43$
   C. $43 + n = 12$ D. $43 \div n = 12$

11. Eight less than a number, d, is 15.

   A. $d - 15 = 8$ B. $8 - d = 15$
   C. $d + 8 = 15$ D. $d - 8 = 15$

12. What is the inverse of the operation in the equation $7t = 28$?

A. addition   B. subtraction
C. multiplication   D. division

13. Solve the equation.

$$\frac{y}{5} = 7$$

A. 7   B. 12
C. 21   D. 35

14. How many nickels are there in $11.35?

A. 200 nickels   B. 220 nickels
C. 227 nickels   D. 229 nickels

15. What is 9°C converted to degrees Fahrenheit? Use the formula $F = (\frac{9}{5} \times C) + 32$. Round to the nearest degree.

A. 37°F   B. 45°F
C. 48°F   D. 58°F

16. What is 80°F converted to degrees Celsius? Use the formula $C = \frac{5}{9} \times (F - 32)$. Round to the nearest degree.

A. 18°C   B. 27°C
C. 48°C   D. 240°C

17. On the Fahrenheit scale, freezing is 32°. What is this temperature on the Celsius scale?

A. 0°C   B. 5°C
C. 10°C   D. 32°C

For questions 18–19, use the formula $d = r \times t$.

18. $d = \underline{\ ?\ }$

$r = 10$ mi per hr

$t = 2$ hr

A. 2 mi   B. 5 mi
C. 12 mi   D. 20 mi

19. $d = 400$ m

$r = \underline{\ ?\ }$

$t = 50$ sec

A. 4 m per sec   B. 6 m per sec
C. 8 m per sec   D. 12 m per sec

20. An airplane travels at 500 mi per hr. How far does the airplane travel in 4 hours?

A. 125 mi   B. 500 mi
C. 1,000 mi   D. 2,000 mi

21. The odometer dial on a car measures only in miles. The car was driven 23 mi. How many kilometers is this? (1 mi = 1.6 km)

A. 23.8 mi   B. 36.8 mi
C. 59.8 mi   D. 61 mi

22. Gary needed to buy 15 in. of wood to fix his shelf. The lumber store sold wood measured in centimeters. How many centimeters of wood should he buy? (1 in. = 2.54 cm)

A. 17.54 cm   B. 28.10 cm
C. 38.10 cm   D. 45.54 cm

Name _____

Choose the letter of the correct answer.

1. Which shows 7 thousandths in standard form?

   A. 0.007   B. 0.07
   C. 0.70   D. 7,000

2. Which expression represents 2^3?

   A. $2 + 3$ B. 2×3
   C. $2 \times 2 \times 2$ D. 3×3

3. Which shows the integers in order from least to greatest?

   A. 1, ⁻2, ⁻3, 0   B. 1, ⁻3, ⁻2, 0
   C. ⁻2, ⁻3, 1, 0   D. ⁻3, ⁻2, 0, 1

4. Don bought 24 pieces of fruit. He bought 6 pears and 4 more plums than apples. How many apples did he buy?

   A. 4 apples   B. 6 apples
   C. 7 apples   D. 11 apples

5. $27\overline{)1,458}$

   A. 53   B. 53 r6
   C. 54   D. 54 r2

6. $71.36 - 24.58$

   A. 33.22   B. 46.78
   C. 47.78   D. not here

7. Mike earns $4.30 per hr baby-sitting. Last week he worked 7.5 hr. How much did he earn baby-sitting last week?

   A. $32.25   B. $33.25
   C. $322.50   D. $332.50

8. $30.4 \div 4$

   A. 0.76   B. 7.6
   C. 7.66   D. not here

9. Which of these is a prime number?

   A. 15   B. 17
   C. 18   D. 21

10. Find the simplest form of $\frac{25}{30}$.

    A. $\frac{5}{7}$ B. $\frac{3}{4}$ C. $\frac{1}{3}$ D. $\frac{5}{6}$

11. Find the difference in simplest form.

    $\frac{7}{8} - \frac{3}{8}$

    A. $\frac{1}{8}$ B. $\frac{1}{4}$ C. $\frac{1}{2}$ D. $\frac{5}{8}$

12. Estimate the sum.

    $\frac{5}{12} + \frac{4}{7}$

    A. $\frac{1}{2}$ B. 1   C. $1\frac{1}{2}$ D. 2

13. Find the sum in simplest form.

    $3\frac{1}{4} + 1\frac{7}{12}$

    A. $4\frac{5}{12}$ B. $4\frac{5}{6}$
    C. $5\frac{5}{12}$ D. $5\frac{5}{6}$

14. Rob bought $3\frac{7}{8}$ lb of beef and $2\frac{1}{2}$ lb of chicken to grill for a family party. About how many pounds of meat did he buy?

    A. about 5 lb   B. about $5\frac{1}{2}$ lb

    C. about 6 lb   D. about $6\frac{1}{2}$ lb

Form A • Multiple-Choice   A65   **Chapters 1–16**   **Go on.** ▶

15. Find the product in simplest form.

$1\frac{1}{3} \times 3\frac{3}{4}$

A. $\frac{4}{15}$ **B.** 3   **C.** 5   **D.** not here

16. Find the quotient in simplest form.

$\frac{7}{12} \div \frac{2}{3}$

A. $\frac{7}{12}$ **B.** $\frac{2}{3}$ **C.** $\frac{7}{8}$ **D.** $\frac{11}{12}$

17. A flat surface that goes on forever in all directions is called a __?__ .

A. point   **B.** line
C. ray   **D.** plane

18. What is the measure of a right angle?

A. less than 90°
B. 90°
C. between 90° and 180°
D. 180°

19. How many angles does a pentagon have?

A. 4 angles   **B.** 5 angles
C. 6 angles   **D.** 8 angles

20. This figure has rotational symmetry. What is the fraction of each turn?

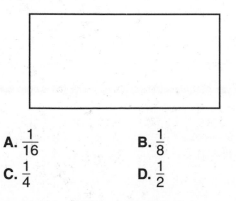

A. $\frac{1}{16}$ **B.** $\frac{1}{8}$
C. $\frac{1}{4}$ **D.** $\frac{1}{2}$

21. Which figure shows a 90° clockwise rotation around the given point?

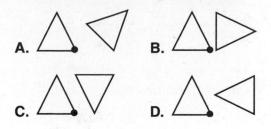

22. Cary wants to make a wallpaper design, using one shape to tessellate a plane. Which of these shapes could she use?

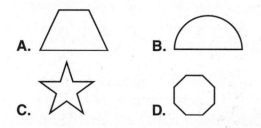

23. A paperweight is in the shape of a triangular pyramid. How many faces does the paperweight have?

A. 3 faces   **B.** 4 faces
C. 6 faces   **D.** 8 faces

24. Rich made a model of a pyramid with 12 edges. How many sides did the base of his pyramid have?

A. 4   **B.** 6   **C.** 8   **D.** 10

25. The sixth-grade class is planning to sell snacks at the next soccer game. Which decision can the students make?

A. the names of the soccer teams
B. the time the game will begin
C. the price to charge for the snacks
D. the number of people who will attend the game

26. The cafeteria staff wants to survey students to see what lunch they like. How can they get a random sample?

   A. Choose students in the salad line.

   B. Have teachers choose students.

   C. Survey all the students in one classroom.

   D. Randomly survey students as they enter the school.

For questions 27–28, use the frequency table.

FAVORITE SCHOOL SUBJECT OF STUDENTS	
Subject	**Frequency**
Reading	14
Science	12
Mathematics	16
Social Studies	10

27. Why is a bar graph the most appropriate graph for this set of data?

   A. The data show changes over time.

   B. The data were gathered in a survey.

   C. The table can be extended to show a cumulative frequency column.

   D. The data show totals for each category.

28. If one axis of the graph is labeled *Number of Students,* what should the other axis be labeled?

   A. Subject   **B.** Favorite

   C. Spelling   **D.** People

29. Is this graph misleading? If so, why?

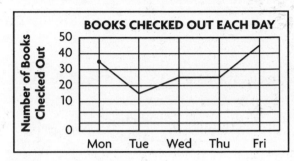

   A. no

   B. Yes; the scale is incorrect.

   C. Yes; only one week is shown.

   D. Yes; the title is wrong.

30. What is the median for this set of data?

11, 15, 14, 20, 20

   A. 11   **B.** 15   **C.** 16   **D.** 20

31. Shirts are sold in white, yellow, red, or blue. They can have long sleeves or short sleeves. How many choices for shirts are there?

   A. 6   **B.** 8   **C.** 10   **D.** not here

32. Tom's class has 5 girls and 15 boys. The teacher puts everyone's name in a bag and then draws one name without looking. What is the probability of choosing a girl's name?

   A. $\frac{1}{4}$ **B.** $\frac{1}{3}$ **C.** $\frac{3}{5}$ **D.** $\frac{3}{4}$

33. Choose the algebraic expression that matches the word expression.

thirty more than *d*

   A. $d + 30$ **B.** $d - 30$

   C. $30 \times d$ **D.** $30 > d$

34. Evaluate $x^2 + 3$ for $x = 5$.

    A. 13   **B.** 25   **C.** 28   **D.** 64

For questions 35–36, use the table.

Input	Algebraic Expression	Output
n	$n + 3$	
5	$5 + 3$	8
6	$6 + 3$	9
7	$7 + 3$	?
8	?	?

35. If the output is 10, what is the input?

    A. 5   **B.** 6   **C.** 7   **D.** 8

36. What is the output when the input is 8?

    A. 8   **B.** 9   **C.** 10   **D.** 11

For questions 37–40, solve each equation.

37. $m - 2 = 10$

    A. $m = 2$ **B.** $m = 8$
    C. $m = 10$ **D.** $m = 12$

38. $15 = k + 3$

    A. $k = 3$ **B.** $k = 15$
    C. $k = 12$ **D.** not here

39. $2w = 12$

    A. $w = 2$ **B.** $w = 6$
    C. $w = 10$ **D.** not here

40. $\frac{b}{4} = 8$

    A. $b = 2$ **B.** $b = 4$
    C. $b = 8$ **D.** not here

41. What is 100 English pounds worth in U.S. dollars? Use the formula $1.6261 \times P = D$.

    A. \$1.63   **B.** \$10.63
    C. \$16.26   **D.** \$162.61

42. To the nearest degree, what is 20°C converted to degrees Fahrenheit? Use the formula $C = \frac{5}{9} \times (F - 32)$.

    A. 12°F **B.** 43°F **C.** 52°F **D.** 68°F

43. A recipe calls for an oven temperature of 325°F. To the nearest degree, what is this temperature in degrees Celsius? Use the formula $C = \frac{5}{9} \times (F - 32)$.

    A. 125°C   **B.** 149°C
    C. 163°C   **D.** 181°C

44. Use the formula $d = r \times t$, for $d = 960$ km and $r = 120$ km per hr.

    A. 4 hr **B.** 8 hr **C.** 16 hr **D.** 24 hr

45. On a recent trip, the Darr family traveled 9 hr at an average speed of 57 mi per hr. How far did they travel on their trip?

    A. 503 mi   **B.** 504 mi
    C. 513 mi   **D.** not here

46. Al's car holds 14 gal of gas. How many liters of gas is this? (1 gal = 3.785 liters)

    A. 5.299 L   **B.** 52.99 L
    C. 529.9 L   **D.** not here

Choose the letter of the correct answer.

1. The length-to-width ratio of a scale drawing is __?__ the length-to-width ratio of the original object.

   A. larger than   **B.** smaller than
   C. the same as   **D.** not here

2. Suppose you want to make a scale drawing of a car. Which of the following would be a good scale to use?

   A. 5 m:1 cm   **B.** 1 in.:2 ft
   C. 2 ft:1 in.   **D.** 1 in.:12 ft

For questions 3–5, find the missing dimension.

3. scale: 1 in.:6 ft

   drawing length: 3 in.

   actual length: ☐ ft

   A. 2   **B.** 3
   C. 12   **D.** 18

4. scale: 5 cm:1 mm

   drawing length: 20 cm

   actual length: ☐ mm

   A. 4   **B.** 15
   C. 25   **D.** 100

5. scale: 1 in.:8 ft

   drawing length: ☐ in.

   actual length: 40 ft

   A. 4   **B.** 5
   C. 10   **D.** 32

6. The scale drawing for a bird feeder is 1 in.:4 in. The drawing length is 2.5 in. What is the actual length of the feeder?

   A. 2.5 in.   **B.** 6.5 in.
   C. 10 in.   **D.** 13 in.

7. A scale drawing of a flower has a width of 10 cm. The actual width of the flower is 2 cm. What is the scale of the drawing?

   A. 1 cm:10 cm
   B. 5 cm:1 cm
   C. 2 cm:10 cm
   D. 5 cm:2 cm

8. A map scale is 1 in. = 50 mi. The map distance is 4 in. What does n represent in the proportion $\frac{1}{50} = \frac{4}{n}$?

   A. the actual distance in miles
   B. the map distance in inches
   C. the straight-line distance in inches
   D. the scale

9. On a map, the straight-line distance between Franklin and Middletown is 6 in. If the scale is 1 in. = 30 mi, which proportion could you use to find the actual distance?

   A. $\frac{1}{30} = \frac{n}{6}$ **B.** $\frac{n}{6} = \frac{1}{3}$

   C. $\frac{1}{3}n = 6$ **D.** $\frac{1}{30} = \frac{6}{n}$

For question 10–11, find the actual miles.

10. scale: 1 in. = 20 mi

    map distance: 4 in.

    A. 5 mi   **B.** 50 mi
    C. 60 mi   **D.** 80 mi

11. scale: 1 in. = 100 mi

    map distance: $5\frac{1}{2}$ in.

    A. 505 mi   **B.** 550 mi
    C. 555 mi   **D.** 650 mi

Form A • Multiple-Choice   A75   **Go on.** ▶

12. Find the actual miles.

scale: $\frac{1}{2}$ in. = 60 mi

map distance: $2\frac{1}{2}$ in.

A. 120 mi   **B.** 150 mi
C. 240 mi   **D.** not here

For questions 13–14 use the scale
1 in. = 3 mi.

13. Mr. Harmon drove from Longwood Acres to Bensley. The map distance for his route was 3 in. How far did he drive?

A. 9 mi   **B.** 18 mi
C. 21 mi   **D.** not here

14. A school bus from Chester went to Richmond for a soccer game and then returned to Chester. The map distance for the one-way trip is 4 in. What is the actual round-trip distance?

A. 12 mi   **B.** 18 mi
C. 24 mi   **D.** not here

For questions 15–18, use the map. Each square equals one city block.

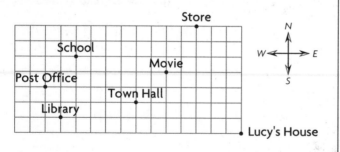

15. Lucy left her house and walked 7 blocks north and 3 blocks west. Where was she?

A. store   **B.** movie
C. school   **D.** library

16. Aaron left the library and went 3 blocks north and 7 blocks east. Where was he?

A. school   **B.** town hall
C. store   **D.** movie

17. Miranda left school and walked 2 blocks south, 4 blocks east, and 1 block south. Where did she go?

A. town hall   **B.** post office
C. library   **D.** movie

18. Lucy's mother left home and drove 10 blocks west, 5 blocks north, and 1 block west. Where did she go?

A. store   **B.** movie
C. school   **D.** library

19. Which is an example of a Golden Ratio?

A. 16:1   **B.** 2:1
C. 5:3   **D.** 6:5

20. A rectangle is 24 in. long. It is a Golden Rectangle. What is its width?

A. 10 in.   **B.** 15 in.
C. 16 in.   **D.** 20 in.

21. Which rectangle is a Golden Rectangle?

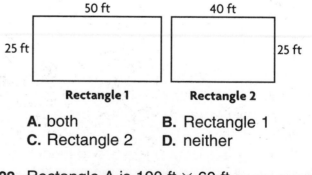

A. both   **B.** Rectangle 1
C. Rectangle 2   **D.** neither

22. Rectangle A is 100 ft × 60 ft. Rectangle B is 200 ft × 120 ft. Which is a Golden Rectangle?

A. both   **B.** Rectangle B
C. Rectangle A   **D.** neither

Form A • Multiple-Choice
▶ **Stop!**

Name _____

Choose the letter of the correct answer.

1. Which of the following are two equivalent ratios that compare the number of circles to the number of squares?

   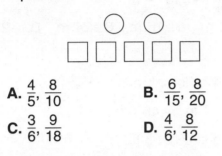

   A. $\frac{4}{5}, \frac{8}{10}$ **B.** $\frac{6}{15}, \frac{8}{20}$

   C. $\frac{3}{6}, \frac{9}{18}$ **D.** $\frac{4}{6}, \frac{8}{12}$

2. What is the ratio for 125 mi in 5 gal written as a fraction?

   A. $\frac{1}{25}$ **B.** $\frac{5}{125}$

   C. $\frac{25}{5}$ **D.** $\frac{125}{5}$

3. What is $\frac{13}{20}$ written as a percent?

   A. 13%   **B.** 52%
   C. 65%   **D.** 75%

4. What percent of the figure is shaded?

   A. 8%   **B.** 33.3%
   C. 45%   **D.** 66.6%

5. Wayne bought 4 tickets to the show for $26. How much would 7 tickets cost?

   A. $32.50   **B.** $39.00
   C. $45.50   **D.** $52.00

6. A music group sold 16 million copies of their newest album. Of the people who bought the album, 45% were adults. How many adults bought the group's new album?

   A. 4.5 million   **B.** 6 million
   C. 7.2 million   **D.** 45 million

For questions 7–8, use the data in the table below for a circle graph.

Favorite Movies of Teenagers	
Movie Type	**Percent**
Action	45%
Comedy	25%
Drama	30%

7. What angle measure should you use for the Drama section of the graph?

   A. 30°   **B.** 60°
   C. 90°   **D.** 108°

8. What angle measure should you use for the Action section of the graph?

   A. 45°   **B.** 90°
   C. 162°   **D.** 198°

9. A clothing store had a Spring sale. All shorts were 20% off the regular price of $18. If Tamara bought 2 pairs of shorts, what would her total discount be?

   A. $3.60   **B.** $7.20
   C. $10.80   **D.** $14.40

10. What is the interest for 1 year if the principal is $1,400 and the simple interest rate is 4.5%?

   A. $63   **B.** $75
   C. $97   **D.** $113

Form A • Multiple-Choice   A77   **Go on.** ▶

11. Identify the pair of figures.

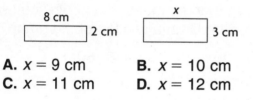

A. similar   B. congruent
C. circular   D. neither

12. One picture frame is 6 in. $\times$ 8 in. Another frame is 18 in. $\times$ 24 in. The frames are __?__.

A. congruent
B. congruent and similar
C. similar
D. not alike

13. Find x for the pair of similar figures.

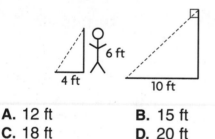

A. $x = 9$ cm   B. $x = 10$ cm
C. $x = 11$ cm   D. $x = 12$ cm

14. What is the height of the flagpole?

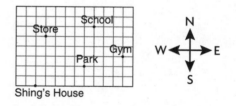

A. 12 ft   B. 15 ft
C. 18 ft   D. 20 ft

15. A building casts a shadow 75 ft long. At the same time an 18 ft statue casts a shadow 30 ft long. How tall is the building?

A. 45 ft   B. 60 ft
C. 90 ft   D. 105 ft

16. Find the missing dimension.

scale: 8 m:1 cm

drawing length: 4 cm

actual length: = m

A. 12 m   B. 16 m   C. 24 m   D. 32 m

17. Find the actual miles.

scale: 1 in. = 45 mi

map distance: 5 in.

A. 90 mi   B. 135 mi
C. 225 mi   D. 315 mi

For questions 18–19, use the map. Each square equals one city block.

18. Shing left his house and walked 2 blocks north, 6 blocks east, and 4 blocks north. Where was he?

A. park   B. gym
C. school   D. store

19. Ema left the gym and walked 3 blocks west, 2 blocks north, and 5 blocks west. Where did she go?

A. store   B. school
C. Shing's house D. park

20. Rectangle A is 112 m $\times$ 80 m. Rectangle B is 250 m $\times$ 150 m. Which is a Golden Rectangle?

A. Rectangle A B. Rectangle B
C. both   D. neither

Form A • Multiple-Choice   A78   ▶ **Stop!**

Name _____

Choose the letter of the correct answer.

1. What is $\frac{7}{8}$ written as a decimal?

   A. 0.07   **B.** 0.70

   C. 0.875   **D.** 0.0875

2. What is the opposite of $^-9$?

   A. $\frac{-1}{9}$ **B.** $\frac{+1}{9}$

   C. $^+9$ **D.** $^-9^2$

3. Use mental math to find the sum.

   $8 + 47 + 12$

   A. 55   **B.** 57

   C. 65   **D.** 67

4. There were 215 laser light shows held in the museum theater last year. The theater holds 280 people and was full for every show. About how many people attended the shows?

   A. about 4,000 people

   B. about 6,000 people

   C. about 40,000 people

   D. about 60,000 people

5. $15.5 + 1.856$

   A. 16.256   **B.** 16.356

   C. 17.256   **D.** 17.356

6. $66.5 \div 7$

   A. 0.95   **B.** 9.5

   C. 9.55   **D.** 95

7. What is the prime factorization of 40?

   A. $3^2 \times 5$ **B.** $2^3 \times 5$

   C. 3×5^2 **D.** $2^4 \times 5$

8. What is $\frac{17}{4}$ written as a mixed number?

   A. $4\frac{1}{7}$ **B.** $4\frac{1}{4}$

   C. $6\frac{1}{7}$ **D.** not here

9. Find the sum in simplest form.

   $\frac{4}{9} + \frac{2}{9}$

   A. $\frac{1}{3}$ **B.** $\frac{5}{9}$

   C. $\frac{2}{3}$ **D.** $\frac{3}{4}$

For questions 10–11, find the answer in simplest form.

10. $3\frac{3}{4} - 2\frac{3}{8}$

    A. $\frac{3}{8}$ **B.** $1\frac{3}{8}$

    C. $1\frac{3}{4}$ **D.** $1\frac{1}{4}$

11. $1\frac{1}{2} \times 1\frac{3}{5}$

    A. $1\frac{2}{5}$ **B.** $2\frac{1}{5}$

    C. $2\frac{2}{5}$ **D.** not here

12. Kent has $3\frac{3}{4}$ lb of sausage. He wants to allow $\frac{1}{4}$ lb of sausage for each individual pizza he makes. How many pizzas can he make?

    A. 12 pizzas   **B.** 15 pizzas

    C. 18 pizzas   **D.** 21 pizzas

13. An angle that measures 120° is classified as a(n) __?__.

    A. obtuse angle   **B.** right angle

    C. acute angle   **D.** straight angle

14. What construction do the figures below represent?

A. congruent line segments
B. bisected line segments
C. congruent angles
D. perpendicular line segments

15. How many lines of symmetry does this figure have?

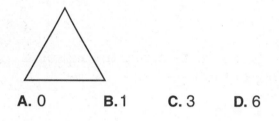

A. 0   **B.** 1   **C.** 3   **D.** 6

16. Which polygon will *not* tessellate a plane?

A. rhombus   B. triangle
C. hexagon   D. not here

17. Name this figure.

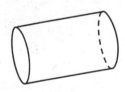

A. cone
B. triangular prism
C. cylinder
D. rectangular prism

18. The top and bottom views of a solid figure are triangles. The front view is a rectangle. What kind of figure is it?

A. triangular prism
B. triangular pyramid
C. rectangular prism
D. rectangular pyramid

19. The sixth graders at Laurel School are being surveyed to find out where they want to go on their class trip. Which question is biased?

A. Do you have a favorite on the list of suggested places?
B. Which day of the week would you prefer to have the trip?
C. Do you agree with the teacher that the museum is the best place to go?
D. Can you suggest other places to go?

For questions 20–21, use the graph.

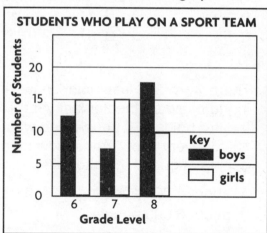

20. What tells you which bars represent girls and which bars represent boys?

A. the data   B. the key
C. the scale   D. the grade

21. Which statement is true?

A. There are more 6th-grade boys than 6th-grade girls who play on a sport team.
B. There are fewer 7th-grade girls than 7th-grade boys who play on a sport team.
C. There are more 8th-grade boys than 8th-grade girls who play on a sport team
D. not here

Name _____

For questions 22–23, use the line graph.

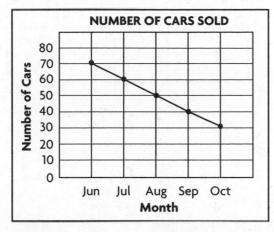

22. What has been the trend in car sales?

A. decreasing   C. increasing

B. staying the same   D. not here

23. Based on the graph, predict how many cars will be sold in November.

A. 10 cars   B. 20 cars

C. 30 cars   D. 40 cars

24. Michelle has gotten a hit in 30 of the last 100 times at bat. How many hits can she expect to get in her next 50 times at bat?

A. 10   B. 15   C. 20   D. 25

25. Evaluate $3 + \frac{1}{4}y$ for $y = 8$.

A. 5   B. 7   C. 11   D. not here

26. $10 = s + 2$

A. $s = 2$ B. $s = 8$

C. $s = 10$ D. $s = 12$

27. $3w = 15$

A. $w = 3$ B. $w = 5$

C. $w = 12$ D. $w = 30$

28. $\frac{b}{3} = 12$

A. $b = 3$ B. $b = 4$

C. $b = 24$ D. $b = 36$

29. What are 10 German marks worth in U.S. dollars? Use the formula $0.6200 \times M = D$. (M = marks; D = dollars)

A. $0.62   B. $6.20

C. $62.00   D. $620.00

30. To the nearest degree, what is 30°C in degrees Fahrenheit? Use the formula $F = (\frac{9}{5} \times C) + 32$.

A. 30°F   B. 49°F

C. 54°F   D. 86°F

31. Todd drove an average of 45 mi per hr from his home to the beach. He drove 2.5 hr to get there. How far does Todd live from the beach? Use the formula $d = r \times t$.

A. 11.25 mi   B. 18 mi

C. 112.5 mi   D. 180 mi

32. Jill weighs 38 kg. Jan weighs 98 lb. How many pounds more does Jan weigh than Jill? (1 kg = 2.2 lb)

A. 1.44 lb   B. 6.55 lb

C. 14.4 lb   D. 65.5 lb

33. Which is another way to write the ratio 3 to 7?

A. 7:3   B. 3:10

C. $\frac{7}{3}$ D. $\frac{3}{7}$

34. What is 20% written as a fraction in simplest form?

A. $\frac{1}{20}$ B. $\frac{1}{5}$

C. $\frac{1}{4}$ D. $\frac{1}{2}$

35. What percent of the figure is shaded?

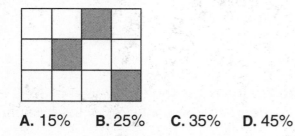

A. 15%   B. 25%   C. 35%   D. 45%

36. The Brown family spent $8,000 remodeling their home. They spent 60% of this on improvements to their kitchen. How much did the Browns spend remodeling their kitchen?

A. $4,200   B. $4,800

C. $5,400   D. not here

37. Books are on sale for 25% off the regular price of $8.00. If Joan buys two books, what is her total discount?

A. $2   B. $4

C. $6   D. $8

38. Andy put $1,800 in the bank for a year. He earned interest at the rate of 5% a year. How much interest did he earn?

A. $50   B. $90

C. $150   D. $180

39. Use the figures below.

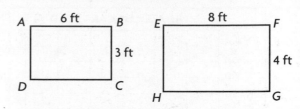

What is the ratio in simplest form of $\frac{AB}{EF}$?

A. $\frac{1}{6}$ B. $\frac{1}{8}$ C. $\frac{1}{2}$ D. $\frac{3}{4}$

40. A photograph is 3 in. wide by 4 in. long. James wants to have the photo enlarged so the length measures 12 in. How wide will the enlarged photo be?

A. 8 in.   B. 9 in.   C. 16 in.   D. 24 in.

41. A tree casts a shadow 48 ft long. At the same time a 3-ft pole nearby casts a shadow 4 ft long. How tall is the tree?

A. 30 ft   B. 36 ft   C. 40 ft   D. 54 ft

42. A scale drawing of a cabin has a scale of 1 in.:2.5 ft. The width in the drawing is 11.5 in. What is the actual width?

A. 11.5 in.   B. 23 ft

C. 28.75 ft   D. 29 ft

43. A map scale is 1 in. = 25 mi. The map distance is 5 in. Find the actual miles.

A. 5 mi   B. 50 mi   C. 100 mi   D. 125 mi

44. A rectangle is 48 in. long. It is a Golden Rectangle. What is its width?

A. 20 in.   B. 30 in.

C. 32 in.   D. 40 in.

Choose the letter of the correct answer.

1. To change pounds to ounces, you should __?__.

   A. multiply by 10   **B.** multiply by 16
   C. divide by 10   **D.** divide by 16

Change to the given unit.

2. 48 pt = ☐ gal

   A. 6   **B.** 8   **C.** 12   **D.** 16

3. For the holiday meal at the Senior Center, juice glasses are filled with 4 fl oz of cranberry juice. How many glasses can be filled with 1 gal of cranberry juice?

   A. 8 glasses   **B.** 16 glasses
   C. 24 glasses   **D.** 32 glasses

4. To get to school, Marco walks 1 mi to the park. Then he walks 1,500 ft to the front door of the school. How many feet does he walk in all?

   A. 2,028 ft   **B.** 3,260 ft
   C. 3,500 ft   **D.** 6,780 ft

5. To change kilometers to meters, you multiply by __?__.

   A. 10   **B.** 100
   C. 1,000   **D.** 10,000

For questions 6–7, change to the given units.

6. 200 g = ☐ kg

   A. 0.02   **B.** 0.2   **C.** 2   **D.** 20

7. 5 L = ☐ mL

   A. 0.5   **B.** 50   **C.** 500   **D.** 5,000

8. Nadia is going to run in a 10K Fun Run. She will run 10 km. How many meters will she run?

   A. 100 m   **B.** 1,000 m
   C. 10,000 m   **D.** 100,000 m

9. When Jerome fills his backpack for school, it weighs 4,500 g. How many kilograms does it weigh?

   A. 0.45 kg   **B.** 4.5 kg
   C. 45 kg   **D.** 450 kg

10. Which is the most precise measurement for the length of a board?

    A. 4 ft   **B.** 44 in.
    C. $3\frac{1}{2}$ ft   **D.** 2 yd

11. Which is the most precise measurement for the height of a kitchen table?

    A. 110 cm   **B.** 1.12 m
    C. 1 m   **D.** 1,118 mm

12. Which is the most precise measurement for the length of a car?

    A. 3 yd   **B.** $9\frac{1}{3}$ ft
    C. $106\frac{1}{4}$ in.   **D.** 108 in.

13. Which is the most precise measurement for the height of a bedroom ceiling?

    A. $112\frac{1}{2}$ in.

    B. 8 ft

    C. $8\frac{1}{2}$ ft

    D. $3\frac{1}{3}$ yd

For questions 14–15, use the network below.

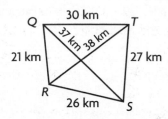

14. What is the length of the route *TSRQ*?

A. 74 km   B. 104 km
C. 111 km   D. 179 km

15. What is the length of the route *QTSR*?

A. 83 km   B. 104 km
C. 121 km   D. 179 km

For questions 17–18, use the network below.

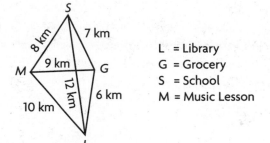

L = Library
G = Grocery
S = School
M = Music Lesson

16. Mrs. Monroe has to go from the school to the grocery store and the library before going to a music lesson. How much difference is there between the routes *SGLM* and *SLGM*?

A. *SLGM* is 1 km shorter.
B. *SLGM* is 2 km shorter.
C. *SGLM* is 4 km shorter.
D. *SGLM* is 1 km shorter.

17. If Mrs. Monroe chooses the shorter route, how many kilometers will she travel?

A. 21 km   B. 23 km
C. 25 km   D. 27 km

18. What is the perimeter?

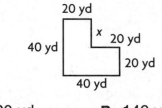

A. 5 cm
B. 5.5 cm
C. 6.5 cm
D. 7 cm

19. Find the missing length. Then find the perimeter.

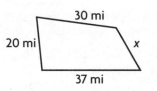

A. 120 yd   B. 140 yd
C. 160 yd   D. 180 yd

20. The perimeter is 103 mi. What is the missing length?

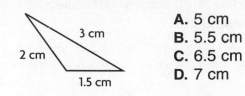

A. 16 mi   B. 20 mi   C. 22 mi   D. 26 mi

21. The Four Corners city garden is located in the center of town. The garden is rectangular and is 1,150 ft by 820 ft. What is its perimeter?

A. 1,970 ft   B. 2,790 ft
C. 2,940 ft   D. 3,940 ft

22. A puzzle is in the shape of a regular hexagon. The perimeter of the puzzle is 48 in. What is the length of each side?

A. 6 in.   B. 8 in.
C. 12 in.   D. 16 in.

Choose the letter of the correct answer.

For questions 1–4, estimate the area of the figure. Each square is 1 cm².

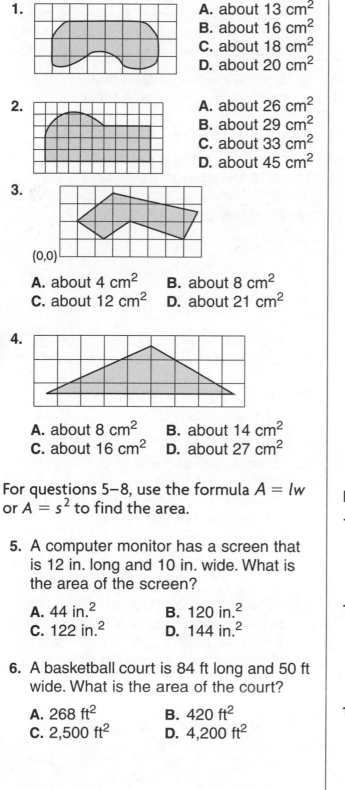

1.
A. about 13 cm²
B. about 16 cm²
C. about 18 cm²
D. about 20 cm²

2.
A. about 26 cm²
B. about 29 cm²
C. about 33 cm²
D. about 45 cm²

3.
(0,0)
A. about 4 cm²   B. about 8 cm²
C. about 12 cm²   D. about 21 cm²

4.
A. about 8 cm²   B. about 14 cm²
C. about 16 cm²   D. about 27 cm²

For questions 5–8, use the formula $A = lw$ or $A = s^2$ to find the area.

5. A computer monitor has a screen that is 12 in. long and 10 in. wide. What is the area of the screen?

A. 44 in.²   B. 120 in.²
C. 122 in.²   D. 144 in.²

6. A basketball court is 84 ft long and 50 ft wide. What is the area of the court?

A. 268 ft²   B. 420 ft²
C. 2,500 ft²   D. 4,200 ft²

7. Tia is laying tile on an 8-ft × 8-ft kitchen floor. Each tile is 1 ft² and costs $2.25. What is the total cost of the tile?

A. $64   B. $128   C. $144   D. $180

8. Yolanda is buying wall-to-wall carpet for her bedroom. The room is 14 ft long and 11 ft wide. The carpet costs $6 per square foot. What will be the total cost?

A. $154   B. $500   C. $724   D. $924

9. What is the relationship between parallelogram QRST and △RST?

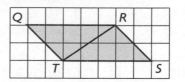

A. Triangle RST is one fourth of parallelogram QRST.
B. Triangle RST is one third of parallelogram QRST.
C. Triangle RST is one half of parallelogram QRST.
D. Triangle RST is two thirds of parallelogram QRST.

For questions 10–12, find the area.

10.
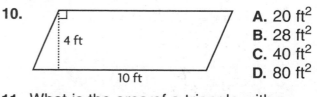
4 ft
10 ft
A. 20 ft²
B. 28 ft²
C. 40 ft²
D. 80 ft²

11. What is the area of a triangle with a base of 12 in. and a height of 6 in.?

A. 9 in.²   B. 18 in.²
C. 36 in.²   D. 72 in.²

12. What is the area of a parallelogram with a base 6.2 m and a height of 3.3 m?

A. 9.5 m²   B. 10.23 m²
C. 19.0 m²   D. 20.46 m²

For questions 13–14, use the figure below.

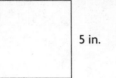

5 in.

13. If you double the length of each side of this square, what will be the area?

A. $12\frac{1}{2}$ in.^{2} **B.** 20 in.^{2}

C. 25 in.^{2} **D.** 100 in.^{2}

14. If you halve the length of each side, what will be the perimeter?

A. 5 in.   **B.** 10 in.
C. 20 in.   **D.** 40 in.

For questions 15–16, use the figure below.

15 cm   25 cm
20 cm

15. If you double the dimensions of this figure, what will be the perimeter?

A. 35 cm   **B.** 60 cm
C. 70 cm   **D.** 120 cm

16. If you halve the dimensions of the figure, what will be the area?

A. 37.5 cm^2 **B.** 75 cm^2
C. 150 cm^2 **D.** 300 cm^2

17. Last year the Wong family had a vegetable garden that was 20 ft × 12 ft. They have decided to double the area of their garden this year. Which of the following sets of dimensions will give them twice the area they had last year?

A. 30 ft × 12 ft   **B.** 40 ft × 12 ft
C. 40 ft × 24 ft   **D.** 80 ft × 24 ft

18. Lia made a square table that was 4 ft on each side. She used 16 tiles to cover the top of the table. Now she has made another square table, and it is 2 ft on each side. She wants to use the same kind of tiles to cover the top of the new table. How many tiles will she need?

A. 4 tiles   **B.** 8 tiles
C. 12 tiles   **D.** 14 tiles

For questions 19–22, use the formula $A = \pi r^2$ to find the area. Use 3.14 for π. Round to the nearest whole unit.

19. What is the area of this figure?

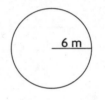

6 m

A. about 36 m^2 **B.** about 108 m^2
C. about 113 m^2 **D.** about 144 m^2

20. What is the area of a circle with a diameter of 10 in.?

A. about 79 in.^{2} **B.** about 100 in.^{2}
C. about 157 in.^{2} **D.** about 314 in.^{2}

21. A circular medal has a radius of 3 cm. What is the area of the medal?

A. about 9 cm^2 **B.** about 28 cm^2
C. about 36 cm^2 **D.** about 108 cm^2

22. For a crafts project, Julian is covering one side of circular disks of cardboard with handmade paper. If each disk has a diameter of 24 in., what is the area to be covered?

A. about 144 in.^{2} **B.** about 288 in.^{2}
C. about 452 in.^{2} **D.** about 576 in.^{2}

Name _____

Choose the letter of the correct answer.

1. About how many of the cubes will it take to fill the prism?

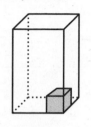

   A. about 5 units^3
   B. about 15 units^3
   C. about 30 units^3
   D. about 90 units^3

2. This figure shows that __?__.

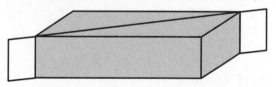

   A. two identical rectangular prisms can be formed by cutting a triangular prism in half
   B. two identical triangular prisms can be formed by cutting a rectangular prism in half
   C. $V = l \times w$
   D. $A = \frac{1}{2} \times l \times w \times h$

For questions 3–4, find the volume of each figure.

3.

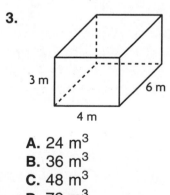

   A. 24 m^3
   B. 36 m^3
   C. 48 m^3
   D. 72 m^3

4.

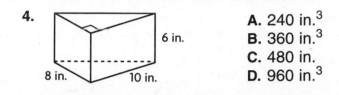

   A. 240 in.^{3}
   B. 360 in.^{3}
   C. 480 in.
   D. 960 in.^{3}

5. A cereal box is 18 cm long, 5 cm wide, and 23 cm high. What is the volume of the box?

   A. 990 cm^3 B. 1,980 cm^3
   C. 2,070 cm^3 D. 8,000 cm^3

6. Firewood is sold by the cord. A cord is a stack of wood that is 8 ft long by 4 ft wide by 4 ft high. What is the volume of a cord of wood?

   A. 32 ft^3 B. 64 ft^3
   C. 128 ft^3 D. 320 ft^3

7. If each side of the cube is doubled, how does its volume change?

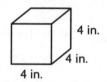

   A. It is twice that of the original cube.
   B. It is 4 times that of the original.
   C. It is 8 times that of the original.
   D. It is 16 times that of the original.

8. How can you change this box so that it will hold twice as much?

   A. Double only one dimension.
   B. Double only two dimensions.
   C. Double all three dimensions.
   D. Add 2 in. to each dimension.

Harcourt Brace School Publishers

Form A • Multiple-Choice   A87   **Go on.** ▶

Name _____

For questions 9–10, use the figure below.

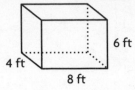

6 ft
4 ft
8 ft

9. If you double all the dimensions of this figure, what is the volume of the larger prism?

   A. 192 ft³
   B. 384 ft³
   C. 768 ft³
   D. 1,536 ft³

10. If you halve all the dimensions of the figure, what is the volume of the smaller prism?

    A. 12 ft³
    B. 24 ft³
    C. 81 ft³
    D. 192 ft³

For questions 11–12, use the figure below.

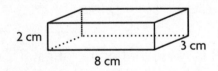

2 cm
3 cm
8 cm

11. If you halve the height of the figure, what is the volume of the smaller prism?

    A. 6 cm³
    B. 12 cm³
    C. 24 cm³
    D. 48 cm³

12. If you double the height of the figure, what is the volume of the larger prism?

    A. 96 cm³
    B. 128 cm³
    C. 192 cm³
    D. 384 cm³

For questions 13–16, find the volume of each cylinder to the nearest whole unit. Use the formula $V = \pi r^2 \times h$.

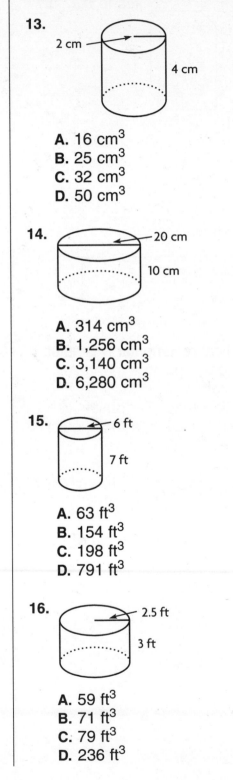

13.
2 cm
4 cm

   A. 16 cm³
   B. 25 cm³
   C. 32 cm³
   D. 50 cm³

14.
20 cm
10 cm

   A. 314 cm³
   B. 1,256 cm³
   C. 3,140 cm³
   D. 6,280 cm³

15.
6 ft
7 ft

   A. 63 ft³
   B. 154 ft³
   C. 198 ft³
   D. 791 ft³

16.
2.5 ft
3 ft

   A. 59 ft³
   B. 71 ft³
   C. 79 ft³
   D. 236 ft³

Form A • Multiple-Choice

Go on. ▶

17. A juice glass in the shape of a cylinder has a height of 4 in. and a diameter of 2 in. About how many cubic inches of juice can it hold if it is filled to the rim?

A. about 8 in.^{3}
B. about 13 in.^{3}
C. about 50 in.^{3}
D. about 100 in.^{3}

18. A flower pot in the shape of a cylinder is 10 cm high and has a radius of 2 cm. About how many cubic centimeters of potting soil will fill the pot?

A. about 13 cm^3
B. about 31 cm^3
C. about 65 cm^3
D. about 126 cm^3

For questions 19–22, find the surface area of each prism.

19.

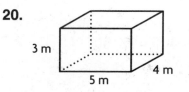

3 in.
3 in.
3 in.

A. 54 in.^{2}
B. 72 in.^{2}
C. 81 in.^{2}
D. 99 in.^{2}

20.

3 m
5 m
4 m

A. 47 m^2
B. 60 m^2
C. 92 m^2
D. 94 m^2

21.

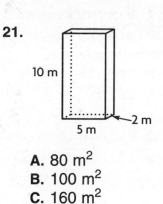

10 m
5 m
2 m

A. 80 m^2
B. 100 m^2
C. 160 m^2
D. 240 m^2

22.

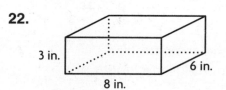

3 in.
6 in.
8 in.

A. 144 in.^{2}
B. 180 in.^{2}
C. 238 in.^{2}
D. 288 in.^{2}

23. For their play, the students are covering wooden cubes with shiny paper. Each cube is 2 ft long. The students cover each side except the bottom. How many square feet of paper does it take to cover each cube?

A. 20 ft^2
B. 24 ft^2
C. 32 ft^2
D. 36 ft^2

24. Thora is planning to paint her bedroom, which is 13 ft long, 11 ft wide, and 9 ft high. She will paint the walls, but not the floor or the ceiling. How much surface area will she paint?

A. 143 ft^2
B. 432 ft^2
C. 484 ft^2
D. 520 ft^2

Form A • Multiple-Choice

▶ **Stop!**

Choose the letter of the correct answer.

1. Nan found a container that holds exactly 16 pt of lemonade. How many cups of lemonade must she make to fill this container?

   A. 2   **B.** 8   **C.** 24   **D.** 32

2. Change to the given units.

   0.15 m = cm

   A. 0.015   **B.** 1.5   **C.** 15   **D.** 150

3. Which is the most precise measurement for the length of a bedroom floor?

   A. $150\frac{1}{2}$ in.   **B.** 4 yd

   C. 12 ft   **D.** $12\frac{1}{2}$ ft

For questions 4–5, use the network below. Distances are expressed in km.

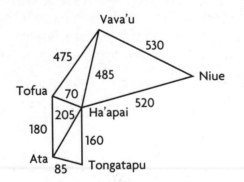

4. What is the length of the route from Vava'u to Tongatapu, through Ha'apai?

   A. 160 km   **B.** 485 km
   C. 645 km   **D.** 1,210 km

5. What is the length of the route from Tofua to Ha'apai through Ata and Tongatapu?

   A. 340 km   **B.** 425 km
   C. 635 km   **D.** 725 km

6. What is the perimeter?

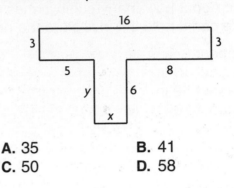

   A. 35   **B.** 41
   C. 50   **D.** 58

For questions 7–8, use the formula $A = lw$ or $A = s^2$ to find the area.

7. Leslie wants to cover four rectangular faces of a box with blue paper. Each face is 12 in. high and 8 in. wide. How much paper will Leslie need?

   A. 48 in.^{2} **B.** 96 in.^{2}
   C. 144 in.^{2} **D.** 384 in.^{2}

8. Charlie has to wax the dance floor. The floor has equal sides of 40 ft. What is the area of the dance floor?

   A. 160 ft^2 **B.** 400 ft^2
   C. 1,000 ft^2 **D.** 1,600 ft^2

9. What is the area of a triangle that has a base of 9 in. and a height of 6 in.?

   A. 15 in.^{2} **B.** 27 in.^{2}
   C. 33 in.^{2} **D.** 54 in.^{2}

10. What is the area of a parallelogram that has a base of 15.5 cm and a height of 4.4 cm?

   A. 19.9 cm^2 **B.** 34.1 cm^2
   C. 68.2 cm^2 **D.** 72.9 cm^2

For questions 11–12, use the figure below.

11. If you double the dimensions of this figure, what is the perimeter?

A. 10 cm　　　　B. 20 cm
C. 24 cm　　　　D. 40 cm

12. If you halve the dimensions of this figure, what is the area?

A. 6 cm^2　　　　B. 10 cm^2
C. 24 cm^2　　　　D. 96 cm^2

For questions 13–14, use the formula $A = \pi r^2$ to find the area. Use 3.14 for π. Round to the nearest whole unit.

13. A circle has a radius of 5 in. What is the approximate area of the circle?

A. about 5 in^2　　B. about 10 in^2
C. about 25 in^2　D. about 79 in^2

14. Nathan was trying to invent a more efficient Frisbee®. The top of his Frisbee® had a diameter of 20 cm. What is the area of the top of his Frisbee®?

A. about 31.4 cm^2　B. about 100 cm^2
C. about 300 cm^2　D. about 314 cm^2

15. A packing crate is 6 ft long, 8 ft wide, and 4 ft high. What is the volume of this box?

A. 18 ft^3　　　　B. 192 ft^3
C. 384 ft^3　　　　D. 400 ft^3

For questions 16–17, use the figure below.

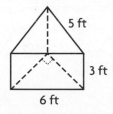

16. If you halve the dimensions of this figure, what is the volume of the smaller prism?

A. 5.625 ft^3　　B. 11.25 ft^3
C. 14 ft^3　　　　D. 45 ft^3

17. If you double the dimensions of this figure, what is the volume of the larger prism?

A. 90 ft^3　　　　B. 180 ft^3
C. 360 ft^3　　　　D. 720 ft^3

18. Find the volume of the given cylinder to the nearest whole unit.

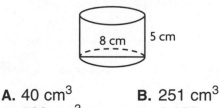

A. 40 cm^3　　　　B. 251 cm^3
C. 502 cm^3　　　　D. 1,005 cm^3

19. A paint can shaped as a cylinder is filled to the top. The can has a height of 10 in. and a diameter of 6 in. About how much paint does the can hold?

A. about 28 in.^{3}　B. about 90 in.^{3}
C. about 283 in.^{3}　D. about 1,130 in.^{3}

20. Trish covered only the outside of a shoe box with paper. The box is 10 in. long, 5 in. tall, and 6 in. wide. How many square inches of paper will she need?

A. 80 in.^{2}　　　　B. 160 in.^{2}
C. 210 in.^{2}　　　　D. 280 in.^{2}

Name _____

Choose the letter of the correct answer.

1. What is the value of the digit 9 in the number 8.369?

   A. 9 thousands   **B.** 9 hundreds
   C. 9 hundredths   **D.** 9 thousandths

2. What is the value of 5^3?

   A. 15   **B.** 25   **C.** 125   **D.** 500

3. Gigi baked a total of 48 peanut butter and chocolate chip cookies. She baked 8 more peanut butter cookies than chocolate chip cookies. How many peanut butter cookies did she bake?

   A. 20 peanut butter cookies
   B. 24 peanut butter cookies
   C. 28 peanut butter cookies
   D. 32 peanut butter cookies

4. $5\overline{)3,240}$

   A. 640   **B.** 640 r2   **C.** 648   **D.** 648 r2

5. $5.52 - 1.05$

   A. 4.47   **B.** 4.53   **C.** 4.57   **D.** not here

6. 3.47×7.3

   A. 2.5331   **B.** 25.331
   C. 253.31   **D.** 2533.1

7. What is the GCF of 12 and 18?

   A. 2   **B.** 4
   C. 6   **D.** 10

8. Which fraction is the simplest form of $\frac{8}{20}$?

   A. $\frac{2}{5}$ **B.** $\frac{2}{3}$
   C. $\frac{4}{5}$ **D.** not here

9. Find the sum in simplest form.

   $$\frac{1}{6} + \frac{1}{12}$$

   A. $\frac{1}{4}$ **B.** $\frac{1}{3}$ **C.** $\frac{3}{8}$ **D.** $\frac{2}{3}$

10. Estimate the difference.
    $$\frac{7}{8} - \frac{1}{10}$$

    A. 0   **B.** $\frac{1}{2}$
    C. 1   **D.** $1\frac{1}{2}$

11. Choose the best estimate for the word problem.

    Last week Jen bought $5\frac{7}{8}$ lb of meat for her family, and this week she bought $2\frac{1}{4}$ lb of meat. How many more pounds did she buy last week than this week?

    A. about 3 lb more
    B. about $3\frac{1}{2}$ lb more
    C. about 4 lb more
    D. about $4\frac{1}{2}$ lb more

12. Find the quotient in simplest form.
    $$\frac{5}{6} \div \frac{1}{3}$$

    A. $\frac{5}{9}$ **B.** $\frac{1}{4}$
    C. $2\frac{1}{4}$ **D.** $2\frac{1}{2}$

13. What does the symbol $\overline{AB}$ refer to?

A. plane *AB*   **C.** line *AB*

B. line segment *AB*   **D.** ray *AB*

14. How many angles does an octagon have?

A. 5   **B.** 6   **C.** 8   **D.** 12

15. Choose the figure that is a translation of the original figure.

R   Я   Я   R

original   figure 1   figure 2   figure 3

A. figure 1   **B.** figure 2

C. figure 3   **D.** not here

16. Alex wants to use small tiles to make a design for a tabletop. He wants the design to tessellate. Which shape can the tiles be?

A. octagon   **B.** hexagon

C. pentagon   **D.** circle

17. Name this figure.

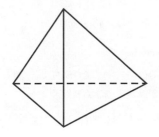

A. triangular pyramid

B. triangular prism

C. rectangular pyramid

D. rectangular prism

18. Cindi is making a model of a prism whose base has 6 sides. She is using sticks of wood for the edges and putty for the vertices. How many sticks of wood will she need?

A. 12 sticks

B. 18 sticks

C. 24 sticks

D. 36 sticks

19. There are 700 people who will vote on a new name for your school. How many voters should you survey if you want to survey 1 out of every 10 voters for a sample?

A. 7 voters

B. 35 voters

C. 70 voters

D. 140 voters

20. The table shows the scores students received on their last math quiz. What is the range in scores?

Scores on Math Quiz							
94	78	84	88	96	92	76	62
76	94	96	83	88	96	98	94

A. 16   **B.** 26

C. 36   **D.** 96

21. A histogram is a special kind of __?__.

A. bar graph

B. stem-and-leaf plot

C. survey data

D. circle graph

22. Use the graph to find the trend in sales of CDs.

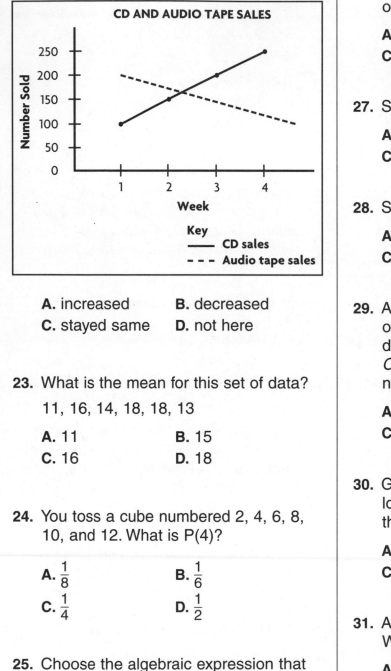

CD AND AUDIO TAPE SALES

Number Sold (vertical axis): 0, 50, 100, 150, 200, 250
Week (horizontal axis): 1, 2, 3, 4

Key
——— CD sales
- - - Audio tape sales

A. increased   B. decreased
C. stayed same   D. not here

23. What is the mean for this set of data?

11, 16, 14, 18, 18, 13

A. 11   B. 15
C. 16   D. 18

24. You toss a cube numbered 2, 4, 6, 8, 10, and 12. What is P(4)?

A. $\frac{1}{8}$ B. $\frac{1}{6}$

C. $\frac{1}{4}$ D. $\frac{1}{2}$

25. Choose the algebraic expression that matches this word expression:

four less than a

A. $a - 4$ B. $4 - a$
C. $4 \div a$ D. $4 \times a$

26. Determine the input for the given output for the expression $m - 6$.

output = 9   input = __?__

A. $m = 3$ B. $m = 8$
C. $m = 11$ D. $m = 15$

27. Solve. $k - 3 = 8$

A. $k = 3$ B. $k = 5$
C. $k = 8$ D. $k = 11$

28. Solve. $4w = 12$

A. $w = 3$ B. $w = 4$
C. $w = 24$ D. $w = 48$

29. A recipe calls for an oven temperature of 375°F. What is this temperature in degrees Celsius? Use the formula $C = \frac{5}{9} \times (F - 32)$. Round to the nearest degree.

A. 163°C   B. 176°C
C. 191°C   D. not here

30. Gretchen has a ribbon that is 15 in. long. How many centimeters long is the ribbon? (1 in. = 2.54 cm)

A. 0.381 cm   B. 3.81 cm
C. 38.1 cm   D. 381 cm

31. A 10-lb bag of potatoes costs $2.90. What is the cost per pound?

A. $0.03   B. $0.29   C. $0.30   D. $0.90

32. If 6 apples cost $1.20, how much will 9 apples cost?

A. $0.90   B. $1.35   C. $1.60   D. $1.80

Name _____

For questions 33–34, use the circle graph.

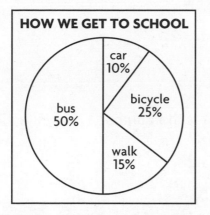

HOW WE GET TO SCHOOL

bus 50%
car 10%
bicycle 25%
walk 15%

33. If 300 students were surveyed, how many ride a bicycle to school?

A. 50 students   **B.** 75 students
C. 100 students   **D.** 150 students

34. If 200 students were surveyed, how many get to school in a car?

A. 20 students   **B.** 40 students
C. 50 students   **D.** 100 students

35. Which pair of figures is congruent?

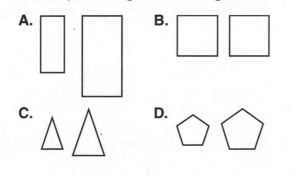

A.   **B.**

C.   **D.**

36. Change to the given unit.

3 ft = _?_ in.

A. 4 in.   **B.** 12 in.
C. 24 in.   **D.** 36 in.

37. The perimeter is 85 ft. What is the missing length?

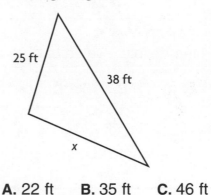

25 ft   38 ft   x

A. 22 ft   **B.** 35 ft   **C.** 46 ft   **D.** 63 ft

38. What is the area of a triangle with a base of 16 in. and a height of 10 in.?

A. 40 in.^{2} **B.** 60 in.^{2}
C. 80 in.^{2} **D.** 160 in.^{2}

39. Use the formula $A = \pi r^2$ to find the area of this circle. Use 3.14 for π. Round to the nearest whole unit.

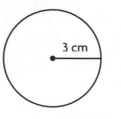

3 cm

A. about 9 cm^2 **B.** about 19 cm^2
C. about 28 cm^2 **D.** about 85 cm^2

40. Find the volume of the figure.

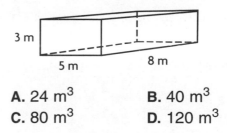

3 m   5 m   8 m

A. 24 m^3 **B.** 40 m^3
C. 80 m^3 **D.** 120 m^3

Name _____

Choose the letter of the correct answer.

1. What is the opposite of $^+2$?

   A. 0   **B.** $\frac{1}{2}$ **C.** $^-2$ **D.** 2^2

2. What is the absolute value of $^-10$?

   A. $\frac{1}{10}$ **B.** 1   **C.** $^-10$ **D.** 10

3. Which integer should you write to represent 15 degrees below zero?

   A. $^-15$ **B.** 15   **C.** $^+15$ **D.** 0

4. What is the absolute value of $^+36$?

   A. $\frac{1}{36}$ **B.** 1   **C.** $^-36$ **D.** 36

For questions 5–6, use the Venn diagram below.

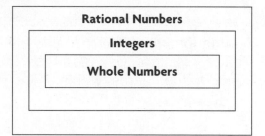

5. In which set or sets does the number $^-50$ belong?

   A. The sets of whole numbers, integers, and rational numbers
   B. The sets of integers and rational numbers
   C. The set of rational numbers
   D. The set of whole numbers

6. In which set or sets does the number 2.25 belong?

   A. The sets of whole numbers, integers, and rational numbers
   B. The sets of integers and rational numbers
   C. The set of rational numbers
   D. The set of whole numbers

7. What is the number 5 written in the form $\frac{a}{b}$?

   A. $\frac{5}{1}$ **B.** $\frac{1}{5}$

   C. $\frac{5}{10}$ **D.** $\frac{5}{5}$

8. What is the number 1.19 written in the form $\frac{a}{b}$?

   A. $\frac{1}{19}$ **B.** $\frac{100}{119}$

   C. $\frac{119}{100}$ **D.** $\frac{19}{10}$

For questions 9–12, find the repeating or terminating decimal for the fraction.

9. $\frac{2}{5}$

   A. 0.2   **B.** $0.\overline{4}$
   C. 0.4   **D.** 2.5

10. $\frac{1}{3}$

   A. 0.3   **B.** $0.\overline{3}$
   C. 0.34   **D.** 1.3

11. $\frac{7}{11}$

   A. $0.\overline{6}$ **B.** $0.6\overline{3}$
   C. $0.\overline{63}$ **D.** $0.6\overline{3}$

12. $\frac{1}{90}$

   A. $0.0\overline{1}$ **B.** $0.0\overline{1}$
   C. $0.\overline{01}$ **D.** 1.90

13. Which rational number is between $1\frac{1}{8}$ and $1\frac{3}{8}$?

   A. $1\frac{1}{2}$ **B.** $1\frac{1}{16}$

   C. $1\frac{1}{4}$ **D.** $1\frac{7}{16}$

Form A • Multiple-Choice   **Go on.** ▶

14. Which rational number is between 0 and $-\frac{1}{2}$?

A. $\frac{-2}{10}$ B. $\frac{-5}{8}$

C. $\frac{1}{4}$ D. $\frac{-5}{10}$

15. Which rational number is between $^-1.5$ and $^-1.6$?

A. $^-1.7$ B. 1.55
C. $^-1.65$ D. $^-1.59$

16. Which rational number is between $^-2\frac{3}{4}$ and $^-3$?

A. $2\frac{7}{8}$ B. $^-2\frac{15}{16}$

C. $^-2\frac{5}{8}$ D. $^-3\frac{1}{16}$

17. In a race, the winner's time was 10.3 sec. The third-place finisher's time was 10.4 sec. What could have been the time for the second-place finisher?

A. 10.0 sec   B. 10.5 sec
C. 10.25 sec   D. 10.33 sec

18. At 6 P.M. a snail was at $^-8.5$ m in a well. By 7 P.M. it was at $^-9.5$ m. At 6:30 P.M. the snail was between these two levels. At what level could the snail have been at 6:30 P.M.?

A. $^-9.1$ m   B. $^-8.4$ m
C. 9.0 m   D. $^-10.0$ m

For questions 19–20, compare the numbers. Choose $<$, $>$, or $=$.

19. $\frac{3}{5}$ ◯ 0.6

A. $<$ B. $>$ C. $=$

20. $-\frac{3}{8}$ ◯ 0.375

A. $<$ B. $>$ C. $=$

For questions 21–22, order the rational numbers from least to greatest.

21. $\frac{1}{2}$, $\frac{-3}{4}$, 0.3

A. $\frac{-3}{4}$, $\frac{1}{2}$, 0.3   B. $\frac{-3}{4}$, 0.3, $\frac{1}{2}$

C. 0.3, $\frac{1}{2}$, $\frac{-3}{4}$ D. $\frac{1}{2}$, 0.3, $\frac{-3}{4}$

22. $\frac{-2}{3}$, $^-1$, $^-1.4$

A. $\frac{-2}{3}$, $^-1$, $^-1.4$ B. $^-1$, $\frac{-2}{3}$, $^-1.4$

C. $^-1.4$, $\frac{-2}{3}$, $^-1$ D. $^-1.4$, $^-1$, $\frac{-2}{3}$

23. Nora, Harry, Jinn, and Tamika each have a solo at the concert. Nora's solo lasts $1\frac{1}{2}$ min, Harry's lasts 1.2 min, Jinn's lasts $1\frac{4}{5}$ min, and Tamika's lasts 1.85 min. Who has the longest solo?

A. Nora
B. Harry
C. Jinn
D. Tamika

24. LeeAnne recorded the time it took her to walk a mile on four different days. The times were $12\frac{4}{5}$ min on Monday, 11.3 min on Tuesday, $12\frac{1}{4}$ min on Wednesday, and $11\frac{2}{5}$ min on Thursday. On which day did she walk the fastest?

A. Monday
B. Tuesday
C. Wednesday
D. Thursday

Name _____

Choose the letter of the correct answer.

1. Which addition equation is modeled on the number line below?

$$-9 \;-8 \;-7 \;-6 \;-5 \;-4 \;-3 \;-2 \;-1 \;\;0 \;+1 \;+2$$

   A. $^+3 + ^-2 = ^+1$
   B. $^-3 + ^-2 = ^-5$
   C. $^+3 + ^+2 = ^+5$
   D. $^-3 + ^+2 = ^-1$

For questions 2–4, find the sum.

2. $^-10 + ^+5$

   A. $^-15$ **B.** $^-5$
   C. $^+5$ **D.** $^+10$

3. $^-7 + ^+9$

   A. $^-16$ **B.** $^-2$
   C. $^+2$ **D.** $^+16$

4. $^-21 + ^-11$

   A. $^-32$ **B.** $^-10$
   C. $^+10$ **D.** $^+32$

5. The day's low temperature was $^-5°F$. The high temperature was 25° greater. What was the high temperature?

   A. $^-30°F$
   B. $^-20°F$
   C. $^+20°F$
   D. $^+30°F$

6. On its first play, a football team lost 3 yd. On its second play, it lost 2 yd. Which integer shows the total gain or loss on the two plays?

   A. $^-5$ yd
   B. $^-1$ yd
   C. $^+1$ yd
   D. $^+5$ yd

7. Which of the following problems has the same solution as $^+4 - ^+6$?

   A. $^-4 + ^+6$
   B. $^-4 + ^-6$
   C. $^+4 + ^+6$
   D. $^+4 + ^-6$

For questions 8–10, find the difference.

8. $^+8 - ^+12$

   A. $^-20$ **B.** $^-4$
   C. $^+4$ **D.** $^+20$

9. $^-5 - ^+15$

   A. $^-20$ **B.** $^-10$
   C. $^+10$ **D.** $^+20$

10. $^+20 - ^-15$

   A. $^-35$ **B.** $^-5$
   C. $^+5$ **D.** $^+35$

11. At dinnertime the temperature was 2°F. By midnight the temperature was 10° less. What was the temperature at midnight?

   A. $^+8°F$
   B. $^+12°F$
   C. $^-8°F$
   D. $^-12°F$

12. On a winter day in Maine, the high temperature was $^-3°F$. The low temperature was 13° less. What was the low temperature?

   A. $^-16°F$
   B. $^-10°F$
   C. $^+10°F$
   D. $^+16°F$

Form A • Multiple-Choice   A98   **Go on. ▶**

13. The product of a positive integer and a negative integer is __?__ .

    A. a positive integer
    B. a negative integer
    C. zero
    D. the same sign as the larger integer

For questions 14–16, find the product.

14. $^-12 \times ^-3$

    A. $^-36$ **B.** $^-4$
    C. $^+4$ **D.** $^+36$

15. $^-8 \times ^+2$

    A. $^-16$ **B.** $^-6$
    C. $^+6$ **D.** $^+16$

16. $^-10 \times ^-5$

    A. $^-50$ **B.** $^-2$
    C. $^+2$ **D.** $^+50$

17. A medical textbook suggests that a safe weight loss is 3 lb per month. Mrs. Hudson lost weight at that rate for 6 months. How do you express the change in her weight as a negative number?

    A. $^-18$ lb   **B.** $^-9$ lb
    C. $^-3$ lb   **D.** $^-2$ lb

18. A container filled with water at a temperature of 70°F was put in a refrigerator. The water temperature fell 5° each hour for the next 4 hr. What was the temperature then?

    A. $^-20$°F   **B.** $^+20$°F
    C. $^+50$°F   **D.** $^+65$°F

19. If you divide a negative integer by a negative integer, the quotient __?__ .

    A. is a positive integer
    B. is a negative integer
    C. is zero
    D. has the same sign of the larger integer

For questions 20–22, find the quotient.

20. $^-15 \div ^-5$

    A. $^-10$ **B.** $^-3$
    C. $^+3$ **D.** $^+10$

21. $^-24 \div ^+4$

    A. $^-20$ **B.** $^-6$
    C. $^+6$ **D.** $^+20$

22. $^-12 \div ^-3$

    A. $^-9$ **B.** $^-4$
    C. $^+4$ **D.** $^+9$

23. Which of the following problems has the greatest quotient?

    A. $^+12 \div ^-4$
    B. $^+60 \div ^-10$
    C. $^-36 \div ^-9$
    D. $^-20 \div ^-4$

24. In 8 hr the temperature fell 24°. If it fell the same number of degrees every hour, how many degrees did it change every hour?

    A. $^-16$°F   **B.** $^-3$°F
    C. $^+3$°F   **D.** $^+16$°F

Harcourt Brace School Publishers

Choose the letter of the correct answer.

1. Evaluate $20 - 10 \div {}^-2$.

   A. $^-5$ B. 5
   C. 15   D. 25

2. Evaluate $y - 10$ for $y = 2$.

   A. $^-12$ B. $^-8$
   C. 8   D. 12

3. Evaluate $4x$ for $x = {}^-3$.

   A. $^-12$ B. $^-7$
   C. 7   D. 12

4. Evaluate $t^2 + 2$ for $t = {}^-1$.

   A. $^-3$ B. $^-1$
   C. 1   D. 3

For questions 5–8, solve the equation.

5. $4p = {}^-16$

   A. $p = {}^-20$ B. $p = {}^-12$
   C. $p = {}^-4$ D. $p = 4$

6. $m + 5 = 2$

   A. $m = {}^-3$

   B. $m = \dfrac{2}{5}$

   C. $m = 3$

   D. $m = 7$

7. $\dfrac{x}{^-2} = {}^-6$

   A. $x = {}^-12$
   B. $x = {}^-3$
   C. $x = 3$
   D. $x = 12$

8. $10 = y + 25$

   A. $y = {}^-35$
   B. $y = {}^-15$
   C. $y = 15$
   D. $y = 35$

9. Which equation should you write for this word sentence?

   Six less than a number, y, is negative twenty-four.

   A. $6y = {}^-24$
   B. $y + 6 = {}^-24$
   C. $y - 6 = {}^-24$
   D. $\dfrac{y}{6} = {}^-24$

10. This morning the temperature increased 4°F to the current temperature of $^-16$°F. Which equation shows how to find the original temperature, t?

    A. $t = {}^-16$
    B. $t + 4 = {}^-16$
    C. $t - 4 = {}^-16$
    D. $4t = {}^-16$

11. What are the whole-number solutions of $x < 4$?

    A. 0, 1, 2, 3, 4
    B. 1, 2, 3, 4
    C. 1, 2, 3
    D. 0, 1, 2, 3

12. What are the whole-number solutions of $a \le 1$?

    A. 0
    B. 1
    C. 0 and 1
    D. all whole numbers except 0

13. Which algebraic inequality is represented by the integers graphed on the number line?

    A. $x > 2$ B. $x < 2$
    C. $x \ge 2$ D. $x \le 2$

14. Which graph represents the algebraic inequality $x < {}^-1$?

A.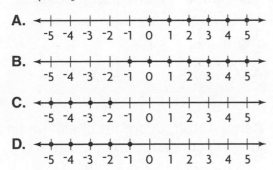
-5 -4 -3 -2 -1 0 1 2 3 4 5

B.
-5 -4 -3 -2 -1 0 1 2 3 4 5

C.
-5 -4 -3 -2 -1 0 1 2 3 4 5

D.
-5 -4 -3 -2 -1 0 1 2 3 4 5

15. Which algebraic inequality represents this word sentence?

All numbers y are greater than or equal to eight.

A. $y < 8$ **B.** $y \geq 8$
C. $y \leq 8$ **D.** $y > 8$

16. The speed limit in front of a school is 20 mi per hour. Which inequality represents the speeds that a driver can legally go?

A. $x < 20$ **B.** $x \leq 20$
C. $x \geq 20$ **D.** $x > 20$

Use the coordinate plane to answer questions 17–20.

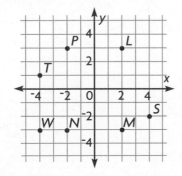

17. Which point is located by the ordered pair $({}^-2,3)$?

A. point L **B.** point M
C. point N **D.** point P

18. Which point is located by the ordered pair $(2,{}^-3)$?

A. point L **B.** point M
C. point N **D.** point P

19. What is the ordered pair for point W?

A. $({}^-4,{}^-3)$ **B.** $({}^-3,{}^-4)$
C. $({}^-4,3)$ **D.** $(3,{}^-4)$

20. What is the ordered pair for point T?

A. $({}^-4,1)$ **B.** $(4,{}^-1)$
C. $(1,{}^-4)$ **D.** $({}^-1,4)$

For questions 21–22, use the table.

x	-3	-2	-1	0	1	2	3
y	-4	-3	-2	-1	0	1	?

21. Which number completes the table?

A. $^-4$ **B.** 2   **C.** 3   **D.** 4

22. Which expression gives each value of y?

A. $x - 1$ **B.** $x + 1$
C. $2x$ **D.** $\dfrac{x}{2}$

For questions 23–24, use the table.

x	2	1	0	-1
y	6	3	0	?

23. Which number completes the table?

A. $^-3$ **B.** $^-1$ **C.** 1   **D.** 3

24. Which expression gives each value of y?

A. $x - 3$ **B.** $x + 4$
C. $3x$ **D.** $3 - x$

Name _____

Choose the letter of the correct answer.

1. What is the opposite of ⁻6?

   A. 0   **B.** $^+\frac{1}{6}$

   C. ⁺6   **D.** 6^2

2. What is the number 8 written in the form $\frac{a}{b}$?

   A. $\frac{1}{8}$ **B.** $\frac{8}{1}$

   C. $\frac{8}{10}$ **D.** $\frac{8}{8}$

For questions 3–4, find the repeating or terminating decimal for the fraction.

3. $\frac{6}{11}$

   A. 0.54   **B.** 0.58   **C.** 0.60   **D.** 0.61

4. $\frac{5}{8}$

   A. 0.56   **B.** 0.625   **C.** 0.80   **D.** 0.83

5. Which rational number is between $2\frac{1}{6}$ and $2\frac{1}{3}$?

   A. $1\frac{1}{4}$ **B.** $2\frac{1}{4}$

   C. $2\frac{3}{4}$ **D.** $3\frac{1}{4}$

6. A campsite is located 8.43 mi from parking Lot B. A picnic area is 8.48 mi from parking lot B. A waterfall is between the campsite and the picnic area. How far from parking lot B could the waterfall be?

   A. 4.24 mi   **B.** 8.40 mi

   C. 8.47 mi   **D.** 16.91 mi

7. Compare the numbers. Choose <, >, or =.

   $\frac{3}{8}$ ● 0.365

   A. <   **B.** >   **C.** =

8. Kane, Aaron, Leon, and Keith had a juggling contest. Kane juggled for $8\frac{3}{8}$ sec, Aaron for 8.45 sec, Leon for $8\frac{1}{6}$ sec, and Keith for 8.08 sec. Who juggled the longest?

   A. Kane   **B.** Aaron

   C. Leon   **D.** Keith

For questions 9–10, find each sum.

9. ⁻6 + ⁺4

   A. ⁻2   **B.** ⁺2

   C. ⁺4   **D.** ⁺10

10. ⁻11 + ⁻4

   A. ⁻15   **B.** ⁻7

   C. ⁺11   **D.** ⁺15

11. Find the difference.

   ⁺6 − ⁻5

   A. ⁻11   **B.** ⁻1

   C. ⁺1   **D.** ⁺11

12. When Yoshi went to bed, it was ⁻5°F. In the morning it was 20° warmer. What was the temperature in the morning?

   A. ⁻15°F   **B.** ⁻5°F

   C. ⁺15°F   **D.** ⁺25°F

13. The product of a negative integer and a negative integer is __?__.

A. a positive integer
B. a negative integer
C. zero
D. the same sign as the larger integer

14. Find the product.

$^-5 \times {}^+3$

A. $^-15$ B. $-\dfrac{3}{5}$

C. $\dfrac{3}{5}$ D. 15

15. Find the quotient.

$^+24 \div {}^-3$

A. $^-21$ B. $^-8$

C. $-\dfrac{1}{8}$ D. 8

16. At 4:00 P.M. the temperature dropped by 21°. If the temperature was 15°F at noon, what was the temperature at 4:00 P.M.?

A. $^-20°F$ B. $^-14°F$
C. $^-6°F$ D. $^-4°F$

17. Evaluate $t + 12$ for $t = {}^-3$.

A. $^-15$ B. $^-9$
C. 9   D. 15

18. Evaluate $7y$ for $y = {}^-2$.

A. $^-14$ B. $-3\dfrac{1}{2}$

C. 9   D. 14

19. Solve the equation.

$a + 3 = {}^-9$

A. $a = {}^-15$ B. $a = {}^-12$
C. $a = {}^-6$ D. $a = {}^+12$

20. Which equation should you write for this word sentence?

3 more than a number, c, is negative 18.

A. $c - 3 = {}^-18$ B. $3 - c = 18$
C. $3 - c = {}^-18$ D. $c + 3 = {}^-18$

21. What are the whole-number solutions to the inequality $x \leq 5$?

A. 0, 1, 2, 3, 4   B. 0, 1, 2, 3, 4, 5
C. 1, 2, 3, 4, 5   D. 1, 2, 3, 4

22. A roller coaster can travel at speeds up to and including, but not greater than, 35 mi per hr. Which inequality represents the speeds that the roller coaster can travel?

A. $x < 35$ B. $x > 35$
C. $x \geq 35$ D. $x \leq 35$

For questions 23–24, use the table.

x	$^-2$	$^-1$	0	1	2
y	$^-1$	0	1	2	?

23. Which number completes the table?

A. $^-2$ B. $^-1$
C. 0   D. 3

24. Which expression, using x, gives the value of y?

A. $x - 1$ B. $\dfrac{^-1}{2}x + 1$

C. $x + 1$ D. $2x - 1$

Form A • Multiple-Choice   A103   ▶ **Stop!**

Name _____

Choose the letter of the correct answer.

1. What is 0.2 written as a fraction?

   A. $\frac{1}{20}$ **B.** $\frac{2}{100}$

   C. $\frac{1}{2}$ **D.** $\frac{2}{10}$

2. Which of these shows the integers written in order from least to greatest?

   A. 0, ⁻1, 3, 2   **B.** 0, 2, ⁻1, 3
   C. ⁻1, 0, 2, 3   **D.** ⁻1, 2, 0, ⁻3

3. Use mental math to find the difference.

   62 − 19

   A. 41   **B.** 42   **C.** 43   **D.** 44

4. Choose the best estimate of the sum.

   4,188
   2,204
   + 3,829

   A. 9,000   **B.** 10,000
   C. 11,000   **D.** 12,000

5. 27.26 ÷ 0.58

   A. 0.047   **B.** 0.47
   C. 4.7   **D.** 47

6. Which of these numbers is a composite number?

   A. 7   **B.** 11   **C.** 15   **D.** 17

7. What is $2\frac{3}{8}$ written as an improper fraction?

   A. $\frac{5}{8}$ **B.** $\frac{17}{8}$ **C.** $\frac{19}{8}$ **D.** $\frac{21}{8}$

8. Find the difference in simplest form.

   $\frac{11}{12} - \frac{1}{12}$

   A. $\frac{4}{5}$ **B.** $\frac{5}{6}$
   C. $\frac{7}{8}$ **D.** not here

9. Find the sum in simplest form.

   $1\frac{1}{4} + 2\frac{5}{12}$

   A. $3\frac{5}{8}$ **B.** $3\frac{2}{3}$
   C. $4\frac{5}{8}$ **D.** not here

10. Find the product in simplest form.

   $\frac{1}{4} \times 2\frac{2}{3}$

   A. $\frac{1}{3}$ **B.** $\frac{2}{3}$ **C.** 1   **D.** 2

11. Which of these statements about pairs of lines is true?

   A. Parallel lines sometimes intersect.
   B. Parallel lines form right angles.
   C. All intersecting lines are parallel.
   D. Some intersecting lines are perpendicular.

12. What construction do the figures below represent?

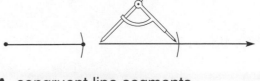

   A. congruent line segments
   B. bisected line segments
   C. congruent angles
   D. perpendicular line segments

13. This figure has rotational symmetry. What is the angle measure of each turn?

A. 45°   **B.** 90°   **C.** 120°   **D.** 180°

14.

figure A   figure B   figure C   figure D

Which polygon(s) will tessellate a plane?

A. figures A and B
B. figures A and C
C. figures B and C
D. figures B and D

15. The bottom view of a solid figure is a rectangle. The front view is a triangle. What kind of figure is it?

A. triangular pyramid
B. triangular prism
C. rectangular pyramid
D. rectangular prism

16. A survey of students who ride bicycles to school is conducted to find out if a new bicycle rack is needed. Which is a useful survey question?

A. How far do you live from school?
B. What color is your bicycle?
C. Can you lock up your bicycle every school day in the rack provided?
D. How old is your bicycle?

For questions 17–18, use this stem-and-leaf plot of test scores for a math test.

Mathematics Test Scores

Stem	Leaves
6	8 9 9
7	0 1 2 2 4 6
8	2 2 4 6 6 8
9	0 2 4 8 8

17. What score is shown by the third stem and its fourth leaf?

A. 72   **B.** 86   **C.** 94   **D.** not here

18. Where should a score of 60 be placed on this plot?

A. the first stem and its first leaf
B. the first stem and its second leaf
C. the first stem and its fourth leaf
D. not here

19. Why is this graph misleading?

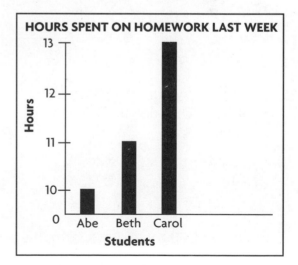

A. The labels are wrong.
B. It shows only one week of data.
C. The scale is misleading.
D. The title is wrong.

20. You can have sausage, mushroom, pepperoni, tomato, or onion on your pizza. You can have a thin crust or a thick crust. How many choices do you have for a one-topping pizza?

A. 7 choices   **B.** 8 choices
C. 10 choices   **D.** 12 choices

21. Evaluate $w^2 - 2$ for $w = 3$.

A. 1   **B.** 4
C. 7   **D.** not here

For questions 22–23, solve each equation.

22. $8 = m + 5$

A. $m = 3$ **B.** $m = 5$
C. $m = 13$ **D.** $m = 15$

23. $\frac{b}{2} = 4$

A. $b = \frac{1}{2}$ **B.** $b = 2$
C. $b = 8$ **D.** $b = 16$

24. What is the value of 150 English pounds in U.S. dollars? Use the formula $1.6261 \times P = D$.

A. $9.23   **B.** $24.39
C. $92.25   **D.** $243.92

25. Ina drove 390 mi to Jan's farm. If she traveled at a rate of 60 miles per hour, how long did it take her?

A. 6 hr   **B.** $6\frac{1}{4}$ hr
C. 7 hr   **D.** not here

26. Which ratio is equivalent to 3:4?

A. 2:3   **B.** 4:3
C. 1:4   **D.** 6:8

27. Maggie has 10 fish in a tank. Of them, 4 are yellow, 2 are black, and the rest are blue. What percent of the fish are blue?

A. 20%   **B.** 30%
C. 40%   **D.** 60%

28. What is the sale price on a jacket that costs $40 if the discount rate is 30%?

A. $12   **B.** $24
C. $28   **D.** not here

29. A flagpole casts a shadow that is 6 m long. At the same time a nearby pole that is 4 m high casts a 2-m shadow. What is the height of the flagpole?

A. 8 m   **B.** 10 m
C. 12 m   **D.** 16 m

30. The scale for a drawing of a patio is 1 in. = 4 ft. The drawing length is 3.5 in. What is the actual length of the patio?

A. 7.5 ft   **B.** 12 ft
C. 14 ft   **D.** not here

31. When Becky packed her suitcase for vacation, it weighed 9,500 g. How many kilograms did it weigh?

A. 0.95 kg   **B.** 9.5 kg
C. 95 kg   **D.** 950 kg

For questions 32–33, use the figure below.

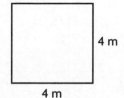

4 m

4 m

32. If you double the length of each side, what will be the area?

A. 16 m²   **B.** 24 m²

C. 36 m²   **D.** 64 m²

33. If you halve the length of each side, what will be the new perimeter?

A. 2 m   **B.** 4 m

C. 8 m   **D.** 32 m

34. Find the volume of the cylinder to the nearest whole unit. Use the formula $V = \pi r^2 \times h$. Use 3.14 for π.

8 cm

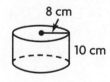

10 cm

A. about 251 cm³

B. about 502 cm³

C. about 2,010 cm³

D. not here

35. Julie is planning to paint her bedroom, which is 12 ft long, 14 ft wide, and 9 ft high. She will paint the walls, but not the floor or the ceiling. How much surface area will she paint?

A. 468 ft²   **B.** 636 ft²

C. 804 ft²   **D.** 1,512 ft²

36. What is the absolute value of ⁺24?

A. $\frac{1}{24}$ **B.** 1   **C.** ⁻24   **D.** 24

37. The winner of a race ran it in 12.5 sec. The third-place runner finished in 12.6 sec. Which could have been the time for the second-place runner?

A. 12.38 sec   **B.** 12.48 sec

C. 12.58 sec   **D.** 12.68 sec

38. Find the sum. ⁻4 + 5

A. ⁻9   **B.** ⁻1

C. ⁺1   **D.** ⁺9

39. On a winter day, the high temperature was ⁻5°F. The low temperature was 12° less. What was the low temperature?

A. ⁻17°F   **B.** ⁻7°F

C. 7°F   **D.** 17°F

40. Find the product. ⁻16 × ⁻2

A. ⁻32   **B.** ⁻8

C. ⁺8   **D.** ⁺32

41. Evaluate $y^2 - 1$ for $y = 3$.

A. ⁻8   **B.** ⁻5

C. ⁺5   **D.** ⁺8

42. Solve the equation. $2n = ⁻8$

A. $n = ⁻16$ **B.** $n = ⁻4$

C. $n = ⁺4$ **D.** $n = ⁺16$

Name _____

Choose the letter of the correct answer.

For questions 1–4, use triangle *RST*. Its coordinates are (1,1), (3,4) and (3,1).

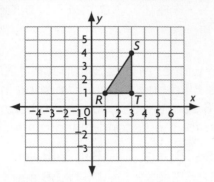

1. If you translate triangle *RST* 2 units to the left, which coordinates will change?

   A. both *x*- and *y*- coordinates
   B. only *x*-coordinates
   C. only *y*-coordinates
   D. neither *x*- nor *y*-coordinates

2. If you translate triangle *RST* 3 units to the left and 2 units down, what are the coordinates of the new triangle?

   A. $R'(^-2,^-1)$, $S'(0,2)$, $T'(0,^-1)$
   B. $R'(^-1,^-2)$, $S'(2,0)$, $T'(^-1,0)$
   C. $R'(^-1,^-2)$, $S'(1,1)$, $T'(^-2,^-1)$
   D. $R'(^-2,1)$, $S'(0,4)$, $T'(0,1)$

3. If you reflect triangle *RST* across the *x*-axis, you create triangle $R'S'T'$. What are the coordinates of S'?

   A. (3,0)
   B. $(3,^-1)$
   C. $(3,^-4)$
   D. $(1,^-4)$

4. If you reflect triangle *RST* across the *y*-axis, what are the coordinates of the new triangle?

   A. $R'(1,^-1)$, $S'(1,^-4)$, $T'(3,^-1)$
   B. $R'(1,^-1)$, $S'(3,^-4)$, $T'(3,^-1)$
   C. $R'(^-1,1)$, $S'(^-1,4)$, $T'(^-3,1)$
   D. $R'(^-1,1)$, $S'(^-3,4)$, $T'(^-3,1)$

For questions 5–6, use parallelogram *MNOP* with coordinates (0,0), (1,2), (4,2), and (3,0).

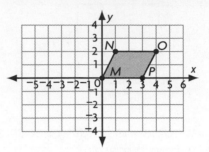

5. If you rotate this figure 90° clockwise around the origin, which vertex of the new figure will have the same coordinates it had in the original figure?

   A. vertex *M*   B. vertex *N*
   C. vertex *O*   D. vertex *P*

6. If you rotate this figure 90° clockwise around the origin, what are the coordinates of the new figure?

   A. $M'(0,0)$, $N'(^-1,^-2)$, $O'(^-2,^-4)$, $P'(0,^-3)$
   B. $M'(0,0)$, $N'(^-1,2)$, $O'(^-2,4)$, $P'(0,3)$
   C. $M'(0,0)$, $N'(2,^-1)$, $O'(2,^-4)$, $P'(0,^-3)$
   D. $M'(0,0)$, $N'(2,1)$, $O'(4,2)$, $P'(3,0)$

For question 7, use the pattern on the grid.

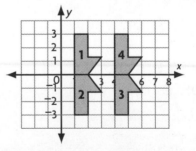

7. What pattern of transformations was used to move the figure from position 1 to position 4?

   A. rotation, reflection, rotation
   B. translation, reflection, translation
   C. reflection, translation, reflection
   D. rotation, translation, reflection

Form A • Multiple-Choice   **Go on.** ▶

For questions 8–10, use the pattern.

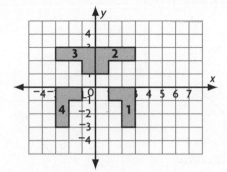

8. What pattern of transformations was used to move the figure from position 1 to position 4?

    A. rotation, reflection, rotation
    B. reflection, translation, reflection
    C. translation, reflection, translation
    D. rotation, translation, reflection

9. What transformation would be used to move the figure to the next position?

    A. translation
    B. reflection
    C. rotation
    D. not here

10. What transformation would be used to move the figure to position 6?

    A. translation
    B. reflection
    C. rotation
    D. not here

11. Describe how many cubes are in the next figure in the pattern.

    A. 3 × 2   B. 4 × 2
    C. 6 × 2   D. not here

For questions 12–14, choose the figure that comes next in the pattern.

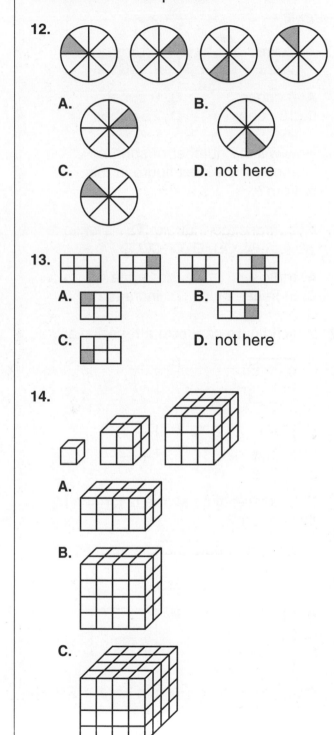

12.

    A.   B.

    C.   D. not here

13.

    A.   B.

    C.   D. not here

14.

    A.

    B.

    C.

    D. not here

15. How many cubes would there be in the next figure in this sequence?

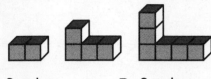

A. 8 cubes   **B.** 9 cubes
C. 16 cubes   **D.** 25 cubes

16. How will the number of spheres change for the next figure in this pattern?

A. triple   **B.** double
C. increase by 5   **D.** increase by 6

17. Which figure can form a tessellation?

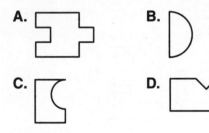

18. What tessellation shape is formed by this pattern?

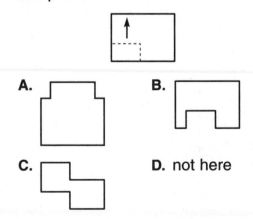

A.

B.

C.   **D.** not here

19. Which tessellation shape is formed by this pattern?

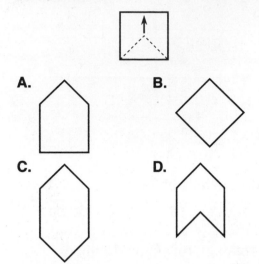

A.   **B.**

C.   **D.**

20. From which shape was this tessellation formed?

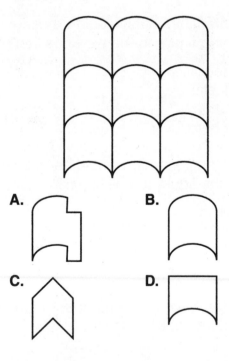

A.   **B.**

C.   **D.**

Choose the letter of the correct answer.

1. Each number in a sequence is called
  __?__.

  A. a pattern
  B. an integer
  C. a term
  D. a triangular number

2. What pattern is used to make the
  sequence?

  128, 64, 32, 16, . . .

  A. subtract 16   **B.** divide by 2
  C. multiply by 2   **D.** add 16

For questions 3–6, find the next term in
the sequence.

3. 5, 10, 15, 20, . . .

  A. 21   **B.** 25
  C. 30   **D.** not here

4. 81, 72, 63, 54, . . .

  A. 36   **B.** 44
  C. 45   **D.** not here

5. 3.5, 5.4, 7.3, 9.2, . . .

  A. 10.1   **B.** 10.9
  C. 11.0   **D.** not here

6. 800, 80, 8, 0.8, . . .

  A. 0.08   **B.** 0.088
  C. 0.80   **D.** not here

7. Racquel is practicing to run a 1,000 m
  race. She runs 500 m the first day. If
  she increases the distance she runs by
  50 m each day, in how many days will
  she be running 1,000 m?

  A. 5 days   **B.** 10 days
  C. 15 days   **D.** 20 days

8. Mikail walks dogs to earn money. He
  made $32 the first week, $39 the
  second week, and $46 the third week.
  If this pattern continues, how much
  money will he earn the sixth week?

  A. $53
  B. $60
  C. $64
  D. $67

9. To identify the pattern of a sequence
  with fractions, __?__.

  A. find a common denominator
  B. convert to decimals
  C. add the fractions
  D. multiply the fractions

For questions 10–12, find the next term in
the sequence.

10. $\frac{1}{10}, \frac{3}{10}, \frac{1}{2}, \cdots$

  A. $\frac{3}{5}$ **B.** $\frac{7}{10}$

  C. $\frac{3}{4}$ **D.** $\frac{4}{5}$

11. $\frac{15}{16}, \frac{3}{4}, \frac{9}{16}, \cdots$

  A. $\frac{3}{8}$ **B.** $\frac{1}{2}$

  C. $\frac{5}{8}$ **D.** $\frac{11}{16}$

12. $1\frac{1}{8}, 1\frac{3}{4}, 2\frac{3}{8}, \cdots$

  A. $2\frac{3}{4}$ **B.** $2\frac{7}{8}$

  C. 3   **D.** $3\frac{1}{8}$

13. On Thursday, Lara read for $\frac{1}{4}$ hr. On Friday, she read for $\frac{3}{4}$ hr. On Saturday, she read for $1\frac{1}{4}$ hr. If this pattern continues, for how much time will she read on Monday?

   A. 2 hr

   B. $2\frac{1}{8}$ hr

   C. $2\frac{1}{4}$ hr

   D. not here

14. What pattern is used to make the sequence?

   $\frac{7}{3}, \frac{7}{9}, \frac{7}{27}, \dots$

   A. multiply by $\frac{1}{3}$

   B. subtract 3

   C. multiply by 3

   D. subtract $\frac{1}{3}$

For questions 15–17, find the next term in the sequence.

15. $\frac{4}{7}, \frac{8}{7}, \frac{16}{7}, \dots$

   A. $\frac{20}{7}$ B. $\frac{24}{7}$

   C. $\frac{28}{7}$ D. $\frac{32}{7}$

16. $\frac{3}{5}, \frac{3}{10}, \frac{3}{20}, \dots$

   A. $\frac{3}{30}$ B. $\frac{3}{40}$

   C. $\frac{3}{50}$ D. $\frac{3}{60}$

17. $\frac{1}{9}, \frac{1}{3}, 1, \dots$

   A. $1\frac{1}{3}$ B. $2\frac{2}{3}$

   C. 3   D. 9

18. A multiplication sequence with a pattern of multiplying by 5 has a first term of $\frac{1}{50}$. What is the fourth term?

   A. $\frac{1}{10}$ B. $\frac{5}{20}$

   C. $\frac{1}{2}$ D. $\frac{5}{2}$

19. What pattern is used in this sequence of integers?

   $^-1, {}^+3, {}^-9, {}^+27, \dots$

   A. multiply by $^-3$
   B. multiply by $^+3$
   C. add $^+4$
   D. not here

For questions 20–21, find the next term in the sequence.

20. $^-4, {}^+8, {}^-16, \dots$

   A. $^-32$ B. $^-24$
   C. $^+24$ D. $^+32$

21. $^+324, {}^-108, {}^+36, \dots$

   A. $^-12$ B. $^-3$
   C. $^+3$ D. $^+12$

22. A scuba diving class lasts for 10 days. On the first day, the class dives to a level of $^-10$ ft. On each of the following days, the class dives 5 ft below the level of the day before. How deep is the dive on the 8th day of class?

   A. $^-35$ ft   B. $^-40$ ft
   C. $^-45$ ft   D. $^-50$ ft

Form A • Multiple-Choice   A112   ▶ **Stop!**

Name _____

Choose the letter of the correct answer.

For questions 1–2, use triangle *JKL*. Its coordinates are (2,2), (2,4), and (6,2).

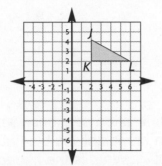

1. If you reflect triangle *JKL* across the x-axis, which coordinates will change?

  A. both x- and y-coordinates
  B. only x-coordinates
  C. only y-coordinates
  D. neither x- nor y-coordinates

2. If you rotate triangle *JKL* around the origin 90° clockwise, what are the coordinates of the new triangle?

  A. (⁻2,2), (⁻2,4), (⁻6,2)
  B. (2,⁻2), (4,⁻2), (2,⁻6)
  C. (4,⁻2), (⁻6,⁻2), (⁻2,⁻2)
  D. (⁻2,⁻2), (4,⁻2), (⁻6,2)

For questions 3–5, use the pattern below.

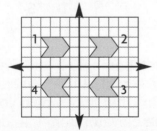

3. What transformations were used to move the figure from 1 to position 4?

  A. rotation, translation, rotation
  B. translation, reflection, translation
  C. rotation, reflection, rotation
  D. translation, rotation, translation

4. What transformation would be used to move the figure to the next position?

  A. 180° rotation   **B.** translation
  C. reflection   **D.** 90° rotation

5. What transformation would be used to move the figure to position 6?

  A. 180° rotation   **B.** translation
  C. reflection   **D.** 90° rotation

6. Describe the next figure in the pattern.

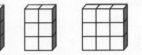

  A. 10 cubes   **B.** 12 cubes
  C. 14 cubes   **D.** 18 cubes

7. How many cubes would there be in the next figure in this sequence?

  A. 9 cubes   **B.** 10 cubes
  C. 16 cubes   **D.** 18 cubes

8. Which figure does not form a tessellation?

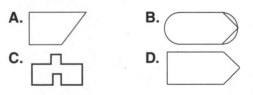

9. Which tessellation shape is formed by this pattern?

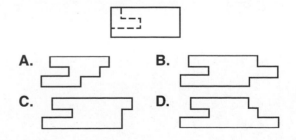

Form A • Multiple-Choice   A113   **Go on. ▶**

Name _____

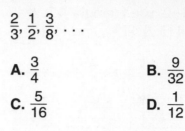

For questions 10–11, find the next term in the sequence.

10. 8, 16, 24, 32, . . .

　　A. 34　　　　　**B.** 38
　　C. 40　　　　　**D.** 48

11. 0.375, 0.75, 1.5, 3, . . .

　　A. 3.75　　　　**B.** 4.5
　　C. 5.25　　　　**D.** 6

For questions 12–13, find the next term in the sequence.

12. $\frac{1}{8}, \frac{1}{4}, \frac{3}{8},$ . . .

　　A. $\frac{1}{2}$　　**B.** $\frac{1}{4}$　　**C.** $\frac{3}{4}$　　**D.** $\frac{5}{8}$

13. $4\frac{1}{2}, 3\frac{3}{4}, 3,$ . . .

　　A. 2　　**B.** $2\frac{1}{4}$　　**C.** $2\frac{1}{2}$　　**D.** $2\frac{3}{4}$

14. On Monday Nick and Lian hiked $\frac{4}{5}$ mi. On Tuesday they hiked $1\frac{3}{5}$ mi and on Wednesday they hiked $2\frac{2}{5}$ mi. If this pattern continues, how far will they hike on Thursday?

　　A. $2\frac{3}{5}$　　　　　**B.** $2\frac{4}{5}$

　　C. $3\frac{1}{5}$　　　　　**D.** $3\frac{2}{5}$

15. What pattern is used to make the sequence?

　　$\frac{3}{8}, \frac{3}{4}, \frac{3}{2},$ . . .

　　A. add 6　　　　　**B.** subtract 6
　　C. multiply by 2　**D.** divide by 2

16. Find the next term in the sequence.

　　$\frac{2}{3}, \frac{1}{2}, \frac{3}{8},$ . . .

　　A. $\frac{3}{4}$　　　　　**B.** $\frac{9}{32}$

　　C. $\frac{5}{16}$　　　　**D.** $\frac{1}{12}$

17. A multiplication sequence with a pattern of multiplying by 4 has a first term of $\frac{1}{64}$. What is the fifth term?

　　A. $\frac{1}{32}$　　　　**B.** $\frac{1}{16}$

　　C. $\frac{1}{4}$　　　　　**D.** $\frac{16}{4}$

For questions 18–19, find the next term in the sequence.

18. ⁻24, ⁺12, ⁻6, . . .

　　A. 0　　　　　　**B.** ⁻3
　　C. ⁺3　　　　　**D.** ⁺6

19. ⁻729, ⁻243, ⁻81, . . .

　　A. ⁻27　　　　　**B.** ⁻9
　　C. ⁻3　　　　　**D.** ⁺3

20. A skyscraper is 80 ft tall. Every 10 ft below the roof of the skyscraper is a floor. On what floor would you be if you took the elevator from the top floor of the skyscraper 60 ft down?

　　A. 1st floor　　　**B.** 2nd floor
　　C. 3rd floor　　　**D.** 6th floor

Choose the letter of the correct answer.

1. What is the value of the digit 2 in the number 204,567.98?

   A. 2 hundreds
   B. 2 thousands
   C. 2 ten thousands
   D. 2 hundred thousands

2. $4\overline{)2{,}542}$

   A. 635   B. 635 r1
   C. 635 r2   D. not here

3. $4.607 + 1.85$

   A. 4.775   B. 5.457
   C. 6.457   D. not here

4. Jason bought 5.5 lb of ground meat at $1.10 a pound. How much did the meat cost?

   A. $5.50   B. $6.05
   C. $6.50   D. $6.60

5. Solve for n to complete the prime factorization.

   $5^n = 125$

   A. $n = 2$ B. $n = 3$
   C. $n = 4$ D. $n = 5$

6. Find the difference in simplest form.

   $\frac{8}{9} - \frac{1}{3}$

   A. $\frac{1}{3}$ B. $\frac{4}{9}$

   C. $\frac{5}{9}$ D. $\frac{2}{3}$

7. Choose the best estimate for the word problem.

   On a hike, Aaron hiked $7\frac{7}{8}$ mi on the first day and $6\frac{1}{10}$ mi on the second day. About how far did he hike in all?

   A. about 13 mi
   B. about $13\frac{1}{2}$ mi
   C. about 14 mi
   D. about $14\frac{1}{2}$ mi

8. Jean wants to make a rectangular flower garden with an area of $35\frac{1}{2}$ sq ft. The length of the garden will be 5 ft. How wide should the garden be?

   A. $7\frac{1}{10}$ ft   B. $7\frac{1}{5}$ ft

   C. $7\frac{7}{10}$ ft   D. not here

9. How many angles does a quadrilateral have?

   A. 3 angles   B. 4 angles
   C. 6 angles   D. 8 angles

10. Choose the figure that is a reflection of the original figure.

original   figure 1   figure 2   figure 3

A. figure 1   **B.** figure 2
C. figure 3   **D.** not here

11. Name this figure.

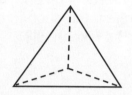

A. triangular pyramid
B. triangular prism
C. rectangular pyramid
D. rectangular prism

12. Maggie is making a model of a pyramid whose base has 6 sides. She is using toothpicks for the edges and balls of putty for the vertices. How many toothpicks does she need?

A. 6 toothpicks   **B.** 12 toothpicks
C. 18 toothpicks   **D.** 24 toothpicks

13. Which of the following questions in a sports survey is biased?

A. What is your favorite sports event?
B. How often do you attend sporting events?
C. How often do you watch sports on TV?
D. Do you agree with the basketball coach that sports events should be full of action?

14. Use the graph.

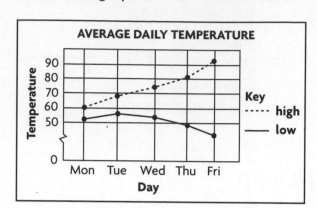

What was the trend for high temperatures?

A. increased   **B.** decreased
C. stayed same   **D.** not here

15. The box-and-whisker graph shows the number of problems that 25 students got correct on a science quiz with 50 problems. What is the median?

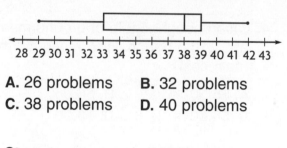

28 29 30 31 32 33 34 35 36 37 38 39 40 41 42 43

A. 26 problems   **B.** 32 problems
C. 38 problems   **D.** 40 problems

16. Steve tosses a coin 100 times. Heads comes up 60 times. What is the experimental probability of tossing heads?

A. $\frac{1}{6}$ **B.** $\frac{2}{5}$ **C.** $\frac{1}{2}$ **D.** $\frac{3}{5}$

17. Determine the input for the given output for this expression: $w + 4$.

output = 10   input = __?__

A. $w = 6$ **B.** $w = 8$
C. $w = 10$ **D.** $w = 14$

18. $b - 2 = 6$

   A. $b = 4$ **B.** $b = 6$
   C. $b = 8$ **D.** $b = 12$

19. $2m = 8$

   A. $m = 4$ **B.** $m = 6$
   C. $m = 10$ **D.** $m = 16$

20. What is 23°C converted to degrees Fahrenheit? Use the formula $F = (\frac{9}{5} \times C) + 32$. Round to the nearest degree.

   A. 41°F   **B.** 45°F
   C. 65°F   **D.** 73°F

21. Mike is in a 20-mi bike race. How long is this ride in kilometers?
(1 mi = 1.609 km)

   A. 12.43 km   **B.** 32.18 km
   C. 123.4 km   **D.** 321.8 km

22. Paulo answered 45 of the 50 problems on his math test correctly. What percent did he answer correctly?

   A. 45%   **B.** 80%
   C. 90%   **D.** 95%

23. What is 60% of 80?

   A. 40   **B.** 60
   C. 80   **D.** not here

24. Beatrice had $200 that earned 5% simple interest a year in a bank. After 2 years, she withdrew her money. How much did she withdraw?

   A. $10   **B.** $20   **C.** $210   **D.** $220

25. Find n in this pair of similar triangles.

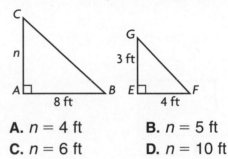

   A. $n = 4$ ft   **B.** $n = 5$ ft
   C. $n = 6$ ft   **D.** $n = 10$ ft

26. A map scale is 1 in. = 20 mi. The map distance is 6.5 in. Find the actual miles.

   A. 100 mi   **B.** 120 mi
   C. 130 mi   **D.** not here

27. Which is the most precise measurement for the height of a bench?

   A. 2 ft   **B.** $2\frac{1}{2}$ ft

   C. 32 in.   **D.** $32\frac{1}{2}$ in.

28. Estimate the area of the figure. Each square is 1 cm².

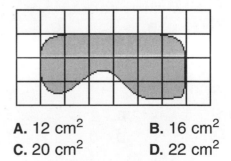

   A. 12 cm²   **B.** 16 cm²
   C. 20 cm²   **D.** 22 cm²

29. Jo is buying wall-to-wall carpet for her bedroom. The room is 12 ft by 12 ft. The carpet costs $5 per sq ft. What will be the total cost of the carpet? (Use the formula $A = s^2$.)

A. $144   **B.** $650
C. $720   **D.** not here

30. Use the figure below.

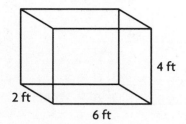

4 ft

2 ft

6 ft

If you double all the dimensions of this figure, what is the volume of the larger prism?

A. 48 ft^3 **B.** 96 ft^3
C. 192 ft^3 **D.** 384 ft^3

31. Choose the repeating or terminating decimal for $\frac{2}{3}$.

A. 0.6   **B.** $0.\overline{6}$
C. 0.66   **D.** 0.67

32. Compare the numbers. Choose $<$, $>$, or $=$.

$\frac{1}{5}$ ● $^-0.5$

A. $<$ **B.** $>$ **C.** $=$

33. Find the difference. $^-4 - {}^+6$

A. $^-10$ **B.** $^-2$
C. 2   **D.** 10

34. Find the product. $^-3 \times 12$

A. $^-36$ **B.** $^-4$
C. $^+4$ **D.** $^+36$

35. Solve the equation. $d + 2 = {}^-8$

A. $d = {}^-10$ **B.** $d = {}^-6$
C. $d = {}^+6$ **D.** $d = {}^+10$

36. How will the number of circles change for the next figure in this pattern?

A. triple
B. double
C. increase by 1
D. increase by 2

For questions 37–38, find the next term in the sequence.

37. 27, 36, 45, 54, . . .

A. 55   **B.** 58
C. 63   **D.** 65

38. $\frac{1}{8}, \frac{1}{4}, \frac{1}{2}, 1, . . .$

A. $1\frac{1}{4}$ **B.** $1\frac{1}{2}$
C. 2   **D.** 4

Choose the letter of the correct answer.

1. What is the value of the digit 5 in the number 150,987,432?

- **A.** 5 thousands
- **B.** 5 ten thousands
- **C.** 5 millions
- **D.** 5 ten millions

1-A.3

2. Which shows the three numbers ordered from least to greatest?

- **A.** 20,084; 20,408; 20,480
- **B.** 20,480; 20,084; 20,408
- **C.** 20,408; 20,480; 20,084
- **D.** not here

1-A.4

3. Joel has 1,200 baseball cards. His sister has 725 baseball cards. How many more cards does Joel have than his sister?

- **A.** 475 more
- **B.** 1,525 more
- **C.** 1,925 more
- **D.** not here

2-A.3

4. What is 5,000 + 300 + 0 + 4 + 0 + 0.08 + 0.002 in standard form?

- **A.** 534.082
- **B.** 5,304.082
- **C.** 5,304.82
- **D.** not here

3-A.2

5. 5.6 − 0.246 = n

- **A.** 5.354
- **B.** 5.364
- **C.** 5.446
- **D.** not here

4-A.1

6. Estimate the sum to the nearest tenth.

3.12
+2.78

- **A.** about 5.8
- **B.** about 5.9
- **C.** about 6.0
- **D.** about 6.1

4-A.2

7. Find the area of the rectangle.

8 ft

24 ft

- **A.** 162 sq ft
- **B.** 182 sq ft
- **C.** 192 sq ft
- **D.** not here

5-A.3

8. 205
× 24

- **A.** 4,820
- **B.** 4,920
- **C.** 4,924
- **D.** 5,920

6-A.1

9. Estimate the product by rounding each factor to its greatest place-value position.

29 × 537 = n

- **A.** 10,000
- **B.** 12,000
- **C.** 15,000
- **D.** not here

6-A.2

10. Estimate the quotient.

4)174

- **A.** about 30
- **B.** about 40
- **C.** about 50
- **D.** about 60

7-A.1

11. 45)374

- **A.** 7 r14
- **B.** 7 r16
- **C.** 8 r16
- **D.** not here

8-A.3

Form A • Multiple-Choice   A1   Go on. ▶

12. Choose the number sentence that can be used to solve the word problem.

Mel bought a new stereo that cost $1,380. She paid for it in 12 monthly payments. How much was each payment?

- **A.** $1,380 + 12 = n
- **B.** $1,380 − 12 = n
- **C.** $1,380 × 12 = n
- **D.** $1,380 ÷ 12 = n

8-A.4

13. What is the mean for the set of data?

24, 13, 12, 14, 12

- **A.** 12
- **B.** 13
- **C.** 14
- **D.** 15

9-A.1

14. Use the graph.

HOW MAGGIE SPENT $8.00

snacks books
snacks books
snacks books
paper books

What fraction of her money did Maggie spend on snacks?

- **A.** $\frac{1}{8}$
- **B.** $\frac{2}{8}$
- **C.** $\frac{3}{8}$
- **D.** $\frac{4}{8}$

10-A.1

15. From a bag that has 7 red marbles and 2 blue marbles, pulling a red marble is __?__ .

- **A.** certain
- **B.** impossible
- **C.** likely
- **D.** unlikely

11-A.1

16. Use the spinner.

What is the probability the pointer will stop on the darker shaded section?

- **A.** $\frac{1}{6}$
- **B.** $\frac{2}{6}$
- **C.** $\frac{3}{6}$
- **D.** $\frac{4}{6}$

11-A.3

17. 3.46
× 2.8

- **A.** 0.9688
- **B.** 9.688
- **C.** 96.88
- **D.** 968.8

12-A.4

18. 2)17.42

- **A.** 0.871
- **B.** 8.71
- **C.** 87.1
- **D.** not here

13-A.2

19. Which is the most reasonable unit for finding the length of a piece of notebook paper?

- **A.** millimeter
- **B.** centimeter
- **C.** meter
- **D.** kilometer

14-A.1

20. In a 5-person relay race, each person on the relay team must run 600 m. How many kilometers long is the whole race?

- **A.** 0.3 km
- **B.** 3 km
- **C.** 30 km
- **D.** not here

14-A.3

Form A • Multiple-Choice   A2   Go on. ▶

21. Choose the fraction shown on the fraction strip.

- **A.** $\frac{1}{4}$
- **B.** $\frac{1}{3}$
- **C.** $\frac{2}{4}$
- **D.** $\frac{2}{3}$

15-A.1

22. Compare the fractions using the LCM.

$\frac{3}{4}$ ○ $\frac{2}{3}$

- **A.** $\frac{6}{8} > \frac{5}{8}$
- **B.** $\frac{3}{4} < \frac{4}{3}$
- **C.** $\frac{30}{40} > \frac{20}{40}$
- **D.** $\frac{9}{12} > \frac{8}{12}$

15-A.3

23. Use division to find an equivalent fraction for $\frac{8}{24}$.

- **A.** $\frac{1}{3}$
- **B.** $\frac{1}{2}$
- **C.** $\frac{4}{8}$
- **D.** $\frac{2}{3}$

16-A.2

24. Mike made some bread. He used 2 cups of whole wheat flour. He used 8 cups of flour in all. In simplest terms, what fraction of the flour was whole wheat flour?

- **A.** $\frac{1}{8}$
- **B.** $\frac{1}{4}$
- **C.** $\frac{1}{3}$
- **D.** $\frac{1}{2}$

16-A.3

For questions 25–26, use fraction strips to find the sum or difference expressed in simplest form.

25. $\frac{1}{2} + \frac{3}{10}$ = __?__

- **A.** $\frac{3}{8}$
- **B.** $\frac{3}{4}$
- **C.** $\frac{4}{5}$
- **D.** $\frac{5}{10}$

17-A.2

26. $\frac{3}{4} - \frac{1}{3}$ = __?__

- **A.** $\frac{1}{6}$
- **B.** $\frac{5}{12}$
- **C.** $\frac{7}{12}$
- **D.** $\frac{5}{8}$

18-A.2

27. Estimate the sum. $\frac{8}{9} + \frac{1}{6}$

- **A.** about $\frac{1}{2}$
- **B.** about 1
- **C.** about $1\frac{1}{2}$
- **D.** about 2

19-A.1

28. Find the answer in simplest form.

$2\frac{1}{3}$
$+3\frac{5}{6}$

- **A.** $5\frac{1}{6}$
- **B.** $5\frac{2}{3}$
- **C.** $6\frac{1}{6}$
- **D.** $6\frac{2}{3}$

20-A.2

29. Book reports are due on May 15. Jen will work on her report for 1 week. When should she begin working on the report?

- **A.** April 15
- **B.** May 1
- **C.** May 8
- **D.** May 16

21-A.2

30. Find the product in simplest form.

$\frac{3}{4} × 2\frac{1}{2}$ = n

- **A.** $n = \frac{3}{4}$
- **B.** $n = \frac{7}{8}$
- **C.** $n = 1\frac{3}{4}$
- **D.** $n = 1\frac{7}{8}$

22-A.3

Form A • Multiple-Choice   A3   Go on. ▶

31. Use this figure.

Which of these angles is not a right angle?

- **A.** ∠AFB
- **B.** ∠AFD
- **C.** ∠CFE
- **D.** ∠DFE

23-A.1

32. Which quadrilateral has 4 congruent sides and 4 right angles?

- **A.** rhombus
- **B.** parallelogram
- **C.** rectangle
- **D.** square

23-A.3

33. A cake platter has a diameter of 12 in. What is the radius of the platter?

- **A.** 1 in.
- **B.** 4 in.
- **C.** 6 in.
- **D.** 12 in.

25-A.1

34. Identify the solid figure.

- **A.** rectangular prism
- **B.** pentagonal pyramid
- **C.** rectangular pyramid
- **D.** triangular pyramid

26-A.1

35. Which ratio is equivalent to 4:24?

- **A.** 1:4
- **B.** 6:1
- **C.** 2:12
- **D.** not here

27-A.2

36. Find the length of the missing side in the similar triangles.

3 5   6   x
   4   8

- **A.** 5
- **B.** 9
- **C.** 10
- **D.** not here

27-A.4

37. What is 25% written as a decimal?

- **A.** 0.025
- **B.** 0.25
- **C.** 2.5
- **D.** 25

28-A.1

38. What is $\frac{3}{10}$ written as a percent?

- **A.** 3%
- **B.** 10%
- **C.** 30%
- **D.** 100%

28-A.2

Form A • Multiple-Choice   A4   ▶ **Stop!**

Multiple-Choice Format • Test Answers   **119**

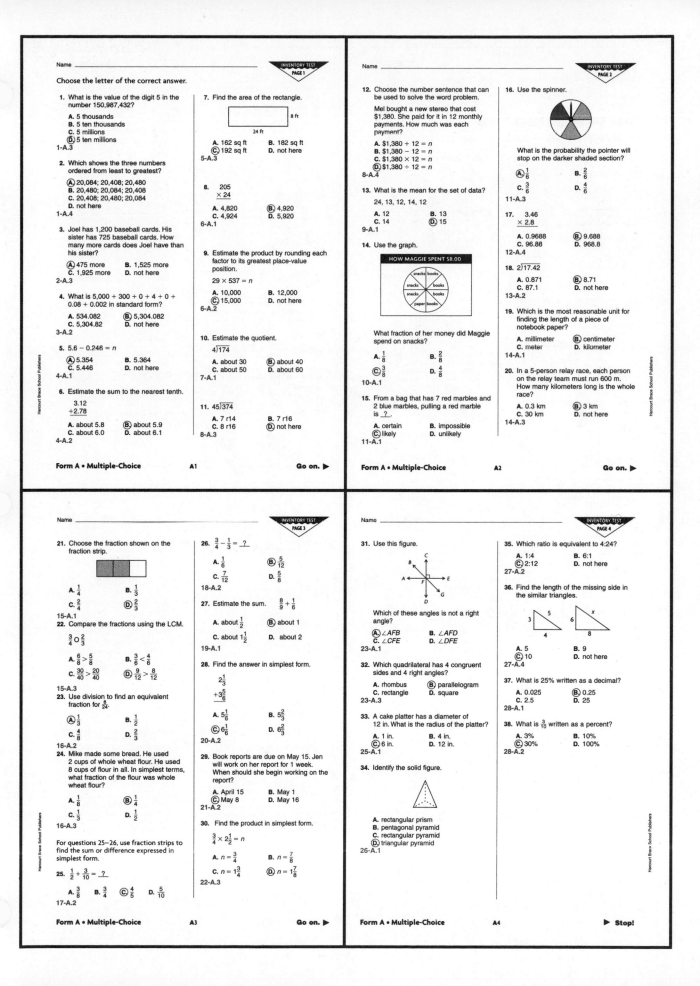

Choose the letter of the correct answer.

For questions 1–2, use the place-value chart below.

PLACE VALUE									
Millions	Hundred Thousands	Ten Thousands	Thousands	Hundreds	Tens	Ones	Tenths	Hundredths	Thousandths
1	4	2	6	3	2	1	.0	7	9

1. What is the value of the digit 4?

   A. 4 tens
   B. 4 thousands
   C. 4 ten thousands
   D. 4 hundred thousands

2. What is the value of the digit 7 in the place-value chart?

   A. 7 tenths
   B. 7 hundredths
   C. 7 thousandths
   D. 7 ten-thousandths

3. What is the value of the digit 8 in the number 407,836.21?

   A. 8 hundreds
   B. 8 thousands
   C. 8 ten thousands
   D. 8 hundred thousands

4. What is the value of the digit 5 in the number 1.275?

   A. 5 tens   B. 5 hundreds
   C. 5 hundredths   D. 5 thousandths

5. What is the standard form of four million, sixty thousand, one hundred two?

   A. 4,060,102   B. 460,102
   C. 46,000,102   D. 4,006,102,000

6. Which shows six hundredths written in standard form?

   A. 0.006
   B. 0.06
   C. 0.60
   D. 600.0

7. Which is greater than 10.25?

   A. 10.4
   B. 1.40
   C. 0.14
   D. 10.04

8. Which shows the numbers written in order from least to greatest?

   A. 2.2, 2.02, 2.12
   B. 2.2, 2.12, 2.02
   C. 2.12, 2.02, 2.2
   D. 2.02, 2.12, 2.2

9. The batting averages of three players are 0.240, 0.229, and 0.252. Which shows these averages written in order from greatest to least?

   A. 0.229, 0.240, 0.252
   B. 0.252, 0.229, 0.240
   C. 0.252, 0.240, 0.229
   D. 0.240, 0.252, 0.229

10. A rabbit can run 56.3 km per hour, a coyote 69.2 km per hour, a giraffe 51.3 km per hour, and a greyhound 63.3 km per hour. Which of the four animals runs the fastest?

    A. rabbit
    B. coyote
    C. giraffe
    D. greyhound

Form A • Multiple-Choice   A5   Go on. ▶

11. How can you change the fraction $\frac{1}{6}$ to a decimal?

    A. Multiply 10 by $\frac{1}{6}$.
    B. Divide 10 by $\frac{1}{6}$.
    C. Divide 6 by 1.
    D. Divide 1 by 6.

12. What is 0.07 written as a fraction?

    A. $\frac{7}{10}$ B. $\frac{1}{7}$
    C. $\frac{7}{100}$ D. $\frac{1}{70}$

13. What is $\frac{2}{5}$ written as a decimal?

    A. 0.10   B. 0.20
    C. 0.25   D. 0.40

14. What decimal makes the following inequality true?

    $\frac{15}{25} < \underline{\ ?\ }$

    A. 0.20   B. 0.45
    C. 0.50   D. 0.8

15. The lake was 1 mi away. Terry rode his bike 0.25 of the way. What is the distance Terry rode, expressed as a fraction?

    A. $\frac{1}{8}$ mi   B. $\frac{1}{5}$ mi
    C. $\frac{1}{4}$ mi   D. $\frac{1}{3}$ mi

16. Katie walked $\frac{3}{5}$ mi. What is the distance she walked, expressed as a decimal?

    A. 0.006 mi
    B. 0.06 mi
    C. 0.6 mi
    D. 6.0 mi

17. How many zeros are in the standard form of 10^6?

    A. 4   B. 5
    C. 6   D. 7

18. Which expression represents 5^2?

    A. 5 + 2
    B. 5 × 2
    C. 5 × 5
    D. 2 × 2 × 2 × 2 × 2

19. What is 4 × 4 × 4 × 4 × 4 written in exponent form?

    A. 4^3 B. 3^4
    C. 4^5 D. 5^4

20. What is the value of 6^3?

    A. 18   B. 36
    C. 42   D. 216

21. Which is less than 0?

    A. ⁻2   B. 0
    C. 4

22. Which of these shows the integers written in order from least to greatest?

    A. 0, ⁻4, 2, 4
    B. 0, 2, ⁻2, 4
    C. ⁻4, 0, 2, 4
    D. ⁻2, 2, 0, ⁻4

23. Which of these shows the integers written in order from least to greatest?

    A. 1, ⁻3, ⁻5, 0
    B. 1, ⁻5, ⁻3, 0
    C. ⁻3, ⁻5, 1, 0
    D. ⁻5, ⁻3, 0, 1

24. What is the opposite of ⁻4?

    A. $-\frac{1}{4}$ B. $+\frac{1}{4}$
    C. ⁺4   D. $+4^2$

Form A • Multiple-Choice   A6   ▶ Stop!

Choose the letter of the correct answer.

For questions 1–4, use mental math.

1. 7 + 18 + 13

   A. 28   B. 31
   C. 35   D. 38

2. 29 + 41 + 31 + 9

   A. 99   B. 100
   C. 110   D. 113

3. 53 − 29

   A. 21   B. 22
   C. 23   D. 24

4. 62 − 17

   A. 27   B. 38
   C. 40   D. 45

5. A rectangular box has a perimeter of 50 ft. The box is 5 ft longer than it is wide. What is the width of the box?

   A. 10 ft   B. 15 ft
   C. 20 ft   D. 40 ft

6. Barry sold a total of 42 green or red banners. He sold 10 more green banners than red banners. How many green banners did he sell?

   A. 16 banners
   B. 22 banners
   C. 26 banners
   D. 32 banners

7. The Rogers hockey team played a total of 20 games. They tied in 3 games and lost 1 more game than they won. How many games did they win?

   A. 7 games
   B. 8 games
   C. 9 games
   D. 10 games

8. Ms. Lee baked a total of 60 pies. She baked a dozen more apple pies than lemon pies. How many apple pies did she bake?

   A. 18 pies   B. 24 pies
   C. 36 pies   D. 48 pies

9. Which property of multiplication is being used below?

   7 × 25 = (7 × 20) + (7 × 5)

   A. Distributive Property
   B. Property of One
   C. Commutative Property
   D. Associative Property

For questions 10–11, use mental math to find the product.

10. 4 × 44

    A. 156   B. 160   C. 176   D. 180

11. 4 × 10 × 6

    A. 240   B. 260   C. 360   D. 400

12. Find the missing factor:

    27 × 43 = (27 × ■) + (27 × 3)

    A. 34   B. 40   C. 43   D. 74

13. Rob is solving the multiplication problem below. What mistake, if any, has Rob made?

    126
    × 23
    ─────
    378
    252

    A. His work has no mistake.
    B. The product 3 × 126 is 370.
    C. The products are lined up incorrectly.
    D. He did not multiply by the hundreds.

Form A • Multiple-Choice   A7   Go on. ▶

14. In this division problem, where would you put the first digit of the quotient?

    17)1,840

    A. in the ones place
    B. in the tens place
    C. in the hundreds place
    D. in the thousands place

15.   120
    × 35

    A. 960
    B. 3,200
    C. 4,100
    D. not here

16.   437
    ×226

    A. 97,862
    B. 98,762
    C. 106,662
    D. 107,662

17. 6)324

    A. 50 r4   B. 52 r2
    C. 53   D. 54

18. 20)4,060

    A. 203   B. 213
    C. 230   D. 233

19. Clea's parents bought a computer for $1,530.00. They are paying for it in 18 monthly payments. How much is each payment?

    A. $77.50
    B. $85.00
    C. $95.00
    D. $127.50

20. The Stone family spends $125 on groceries each week. How much does the family spend on groceries in one year? (HINT: 1 yr = 52 wk.)

    A. $650   B. $2,500
    C. $5,250   D. $6,500

21. Choose the best estimate of the sum.

       5,199
       4,206
     +3,749

    A. 11,000   B. 12,000
    C. 13,000   D. 15,000

22. Choose the best estimate of the quotient.

    1,765 ÷ 28

    A. 0.6   B. 60
    C. 600   D. 6,000

23. The music store sold 589 CDs of waterfall sounds and 209 audiotapes of the sounds. About how many more CDs were sold than audiotapes?

    A. about 200 more CDs
    B. about 300 more CDs
    C. about 400 more CDs
    D. about 500 more CDs

24. The movie theater at the waterfall park had 213 shows this summer. The theater, which holds 480 people, was full for every show. About how many people attended the shows?

    A. about 10,000 people
    B. about 10,200 people
    C. about 80,000 people
    D. about 100,000 people

Form A • Multiple-Choice   A8   ▶ Stop!

Multiple-Choice Format • Test Answers

120

Choose the letter of the correct answer.

For questions 1–2, estimate the sum.

1. 0.85 + 2.25 + 12.95
   A. 6   B. 14
   C. 16   D. 18

2. 5.42 + 0.76 + 4.06
   A. 7   B. 9
   C. 10   D. 15

For questions 3–4, find the sum.

3. 0.26 + 0.04
   A. 0.03   B. 0.3
   C. 0.36   D. 0.66

4. 3.2 + 10.07 + 0.64
   A. 4.84   B. 9.6
   C. 13.91   D. 19.6

5. A hiking trail has four sections. The lengths of the sections are 1.8 mi, 2.5 mi, 1.05 mi, and 0.75 mi. How many miles long is the hiking trail?
   A. 5.6 mi
   B. 6.1 mi
   C. 7.05 mi
   D. 7.5 mi

6. Rhonda spent $4.50 for a movie ticket. Her bus fare to the movie was $0.85 each way. At the movie, she bought popcorn for $1.60. How much did she spend in all?
   A. $6.10
   B. $6.80
   C. $6.95
   D. $7.80

7. 5.5 − 0.7
   A. 2.2   B. 2.8
   C. 3.2   D. 4.8

8. $7.63 − $1.58
   A. $5.05   B. $5.15
   C. $5.95   D. $6.05

9. 42.09 − 11.6
   A. 30.49   B. 31.03
   C. 31.3   D. 31.49

10. 18 − 10.005
    A. 7.995
    B. 8.995
    C. 16.995
    D. 16.095

11. Mrs. Ruiz drove 127.8 mi on Tuesday and 204.3 mi on Wednesday. How much farther did she drive on Wednesday?
    A. 72.5 mi
    B. 76.5 mi
    C. 77.5 mi
    D. 78.5 mi

12. The winning time in a swimming race was 91.26 sec. The second-place finisher had a time of 92.08 sec. What was the difference between the two times?
    A. 0.66 sec
    B. 0.72 sec
    C. 0.82 sec
    D. 1.14 sec

Form A • Multiple-Choice   A9   Go on. ▶

---

13. Use the decimal square to find 3 × 0.12.

    0.12 0.12 0.12

    A. 0.036   B. 0.36
    C. 3.6   D. 36.0

14. How many decimal places are there in the product 0.055 × 0.07?
    A. 2 decimal places
    B. 3 decimal places
    C. 4 decimal places
    D. 5 decimal places

15. 5 × 0.7
    A. 0.035   B. 0.35
    C. 35   D. not here

16. $2.75 × 8
    A. $16.60   B. $22.00
    C. $22.50   D. not here

17. 0.3 × 0.4
    A. 0.12   B. 1.12
    C. 1.2   D. not here

18. 0.27 × 4.2
    A. 0.1134   B. 1.134
    C. 1.34   D. not here

19. Brittany charges $3.50 per hour for baby-sitting. If she baby-sits for 4.5 hr, how much will she earn?
    A. $14.00   B. $14.75
    C. $15.25   D. $15.75

20. Craig is planning a cookout for 27 students. He needs 0.25 lb of hamburger for each student. How many pounds of hamburger does he need in all?
    A. 6.75 lb B. 12.5 lb
    C. 16.5 lb D. 67.5 lb

21. Which of these numbers should you multiply by to make the divisor in the division problem a whole number?
    0.65)2.145
    A. 1   B. 10
    C. 100   D. not here

22. 15.3 ÷ 9
    A. 0.17   B. 1.7
    C. 1.77   D. 17

23. 0.18)3.96
    A. 0.022   B. 0.22
    C. 2.2   D. 22

24. 13.44 ÷ 0.24
    A. 0.56   B. 5.06
    C. 5.6   D. 56

Form A • Multiple-Choice   A10   ▶ Stop!

Choose the letter of the correct answer.

1. What is the value of the digit 3 in the number 37,529.04?
   A. 3 tens
   B. 3 hundreds
   C. 3 thousands
   D. 3 ten thousands
   1-A.1

2. Which is less than 7.46?
   A. 7.39   B. 7.50
   C. 17.2   D. 70.5
   1-A.1

3. What is $\frac{5}{8}$ written as a decimal?
   A. 0.375   B. 0.58
   C. 0.625   D. 0.75
   1-A.2

4. Mark skated $\frac{5}{6}$ mi. What is the distance he skated, expressed as a decimal?
   A. 0.66 mi B. 0.75 mi
   C. 0.83 mi D. 5.6 mi
   1-A.2

5. How many zeros are there in the standard form of 10^4?
   A. 3   B. 4
   C. 5   D. 6
   1-A.3

6. What is the value of 3^4?
   A. 12   B. 36
   C. 81   D. 243
   1-A.3

7. Which of these shows the integers written in order from least to greatest?
   A. 9, 0, ⁻3, ⁻6
   B. 0, ⁻3, ⁻6, 9
   C. ⁻6, 9, ⁻3, 0
   D. ⁻6, ⁻3, 0, 9
   1-A.4

8. What is the opposite of ⁺16?
   A. ⁻16   B. ⁻$\frac{1}{16}$
   C. ⁺$\frac{1}{16}$ D. ⁺4^2
   1-A.4

9. Julie and Wanda scored a total of 38 points in a basketball game. Wanda scored 8 more points than Julie. How many points did Julie score?
   A. 15 points
   B. 16 points
   C. 23 points
   D. 30 points
   2-A.2

10. Kane made 54 treats for the bake sale. He made 12 brownies and made 6 more chocolate chip cookies than he did sugar cookies. How many sugar cookies did he make?
    A. 12 cookies
    B. 18 cookies
    C. 24 cookies
    D. 36 cookies
    2-A.2

11. Find the missing factor.
    16 × __?__ = (16 × 60) + (16 × 4)
    A. 4   B. 8
    C. 16   D. 64
    2-A.3

12. 350
    × 26
    A. 2,800
    B. 6,300
    C. 9,100
    D. 72,100
    2-A.3

Form A • Multiple-Choice   A11   Go on. ▶

---

13. 35)5,090
    A. 115 r45
    B. 135 r15
    C. 145 r15
    D. 154 r45
    2-A.3

14. The distance between two cities is 2,470 mi round trip. A pilot made the trip 9 times in one month. How many miles did the pilot travel?
    A. 22,230 mi
    B. 23,200 mi
    C. 23,320 mi
    D. 24,330 mi
    2-A.3

15. Choose the best estimate of the difference.
    8,462
    −2,248
    A. 6,000   B. 6,100
    C. 6,200   D. 6,300
    2-A.4

16. Choose the best estimate of the product.
    781
    ×412
    A. 280,000
    B. 320,000
    C. 350,000
    D. 400,000
    2-A.4

17. Find the sum.
    0.48 + 3.32 + 2.55
    A. 4.75   B. 5.25
    C. 6.35   D. 8.67
    3-A.1

18. Each member of a relay team ran 100 yd. The times for each member were 12.23 sec, 12.35 sec, 11.96 sec, and 11.89 sec. What was the total time for the relay team?
    A. 47.33 sec   B. 48.43 sec
    C. 49.34 sec   D. 50.44 sec
    3-A.1

19. 6.5093 − 2.2508
    A. 4.1513   B. 4.2585
    C. 4.3350   D. 4.3422
    3-A.1

20. Alani threw a shot put 12.83 m on his first try and 13.09 m on his second try. How much farther was his second throw?
    A. 0.26 m   B. 0.92 m
    C. 1.26 m   D. 1.83 m
    3-A.1

21. 8 × 4.73
    A. 32.64   B. 35.46
    C. 37.84   D. 38.48
    3-A.2

22. Heather is performing a chemistry experiment using 8 test tubes. She needs 2.50 mL of acid in each test tube. How much acid does she need?
    A. 10.5 mL B. 16.0 mL
    C. 16.5 mL D. 20.0 mL
    3-A.2

23. 2.6)2.08
    A. 0.52   B. 0.80
    C. 0.82   D. 1.10
    3-A.3

24. 53.6 ÷ 8
    A. 6.7   B. 7.6
    C. 7.8   D. 8.6
    3-A.3

Form A • Multiple-Choice   A12   ▶ Stop!

Multiple-Choice Format • Test Answers

Choose the letter of the correct answer.

1. What is the value of the digit 2 in the number 123,456.78?

A. 2 tens
B. 2 thousands
C. 2 ten thousands
D. 2 hundred thousands
1-A.1

2. What is the value of the digit 6 in the number 3.456?

A. 6 tens   B. 6 hundreds
C. 6 hundredths D. 6 thousandths
1-A.1

3. Which is the standard form of 6 million, thirty thousand, four hundred seven?

A. 630,407
B. 6,030,407
C. 63,000,407
D. 6,003,407,000
1-A.1

4. Which shows nine hundredths written in standard form?

A. 0.009   B. 0.09
C. 0.90   D. 900.0
1-A.1

5. Which is greater than 12.50?

A. 1.65   B. 12.06
C. 12.28   D. 12.65
1-A.1

6. Which shows the numbers written in order from least to greatest?

A. 4.5, 4.05, 4.15
B. 4.5, 4.15, 4.05
C. 4.15, 4.05, 4.5
D. 4.05, 4.15, 4.5
1-A.1

7. The batting averages of three players are 0.225, 0.251, 0.215. Which shows these averages written in order from greatest to least?

A. 0.225, 0.251, 0.215
B. 0.251, 0.215, 0.225
C. 0.251, 0.225, 0.215
D. 0.225, 0.215, 0.251
1-A.1

8. The table shows the amount of rainfall that fell in Dixon for three months.

Rainfall in Dixon (in inches)		
Month	Mar	Apr	May
Rainfall	3.85	3.51	3.58

Which shows the rainfall written in order from least rainfall to greatest?

A. 3.85, 3.51, 3.58
B. 3.58, 3.51, 3.85
C. 3.51, 3.85, 3.58
D. 3.51, 3.58, 3.85
1-A.1

9. What is 0.03 written as a fraction?

A. $\frac{3}{10}$ B. $\frac{1}{3}$
C. $\frac{3}{100}$ D. $\frac{1}{30}$
1-A.2

10. What is $\frac{4}{10}$ written as a decimal?

A. 0.10   B. 0.20
C. 0.04   D. 0.40
1-A.2

11. Which decimal makes the following inequality true?
$\frac{10}{25} < \underline{\quad}$?

A. 0.15   B. 0.25
C. 0.35   D. 0.45
1-A.2

12. James ate $\frac{3}{4}$ of the pizza. What is the amount of pizza he ate expressed as a decimal?

A. 0.0075 of the pizza
B. 0.075 of the pizza
C. 0.75 of the pizza
D. 7.5 of the pizza
1-A.2

13. What is $6 \times 6 \times 6 \times 6$ written in exponent form?

A. 4^4 B. 4^6
C. 6^4 D. 6^6
1-A.3

14. What is the value of 5^4?

A. 20   B. 25
C. 125   D. 625
1-A.3

15. Which of these shows the integers written in order from least to greatest?

A. 0, ⁻6, 5, 6   B. 0, 5, ⁻5, 6
C. ⁻6, 0, 5, 6   D. ⁻5, 5, 0, ⁻6
1-A.4

16. Which of these shows the integers written in order from least to greatest?

A. 7, ⁻8, ⁻9, 0   B. 7, ⁻9, ⁻8, 0
C. ⁻8, ⁻9, 7, 0   D. ⁻9, ⁻8, 0, 1
1-A.4

17. What is the opposite of ⁻5?

A. ⁻$\frac{1}{5}$ B. ⁺$\frac{1}{5}$
C. ⁺5   D. ⁺5^2
1-A.4

For questions 18–21, use mental math.

18. 5 + 17 + 25

A. 37   B. 42
C. 45   D. 47
2-A.1

19. 23 + 19 + 17 + 31

A. 70   B. 80
C. 90   D. 100
2-A.1

20. 62 − 39

A. 21   B. 22
C. 23   D. 24
2-A.1

21. 71 − 18

A. 52   B. 53
C. 62   D. 63
2-A.1

22. A rectangular box has a perimeter of 24 ft. The box is 2 ft longer than it is wide. What is the width of the box?

A. 5 ft   B. 7 ft
C. 10 ft   D. 12 ft
2-A.2

23. Max bought a total of 36 cans of apple and orange juice. He bought 6 more cans of apple juice than orange juice. How many cans of apple juice did he buy?

A. 10 cans   B. 15 cans
C. 20 cans   D. not here
2-A.2

For questions 24–25, use mental math to find the product.

24. 5 × 24

A. 100   B. 110
C. 120   D. 140
2-A.3

25. 3 × 10 × 4

A. 30   B. 120
C. 170   D. 300
2-A.3

26. 150
× 27

A. 3,950   B. 4,040
C. 4,050   D. not here
2-A.3

27. 368
× 142

A. 51,256   B. 52,156
C. 52,256   D. 52,456
2-A.3

28. 8)288

A. 30 r6   B. 32 r4
C. 34 r6   D. 36
2-A.3

29. 71)3,765

A. 53   B. 53 r4
C. 54 r6   D. 53 r2
2-A.3

30. Choose the best estimate of the sum.
4,122
3,878
+ 4,033

A. 9,000   B. 10,000
C. 12,000   D. 16,000
2-A.4

31. Choose the best estimate of the quotient.
1,632 ÷ 79

A. 20   B. 40
C. 60   D. 80
2-A.4

32. The Master Movie Theater can seat 289 people. It was filled to capacity for the last 19 shows. About how many people saw the last 19 shows?

A. about 4,000 people
B. about 6,000 people
C. about 8,000 people
D. about 10,000 people
2-A.4

For questions 33–34, estimate the sum.

33. 0.94 + 5.21 + 6.02

A. 10   B. 12
C. 14   D. 16
3-A.1

34. 2.95 + 0.89 + 2.09

A. 4   B. 6
C. 8   D. 10
3-A.1

35. 0.67 + 0.03

A. 0.07   B. 0.08
C. 0.7   D. 0.8
3-A.1

36. 5.3 + 2.04 + 10.65

A. 13.22   B. 16.99
C. 17.99   D. 18.35
3-A.1

37. 5.7 − 0.8

A. 4.1   B. 4.9
C. 5.1   D. 5.9
3-A.1

38. $8.52 − $1.39

A. $6.13   B. $6.27
C. $7.27   D. not here
3-A.1

39. 58.07 − 13.6

A. 44.47   B. 44.67
C. 45.47   D. 45.67
3-A.1

40. Mr. Mills drove 247.8 mi on Sunday and 305.3 mi on Monday. How much farther did he drive on Monday?

A. 57.5 mi farther
B. 59.5 mi farther
C. 157.5 mi farther
D. 159.5 ml farther
3-A.1

41. 8 × 0.4

A. 0.032   B. 0.32
C. 3.2   D. 32
3-A.2

42. 0.6 × 0.8

A. 0.0048   B. 0.48
C. 4.8   D. 48
3-A.2

43. 0.54 × 6.8

A. 0.03672   B. 0.3672
C. 3.672   D. 36.72
3-A.2

44. Joe charges $4.50 per hour to mow lawns. If he spends 2.5 hr mowing a lawn, how much will he earn?

A. $11.00   B. $11.25
C. $11.75   D. $12.25
3-A.2

45. Michele is making costumes for the class play. She needs 2.5 yd of fabric for each costume. How much fabric will she need to make 11 costumes?

A. 25 yd   B. 25.5 yd
C. 27 yd   D. 27.5 yd
3-A.2

46. 18.2 ÷ 7

A. 0.26   B. 2.6
C. 2.66   D. 26
3-A.2

47. 0.14)5.32

A. 0.038   B. 0.38
C. 3.8   D. 38
3-A.2

48. 25.55 ÷ 0.35

A. 0.073   B. 0.73
C. 7.3   D. 73
3-A.2

Multiple-Choice Format • Test Answers

Harcourt Brace School Publishers

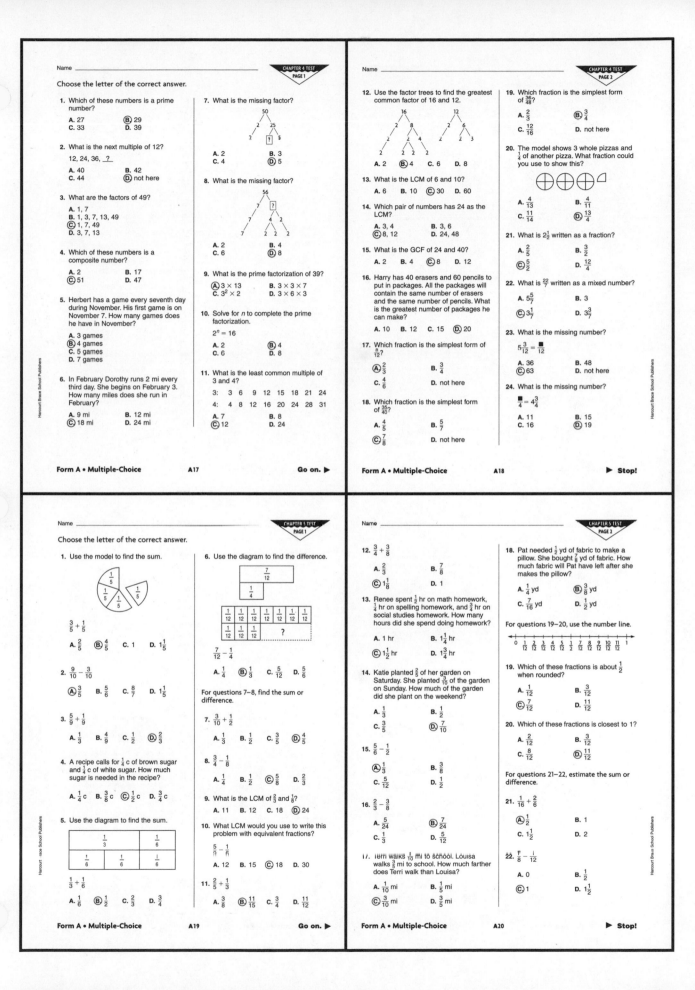

Name _____

Choose the letter of the correct answer.

1. Which of these numbers is a prime number?
   A. 27
   (B) 29
   C. 33
   D. 39

2. What is the next multiple of 12?
   12, 24, 36, __?__
   A. 40
   B. 42
   C. 44
   (D) not here

3. What are the factors of 49?
   A. 1, 7
   B. 1, 3, 7, 13, 49
   (C) 1, 7, 49
   D. 3, 7, 13

4. Which of these numbers is a composite number?
   A. 2
   B. 17
   (C) 51
   D. 47

5. Herbert has a game every seventh day during November. His first game is on November 7. How many games does he have in November?
   A. 3 games
   (B) 4 games
   C. 5 games
   D. 7 games

6. In February Dorothy runs 2 mi every third day. She begins on February 3. How many miles does she run in February?
   A. 9 mi
   B. 12 mi
   (C) 18 mi
   D. 24 mi

7. What is the missing factor?
   A. 2
   B. 3
   C. 4
   (D) 5

8. What is the missing factor?
   A. 2
   B. 4
   C. 6
   (D) 8

9. What is the prime factorization of 39?
   (A) 3×13
   B. $3 \times 3 \times 7$
   C. $3^2 \times 2$
   D. $3 \times 6 \times 3$

10. Solve for n to complete the prime factorization.
    $2^n = 16$
    A. 2
    (B) 4
    C. 6
    D. 8

11. What is the least common multiple of 3 and 4?
    3: 3 6 9 12 15 18 21 24
    4: 4 8 12 16 20 24 28 31
    A. 7
    B. 8
    (C) 12
    D. 24

Form A • Multiple-Choice   A17   Go on. ▶

Name _____

12. Use the factor trees to find the greatest common factor of 16 and 12.
    A. 2
    (B) 4
    C. 6
    D. 8

13. What is the LCM of 6 and 10?
    A. 6
    B. 10
    (C) 30
    D. 60

14. Which pair of numbers has 24 as the LCM?
    A. 3, 4
    B. 3, 6
    (C) 8, 12
    D. 24, 48

15. What is the GCF of 24 and 40?
    A. 2
    B. 4
    (C) 8
    D. 12

16. Harry has 40 erasers and 60 pencils to put in packages. All the packages will contain the same number of erasers and the same number of pencils. What is the greatest number of packages he can make?
    A. 10
    B. 12
    C. 15
    (D) 20

17. Which fraction is the simplest form of $\frac{8}{12}$?
    (A) $\frac{2}{3}$
    B. $\frac{3}{4}$
    C. $\frac{4}{6}$
    D. not here

18. Which fraction is the simplest form of $\frac{35}{40}$?
    A. $\frac{4}{5}$
    B. $\frac{5}{7}$
    (C) $\frac{7}{8}$
    D. not here

19. Which fraction is the simplest form of $\frac{36}{48}$?
    A. $\frac{2}{3}$
    (B) $\frac{3}{4}$
    C. $\frac{12}{16}$
    D. not here

20. The model shows 3 whole pizzas and $\frac{1}{4}$ of another pizza. What fraction could you use to show this?
    A. $\frac{4}{13}$
    B. $\frac{4}{11}$
    C. $\frac{11}{14}$
    (D) $\frac{13}{4}$

21. What is $2\frac{2}{5}$ written as a fraction?
    A. $\frac{2}{5}$
    B. $\frac{3}{2}$
    (C) $\frac{5}{2}$
    D. $\frac{12}{4}$

22. What is $\frac{22}{7}$ written as a mixed number?
    A. $5\frac{5}{7}$
    B. 3
    (C) $3\frac{1}{7}$
    D. $3\frac{3}{7}$

23. What is the missing number?
    $5\frac{3}{12} = \frac{\blacksquare}{12}$
    A. 36
    B. 48
    (C) 63
    D. not here

24. What is the missing number?
    $\frac{\blacksquare}{4} = 4\frac{3}{4}$
    A. 11
    B. 15
    C. 16
    (D) 19

Form A • Multiple-Choice   A18   ▶ Stop!

Name _____

Choose the letter of the correct answer.

1. Use the model to find the sum.
   $\frac{3}{5} + \frac{1}{5}$
   A. $\frac{2}{5}$
   (B) $\frac{4}{5}$
   C. 1
   D. $1\frac{1}{5}$

2. $\frac{9}{10} - \frac{3}{10}$
   (A) $\frac{3}{5}$
   B. $\frac{5}{6}$
   C. $\frac{8}{7}$
   D. $1\frac{1}{5}$

3. $\frac{5}{9} + \frac{1}{9}$
   A. $\frac{1}{3}$
   B. $\frac{4}{9}$
   C. $\frac{1}{2}$
   (D) $\frac{2}{3}$

4. A recipe calls for $\frac{1}{4}$ c of brown sugar and $\frac{1}{4}$ c of white sugar. How much sugar is needed in the recipe?
   A. $\frac{1}{4}$ c   B. $\frac{3}{8}$ c   (C) $\frac{1}{2}$ c   D. $\frac{3}{4}$ c

5. Use the diagram to find the sum.
   $\frac{1}{3} + \frac{1}{6}$
   A. $\frac{1}{6}$
   (B) $\frac{1}{2}$
   C. $\frac{2}{3}$
   D. $\frac{3}{4}$

6. Use the diagram to find the difference.
   $\frac{7}{12} - \frac{1}{4}$
   A. $\frac{1}{4}$
   (B) $\frac{1}{3}$
   C. $\frac{5}{12}$
   D. $\frac{5}{6}$

For questions 7–8, find the sum or difference.

7. $\frac{3}{10} + \frac{1}{2}$
   A. $\frac{1}{3}$
   B. $\frac{1}{2}$
   C. $\frac{3}{5}$
   (D) $\frac{4}{5}$

8. $\frac{3}{4} - \frac{1}{8}$
   A. $\frac{1}{4}$
   B. $\frac{1}{2}$
   (C) $\frac{5}{8}$
   D. $\frac{2}{3}$

9. What is the LCM of $\frac{2}{3}$ and $\frac{1}{8}$?
   A. 11
   B. 12
   C. 18
   (D) 24

10. What LCM would you use to write this problem with equivalent fractions?
    $\frac{5}{n} - \frac{1}{6}$
    A. 12
    B. 15
    (C) 18
    D. 30

11. $\frac{2}{5} + \frac{1}{3}$
    A. $\frac{3}{8}$
    (B) $\frac{11}{15}$
    C. $\frac{3}{4}$
    D. $\frac{11}{12}$

Form A • Multiple-Choice   A19   Go on. ▶

Name _____

12. $\frac{3}{4} + \frac{3}{8}$
    A. $\frac{2}{3}$
    B. $\frac{7}{8}$
    (C) $1\frac{1}{8}$
    D. 1

13. Renee spent $\frac{1}{2}$ hr on math homework, $\frac{1}{4}$ hr on spelling homework, and $\frac{3}{4}$ hr on social studies homework. How many hours did she spend doing homework?
    A. 1 hr
    B. $1\frac{1}{4}$ hr
    (C) $1\frac{1}{2}$ hr
    D. $1\frac{3}{4}$ hr

14. Katie planted $\frac{2}{5}$ of her garden on Saturday. She planted $\frac{3}{10}$ of the garden on Sunday. How much of the garden did she plant on the weekend?
    A. $\frac{1}{3}$
    B. $\frac{1}{2}$
    C. $\frac{3}{5}$
    (D) $\frac{7}{10}$

15. $\frac{5}{6} - \frac{1}{2}$
    (A) $\frac{1}{3}$
    B. $\frac{3}{8}$
    C. $\frac{5}{12}$
    D. $\frac{1}{2}$

16. $\frac{2}{3} - \frac{3}{8}$
    A. $\frac{5}{24}$
    (B) $\frac{7}{24}$
    C. $\frac{1}{3}$
    D. $\frac{5}{12}$

17. Terri walks $\frac{1}{10}$ mi to school. Louisa walks $\frac{3}{5}$ mi to school. How much farther does Terri walk than Louisa?
    A. $\frac{1}{10}$ mi
    B. $\frac{1}{5}$ mi
    (C) $\frac{3}{10}$ mi
    D. $\frac{3}{5}$ mi

18. Pat needed $\frac{1}{2}$ yd of fabric to make a pillow. She bought $\frac{7}{8}$ yd of fabric. How much fabric will Pat have left after she makes the pillow?
    A. $\frac{1}{4}$ yd
    (B) $\frac{3}{8}$ yd
    C. $\frac{7}{16}$ yd
    D. $\frac{1}{2}$ yd

For questions 19–20, use the number line.

19. Which of these fractions is about $\frac{1}{2}$ when rounded?
    A. $\frac{1}{12}$
    B. $\frac{3}{12}$
    (C) $\frac{7}{12}$
    D. $\frac{11}{12}$

20. Which of these fractions is closest to 1?
    A. $\frac{2}{12}$
    B. $\frac{3}{12}$
    C. $\frac{8}{12}$
    (D) $\frac{11}{12}$

For questions 21–22, estimate the sum or difference.

21. $\frac{1}{16} + \frac{2}{6}$
    (A) $\frac{1}{2}$
    B. 1
    C. $1\frac{1}{2}$
    D. 2

22. $\frac{7}{8} - \frac{1}{12}$
    A. 0
    B. $\frac{1}{2}$
    (C) 1
    D. $1\frac{1}{2}$

Form A • Multiple-Choice   A20   ▶ Stop!

Multiple-Choice Format • Test Answers

Choose the letter of the correct answer.

For questions 1–2, choose the addition problem shown by the diagram.

1.
| 1 | | $\frac{1}{7}$ | | 1 | | $\frac{1}{7}$ |
| 1 | | $\frac{1}{7}$ |

A. $3\frac{1}{7} + 1\frac{1}{7}$ Ⓑ $3\frac{2}{7} + 1\frac{1}{7}$

C. $3\frac{3}{7} + 1$ D. $3 + 1\frac{3}{7}$

2.
| 1 | | 1 |
| 1 | | $\frac{1}{8}\frac{1}{8}\frac{1}{8}$ |
| $\frac{1}{4}$ |

A. $\frac{3}{4} + \frac{7}{8}$ B. $1\frac{2}{8} + 2\frac{1}{4}$

Ⓒ $2\frac{1}{4} + 1\frac{3}{8}$ D. $2\frac{1}{8} + 1\frac{3}{4}$

For questions 3–4, draw a diagram to help you find the sum.

3. $3\frac{1}{6} + 2\frac{1}{3}$

A. $5\frac{2}{9}$ B. $5\frac{1}{3}$ Ⓒ $5\frac{1}{2}$ D. $5\frac{2}{3}$

4. $1\frac{1}{2} + 2\frac{1}{4}$

A. $3\frac{1}{3}$ Ⓑ $3\frac{3}{4}$ C. $3\frac{5}{6}$ D. $4\frac{1}{4}$

5. Which diagram matches the mixed number $2\frac{2}{3}$?

A.
| 1 |
| $\frac{1}{2}$ |

B.
| 1 |
| 1 |
| $\frac{1}{4}$ |

C.
| 1 |
| 1 |
| $\frac{1}{8}\frac{1}{8}\frac{1}{8}$ |

Ⓓ
| 1 |
| $\frac{1}{3}\frac{1}{3}\frac{1}{3}$ |
| $\frac{1}{3}$ |

6. Use the diagram to find the difference.

| 1 |
| 1 |
| $\frac{1}{4}$ $\frac{1}{4}$ $\frac{1}{4}$ $\frac{1}{4}$ |
| $\frac{1}{4}$ |

$3\frac{1}{2} - 1\frac{1}{2}$

Ⓐ $1\frac{3}{4}$ B. $1\frac{7}{8}$

C. $2\frac{1}{4}$ D. $2\frac{3}{4}$

For questions 7–8, draw a diagram to help you find the difference. Answers are in simplest form.

7. $4\frac{4}{5} - 3\frac{2}{5}$

A. $\frac{2}{5}$ B. $1\frac{1}{5}$

Ⓒ $1\frac{2}{5}$ D. $2\frac{1}{5}$

8. $5\frac{5}{12} - 3\frac{1}{2}$

A. $1\frac{1}{5}$ Ⓑ $1\frac{11}{12}$

C. $2\frac{1}{12}$ D. $2\frac{2}{5}$

9. $3\frac{3}{4} + 1\frac{3}{8}$

A. $2\frac{1}{8}$ B. $4\frac{1}{2}$

C. $4\frac{3}{4}$ Ⓓ not here

10. $4\frac{2}{3} + 2\frac{5}{6}$

A. $6\frac{1}{2}$ Ⓑ $7\frac{1}{2}$

C. $7\frac{2}{3}$ D. not here

11. A costume requires $2\frac{1}{2}$ yd of fabric for the jacket and $1\frac{7}{8}$ yd for the pants. How much fabric is required in all?

A. $3\frac{5}{8}$ yd   B. $3\frac{4}{6}$ yd

C. 4 yd   Ⓓ $4\frac{3}{8}$ yd

12. Last week the basketball team practiced for $6\frac{1}{2}$ hr. It usually practices for $9\frac{1}{4}$ hr. How many hours less did the team practice last week?

Ⓐ $2\frac{3}{4}$ hr   B. $2\frac{7}{8}$ hr

C. $3\frac{1}{4}$ hr   D. $3\frac{3}{4}$ hr

13. In March it rained $5\frac{3}{10}$ in. In April it rained $3\frac{4}{5}$ in. How much more did it rain in March than in April?

A. $1\frac{1}{5}$ in.   Ⓑ $1\frac{1}{2}$ in.

C. $2\frac{1}{10}$ in.   D. $2\frac{1}{2}$ in.

14. For a class party, $2\frac{3}{4}$ gal of apple juice and $1\frac{1}{2}$ gal of ginger ale were combined to make punch. How many gallons of punch were made?

A. $1\frac{1}{4}$ gal   B. $3\frac{7}{8}$ gal

C. 4 gal   Ⓓ $4\frac{1}{4}$ gal

15. Which will give the best estimate of the sum?

$5\frac{7}{8} + 2\frac{3}{4}$

A. $5 + 2$ B. $6 + 2$

C. $5 + 3$ Ⓓ $6 + 3$

16. Which will give the best estimate of the difference?

$9\frac{1}{6} - 2\frac{9}{10}$

Ⓐ $9 - 3$ B. $9 - 2$

C. $10 - 2$ D. $10 - 3$

For questions 17–18, choose the best estimate for each sum or difference.

17. $3\frac{2}{9} + 2\frac{1}{7}$

A. about 1   Ⓑ about 5

C. about 7   D. about 8

18. $7\frac{1}{8} - 2\frac{1}{12}$

A. about $4\frac{1}{2}$ Ⓑ about $5\frac{1}{2}$

C. about $6\frac{1}{2}$ D. about 10

For questions 19–20, choose the best estimate for the word problem.

19. At a fruit stand, the Raleigh family bought $4\frac{1}{8}$ lb of cooking apples and $2\frac{9}{10}$ lb of apples to eat. About how many pounds of apples did the family buy altogether?

A. about 6 lb   Ⓑ about 7 lb

C. about 9 lb   D. about 10 lb

20. On a hike, the scout troop hiked $13\frac{5}{8}$ mi on the first day. They hiked $9\frac{1}{10}$ mi on the second day. About how much farther did they hike the first day than the second day?

A. about $3\frac{1}{2}$ mi   Ⓑ about $4\frac{1}{2}$ mi

C. about 5 mi   D. about 21 mi

Choose the letter of the correct answer.

1. Use the model to help you find the product.

$\frac{1}{3} \times \frac{1}{2}$

Ⓐ $\frac{1}{6}$ B. $\frac{1}{3}$ C. $\frac{5}{12}$ D. $\frac{1}{2}$

2. Which multiplication sentence shows a reasonable estimate for $1\frac{4}{5} \times 5$?

A. $\frac{4}{5} \times 5 = 4$

B. $1 \times 5 = 5$

Ⓒ $2 \times 5 = 10$

D. $4 \times 5 = 20$

3. $\frac{1}{2} \times \frac{1}{2}$

A. $\frac{1}{8}$ Ⓑ $\frac{1}{4}$ C. $\frac{11}{16}$ D. not here

4. $\frac{2}{5} \times \frac{3}{4}$

Ⓐ $\frac{3}{10}$ B. $\frac{1}{3}$ C. $\frac{1}{2}$ D. not here

5. $3 \times \frac{5}{6}$

A. $\frac{2}{5}$ Ⓑ $2\frac{1}{2}$ C. $2\frac{3}{5}$ D. not here

6. $\frac{2}{3} \times \frac{7}{10}$

A. $\frac{3}{10}$ B. $\frac{1}{3}$ C. $\frac{13}{30}$ Ⓓ not here

7. In which of these multiplication problems could you use two GCFs to simplify fractions?

A. $\frac{3}{4} \times \frac{1}{12}$ B. $\frac{1}{6} \times \frac{1}{12}$

C. $\frac{2}{3} \times \frac{3}{5}$ Ⓓ $\frac{3}{5} \times \frac{5}{9}$

For questions 8–9, choose the GCF you should use to simplify the fractions.

8. $\frac{3}{7} \times \frac{5}{12}$

Ⓐ 3   B. 5   C. 7   D. 12

9. $\frac{5}{6} \times \frac{4}{7}$

Ⓐ 2   B. 4   C. 5   D. 6

10. Solve. Use GCFs to simplify the factors. Answers are in simplest form.

$\frac{3}{8} \times \frac{4}{9}$

A. $\frac{1}{12}$ B. $\frac{1}{9}$ Ⓒ $\frac{1}{6}$ D. $\frac{1}{3}$

11. What is the first step in finding this product?

$2\frac{1}{2} \times 1\frac{1}{3}$

A. Find the GCF.

B. Estimate the product by using whole numbers.

C. Round the mixed numbers to whole numbers.

Ⓓ Write the mixed numbers as fractions.

12. $4\frac{1}{2} \times \frac{2}{3}$

A. $1\frac{1}{3}$ B. $1\frac{1}{2}$

C. $2\frac{2}{3}$ Ⓓ 3

13. $1\frac{4}{5} \times 1\frac{1}{3}$

A. $1\frac{9}{10}$ Ⓑ $2\frac{2}{5}$

C. $2\frac{8}{15}$ D. $2\frac{4}{5}$

14. $4\frac{1}{6} \times 2\frac{2}{5}$

A. $6\frac{17}{30}$ B. $8\frac{1}{15}$

Ⓒ 10   D. $12\frac{1}{2}$

15. A hiking trail around a lake is $6\frac{3}{4}$ mi long. Frederico has hiked $\frac{1}{3}$ of the way. How far has he hiked?

Ⓐ $2\frac{1}{4}$ mi   B. $2\frac{3}{4}$ mi

C. $3\frac{1}{2}$ mi   D. $4\frac{1}{2}$ mi

16. Some friends made 4 batches of chocolate chip cookies. They used $1\frac{2}{3}$ c of chocolate chips in each batch. How many cups of chips did they use to make all the cookies?

A. $4\frac{2}{3}$ c   B. $5\frac{1}{2}$ c

Ⓒ $6\frac{2}{3}$ c   D. $7\frac{1}{3}$ c

17. What is the reciprocal of $\frac{3}{4}$?

A. $\frac{1}{4}$ B. 1

C. $\frac{5}{4}$ Ⓓ $\frac{4}{3}$

18. How can you rewrite this division problem as a multiplication problem?

$\frac{4}{5} \div \frac{2}{3}$

A. $\frac{4}{5} \times \frac{2}{3}$ Ⓑ $\frac{4}{5} \times \frac{3}{2}$

C. $\frac{5}{4} \times \frac{2}{3}$ D. $\frac{5}{4} \times \frac{3}{2}$

19. $\frac{7}{8} \div \frac{1}{2}$

A. $\frac{7}{16}$ B. $1\frac{1}{2}$

Ⓒ $1\frac{3}{4}$ D. $2\frac{2}{7}$

20. $8 \div \frac{4}{5}$

A. $\frac{1}{10}$ B. $\frac{1}{6}$

C. 6   Ⓓ 10

21. The area of a rectangular rug is $19\frac{1}{4}$ ft². The rug is $5\frac{1}{2}$ ft long. What is the width?

Ⓐ $3\frac{1}{2}$ ft   B. $3\frac{3}{4}$ ft

C. $4\frac{1}{4}$ ft   D. $4\frac{1}{2}$ ft

22. Gerri bought a piece of salmon that weighs $2\frac{3}{4}$ lb. She wants each serving to be $\frac{1}{4}$ lb. How many servings can she make?

A. 5 servings   B. 9 servings

C. 10 servings   Ⓓ 11 servings

23. Claude has a piece of wood $5\frac{5}{8}$ ft long. It is 3 times the length he needs to make a small shelf. How long will the shelf be?

A. $1\frac{1}{8}$ ft   Ⓑ $1\frac{7}{8}$ ft

C. $2\frac{1}{4}$ ft   D. $2\frac{3}{8}$ ft

24. A DJ plays songs for $12\frac{1}{2}$ min without interruption. Each song lasts $2\frac{1}{2}$ min. How many songs does the DJ play?

A. 4 songs   Ⓑ 5 songs

C. $5\frac{1}{2}$ songs   D. 6 songs

Multiple-Choice Format • Test Answers

Name _____

Choose the letter of the correct answer.

1. What are the factors of 25?
(A) 1, 5, 25
B. 1, 2, 5, 25
C. 1, 25
D. 1, 2, 5, 10, 25
4-A.1

2. What is the prime factorization of 58?
(A) 2×29
B. $2 \times 4 \times 8$
C. $2^2 \times 29$
D. $2 \times 5 \times 8$
4-A.2

3. What is the LCM of 8 and 18?
A. 8
B. 26
C. 36
(D) 72
4-A.3

4. Which fraction is the simplest form of $\frac{10}{16}$?
A. $\frac{4}{8}$
(B) $\frac{5}{8}$
C. $\frac{5}{9}$
D. $\frac{6}{10}$
4-A.4

5. What is $4\frac{3}{5}$ written as a fraction?
A. $\frac{3}{5}$
B. $\frac{4}{5}$
C. $\frac{12}{5}$
(D) $\frac{23}{5}$
4-A.5

6. What is the missing number?
$\frac{\square}{9} = 3\frac{7}{9}$
A. 7
B. 19
C. 27
(D) 34
4-A.5

7. $\frac{4}{11} + \frac{9}{11}$
A. $\frac{5}{11}$
B. $\frac{12}{11}$
(C) $\frac{13}{11}$
D. $13\frac{1}{11}$
5-A.1

8. Mika's box of pencils was full. She used $\frac{3}{7}$ of the pencils and gave away $\frac{2}{7}$ to her friends. What fraction of the pencils did she have remaining?
A. $\frac{1}{7}$
(B) $\frac{2}{7}$
C. $\frac{2}{3}$
D. $\frac{5}{7}$
5-A.1

9. $\frac{4}{5} - \frac{2}{3}$
A. $\frac{1}{15}$
(B) $\frac{2}{15}$
C. $\frac{4}{15}$
D. $\frac{2}{3}$
5-A.2

10. $\frac{7}{10} - \frac{3}{5}$
(A) $\frac{1}{10}$
B. $\frac{4}{10}$
C. $\frac{2}{5}$
D. $\frac{4}{5}$
5-A.2

11. Which of these fractions is about $\frac{1}{2}$ when rounded?
A. $\frac{2}{9}$
(B) $\frac{4}{9}$
C. $\frac{7}{9}$
D. $\frac{8}{9}$
5-A.3

12. Which of these fractions is closest to 1?
(A) $\frac{7}{8}$
B. $\frac{2}{11}$
C. $\frac{5}{32}$
D. $1\frac{7}{8}$
5-A.3

Form A • Multiple-Choice   A25   Go on. ▶

Name _____

13. Choose the addition problem shown by the diagram.

A. $1\frac{1}{3} + 1\frac{2}{3}$
B. $2\frac{1}{3} + 1\frac{1}{3}$
(C) $2\frac{1}{3} + 1\frac{2}{3}$
D. $2\frac{2}{3} + 1\frac{1}{3}$
6-A.1

14. Use the diagram to find the difference.

$2\frac{3}{5} - 1\frac{4}{5}$
A. $\frac{1}{5}$
(B) $\frac{4}{5}$
C. $1\frac{1}{5}$
D. $1\frac{4}{5}$
6-A.1

15. Which will give the best estimate of the sum?
$3\frac{1}{7} + 4\frac{5}{6}$
A. $4 + 4$
(B) $3 + 5$
C. $4 + 5$
D. $6 + 7$
6-A.1

16. Cara and Jean went to the market. Jean drove $4\frac{5}{8}$ mi and Cara drove $8\frac{3}{8}$ mi. About how many more miles did Cara drive than Jean?
(A) about 4 mi
B. about 5 mi
C. about 6 mi
D. about 5 mi
6-A.2

17. It rained $8\frac{4}{5}$ in. during June. The average rainfall for June is $6\frac{1}{10}$ in. About how much more did it rain above the average?
A. about 1 in.
B. about 2 in.
C. about $2\frac{1}{7}$ in.
(D) about 3 in.
6-A.2

18. $\frac{4}{7} \times \frac{1}{2}$
(A) $\frac{2}{7}$
B. $\frac{4}{9}$
C. $\frac{5}{9}$
D. $\frac{5}{14}$
7-A.1

19. Van needed to hang 3 bird feeders, using wire. He used $\frac{8}{9}$ yd for each bird feeder. How many yards of wire did he use in all?
A. $\frac{24}{27}$ yd
B. $1\frac{2}{3}$ yd
C. $2\frac{2}{9}$ yd
(D) $2\frac{2}{3}$ yd
7-A.1

20. $\frac{3}{8} \div \frac{1}{3}$
A. $\frac{1}{8}$
B. $1\frac{1}{8}$
C. $1\frac{5}{8}$
D. $2\frac{1}{8}$
7-A.2

21. $12 \div \frac{3}{5}$
A. $5\frac{1}{3}$
B. $10\frac{3}{5}$
C. $15\frac{4}{5}$
(D) 20
7-A.2

22. A relay team finished in $6\frac{2}{3}$ min. Each of the 4 runners on the team had the same time. How long did each person run?
A. $\frac{2}{3}$ min
B. 1 min
(C) $1\frac{2}{3}$ min
D. $1\frac{3}{4}$ min
7-A.2

Form A • Multiple-Choice   A26   ▶ Stop!

Name _____

Choose the letter of the correct answer.

1. What is the value of the digit 4 in the number 405,321.98?
A. 4 hundreds
B. 4 thousands
C. 4 ten thousands
(D) 4 hundred thousands
1-A.1

2. Which shows 3 thousandths written in standard form?
(A) 0.003
B. 0.03
C. 0.30
D. 3,000
1-A.1

3. Which shows the numbers written in order from least to greatest?
A. 3.02, 3.002, 3.2
B. 3.2, 3.002, 3.002
(C) 3.002, 3.02, 3.2
D. 3.002, 3.2, 3.02
1-A.1

4. What is 0.08 written as a fraction?
A. $\frac{8}{10}$
B. $\frac{1}{8}$
(C) $\frac{8}{100}$
D. $\frac{1}{80}$
1-A.2

5. What is $\frac{3}{5}$ written as a decimal?
A. 0.10
B. 0.20
C. 0.40
(D) 0.60
1-A.2

6. What is the value of 3^5?
A. 15
B. 81
(C) 243
D. 729
1-A.3

7. Which of these shows the integers written in order from least to greatest?
A. 5, $^-7$, $^-9$, 0
B. 5, $^-9$, $^-7$, 0
C. $^-7$, $^-9$, 5, 0
(D) $^-9$, $^-7$, 0, 5
1-A.4

8. What is the opposite of $^+2$?
A. $^-\frac{1}{2}$
B. $^+\frac{1}{2}$
(C) $^-2$
D. $^+2^2$
1-A.4

For questions 9–10, use mental math.

9. $8 + 15 + 32$
A. 45
B. 47
(C) 55
D. 57
2-A.1

10. $74 - 28$
A. 36
B. 44
(C) 46
D. 54
2-A.1

11. The Eagles soccer team played a total of 16 games. They tied in 4 games and won 2 more games than they lost. How many games did they lose?
(A) 5 games
B. 7 games
C. 12 games
D. 16 games
2-A.2

12. 372×251
A. 82,372
B. 83,372
C. 92,372
(D) 93,372
2-A.3

Form A • Multiple-Choice   A27   Chapters 1–7   Go on. ▶

Name _____

13. $43)\overline{2,887}$
A. 67
B. 67 r1
(C) 67 r6
D. not here
2-A.3

14. Choose the best estimate of the difference.
$4,821 - 2,045$
A. 2,000
(B) 3,000
C. 4,000
D. 5,000
2-A.4

15. Mark has a coin collection. He has 493 United States coins and 115 foreign coins. About how many more United States coins than foreign coins does he have?
A. about 300 more
(B) about 400 more
C. about 500 more
D. about 600 more
2-A.4

16. $0.87 + 1.476$
A. 1.246
B. 1.346
C. 2.246
(D) 2.346
3-A.1

17. $73.61 - 24.37$
A. 48.24
B. 51.33
C. 59.24
(D) not here
3-A.1

18. Jake earns $5.70 per hour selling books at Bargain Books. Last week Jake worked 8.5 hours. How much did he earn working at the book store?
A. $47.45
(B) $48.45
C. $474.50
D. $484.50
3-A.2

19. $72.9 \div 9$
A. 0.81
(B) 8.1
C. 8.11
D. 81
3-A.3

20. $7.2)\overline{187.2}$
A. 0.026
B. 0.26
C. 2.6
(D) 26
3-A.3

21. Which of these numbers is a prime number?
A. 18
(B) 31
C. 35
D. 40
4-A.1

22. Anna rode her bike every eighth day in September beginning on September 5th. How many times did she ride her bike in September?
A. 3 times
(B) 4 times
C. 5 times
D. 6 times
4-A.1

23. What is the prime factorization of 45?
(A) $3^2 \times 5$
B. $2^3 \times 5$
C. 3×5^2
D. 5×9
4-A.2

24. Solve for n to complete the prime factorization.
$2^n = 32$
A. 3
B. 4
(C) 5
D. 6
4-A.2

Form A • Multiple-Choice   A28   Chapters 1–7   Go on. ▶

Multiple-Choice Format • Test Answers   **125**

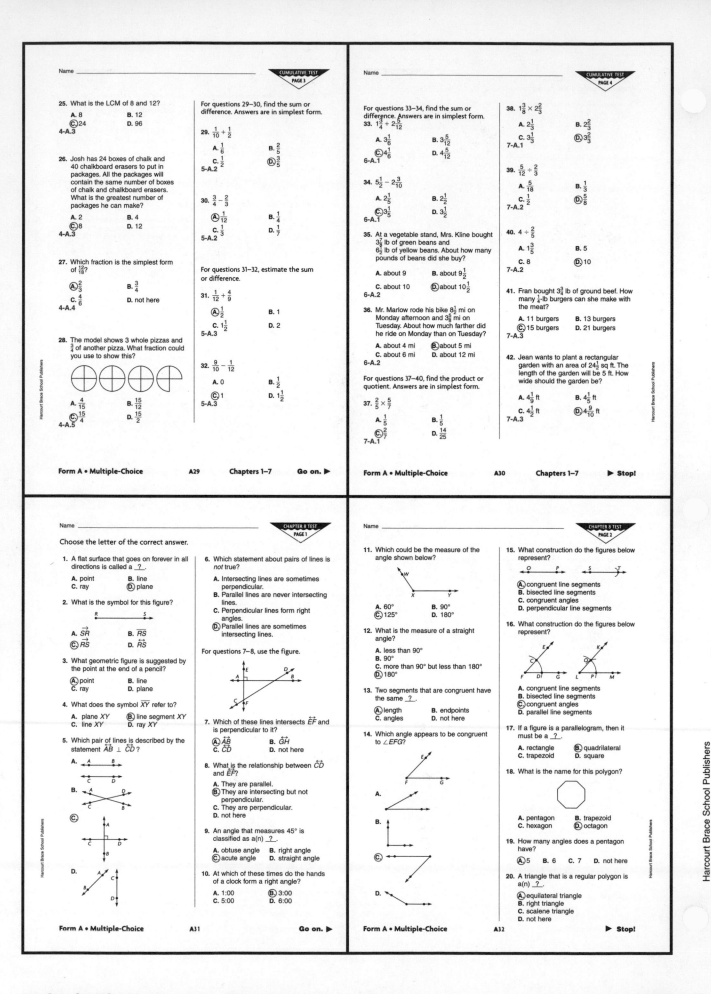

25. What is the LCM of 8 and 12?

  A. 8   B. 12
  C. 24   D. 96
4-A.3

26. Josh has 24 boxes of chalk and 40 chalkboard erasers to put in packages. All the packages will contain the same number of boxes of chalk and chalkboard erasers. What is the greatest number of packages he can make?

  A. 2   B. 4
  C. 8   D. 12
4-A.3

27. Which fraction is the simplest form of $\frac{12}{18}$?

  A. $\frac{2}{3}$ B. $\frac{3}{4}$
  C. $\frac{4}{6}$ D. not here
4-A.4

28. The model shows 3 whole pizzas and $\frac{3}{4}$ of another pizza. What fraction could you use to show this?

  A. $\frac{4}{15}$ B. $\frac{15}{12}$
  C. $\frac{15}{4}$ D. $\frac{15}{2}$
4-A.5

For questions 29–30, find the sum or difference. Answers are in simplest form.

29. $\frac{1}{10} + \frac{1}{2}$

  A. $\frac{1}{6}$ B. $\frac{2}{5}$
  C. $\frac{1}{2}$ D. $\frac{3}{5}$
5-A.2

30. $\frac{3}{4} - \frac{2}{3}$

  A. $\frac{1}{12}$ B. $\frac{1}{4}$
  C. $\frac{1}{3}$ D. $\frac{1}{7}$
5-A.2

For questions 31–32, estimate the sum or difference.

31. $\frac{1}{12} + \frac{4}{9}$

  A. $\frac{1}{2}$ B. 1
  C. $1\frac{1}{2}$ D. 2
5-A.3

32. $\frac{9}{10} - \frac{1}{12}$

  A. 0   B. $\frac{1}{2}$
  C. 1   D. $1\frac{1}{2}$
5-A.3

For questions 33–34, find the sum or difference. Answers are in simplest form.

33. $1\frac{3}{4} + 2\frac{5}{12}$

  A. $3\frac{1}{6}$ B. $3\frac{5}{12}$
  C. $4\frac{1}{6}$ D. $4\frac{5}{12}$
6-A.1

34. $5\frac{1}{2} - 2\frac{3}{10}$

  A. $2\frac{1}{5}$ B. $2\frac{1}{2}$
  C. $3\frac{1}{5}$ D. $3\frac{1}{2}$
6-A.1

35. At a vegetable stand, Mrs. Kline bought $3\frac{7}{8}$ lb of green beans and $6\frac{1}{2}$ lb of yellow beans. About how many pounds of beans did she buy?

  A. about 9   B. about $9\frac{1}{2}$
  C. about 10   D. about $10\frac{1}{2}$
6-A.2

36. Mr. Marlow rode his bike $8\frac{1}{2}$ mi on Monday afternoon and $3\frac{5}{8}$ mi on Tuesday. About how much farther did he ride on Monday than on Tuesday?

  A. about 4 mi   B. about 5 mi
  C. about 6 mi   D. about 12 mi
6-A.2

For questions 37–40, find the product or quotient. Answers are in simplest form.

37. $\frac{2}{5} \times \frac{5}{7}$

  A. $\frac{1}{5}$ B. $\frac{1}{6}$
  C. $\frac{2}{7}$ D. $\frac{14}{25}$
7-A.1

38. $1\frac{3}{8} \times 2\frac{2}{3}$

  A. $2\frac{1}{3}$ B. $2\frac{2}{3}$
  C. $3\frac{1}{3}$ D. $3\frac{2}{3}$
7-A.1

39. $\frac{5}{12} \div \frac{2}{3}$

  A. $\frac{5}{18}$ B. $\frac{1}{3}$
  C. $\frac{1}{2}$ D. $\frac{5}{8}$
7-A.2

40. $4 \div \frac{2}{5}$

  A. $1\frac{3}{5}$ B. 5
  C. 8   D. 10
7-A.2

41. Fran bought $3\frac{3}{4}$ lb of ground beef. How many $\frac{1}{4}$-lb burgers can she make with the meat?

  A. 11 burgers   B. 13 burgers
  C. 15 burgers   D. 21 burgers
7-A.3

42. Jean wants to plant a rectangular garden with an area of $24\frac{1}{2}$ sq ft. The length of the garden will be 5 ft. How wide should the garden be?

  A. $4\frac{1}{9}$ ft   B. $4\frac{1}{5}$ ft
  C. $4\frac{1}{2}$ ft   D. $4\frac{9}{10}$ ft
7-A.3

Choose the letter of the correct answer.

1. A flat surface that goes on forever in all directions is called a __?__.

  A. point   B. line
  C. ray   D. plane

2. What is the symbol for this figure?

  A. $\overrightarrow{SR}$ B. $\overline{RS}$
  C. $\overleftrightarrow{RS}$ D. $\overrightarrow{RS}$

3. What geometric figure is suggested by the point at the end of a pencil?

  A. point   B. line
  C. ray   D. plane

4. What does the symbol $\overline{XY}$ refer to?

  A. plane XY B. line segment XY
  C. line XY D. ray XY

5. Which pair of lines is described by the statement $\overleftrightarrow{AB} \perp \overleftrightarrow{CD}$?

  A.
  B.
  C.
  D.

6. Which statement about pairs of lines is not true?

  A. Intersecting lines are sometimes perpendicular.
  B. Parallel lines are never intersecting lines.
  C. Perpendicular lines form right angles.
  D. Parallel lines are sometimes intersecting lines.

For questions 7–8, use the figure.

7. Which of these lines intersects $\overleftrightarrow{EF}$ and is perpendicular to it?

  A. $\overleftrightarrow{AB}$ B. $\overleftrightarrow{GH}$
  C. $\overleftrightarrow{CD}$ D. not here

8. What is the relationship between $\overleftrightarrow{CD}$ and $\overleftrightarrow{EF}$?

  A. They are parallel.
  B. They are intersecting but not perpendicular.
  C. They are perpendicular.
  D. not here

9. An angle that measures 45° is classified as a(n) __?__.

  A. obtuse angle   B. right angle
  C. acute angle   D. straight angle

10. At which of these times do the hands of a clock form a right angle?

  A. 1:00   B. 3:00
  C. 5:00   D. 6:00

11. Which could be the measure of the angle shown below?

  A. 60°   B. 90°
  C. 125°   D. 180°

12. What is the measure of a straight angle?

  A. less than 90°
  B. 90°
  C. more than 90° but less than 180°
  D. 180°

13. Two segments that are congruent have the same __?__.

  A. length   B. endpoints
  C. angles   D. not here

14. Which angle appears to be congruent to $\angle EFG$?

  A.
  B.
  C.
  D.

15. What construction do the figures below represent?

  A. congruent line segments
  B. bisected line segments
  C. congruent angles
  D. perpendicular line segments

16. What construction do the figures below represent?

  A. congruent line segments
  B. bisected line segments
  C. congruent angles
  D. parallel line segments

17. If a figure is a parallelogram, then it must be a __?__.

  A. rectangle   B. quadrilateral
  C. trapezoid   D. square

18. What is the name for this polygon?

  A. pentagon   B. trapezoid
  C. hexagon   D. octagon

19. How many angles does a pentagon have?

  A. 5   B. 6   C. 7   D. not here

20. A triangle that is a regular polygon is a(n) __?__.

  A. equilateral triangle
  B. right triangle
  C. scalene triangle
  D. not here

Multiple-Choice Format • Test Answers

Choose the letter of the correct answer.

1. A figure that can be rotated less than 360° around a central point and match the original figure has __?__ symmetry.
   A. line
   B. rotational
   C. no
   D. not here

2. This figure has line symmetry, so its two parts __?__.

   A. are congruent
   B. have been rotated
   C. each have the same shape as the original figure
   D. not here

3. In which figure is the dashed line a line of symmetry?
   A.
   B.
   C.
   D.

4. How many lines of symmetry does this figure have?
   A. 0 lines
   B. 1 line
   C. 2 lines
   D. 4 lines

5. This figure has rotational symmetry. What is the fraction of each turn?
   A. $\frac{1}{16}$
   B. $\frac{1}{8}$
   C. $\frac{1}{4}$
   D. $\frac{1}{2}$

6. This figure has rotational symmetry. What is the angle measure of each turn?
   A. 45°
   B. 90°
   C. 120°
   D. 180°

7. A turn of a figure around a point is called a __?__.
   A. rotation
   B. translation
   C. reflection
   D. tessellation

8. What change occurs when a figure is translated?
   A. The size of the figure changes.
   B. The shape of the figure changes.
   C. The location of the figure changes.
   D. The figure turns.

For questions 9–11, choose the figure that is the transformation of the original figure.

Original   Figure 1   Figure 2   Figure 3

9. rotation
   A. Figure 1
   B. Figure 2
   C. Figure 3
   D. not here

10. translation
   A. Figure 1
   B. Figure 2
   C. Figure 3
   D. not here

11. reflection
   A. Figure 1
   B. Figure 2
   C. Figure 3
   D. not here

Form A • Multiple-Choice   A33   Go on. ▶

12. Which figure shows a 90° clockwise rotation around the given point?
   A.
   B.
   C.
   D.

For question 13, use the figures below.

Figure A   Figure B   Figure C   Figure D

13. Which polygon(s) will tessellate a plane?
   A. Figure A
   B. Figure B
   C. Figures A and C
   D. Figures B and D

14. Which polygon will NOT tessellate a plane?
   A. rectangle
   B. hexagon
   C. rhombus
   D. not here

For questions 15–16, use the figure below.

15. What is the measure of each angle that surrounds the circled vertex?
   A. 45°
   B. 60°
   C. 90°
   D. 180°

16. What is the sum of the measures of the angles at the circled vertex?
   A. 100°
   B. 180°
   C. 300°
   D. 360°

17. Nhat wants to make a wallpaper design, using one shape to tessellate a plane. Which of these shapes could she use?
   A.
   B.
   C.
   D.

18. Derek wants to use the shape below to make a floor tile. He wants the shape to tessellate a plane. How could he check to see if the shape will work?

   A. See if paper models of the shape will cluster around a point.
   B. Add up the angles in the shape to be sure they are a multiple of 90°.
   C. Hold up the shape to a mirror to see if it looks the same.
   D. Fold a paper model of the shape to find the lines of symmetry.

19. Amy is designing a greeting card. She wants to use a shape that will tessellate a plane. Which of the two shapes below can she use?

   shape 1   shape 2

   A. both shapes
   B. only shape 1
   C. only shape 2
   D. neither

20. Marco is planning a design that will tessellate a plane. Which shape could he use?
   A. octagon
   B. circle
   C. triangle
   D. not here

Form A • Multiple-Choice   A34   ▶ Stop!

Choose the letter of the correct answer.

1. What question should you ask to find out if a solid figure is a polyhedron?
   A. How many bases are there?
   B. Are all the faces polygons?
   C. Which faces are congruent?
   D. Is there more than 1 vertex?

2. Which statement about the bases of pyramids and prisms is true?
   A. Both pyramids and prisms have 2 bases.
   B. Both pyramids and prisms have only 1 base.
   C. Pyramids have 1 base; prisms have 2 bases.
   D. Prisms have 1 base; pyramids have 2 bases.

For questions 3–5, use this group of figures.

Figure A   Figure B   Figure C   Figure D

3. Which figure is a cone?
   A. Figure A
   B. Figure B
   C. Figure C
   D. Figure D

4. Which figure is a triangular prism?
   A. Figure A
   B. Figure B
   C. Figure C
   D. Figure D

5. How many of these figures are polyhedrons?
   A. 4 of them
   B. 3 of them
   C. 2 of them
   D. not here

For questions 6–8, use the figure below.

6. How many faces does this solid figure have?
   A. 4   B. 5   C. 6   D. 7

7. How many edges does this figure have?
   A. 5   B. 6   C. 8   D. not here

8. Which names a vertex of this figure?
   A. △ABC
   B. BC
   C. CA
   D. point D

9. A piece of cheese is cut in the shape of a triangular prism. How many edges does it have?
   A. 5   B. 6   C. 8   D. 9

10. Horace built a rectangular prism, using toothpicks for edges and miniature marshmallows for vertices. How many marshmallows did he use?
   A. 5   B. 6   C. 8   D. 12

11. What solid figure can you make from this net?
   A. triangular prism
   B. triangular pyramid
   C. rectangular prism
   D. not here

Form A • Multiple-Choice   A35   Go on. ▶

12. What solid figure can you make from this net?
   A. rectangular prism
   B. rectangular pyramid
   C. triangular prism
   D. cube

13. How many faces of this prism have the dimensions 2 in. × 4 in.?

   4 in.   2 in.   3 in.

   A. 1   B. 2   C. 4   D. 6

14. Which arrangement below is NOT a net for a cube?
   A.
   B.
   C.
   D.

15. A solid figure that has a circle as a bottom view and a triangle as a front view is a __?__.
   A. cone
   B. triangular pyramid
   C. triangular prism
   D. not here

16. What solid figure has these views?

   top   side   bottom

   A. octagonal pyramid
   B. pentagonal prism
   C. hexagonal prism
   D. octagonal prism

17. The top, bottom, and side views of a solid figure are all squares. What kind of figure is it?
   A. hexagonal prism
   B. cylinder
   C. triangular pyramid
   D. cube

18. What solid figure has these views?

   top   front   side

   A. rectangular prism
   B. triangular prism
   C. triangular pyramid
   D. not here

19. Jodie wants to make a paperweight by covering each face of an octagonal prism with a separate piece of wrapping paper. How many pieces will she use?
   A. 8   B. 9   C. 10   D. 16

20. Ian is making a model of a pyramid whose base has 12 sides. He is using sticks of wood for the edges and balls of putty for the vertices. How many sticks of wood will he need?
   A. 12   B. 13   C. 18   D. 24

Form A • Multiple-Choice   A36   ▶ Stop!

Multiple-Choice Format • Test Answers   127

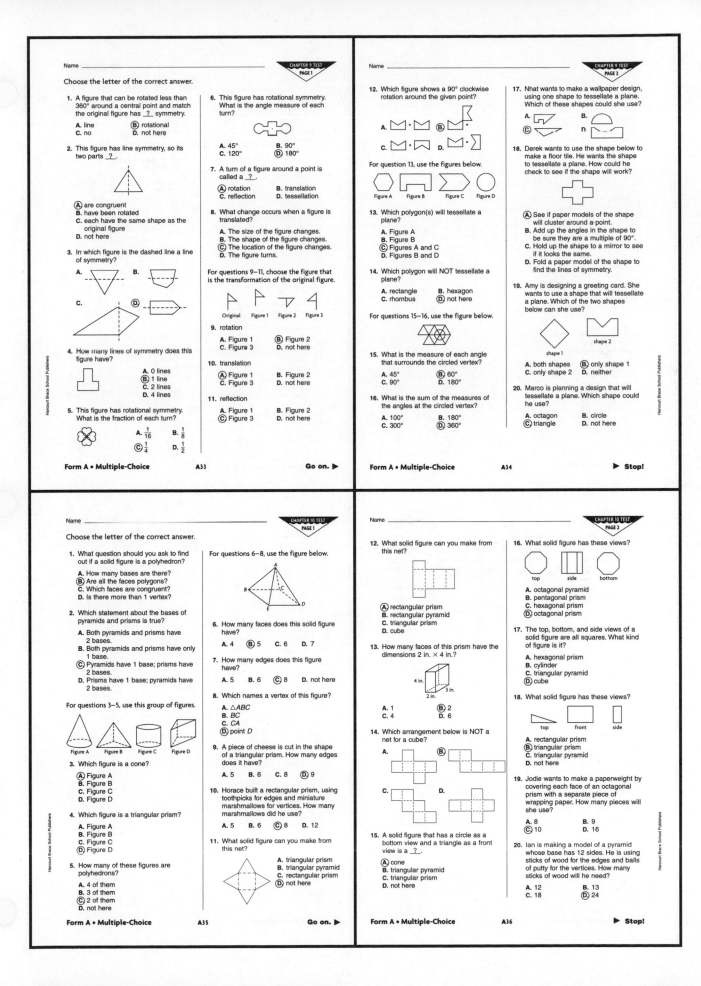

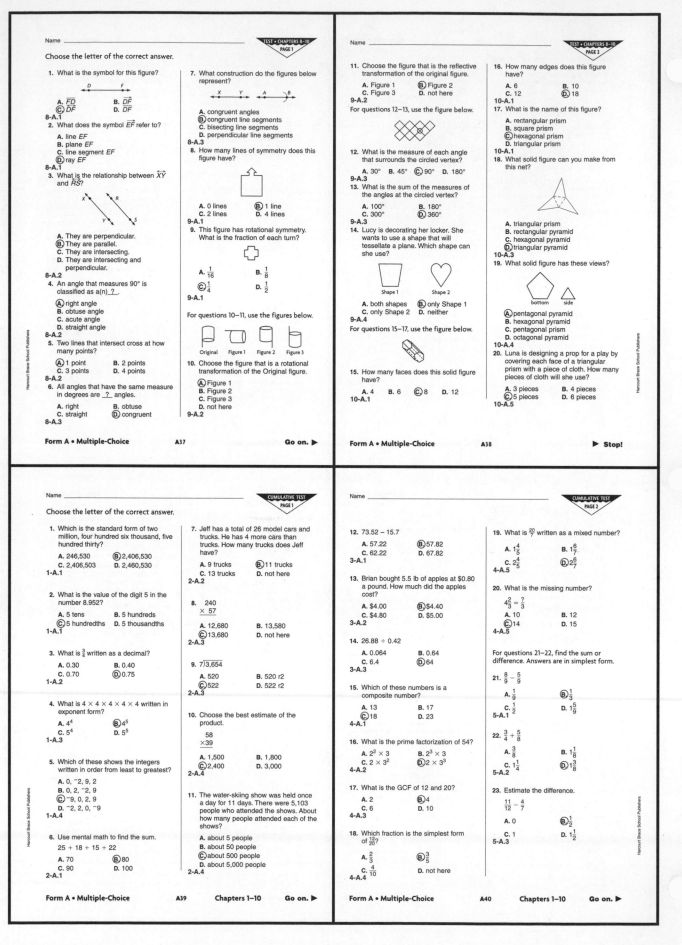

Choose the letter of the correct answer.

1. What is the symbol for this figure?

   D   F

   A. $\overline{FD}$ B. $\overrightarrow{DF}$
   C. $\overleftrightarrow{DF}$ D. $\overrightarrow{DF}$
   8-A.1

2. What does the symbol $\overleftrightarrow{EF}$ refer to?

   A. line EF
   B. plane EF
   C. line segment EF
   D. ray EF
   8-A.1

3. What is the relationship between $\overleftrightarrow{XY}$ and $\overleftrightarrow{RS}$?

   X   R

   Y   S

   A. They are perpendicular.
   B. They are parallel.
   C. They are intersecting.
   D. They are intersecting and perpendicular.
   8-A.2

4. An angle that measures 90° is classified as a(n) _?_.

   A. right angle
   B. obtuse angle
   C. acute angle
   D. straight angle
   8-A.2

5. Two lines that intersect cross at how many points?

   A. 1 point   B. 2 points
   C. 3 points   D. 4 points
   8-A.2

6. All angles that have the same measure in degrees are _?_ angles.

   A. right   B. obtuse
   C. straight   D. congruent
   8-A.3

7. What construction do the figures below represent?

   X   Y   A   B

   A. congruent angles
   B. congruent line segments
   C. bisecting line segments
   D. perpendicular line segments
   8-A.3

8. How many lines of symmetry does this figure have?

   A. 0 lines   B. 1 line
   C. 2 lines   D. 4 lines
   9-A.1

9. This figure has rotational symmetry. What is the fraction of each turn?

   A. $\frac{1}{16}$ B. $\frac{1}{8}$
   C. $\frac{1}{4}$ D. $\frac{1}{2}$
   9-A.1

For questions 10–11, use the figures below.

   Original   Figure 1   Figure 2   Figure 3

10. Choose the figure that is a rotational transformation of the Original figure.

   A. Figure 1
   B. Figure 2
   C. Figure 3
   D. not here
   9-A.2

Form A • Multiple-Choice   A37   **Go on. ▶**

---

11. Choose the figure that is the reflective transformation of the original figure.

   A. Figure 1   B. Figure 2
   C. Figure 3   D. not here
   9-A.2

For questions 12–13, use the figure below.

12. What is the measure of each angle that surrounds the circled vertex?

   A. 30°   B. 45°   C. 90°   D. 180°
   9-A.3

13. What is the sum of the measures of the angles at the circled vertex?

   A. 100°   B. 180°
   C. 300°   D. 360°
   9-A.3

14. Lucy is decorating her locker. She wants to use a shape that will tessellate a plane. Which shape can she use?

   Shape 1   Shape 2

   A. both shapes   B. only Shape 1
   C. only Shape 2   D. neither
   9-A.4

For questions 15–17, use the figure below.

15. How many faces does this solid figure have?

   A. 4   B. 6   C. 8   D. 12
   10-A.1

16. How many edges does this figure have?

   A. 6   B. 10
   C. 12   D. 18
   10-A.1

17. What is the name of this figure?

   A. rectangular prism
   B. square prism
   C. hexagonal prism
   D. triangular prism
   10-A.1

18. What solid figure can you make from this net?

   A. triangular prism
   B. rectangular pyramid
   C. hexagonal pyramid
   D. triangular pyramid
   10-A.3

19. What solid figure has these views?

   bottom   side

   A. pentagonal pyramid
   B. hexagonal pyramid
   C. pentagonal prism
   D. octagonal pyramid
   10-A.4

20. Luna is designing a prop for a play by covering each face of a triangular prism with a piece of cloth. How many pieces of cloth will she use?

   A. 3 pieces   B. 4 pieces
   C. 5 pieces   D. 6 pieces
   10-A.5

Form A • Multiple-Choice   A38   **▶ Stop!**

Choose the letter of the correct answer.

1. Which is the standard form of two million, four hundred six thousand, five hundred thirty?

   A. 246,530   B. 2,406,530
   C. 2,406,503   D. 2,460,530
   1-A.1

2. What is the value of the digit 5 in the number 8.952?

   A. 5 tens   B. 5 hundreds
   C. 5 hundredths   D. 5 thousandths
   1-A.1

3. What is $\frac{3}{4}$ written as a decimal?

   A. 0.30   B. 0.40
   C. 0.70   D. 0.75
   1-A.2

4. What is $4 \times 4 \times 4 \times 4 \times 4$ written in exponent form?

   A. 4^4 B. 4^5
   C. 5^4 D. 5^5
   1-A.3

5. Which of these shows the integers written in order from least to greatest?

   A. 0, ⁻2, 9, 2
   B. 0, 2, ⁻2, 9
   C. ⁻9, 0, 2, 9
   D. ⁻2, 2, 0, ⁻9
   1-A.4

6. Use mental math to find the sum.

   $25 + 18 + 15 + 22$

   A. 70   B. 80
   C. 90   D. 100
   2-A.1

7. Jeff has a total of 26 model cars and trucks. He has 4 more cars than trucks. How many trucks does Jeff have?

   A. 9 trucks   B. 11 trucks
   C. 13 trucks   D. not here
   2-A.2

8.
   240
   $\times\ 57$

   A. 12,680   B. 13,580
   C. 13,680   D. not here
   2-A.3

9. $7\overline{)3,654}$

   A. 520   B. 520 r2
   C. 522   D. 522 r2
   2-A.3

10. Choose the best estimate of the product.

   58
   $\times 39$

   A. 1,500   B. 1,800
   C. 2,400   D. 3,000
   2-A.4

11. The water-skiing show was held once a day for 11 days. There were 5,103 people who attended the shows. About how many people attended each of the shows?

   A. about 5 people
   B. about 50 people
   C. about 500 people
   D. about 5,000 people
   2-A.4

Form A • Multiple-Choice   A39   Chapters 1–10   **Go on. ▶**

---

12. $73.52 - 15.7$

   A. 57.22   B. 57.82
   C. 62.22   D. 67.82
   3-A.1

13. Brian bought 5.5 lb of apples at $0.80 a pound. How much did the apples cost?

   A. $4.00   B. $4.40
   C. $4.80   D. $5.00
   3-A.2

14. $26.88 \div 0.42$

   A. 0.064   B. 0.64
   C. 6.4   D. 64
   3-A.3

15. Which of these numbers is a composite number?

   A. 13   B. 17
   C. 18   D. 23
   4-A.1

16. What is the prime factorization of 54?

   A. $2^2 \times 3$ B. $2^3 \times 3$
   C. 2×3^2 D. 2×3^3
   4-A.2

17. What is the GCF of 12 and 20?

   A. 2   B. 4
   C. 6   D. 10
   4-A.3

18. Which fraction is the simplest form of $\frac{12}{20}$?

   A. $\frac{2}{3}$ B. $\frac{3}{5}$
   C. $\frac{4}{10}$ D. not here
   4-A.4

19. What is $\frac{20}{7}$ written as a mixed number?

   A. $1\frac{4}{5}$ B. $1\frac{6}{7}$
   C. $2\frac{4}{5}$ D. $2\frac{6}{7}$
   4-A.5

20. What is the missing number?

   $4\frac{2}{3} = \frac{?}{3}$

   A. 10   B. 12
   C. 14   D. 15
   4-A.5

For questions 21–22, find the sum or difference. Answers are in simplest form.

21. $\frac{8}{9} - \frac{5}{9}$

   A. $\frac{1}{9}$ B. $\frac{1}{3}$
   C. $\frac{1}{2}$ D. $1\frac{5}{9}$
   5-A.1

22. $\frac{3}{4} + \frac{5}{8}$

   A. $\frac{3}{8}$ B. $1\frac{1}{8}$
   C. $1\frac{1}{4}$ D. $1\frac{3}{8}$
   5-A.2

23. Estimate the difference.

   $\frac{11}{12} - \frac{4}{7}$

   A. 0   B. $\frac{1}{2}$
   C. 1   D. $1\frac{1}{2}$
   5-A.3

Form A • Multiple-Choice   A40   Chapters 1–10   **Go on. ▶**

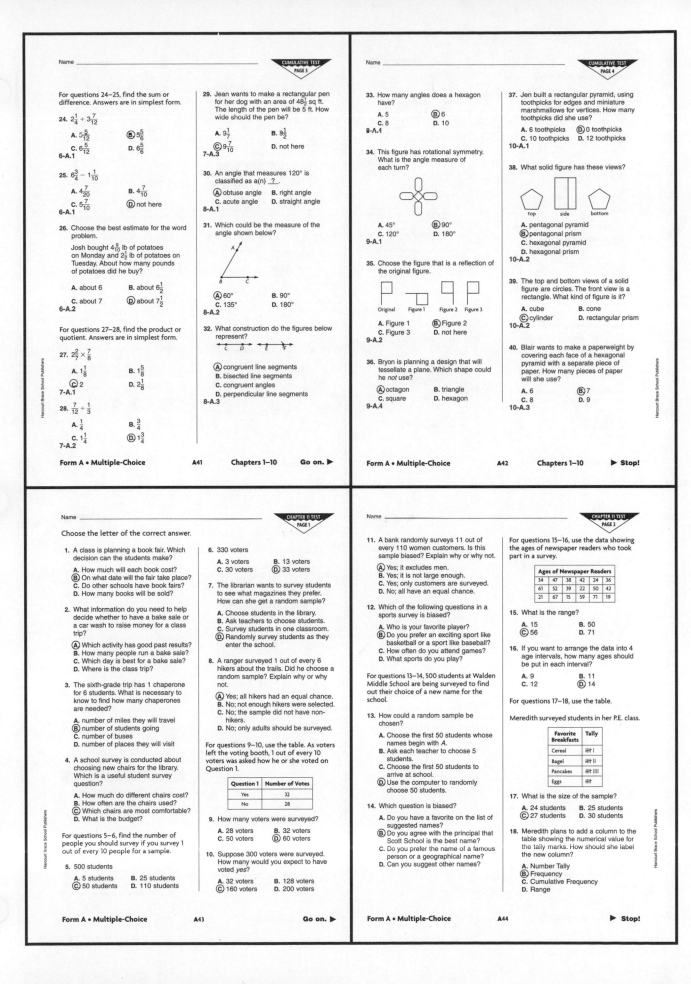

For questions 24–25, find the sum or difference. Answers are in simplest form.

24. $2\frac{1}{4} + 3\frac{7}{12}$

A. $5\frac{5}{12}$ B. $5\frac{5}{6}$

C. $6\frac{5}{12}$ D. $6\frac{5}{6}$

6-A.1

25. $6\frac{3}{4} - 1\frac{1}{10}$

A. $4\frac{7}{20}$ B. $4\frac{7}{10}$

C. $5\frac{7}{10}$ D. not here

6-A.1

26. Choose the best estimate for the word problem.

Josh bought $4\frac{9}{10}$ lb of potatoes on Monday and $2\frac{2}{3}$ lb of potatoes on Tuesday. About how many pounds of potatoes did he buy?

A. about 6   B. about $6\frac{1}{2}$

C. about 7   D. about $7\frac{1}{2}$

6-A.2

For questions 27–28, find the product or quotient. Answers are in simplest form.

27. $2\frac{2}{7} \times \frac{7}{8}$

A. $1\frac{1}{8}$ B. $1\frac{5}{8}$

C. 2   D. $2\frac{1}{8}$

7-A.1

28. $7\frac{1}{12} \div \frac{1}{3}$

A. $\frac{1}{4}$ B. $\frac{3}{4}$

C. $1\frac{1}{4}$ D. $1\frac{1}{3}$

7-A.2

29. Jean wants to make a rectangular pen for her dog with an area of $48\frac{1}{2}$ sq ft. The length of the pen will be 5 ft. How wide should the pen be?

A. $9\frac{1}{7}$ B. $9\frac{1}{2}$

C. $9\frac{7}{10}$ D. not here

7-A.3

30. An angle that measures 120° is classified as a(n) ? .

A. obtuse angle   B. right angle

C. acute angle   D. straight angle

8-A.1

31. Which could be the measure of the angle shown below?

A. 60°   B. 90°

C. 135°   D. 180°

8-A.2

32. What construction do the figures below represent?

A. congruent line segments
B. bisected line segments
C. congruent angles
D. perpendicular line segments

8-A.3

Form A • Multiple-Choice   A41   **Chapters 1–10**   **Go on. ▶**

33. How many angles does a hexagon have?

A. 5   B. 6

C. 8   D. 10

8-A.1

34. This figure has rotational symmetry. What is the angle measure of each turn?

A. 45°   B. 90°

C. 120°   D. 180°

9-A.1

35. Choose the figure that is a reflection of the original figure.

Original   Figure 1   Figure 2   Figure 3

A. Figure 1   B. Figure 2

C. Figure 3   D. not here

9-A.2

36. Bryon is planning a design that will tessellate a plane. Which shape could he not use?

A. octagon   B. triangle

C. square   D. hexagon

9-A.4

37. Jen built a rectangular pyramid, using toothpicks for edges and miniature marshmallows for vertices. How many toothpicks did she use?

A. 6 toothpicks   B. 0 toothpicks

C. 10 toothpicks   D. 12 toothpicks

10-A.1

38. What solid figure has these views?

top   side   bottom

A. pentagonal pyramid
B. pentagonal prism
C. hexagonal pyramid
D. hexagonal prism

10-A.2

39. The top and bottom views of a solid figure are circles. The front view is a rectangle. What kind of figure is it?

A. cube   B. cone

C. cylinder   D. rectangular prism

10-A.2

40. Blair wants to make a paperweight by covering each face of a hexagonal pyramid with a separate piece of paper. How many pieces of paper will she use?

A. 6   B. 7

C. 8   D. 9

10-A.3

Form A • Multiple-Choice   A42   **Chapters 1–10**   **▶ Stop!**

Choose the letter of the correct answer.

1. A class is planning a book fair. Which decision can the students make?

A. How much will each book cost?
B. On what date will the fair take place?
C. Do other schools have book fairs?
D. How many books will be sold?

2. What information do you need to help decide whether to have a bake sale or a car wash to raise money for a class trip?

A. Which activity has good past results?
B. How many people run a bake sale?
C. Which day is best for a bake sale?
D. Where is the class trip?

3. The sixth-grade trip has 1 chaperone for 6 students. What is necessary to know to find how many chaperones are needed?

A. number of miles they will travel
B. number of students going
C. number of buses
D. number of places they will visit

4. A school survey is conducted about choosing new chairs for the library. Which is a useful student survey question?

A. How much do different chairs cost?
B. How often are the chairs used?
C. Which chairs are most comfortable?
D. What is the budget?

For questions 5–6, find the number of people you should survey if you survey 1 out of every 10 people for a sample.

5. 500 students

A. 5 students   B. 25 students

C. 50 students   D. 110 students

6. 330 voters

A. 3 voters   B. 13 voters

C. 30 voters   D. 33 voters

7. The librarian wants to survey students to see what magazines they prefer. How can she get a random sample?

A. Choose students in the library.
B. Ask teachers to choose students.
C. Survey students in one classroom.
D. Randomly survey students as they enter the school.

8. A ranger surveyed 1 out of every 6 hikers about the trails. Did he choose a random sample? Explain why or why not.

A. Yes; all hikers had an equal chance.
B. No; not enough hikers were selected.
C. No; the sample did not have non-hikers.
D. No; only adults should be surveyed.

For questions 9–10, use the table. As voters left the voting booth, 1 out of every 10 voters was asked how he or she voted on Question 1.

Question 1	Number of Votes
Yes	32
No	28

9. How many voters were surveyed?

A. 28 voters   B. 32 voters

C. 50 voters   D. 60 voters

10. Suppose 300 voters were surveyed. How many would you expect to have voted yes?

A. 32 voters   B. 128 voters

C. 160 voters   D. 200 voters

Form A • Multiple-Choice   A43   **Go on. ▶**

11. A bank randomly surveys 11 out of every 110 women customers. Is this sample biased? Explain why or why not.

A. Yes; it excludes men.
B. Yes; it is not large enough.
C. Yes; only customers are surveyed.
D. No; all have an equal chance.

12. Which of the following questions in a sports survey is biased?

A. Who is your favorite player?
B. Do you prefer an exciting sport like basketball or a sport like baseball?
C. How often do you attend games?
D. What sports do you play?

For questions 13–14, 500 students at Walden Middle School are being surveyed to find out their choice of a new name for the school.

13. How could a random sample be chosen?

A. Choose the first 50 students whose names begin with A.
B. Ask each teacher to choose 5 students.
C. Choose the first 50 students to arrive at school.
D. Use the computer to randomly choose 50 students.

14. Which question is biased?

A. Do you have a favorite on the list of suggested names?
B. Do you agree with the principal that Scott School is the best name?
C. Do you prefer the name of a famous person or a geographical name?
D. Can you suggest other names?

For questions 15–16, use the data showing the ages of newspaper readers who took part in a survey.

Ages of Newspaper Readers

34	47	38	42	24	36
61	52	39	22	50	42
21	67	15	59	71	19

15. What is the range?

A. 15   B. 50

C. 56   D. 71

16. If you want to arrange the data into 4 age intervals, how many ages should be put in each interval?

A. 9   B. 11

C. 12   D. 14

For questions 17–18, use the table.

Meredith surveyed students in her P.E. class.

Favorite Breakfasts	Tally
Cereal	ﾗﾗﾗﾗ I
Bagel	ﾗﾗﾗﾗ II
Pancakes	ﾗﾗﾗﾗ IIII
Eggs	ﾗﾗﾗﾗ

17. What is the size of the sample?

A. 24 students   B. 25 students

C. 27 students   D. 30 students

18. Meredith plans to add a column to the table showing the numerical value for the tally marks. How should she label the new column?

A. Number Tally
B. Frequency
C. Cumulative Frequency
D. Range

Form A • Multiple-Choice   A44   **▶ Stop!**

Harcourt Brace School Publishers

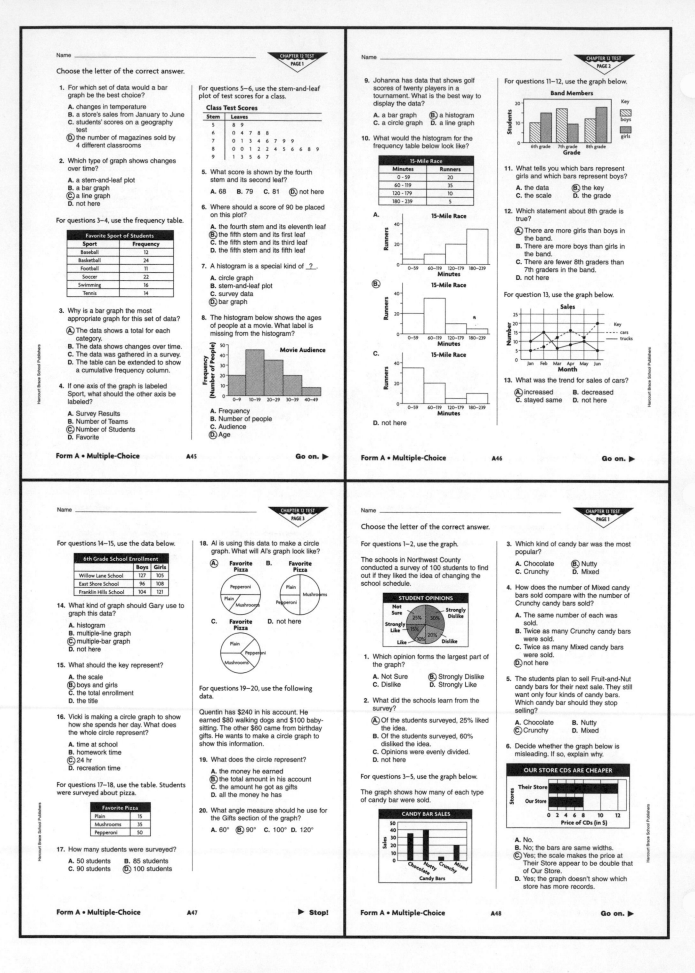

Name _____

Choose the letter of the correct answer.

1. For which set of data would a bar graph be the best choice?

  A. changes in temperature
  B. a store's sales from January to June
  C. students' scores on a geography test
  (D.) the number of magazines sold by 4 different classrooms

2. Which type of graph shows changes over time?

  A. a stem-and-leaf plot
  B. a bar graph
  (C) a line graph
  D. not here

For questions 3–4, use the frequency table.

Favorite Sport of Students	
Sport	**Frequency**
Baseball	12
Basketball	24
Football	11
Soccer	22
Swimming	16
Tennis	14

3. Why is a bar graph the most appropriate graph for this set of data?

  (A) The data shows a total for each category.
  B. The data shows changes over time.
  C. The data was gathered in a survey.
  D. The table can be extended to show a cumulative frequency column.

4. If one axis of the graph is labeled Sport, what should the other axis be labeled?

  A. Survey Results
  B. Number of Teams
  (C) Number of Students
  D. Favorite

For questions 5–6, use the stem-and-leaf plot of test scores for a class.

Class Test Scores

Stem	Leaves
5	8 9
6	0 4 7 8 8
7	0 1 3 4 6 7 9 9
8	0 0 1 2 2 4 5 6 6 8 9
9	1 3 5 6 7

5. What score is shown by the fourth stem and its second leaf?

  A. 68 B. 79 C. 81 **(D.)** not here

6. Where should a score of 90 be placed on this plot?

  A. the fourth stem and its eleventh leaf
  (B.) the fifth stem and its first leaf
  C. the fifth stem and its third leaf
  D. the fifth stem and its fifth leaf

7. A histogram is a special kind of _?_.

  A. circle graph
  B. stem-and-leaf plot
  C. survey data
  (D) bar graph

8. The histogram below shows the ages of people at a movie. What label is missing from the histogram?

  A. Frequency
  B. Number of people
  C. Audience
  (D) Age

Name _____

9. Johanna has data that shows golf scores of twenty players in a tournament. What is the best way to display the data?

  A. a bar graph **(B.)** a histogram
  C. a circle graph D. a line graph

10. What would the histogram for the frequency table below look like?

15-Mile Race	
Minutes	**Runners**
0 - 59	20
60 - 119	35
120 - 179	10
180 - 239	5

A. 15-Mile Race
B. 15-Mile Race
C. 15-Mile Race
D. not here

For questions 11–12, use the graph below.

Band Members

Key: boys, girls

11. What tells you which bars represent girls and which bars represent boys?

  A. the data **(B.)** the key
  C. the scale D. the grade

12. Which statement about 8th grade is true?

  (A.) There are more girls than boys in the band.
  B. There are more boys than girls in the band.
  C. There are fewer 8th graders than 7th graders in the band.
  D. not here

For question 13, use the graph below.

Sales

Key: cars (dashed), trucks (solid)

13. What was the trend for sales of cars?

  (A.) increased B. decreased
  C. stayed same D. not here

Name _____

For questions 14–15, use the data below.

6th Grade School Enrollment	Boys	Girls
Willow Lane School	127	105
East Shore School	96	108
Franklin Hills School	104	121

14. What kind of graph should Gary use to graph this data?

  A. histogram
  B. multiple-line graph
  (C) multiple-bar graph
  D. not here

15. What should the key represent?

  A. the scale
  (B) boys and girls
  C. the total enrollment
  D. the title

16. Vicki is making a circle graph to show how she spends her day. What does the whole circle represent?

  A. time at school
  B. homework time
  (C) 24 hr
  D. recreation time

For questions 17–18, use the table. Students were surveyed about pizza.

Favorite Pizza	
Plain	15
Mushrooms	35
Pepperoni	50

17. How many students were surveyed?

  A. 50 students B. 85 students
  C. 90 students **(D)** 100 students

18. Al is using this data to make a circle graph. What will Al's graph look like?

  (A) Favorite Pizza
  B. Favorite Pizza
  C. Favorite Pizza
  D. not here

For questions 19–20, use the following data.

Quentin has $240 in his account. He earned $80 walking dogs and $100 baby-sitting. The other $60 came from birthday gifts. He wants to make a circle graph to show this information.

19. What does the circle represent?

  A. the money he earned
  (B) the total amount in his account
  C. the amount he got as gifts
  D. all the money he has

20. What angle measure should he use for the Gifts section of the graph?

  A. 60° **(B)** 90° C. 100° D. 120°

Name _____

Choose the letter of the correct answer.

For questions 1–2, use the graph.

The schools in Northwest County conducted a survey of 100 students to find out if they liked the idea of changing the school schedule.

STUDENT OPINIONS

Not Sure 25%, Strongly Dislike 30%, Dislike 20%, Like 10%, Strongly Like 15%

1. Which opinion forms the largest part of the graph?

  A. Not Sure **(B)** Strongly Dislike
  C. Dislike D. Strongly Like

2. What did the schools learn from the survey?

  (A) Of the students surveyed, 25% liked the idea.
  B. Of the students surveyed, 60% disliked the idea.
  C. Opinions were evenly divided.
  D. not here

For questions 3–5, use the graph below.

The graph shows how many of each type of candy bar were sold.

CANDY BAR SALES

Chocolate, Nutty, Crunchy, Mixed

3. Which kind of candy bar was the most popular?

  A. Chocolate **(B)** Nutty
  C. Crunchy D. Mixed

4. How does the number of Mixed candy bars sold compare with the number of Crunchy candy bars sold?

  A. The same number of each was sold.
  B. Twice as many Crunchy candy bars were sold.
  C. Twice as many Mixed candy bars were sold.
  (D) not here

5. The students plan to sell Fruit-and-Nut candy bars for their next sale. They still want only four kinds of candy bars. Which candy bar should they stop selling?

  A. Chocolate B. Nutty
  (C) Crunchy D. Mixed

6. Decide whether the graph below is misleading. If so, explain why.

OUR STORE CDS ARE CHEAPER

Their Store, Our Store — Price of CDs (in $)

  A. No.
  B. No; the bars are same widths.
  (C) Yes; the scale makes the price at Their Store appear to be double that of Our Store.
  D. Yes; the graph doesn't show which store has more records.

Harcourt Brace School Publishers

Multiple-Choice Format • Test Answers

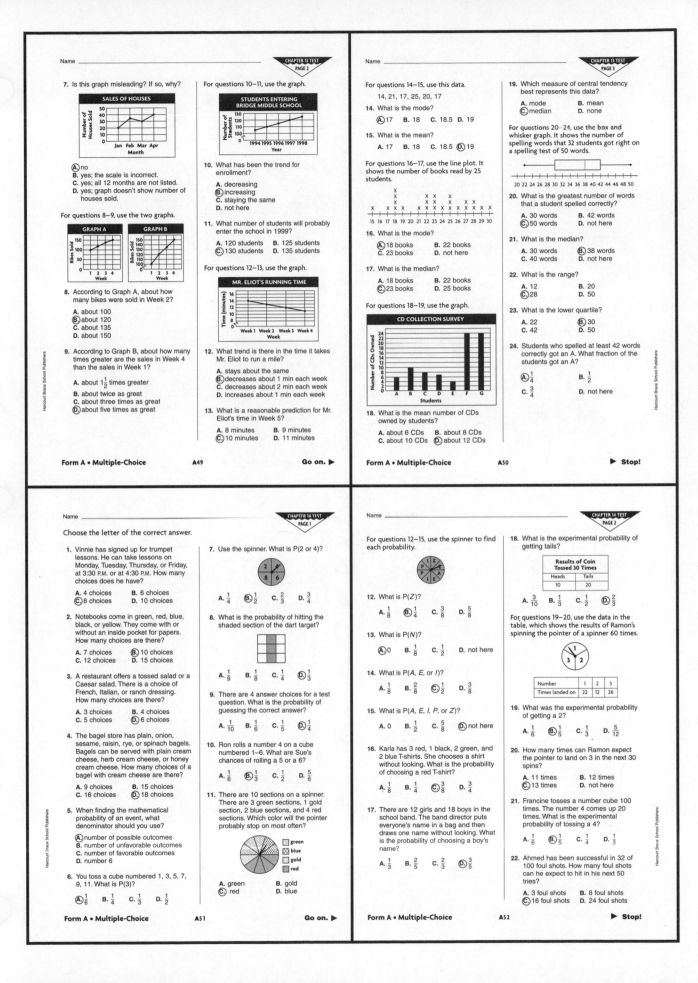

7. Is this graph misleading? If so, why?

SALES OF HOUSES

A. no
B. yes; the scale is incorrect.
C. yes; all 12 months are not listed.
D. yes; graph doesn't show number of houses sold.

For questions 8–9, use the two graphs.

GRAPH A   **GRAPH B**

8. According to Graph A, about how many bikes were sold in Week 2?
   A. about 100
   B. about 120
   C. about 135
   D. about 150

9. According to Graph B, about how many times greater are the sales in Week 4 than the sales in Week 1?
   A. about $1\frac{1}{2}$ times greater
   B. about twice as great
   C. about three times as great
   D. about five times as great

For questions 10–11, use the graph.

STUDENTS ENTERING BRIDGE MIDDLE SCHOOL

10. What has been the trend for enrollment?
    A. decreasing
    B. increasing
    C. staying the same
    D. not here

11. What number of students will probably enter the school in 1999?
    A. 120 students   B. 125 students
    C. 130 students   D. 135 students

For questions 12–13, use the graph.

MR. ELIOT'S RUNNING TIME

12. What trend is there in the time it takes Mr. Eliot to run a mile?
    A. stays about the same
    B. decreases about 1 min each week
    C. decreases about 2 min each week
    D. increases about 1 min each week

13. What is a reasonable prediction for Mr. Eliot's time in Week 5?
    A. 8 minutes   B. 9 minutes
    C. 10 minutes   D. 11 minutes

Form A • Multiple-Choice   A49   **Go on. ▶**

For questions 14–15, use this data.
14, 21, 17, 25, 20, 17

14. What is the mode?
    A. 17   B. 18   C. 18.5   D. 19

15. What is the mean?
    A. 17   B. 18   C. 18.5   D. 19

For questions 16–17, use the line plot. It shows the number of books read by 25 students.

16. What is the mode?
    A. 18 books   B. 22 books
    C. 23 books   D. not here

17. What is the median?
    A. 18 books   B. 22 books
    C. 23 books   D. 25 books

For questions 18–19, use the graph.

CD COLLECTION SURVEY

18. What is the mean number of CDs owned by students?
    A. about 6 CDs   B. about 8 CDs
    C. about 10 CDs   D. about 12 CDs

19. Which measure of central tendency best represents this data?
    A. mode   B. mean
    C. median   D. none

For questions 20–24, use the box and whisker graph. It shows the number of spelling words that 32 students got right on a spelling test of 50 words.

20. What is the greatest number of words that a student spelled correctly?
    A. 30 words   B. 42 words
    C. 50 words   D. not here

21. What is the median?
    A. 30 words   B. 38 words
    C. 40 words   D. not here

22. What is the range?
    A. 12   B. 20
    C. 28   D. 50

23. What is the lower quartile?
    A. 22   B. 30
    C. 42   D. 50

24. Students who spelled at least 42 words correctly got an A. What fraction of the students got an A?
    A. $\frac{1}{4}$ B. $\frac{1}{2}$
    C. $\frac{3}{4}$ D. not here

Form A • Multiple-Choice   A50   **▶ Stop!**

Choose the letter of the correct answer.

1. Vinnie has signed up for trumpet lessons. He can take lessons on Monday, Tuesday, Thursday, or Friday, at 3:30 P.M. or at 4:30 P.M. How many choices does he have?
   A. 4 choices   B. 6 choices
   C. 8 choices   D. 10 choices

2. Notebooks come in green, red, blue, black, or yellow. They come with or without an inside pocket for papers. How many choices are there?
   A. 7 choices   B. 10 choices
   C. 12 choices   D. 15 choices

3. A restaurant offers a tossed salad or a Caesar salad. There is a choice of French, Italian, or ranch dressing. How many choices are there?
   A. 3 choices   B. 4 choices
   C. 5 choices   D. 6 choices

4. The bagel store has plain, onion, sesame, raisin, rye, or spinach bagels. Bagels can be served with plain cream cheese, herb cream cheese, or honey cream cheese. How many choices of a bagel with cream cheese are there?
   A. 9 choices   B. 15 choices
   C. 16 choices   D. 18 choices

5. When finding the mathematical probability of an event, what denominator should you use?
   A. number of possible outcomes
   B. number of unfavorable outcomes
   C. number of favorable outcomes
   D. number 6

6. You toss a cube numbered 1, 3, 5, 7, 9, 11. What is P(3)?
   A. $\frac{1}{6}$ B. $\frac{1}{4}$ C. $\frac{1}{3}$ D. $\frac{1}{2}$

7. Use the spinner. What is P(2 or 4)?
   A. $\frac{1}{4}$ B. $\frac{1}{2}$ C. $\frac{2}{3}$ D. $\frac{3}{4}$

8. What is the probability of hitting the shaded section of the dart target?
   A. $\frac{1}{9}$ B. $\frac{1}{8}$ C. $\frac{1}{4}$ D. $\frac{1}{3}$

9. There are 4 answer choices for a test question. What is the probability of guessing the correct answer?
   A. $\frac{1}{10}$ B. $\frac{1}{6}$ C. $\frac{1}{5}$ D. $\frac{1}{4}$

10. Ron rolls a number 4 on a cube numbered 1–6. What are Sue's chances of rolling a 5 or 6?
    A. $\frac{1}{6}$ B. $\frac{1}{3}$ C. $\frac{1}{2}$ D. $\frac{5}{6}$

11. There are 10 sections on a spinner. There are 3 green sections, 1 gold section, 2 blue sections, and 4 red sections. Which color will the pointer probably stop on most often?
    green
    blue
    gold
    red
    A. green   B. gold
    C. red   D. blue

Form A • Multiple-Choice   A51   **Go on. ▶**

For questions 12–15, use the spinner to find each probability.

12. What is P(Z)?
    A. $\frac{1}{8}$ B. $\frac{1}{4}$ C. $\frac{3}{8}$ D. $\frac{5}{8}$

13. What is P(N)?
    A. 0   B. $\frac{1}{8}$ C. $\frac{1}{2}$ D. not here

14. What is P(A, E, I, or I)?
    A. $\frac{1}{8}$ B. $\frac{2}{8}$ C. $\frac{1}{2}$ D. $\frac{3}{8}$

15. What is P(A, E, I, P, or Z)?
    A. 0   B. $\frac{1}{2}$ C. $\frac{5}{8}$ D. not here

16. Karla has 3 red, 1 black, 2 green, and 2 blue T-shirts. She chooses a shirt without looking. What is the probability of choosing a red T-shirt?
    A. $\frac{1}{8}$ B. $\frac{1}{4}$ C. $\frac{3}{8}$ D. $\frac{3}{4}$

17. There are 12 girls and 18 boys in the school band. The band director puts everyone's name in a bag and then draws one name without looking. What is the probability of choosing a boy's name?
    A. $\frac{1}{3}$ B. $\frac{2}{5}$ C. $\frac{2}{3}$ D. $\frac{3}{5}$

18. What is the experimental probability of getting tails?

Results of Coin Tossed 30 Times	
Heads	Tails
10	20

    A. $\frac{3}{10}$ B. $\frac{1}{3}$ C. $\frac{1}{2}$ D. $\frac{2}{3}$

For questions 19–20, use the data in the table, which shows the results of Ramon's spinning the pointer of a spinner 60 times.

Number	1	2	3
Times landed on	22	12	26

19. What was the experimental probability of getting a 2?
    A. $\frac{1}{6}$ B. $\frac{1}{5}$ C. $\frac{1}{3}$ D. $\frac{5}{12}$

20. How many times can Ramon expect the pointer to land on 3 in the next 30 spins?
    A. 11 times   B. 12 times
    C. 13 times   D. not here

21. Francine tosses a number cube 100 times. The number 4 comes up 20 times. What is the experimental probability of tossing a 4?
    A. $\frac{1}{6}$ B. $\frac{1}{5}$ C. $\frac{1}{4}$ D. $\frac{1}{3}$

22. Ahmed has been successful in 32 of 100 foul shots. How many foul shots can he expect to hit in his next 50 tries?
    A. 3 foul shots   B. 8 foul shots
    C. 16 foul shots D. 24 foul shots

Form A • Multiple-Choice   A52   **▶ Stop!**

Multiple-Choice Format • Test Answers   **131**

Choose the letter of the correct answer.

1. One gallon of gas is needed for every 30 mi of a trip. What is necessary to know to find how many gallons of gas is needed?

   A. number of gallons of gas the car holds
   B. number of people traveling in the car
   C. number of miles of the trip
   D. number of days the trip will take

   11-A.1

2. If you survey 1 out of every 12 students, how many people should you survey from a sample of 420 students?

   A. 12 students   B. 20 students
   C. 24 students   D. 35 students

   11-A.2

3. In a survey about school subjects, which of the following questions is biased?

   A. What subjects do you find hardest?
   B. Do you enjoy geography, a class most students find boring?
   C. What is your favorite subject?
   D. How many subjects do you study a day?

   11-A.3

For questions 4–5, use the data showing the ages of moviegoers who took part in a survey.

Ages of Moviegoers					
53	21	9	42	45	36
61	18	27	33	59	64
12	48	24	15	38	51

4. What is the range?

   A. 9   B. 45   C. 55   D. 64

   11-A.4

5. If you want to arrange the data into 5 age intervals, how many ages should be put in each interval?

   A. 11   B. 13   C. 16   D. 18

   11-A.4

6. What type of graph would be most appropriate for the following data?

1 Month	Nov	Dec	Jan	Feb	Mar
Average Snowfall (in.)	5.5	7.1	8.7	6.4	4.2

   A. line plot
   B. line graph
   C. circle graph
   D. stem-and-leaf plot

   12-A.1

7. What type of graph should Alisa make to show the sales of three different companies over the last 10 years?

   A. single-bar graph
   B. multiple-bar graph
   C. single-line graph
   D. multiple-line graph

   12-A.3

For questions 8–9, use the following data.

Brock wants to make a circle graph showing how much time he spends each week on homework. He spends 2 hr on language arts, 4 hr on math, 1.5 hr on science, and 2.5 hr on reading.

8. In the circle graph, what does the whole circle represent?

   A. the hours spent reading each week
   B. the hours spent in math class
   C. the total hours spent on homework weekly
   D. the hours spent in the science lab

   12-A.2

9. What angle measure should Brock use for the Language Arts section of the graph?

   A. 54°   B. 72°
   C. 90°   D. 144°

   12-A.2

Form A • Multiple-Choice   A53   Go on. ▶

For questions 10–11, use the graph.

SPORTING EQUIPMENT SALES

10. Which type of ball was least popular?

    A. football   B. volleyball
    C. soccer ball D. basketball

    13-A.1

11. How does the number of soccer balls compare with the number of volleyballs sold?

    A. One-fourth as many volleyballs were sold.
    B. Half as many soccer balls were sold.
    C. The same number of each were sold.
    D. Twice as many soccer balls were sold.

    13-A.1

12. A computer sold for $2,500. After 6 months, the computer sold for $2,200. After 12 months it sold for $1,900. What do you think the computer will sell for after 18 months?

    A. $1,400   B. $1,500
    C. $1,600   D. $1,700

    13-A.3

For questions 13–14, use the table below.

6th Grade Basketball Scores				
51	48	39	53	47
44	42	55	43	48

13. What is the median of the basketball scores?

    A. 47   B. 47.5   C. 48   D. 49.5

    13-A.4

14. What is the mean of the basketball scores?

    A. 46.0   B. 46.5
    C. 47.0   D. 47.5

    13-A.4

15. The cafeteria offers a choice of a hamburger or cheeseburger. A choice of toppings for the burger includes ketchup, onions, pickles, and lettuce. How many choices are there?

    A. 6 choices   B. 8 choices
    C. 10 choices   D. 12 choices

    14-A.1

16. You toss a cube labeled Q, R, S, T, U, V. What is P(R, S, T or V)?

    A. $\frac{1}{6}$ B. $\frac{1}{3}$
    C. $\frac{1}{2}$ D. $\frac{2}{3}$

    14-A.2

17. Each lunch bag contains a piece of fruit. Two bags contain bananas, 10 contain apples, 8 contain oranges, and 4 contain plums. What is the probability of choosing a lunch bag with a banana?

    A. $\frac{1}{12}$ B. $\frac{1}{6}$
    C. $\frac{1}{3}$ D. $\frac{5}{12}$

    14-A.2

18. A trivia game is divided up into 2 rounds. In the first round, Ruth answered 9 out of 15 questions correctly. The second round has 35 questions. How many questions can Ruth expect to answer correctly?

    A. 9 questions   B. 15 questions
    C. 21 questions   D. 25 questions

    14-A.3

Form A • Multiple-Choice   A54   ▶ Stop!

Choose the letter of the correct answer.

1. The batting averages of three players are 0.265, 0.250, 0.206. Which shows these averages written in order from greatest to least?

   A. 0.265, 0.250, 0.206
   B. 0.250, 0.206, 0.265
   C. 0.250, 0.265, 0.206
   D. 0.265, 0.206, 0.250

   1-A.1

2. What is 0.5 written as a fraction?

   A. $\frac{1}{50}$ B. $\frac{5}{100}$
   C. $\frac{1}{5}$ D. $\frac{5}{10}$

   1-A.2

3. What is the value of 2^5?

   A. 10   B. 16
   C. 25   D. 32

   1-A.3

4. What is the opposite of ⁻2?

   A. $-\frac{1}{2}$ B. $+\frac{1}{2}$
   C. $^+2$ D. $^+2^2$

   1-A.4

5. Use mental math to find the difference.

   81 − 28

   A. 51   B. 52
   C. 53   D. 54

   2-A.1

6. Marge sold a total of 45 green or gold flags at the football game. She sold 11 more gold flags than green flags. How many gold flags did she sell?

   A. 11 gold flags   B. 17 gold flags
   C. 22 gold flags   D. 28 gold flags

   2-A.2

7. 279
   × 643

   A. 169,297   B. 169,397
   C. 179,397   D. not here

   2-A.3

8. Choose the best estimate of the difference.

   867 − 352

   A. 300   B. 400
   C. 500   D. 600

   2-A.4

9. A bike path has three sections. The lengths of the sections are 2.8 mi, 1.6 mi, and 3.4 mi. How many miles long is the bike path?

   A. 4.4 mi   B. 7.4 mi
   C. 7.8 mi   D. not here

   3-A.1

10. 3.25 × 7.4

    A. 0.2405   B. 2.405
    C. 24.05   D. 240.5

    3-A.2

11. 3.15 ÷ 4.5

    A. 0.07   B. 0.7
    C. 7.0   D. 70

    3-A.3

12. Solve for n to complete the prime factorization.

    $3^n = 81$

    A. 3   B. 4
    C. 5   D. 6

    4-A.2

Form A • Multiple-Choice   A55   Chapters 1–14   Go on. ▶

---

13. What is the LCM of 4 and 6?

    A. 8   B. 12   C. 16   D. 24

    4-A.3

14. What is $2\frac{1}{5}$ written as a fraction?

    A. $\frac{5}{11}$ B. $\frac{1}{2}$
    C. $\frac{11}{5}$ D. $\frac{16}{5}$

    4-A.5

For questions 15–16, find the sum or difference. Answers are in simplest form.

15. $\frac{1}{12} + \frac{5}{12}$

    A. $\frac{1}{6}$ B. $\frac{1}{2}$
    C. $\frac{3}{4}$ D. $\frac{7}{8}$

    5-A.1

16. $\frac{5}{6} - \frac{1}{2}$

    A. $\frac{1}{6}$ B. $\frac{1}{4}$
    C. $\frac{1}{3}$ D. $\frac{3}{4}$

    5-A.2

17. Estimate the sum.

    $\frac{11}{12} + \frac{5}{9}$

    A. $\frac{1}{2}$ B. 1
    C. $1\frac{1}{2}$ D. 2

    5-A.3

18. Find the sum in simplest form.

    $3\frac{3}{10} + 2\frac{1}{2}$

    A. $5\frac{3}{4}$ B. $5\frac{4}{5}$
    C. $6\frac{3}{4}$ D. $6\frac{4}{5}$

    6-A.1

19. Choose the best estimate for the word problem.

    Maria used $4\frac{4}{5}$ lb of peanuts and $2\frac{1}{10}$ lb of pretzels to make a snack mix. About how many more pounds of peanuts than pretzels did she use?

    A. about 2 lb more
    B. about $2\frac{1}{2}$ lb more
    C. about 3 lb more
    D. about $3\frac{1}{2}$ lb more

    6-A.2

For questions 20–21, find the product or quotient. Answers are in simplest form.

20. $\frac{2}{7} \times \frac{7}{9}$

    A. $\frac{1}{7}$ B. $\frac{2}{9}$ C. $\frac{2}{7}$ D. $\frac{7}{18}$

    7-A.1

21. $\frac{5}{12} \div \frac{2}{3}$

    A. $\frac{5}{18}$ B. $\frac{?}{3}$ C. $\frac{1}{2}$ D. $\frac{5}{8}$

    7-A.2

22. Ross bought a piece of wood $5\frac{1}{2}$ ft long. It is 4 times the length he needs to make a book shelf. How long will the book shelf be?

    A. $1\frac{1}{8}$ ft   B. $1\frac{1}{4}$ ft   C. $1\frac{3}{8}$ ft   D. not here

    7-A.3

23. Which statement about pairs of lines is not true?

    A. Parallel lines are always the same distance apart.
    B. Perpendicular lines form right angles.
    C. Parallel lines never intersect.
    D. Intersecting lines sometimes cross at two points.

    8-A.1

Form A • Multiple-Choice   A56   Chapters 1–14   Go on. ▶

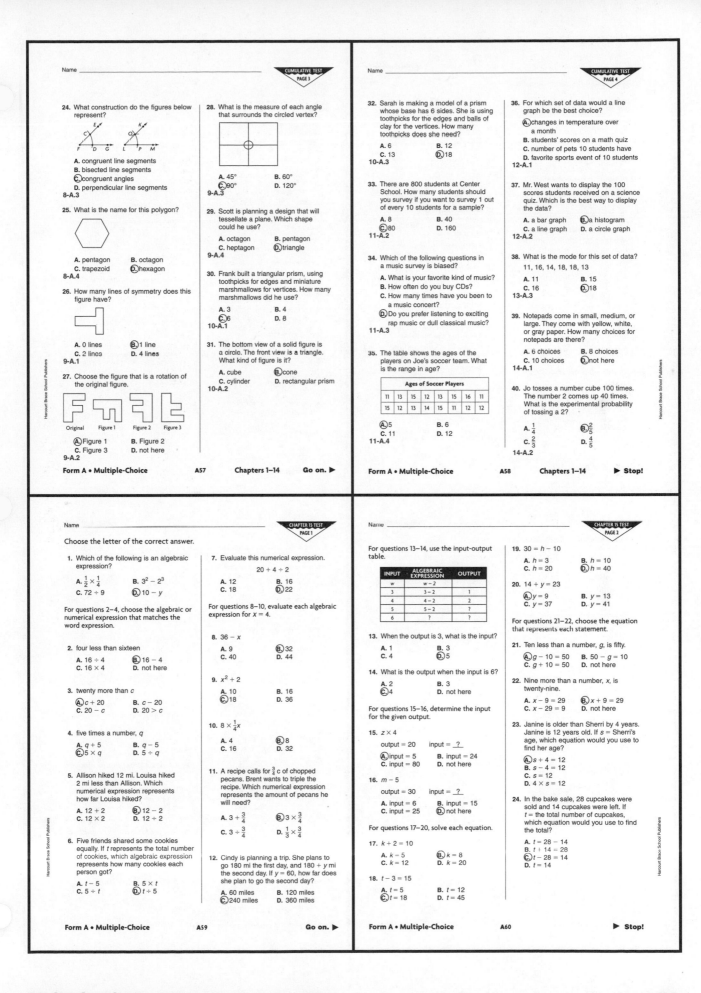

24. What construction do the figures below represent?

A. congruent line segments
B. bisected line segments
C. congruent angles
D. perpendicular line segments
8-A.3

25. What is the name for this polygon?

A. pentagon
B. octagon
C. trapezoid
D. hexagon
8-A.4

26. How many lines of symmetry does this figure have?

A. 0 lines
B. 1 line
C. 2 lines
D. 4 lines
9-A.1

27. Choose the figure that is a rotation of the original figure.

Original   Figure 1   Figure 2   Figure 3

A. Figure 1
B. Figure 2
C. Figure 3
D. not here
9-A.2

28. What is the measure of each angle that surrounds the circled vertex?

A. 45°
B. 60°
C. 90°
D. 120°
9-A.3

29. Scott is planning a design that will tessellate a plane. Which shape could he use?

A. octagon
B. pentagon
C. heptagon
D. triangle
9-A.4

30. Frank built a triangular prism, using toothpicks for edges and miniature marshmallows for vertices. How many marshmallows did he use?

A. 3
B. 4
C. 6
D. 8
10-A.1

31. The bottom view of a solid figure is a circle. The front view is a triangle. What kind of figure is it?

A. cube
B. cone
C. cylinder
D. rectangular prism
10-A.2

Form A • Multiple-Choice   A57   Chapters 1–14   ▶ Go on. ▶

32. Sarah is making a model of a prism whose base has 6 sides. She is using toothpicks for the edges and balls of clay for the vertices. How many toothpicks does she need?

A. 6
B. 12
C. 13
D. 18
10-A.3

33. There are 800 students at Center School. How many students should you survey if you want to survey 1 out of every 10 students for a sample?

A. 8
B. 40
C. 80
D. 160
11-A.2

34. Which of the following questions in a music survey is biased?

A. What is your favorite kind of music?
B. How often do you buy CDs?
C. How many times have you been to a music concert?
D. Do you prefer listening to exciting rap music or dull classical music?
11-A.3

35. The table shows the ages of the players on Joe's soccer team. What is the range in age?

Ages of Soccer Players							
11	13	15	12	13	15	16	11
15	12	13	14	15	11	12	12

A. 5
B. 6
C. 11
D. 12
11-A.4

36. For which set of data would a line graph be the best choice?

A. changes in temperature over a month
B. students' scores on a math quiz
C. number of pets 10 students have
D. favorite sports event of 10 students
12-A.1

37. Mr. West wants to display the 100 scores students received on a science quiz. Which is the best way to display the data?

A. a bar graph
B. a histogram
C. a line graph
D. a circle graph
12-A.2

38. What is the mode for this set of data?

11, 16, 14, 18, 18, 13

A. 11
B. 15
C. 16
D. 18
13-A.3

39. Notepads come in small, medium, or large. They come with yellow, white, or gray paper. How many choices for notepads are there?

A. 6 choices
B. 8 choices
C. 10 choices
D. not here
14-A.1

40. Jo tosses a number cube 100 times. The number 2 comes up 40 times. What is the experimental probability of tossing a 2?

A. $\frac{1}{4}$
B. $\frac{2}{5}$
C. $\frac{2}{3}$
D. $\frac{4}{5}$
14-A.2

Form A • Multiple-Choice   A58   Chapters 1–14   ▶ Stop!

Choose the letter of the correct answer.

1. Which of the following is an algebraic expression?

A. $\frac{1}{2} \times \frac{1}{4}$
B. $3^2 - 2^3$
C. $72 \div 9$
D. $10 - y$

For questions 2–4, choose the algebraic or numerical expression that matches the word expression.

2. four less than sixteen

A. $16 \div 4$
B. $16 - 4$
C. 16×4
D. not here

3. twenty more than c

A. $c + 20$
B. $c - 20$
C. $20 - c$
D. $20 > c$

4. five times a number, q

A. $q + 5$
B. $q - 5$
C. $5 \times q$
D. $5 \div q$

5. Allison hiked 12 mi. Louisa hiked 2 mi less than Allison. Which numerical expression represents how far Louisa hiked?

A. $12 + 2$
B. $12 - 2$
C. 12×2
D. $12 \div 2$

6. Five friends shared some cookies equally. If t represents the total number of cookies, which algebraic expression represents how many cookies each person got?

A. $t - 5$
B. $5 \times t$
C. $5 \div t$
D. $t \div 5$

7. Evaluate this numerical expression.

$20 + 4 \div 2$

A. 12
B. 16
C. 18
D. 22

For questions 8–10, evaluate each algebraic expression for $x = 4$.

8. $36 - x$

A. 9
B. 32
C. 40
D. 44

9. $x^2 + 2$

A. 10
B. 16
C. 18
D. 36

10. $8 \times \frac{1}{4}x$

A. 4
B. 8
C. 16
D. 32

11. A recipe calls for $\frac{3}{4}$ c of chopped pecans. Brent wants to triple the recipe. Which numerical expression represents the amount of pecans he will need?

A. $3 + \frac{3}{4}$
B. $3 \times \frac{3}{4}$
C. $3 \div \frac{3}{4}$
D. $\frac{1}{3} \times \frac{3}{4}$

12. Cindy is planning a trip. She plans to go 180 mi the first day, and $180 + y$ mi the second day. If $y = 60$, how far does she plan to go the second day?

A. 60 miles
B. 120 miles
C. 240 miles
D. 360 miles

Form A • Multiple-Choice   A59   ▶ Go on. ▶

For questions 13–14, use the input-output table.

INPUT	ALGEBRAIC EXPRESSION	OUTPUT
w	$w - 2$	
3	$3 - 2$	1
4	$4 - 2$	2
5	$5 - 2$	?
6	?	?

13. When the output is 3, what is the input?

A. 1
B. 3
C. 4
D. 5

14. What is the output when the input is 6?

A. 2
B. 3
C. 4
D. not here

For questions 15–16, determine the input for the given output.

15. $z \times 4$

output = 20   input = ?

A. input = 5
B. input = 24
C. input = 80
D. not here

16. $m - 5$

output = 30   input = ?

A. input = 6
B. input = 15
C. input = 25
D. not here

For questions 17–20, solve each equation.

17. $k + 2 = 10$

A. $k = 5$
B. $k = 8$
C. $k = 12$
D. $k = 20$

18. $t - 3 = 15$

A. $t = 5$
B. $t = 12$
C. $t = 18$
D. $t = 45$

19. $30 = h - 10$

A. $h = 3$
B. $h = 10$
C. $h = 20$
D. $h = 40$

20. $14 + y = 23$

A. $y = 9$
B. $y = 13$
C. $y = 37$
D. $y = 41$

For questions 21–22, choose the equation that represents each statement.

21. Ten less than a number, g, is fifty.

A. $g - 10 = 50$
B. $50 - g = 10$
C. $g + 10 = 50$
D. not here

22. Nine more than a number, x, is twenty-nine.

A. $x - 9 = 29$
B. $x + 9 = 29$
C. $x - 29 = 9$
D. not here

23. Janine is older than Sherri by 4 years. Janine is 12 years old. If $s =$ Sherri's age, which equation would you use to find her age?

A. $s + 4 = 12$
B. $s - 4 = 12$
C. $s = 12$
D. $4 \times s = 12$

24. In the bake sale, 28 cupcakes were sold and 14 cupcakes were left. If $t =$ the total number of cupcakes, which equation would you use to find the total?

A. $t = 28 - 14$
B. $t + 14 = 28$
C. $t - 28 = 14$
D. $t = 14$

Form A • Multiple-Choice   A60   ▶ Stop!

Multiple-Choice Format • Test Answers

Name _____

Choose the letter of the correct answer.

1. What is the inverse of the operation in the equation $5x = 15$?
   A. addition
   B. subtraction
   C. multiplication
   (D) division

2. To solve the equation $18 = \frac{y}{2}$, __?__.
   A. add 2 to both sides
   B. subtract 2 from both sides
   (C) multiply both sides by 2
   D. divide both sides by 2

For questions 3–6, solve each equation.

3. $3m = 12$
   (A) $m = 4$ B. $m = 9$
   C. $m = 15$ D. $m = 36$

4. $\frac{r}{4} = 16$
   A. $r = 4$ B. $r = 12$
   C. $r = 20$ (D) $r = 64$

5. $\frac{t}{7} = 7$
   A. $t = 1$ B. $t = 7$
   (C) $t = 49$ D. $t = 77$

6. $8p = 24$
   A. $p = 2$ (B) $p = 3$
   C. $p = 32$ D. $p = 192$

7. How many quarters are in $24.50?
   A. 49   B. 94
   (C) 98   D. not here

8. How many nickels are in $18.00?
   A. 300   (B) 360
   C. 400   D. not here

9. What is 10 English pounds in U.S. dollars? Use the formula $1.6261 \times P = D$. Round to the nearest penny.
   A. $1.63   B. $10.63
   (C) $16.26   D. $162.61

10. What is 100 German marks in U.S. dollars? Use the formula $0.6200 \times M = D$.
    A. $6.20   (B) $62.00
    C. $602.00   D. $620.00

11. One roll of quarters is worth $10. One roll of nickels is worth $2. How many coins are in 2 rolls of quarters and 2 rolls of nickels?
    A. 40 coins   B. 80 coins
    C. 96 coins   (D) 160 coins

12. A roll of dimes is worth $10. A roll of nickels is worth $2. If you have two rolls of each, how many coins do you have?
    A. 180 coins   B. 240 coins
    (C) 280 coins   D. 320 coins

13. What is 15°C converted to degrees Fahrenheit? Use the formula $F = (\frac{9}{5} \times C) + 32$. Round to the nearest degree.
    A. 10°F   B. 27°F
    C. 47°F   (D) 59°F

14. What is 90°F converted to degrees Celsius? Use the formula $C = \frac{5}{9} \times (F - 32)$. Round to the nearest degree.
    A. 12°C   (B) 32°C
    C. 50°C   D. 64°C

Name _____

For questions 15–16, use the formula $C = \frac{5}{9} \times (F - 32)$. Round to the nearest degree.

15. Many recipes call for an oven temperature of 350°F. What is this temperature in degrees Celsius?
    A. 63°C   (B) 177°C
    C. 194°C   D. 630°C

16. If a person's temperature is about 100°F, the person has a fever. What is this temperature in degrees Celsius?
    (A) 38°C   B. 56°C
    C. 68°C   D. 72°C

For questions 17–20, use the formula $d = r \times t$.

17. $d = $ __?__
    $r = 20$ mi per hr
    $t = 4$ hr
    A. 5 mi   B. 24 mi
    (C) 80 mi   D. 120 mi

18. $d = 500$ km
    $r = 125$ km per hr
    $t = $ __?__
    A. $\frac{1}{4}$ hr   B. $\frac{1}{2}$ hr
    C. 2 hr   (D) 4 hr

19. A high speed train travels 300 km per hr. How far would the train travel in 2.5 hours?
    A. 120 km   B. 450 km
    C. 600 km   (D) not here

20. The Lawrence family is planning a trip. They want to go 270 miles the first day. If they travel at a rate of 60 mi per hour, how long will it take them?
    A. $3\frac{1}{2}$ hours   B. 4 hours
    (C) $4\frac{1}{2}$ hours   D. not here

21. Vandri is in a 10-mi bike race. How far is this in kilometers? (1 mi = 1.609 km)
    A. 1.6 km   B. 10 km
    (C) 16.09 km   D. not here

22. Gus' car holds 12 gal of gas. If he were in a country where gas is sold in liters, how many liters of gas would Gus need to fill his car? (1 gal = 3.785 L)
    A. 4.542 L   (B) 45.42 L
    C. 454.2 L   D. not here

23. A photograph is 4 in. by 6 in. Thea is putting it in an album that has picture sizes marked in centimeters. What are the dimensions of the photograph in centimeters? (1 in. = 2.54 cm)
    (A) 10.16 cm × 15.24 cm
    B. 15.24 cm × 17.78 cm
    C. 20.32 cm × 30.48 cm
    D. 25.4 cm × 30.48 cm

24. A French recipe calls for 2 kg of potatoes. How many pounds of potatoes is this? (1 kg = 2.2 lb)
    A. 2.4 lb   (B) 4.4 lb
    C. 4.44 lb   D. 44 lb

Name _____

Choose the letter of the correct answer.

1. Which of the following is a numerical expression?
   A. $r^2 - 3$ B. $x + 4$
   (C) $2\frac{1}{2} + \frac{3}{5}$ D. $3a - 1$
   15-A.1

2. Choose the algebraic expression that matches the word expression.
   18 more than x
   A. $x - 18$ B. $18 - x$
   C. $x > 18$ (D) $x + 18$
   15-A.1

3. A baseball team with 20 players ate pizza after a game. The players were given equal amounts of pizza. If y represents the total number of pizza slices, which algebraic expression represents how many pizza slices each player got?
   (A) $y \div 20$ B. $y - 20$
   C. $y + 20$ D. $20 \times y$
   15-A.1

4. Evaluate this numerical expression.
   $15 \div 3 + 15$
   A. 5   (B) 20
   C. 33   D. 75
   15-A.2

5. Evaluate this algebraic expression for $t = 3$.
   $20 - t$
   (A) 17   B. $3 - t$
   C. 20   D. 23
   15-A.2

For questions 6–7, use the input-output table.

Input	Algebraic Expression	Output
v	$v - 8$	
8	$8 - 8$	0
9	?	?
?	$10 - 8$	?

6. What is the output when the input is 9?
   A. 0   (B) 1   C. 2   D. 8
   15-A.3

7. When the output is 2, what is the input?
   A. 8   B. 9   (C) 10   D. 12
   15-A.3

8. $x + 11 = 40$
   A. $x = 11$ (B) $x = 29$
   C. $x = 31$ D. $x = 51$
   15-A.4

9. $22 = b - 5$
   A. 5   B. 17   (C) 27   D. 32
   15-A.4

For questions 10–11, choose the equation that represents each statement.

10. Twelve more than a number, n, is 43.
    (A) $n + 12 = 43$ B. $n - 12 = 43$
    C. $43 + n = 12$ D. $43 \div n = 12$
    15-A.4

11. Eight less than a number, d, is 15.
    A. $d - 15 = 8$ B. $8 - d = 15$
    C. $d + 8 = 15$ (D) $d - 8 = 15$
    15-A.4

Name _____

12. What is the inverse of the operation in the equation $7t = 28$?
    A. addition   B. subtraction
    C. multiplication   (D) division
    16-A.1

13. Solve the equation.
    $\frac{y}{5} = 7$
    A. 7   B. 12
    C. 21   (D) 35
    16-A.1

14. How many nickels are there in $11.35?
    A. 200 nickels   B. 220 nickels
    (C) 227 nickels   D. 229 nickels
    16-A.2

15. What is 9°C converted to degrees Fahrenheit? Use the formula $F = (\frac{9}{5} \times C) + 32$. Round to the nearest degree.
    A. 37°F   B. 45°F
    (C) 48°F   D. 58°F
    16-A.3

16. What is 80°F converted to degrees Celsius? Use the formula $C = \frac{5}{9} \times (F - 32)$. Round to the nearest degree.
    A. 18°C   (B) 27°C
    C. 48°C   D. 240°C
    16-A.3

17. On the Fahrenheit scale, freezing is 32°F. What is this temperature on the Celsius scale?
    (A) 0°C   B. 5°C
    C. 10°C   D. 32°C
    16-A.3

For questions 18–19, use the formula $d = r \times t$.

18. $d = $ __?__
    $r = 10$ mi per hr
    $t = 2$ hr
    A. 2 mi   B. 5 mi
    C. 12 mi   (D) 20 mi
    16-A.4

19. $d = 400$ m
    $r = $ __?__
    $t = 50$ sec
    A. 4 m per sec   B. 6 m per sec
    (C) 8 m per sec   D. 12 m per sec
    16-A.4

20. An airplane travels at 500 mi per hr. How far does the airplane travel in 4 hours?
    A. 125 mi   B. 500 mi
    C. 1,000 mi   (D) 2,000 mi
    16-A.4

21. The odometer dial on a car measures only in miles. The car was driven 23 mi. How many kilometers is this? (1 mi = 1.6 km)
    A. 23.8 mi   (B) 36.8 mi
    C. 59.8 mi   D. 61 mi
    16-A.5

22. Gary needed to buy 15 in. of wood to fix his shelf. The lumber store sold wood measured in centimeters. How many centimeters of wood should he buy? (1 in. = 2.54 cm)
    A. 17.54 cm   B. 28.10 cm
    (C) 38.10 cm   D. 45.54 cm
    16-A.5

Multiple-Choice Format • Test Answers   **134**

CUMULATIVE TEST
PAGE 1

Choose the letter of the correct answer.

1. Which shows 7 thousandths in standard form?
   A. 0.007   B. 0.07
   C. 0.70   D. 7,000
   1-A.1

2. Which expression represents 2^3?
   A. $2 + 3$ B. 2×3
   C. $2 \times 2 \times 2$ D. 3×3
   1-A.3

3. Which shows the integers in order from least to greatest?
   A. 1, −2, −3, 0   B. 1, −3, −2, 0
   C. −2, −3, 1, 0   D. −3, −2, 0, 1
   1-A.4

4. Don bought 24 pieces of fruits. He bought 6 pears and 4 more plums than apples. How many apples did he buy?
   A. 4 apples   B. 6 apples
   C. 7 apples   D. 11 apples
   2-A.2

5. $27\overline{)1,458}$
   A. 53   B. 53 r6
   C. 54   D. 54 r2
   2-A.3

6. $71.36 - 24.58$
   A. 33.22   B. 46.78
   C. 47.78   D. not here
   3-A.1

7. Mike earns $4.30 per hr baby-sitting. Last week he worked 7.5 hr. How much did he earn baby-sitting last week?
   A. $32.25   B. $33.25
   C. $322.50   D. $332.50
   3-A.2

8. $30.4 \div 4$
   A. 0.76   B. 7.6
   C. 7.66   D. not here
   3-A.3

9. Which of these is a prime number?
   A. 15   B. 17
   C. 18   D. 21
   4-A.1

10. Find the simplest form of $\frac{25}{30}$.
    A. $\frac{5}{7}$ B. $\frac{3}{4}$ C. $\frac{1}{3}$ D. $\frac{5}{6}$
    4-A.4

11. Find the difference in simplest form.
    $\frac{7}{8} - \frac{3}{8}$
    A. $\frac{1}{8}$ B. $\frac{1}{4}$ C. $\frac{1}{2}$ D. $\frac{5}{8}$
    5-A.1

12. Estimate the sum.
    $\frac{5}{12} + \frac{4}{7}$
    A. $\frac{1}{2}$ B. 1   C. $1\frac{1}{2}$ D. 2
    5-A.3

13. Find the sum in simplest form.
    $3\frac{1}{4} + 1\frac{7}{12}$
    A. $4\frac{5}{12}$ B. $4\frac{5}{6}$
    C. $5\frac{5}{12}$ D. $5\frac{5}{6}$
    6-A.1

14. Rob bought $3\frac{7}{8}$ lb of beef and $2\frac{1}{2}$ lb of chicken to grill for a family party. About how many pounds of meat did he buy?
    A. about 5 lb   B. about $5\frac{1}{2}$ lb
    C. about 6 lb   D. about $6\frac{1}{2}$ lb
    6-A.2

Form A • Multiple-Choice   A65   Chapters 1–16   Go on. ▶

CUMULATIVE TEST
PAGE 2

15. Find the product in simplest form.
    $1\frac{1}{3} \times 3\frac{3}{4}$
    A. $\frac{4}{15}$ B. 3   C. 5   D. not here
    7-A.1

16. Find the quotient in simplest form.
    $\frac{7}{12} \div \frac{2}{3}$
    A. $\frac{7}{12}$ B. $\frac{2}{3}$ C. $\frac{7}{8}$ D. $\frac{11}{12}$
    7-A.2

17. A flat surface that goes on forever in all directions is called a ___.
    A. point   B. line
    C. ray   D. plane
    8-A.1

18. What is the measure of a right angle?
    A. less than 90°
    B. 90°
    C. between 90° and 180°
    D. 180°
    8-A.2

19. How many angles does a pentagon have?
    A. 4 angles   B. 5 angles
    C. 6 angles   D. 8 angles
    8-A.4

20. This figure has rotational symmetry. What is the fraction of each turn?
    A. $\frac{1}{16}$ B. $\frac{1}{8}$
    C. $\frac{1}{4}$ D. $\frac{1}{2}$
    9-A.1

21. Which figure shows a 90° clockwise rotation around the given point?
    A.   B.
    C.   D.
    9-A.2

22. Cary wants to make a wallpaper design, using one shape to tessellate a plane. Which of these shapes could she use?
    A.   B.
    C.   D.
    9-A.4

23. A paperweight is in the shape of a triangular pyramid. How many faces does the paperweight have?
    A. 3 faces   B. 4 faces
    C. 6 faces   D. 8 faces
    10-A.1

24. Rich made a model of a pyramid with 12 edges. How many sides did the base of his pyramid have?
    A. 4   B. 6   C. 8   D. 10
    10-A.3

25. The sixth-grade class is planning to sell snacks at the next soccer game. Which decision can the students make?
    A. the names of the soccer teams
    B. the time the game will begin
    C. the price to charge for the snacks
    D. the number of people who will attend the game
    11-A.1

Form A • Multiple-Choice   A66   Chapters 1–16   Go on. ▶

CUMULATIVE TEST
PAGE 3

26. The cafeteria staff wants to survey students to see what lunch they like. How can they get a random sample?
    A. Choose students in the salad line.
    B. Have teachers choose students.
    C. Survey all the students in one classroom.
    D. Randomly survey students as they enter the school.
    11-A.2

For questions 27–28, use the frequency table.

FAVORITE SCHOOL SUBJECT OF STUDENTS	
Subject	Frequency
Reading	14
Science	12
Mathematics	16
Social Studies	10

27. Why is a bar graph the most appropriate graph for this set of data?
    A. The data show changes over time.
    B. The data were gathered in a survey.
    C. The table can be extended to show a cumulative frequency column.
    D. The data show totals for each category.
    12-A.1

28. If one axis of the graph is labeled *Number of Students*, what should the other axis be labeled?
    A. Subject   B. Favorite
    C. Spelling   D. People
    12-A.1

29. Is this graph misleading? If so, why?

BOOKS CHECKED OUT EACH DAY
Number of Books Checked Out
50 40 30 20 10
Mon Tue Wed Thu Fri

    A. no
    B. Yes; the scale is incorrect.
    C. Yes; only one week is shown.
    D. Yes; the title is wrong.
    13-A.2

30. What is the median for this set of data?
    11, 15, 14, 20, 20
    A. 11   B. 15   C. 16   D. 20
    13-A.3

31. Shirts are sold in white, yellow, red, or blue. They can have long sleeves or short sleeves. How many choices for shirts are there?
    A. 6   B. 8   C. 10   D. not here
    14-A.1

32. Tom's class has 5 girls and 15 boys. The teacher puts everyone's name in a bag and then draws one name without looking. What is the probability of choosing a girl's name?
    A. $\frac{1}{4}$ B. $\frac{1}{3}$ C. $\frac{3}{5}$ D. $\frac{3}{4}$
    14-A.2

33. Choose the algebraic expression that matches the word expression.
    thirty more than d
    A. $d + 30$ B. $d - 30$
    C. $30 \times d$ D. $30 > d$
    15-A.1

Form A • Multiple-Choice   A67   Chapters 1–16   Go on. ▶

CHAPTER 2 TEST
PAGE 2

14. In this division problem, where would you put the first digit of the quotient?
    $17\overline{)1,840}$
    A. in the ones place
    B. in the tens place
    C. in the hundreds place
    D. in the thousands place

15. 120×35
    A. 960
    B. 3,200
    C. 4,100
    D. not here

16. 437×226
    A. 97,862
    B. 98,762
    C. 106,662
    D. 107,662

17. $6\overline{)324}$
    A. 50 r4   B. 52 r2
    C. 53   D. 54

18. $20\overline{)4,060}$
    A. 203   B. 213
    C. 230   D. 233

19. Clea's parents bought a computer for $1,530.00. They are paying for it in 18 monthly payments. How much is each payment?
    A. $77.50
    B. $85.00
    C. $95.00
    D. $127.50

20. The Stone family spends $125 on groceries each week. How much does the family spend on groceries in one year? (HINT: 1 yr = 52 wk.)
    A. $650   B. $2,500
    C. $5,250   D. $6,500

21. Choose the best estimate of the sum.
    $5,199$
    $4,206$
    $+3,749$
    A. 11,000   B. 12,000
    C. 13,000   D. 15,000

22. Choose the best estimate of the quotient.
    $1,765 \div 28$
    A. 0.6   B. 60
    C. 600   D. 6,000

23. The music store sold 589 CDs of waterfall sounds and 209 audiotapes of the sounds. About how many more CDs were sold than audiotapes?
    A. about 200 more CDs
    B. about 300 more CDs
    C. about 400 more CDs
    D. about 500 more CDs

24. The movie theater at the waterfall park had 213 shows this summer. The theater, which holds 480 people, was full for every show. About how many people attended the shows?
    A. about 10,000 people
    B. about 10,200 people
    C. about 80,000 people
    D. about 100,000 people

Form A • Multiple-Choice   A8   ▶ Stop!

Multiple-Choice Format • Test Answers   135

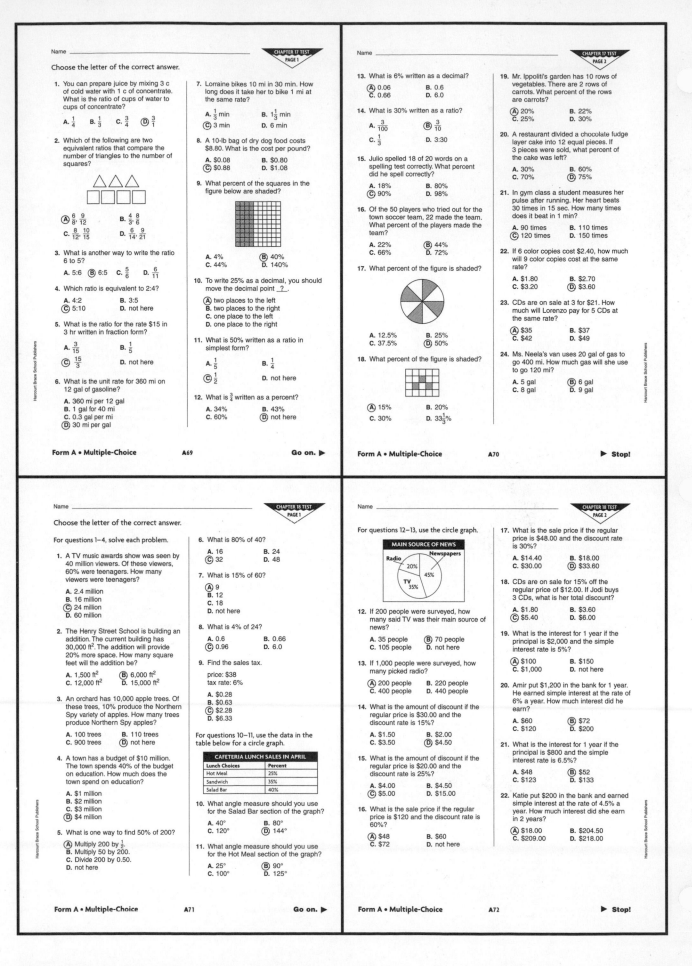

Name _____

Choose the letter of the correct answer.

1. You can prepare juice by mixing 3 c of cold water with 1 c of concentrate. What is the ratio of cups of water to cups of concentrate?

A. $\frac{1}{4}$ B. $\frac{1}{3}$ C. $\frac{3}{4}$ (D) $\frac{3}{1}$

2. Which of the following are two equivalent ratios that compare the number of triangles to the number of squares?

(A) $\frac{6}{8}, \frac{9}{12}$ B. $\frac{4}{3}, \frac{8}{6}$
C. $\frac{8}{12}, \frac{10}{15}$ D. $\frac{6}{14}, \frac{9}{21}$

3. What is another way to write the ratio 6 to 5?

A. 5:6   B. 6:5   C. $\frac{5}{6}$ D. $\frac{6}{11}$

4. Which ratio is equivalent to 2:4?

A. 4:2   B. 3:5
(C) 5:10   D. not here

5. What is the ratio for the rate $15 in 3 hr written in fraction form?

A. $\frac{3}{15}$ B. $\frac{1}{5}$
(C) $\frac{15}{3}$ D. not here

6. What is the unit rate for 360 mi on 12 gal of gasoline?

A. 360 mi per 12 gal
B. 1 gal for 40 mi
C. 0.3 gal per mi
(D) 30 mi per gal

7. Lorraine bikes 10 mi in 30 min. How long does it take her to bike 1 mi at the same rate?

A. $\frac{1}{3}$ min   B. $1\frac{1}{3}$ min
(C) 3 min   D. 6 min

8. A 10-lb bag of dry dog food costs $8.80. What is the cost per pound?

A. $0.08   B. $0.80
(C) $0.88   D. $1.08

9. What percent of the squares in the figure below are shaded?

A. 4%   (B) 40%
C. 44%   D. 140%

10. To write 25% as a decimal, you should move the decimal point __?__ .

(A) two places to the left
B. two places to the right
C. one place to the left
D. one place to the right

11. What is 50% written as a ratio in simplest form?

A. $\frac{1}{5}$ B. $\frac{1}{4}$
(C) $\frac{1}{2}$ D. not here

12. What is $\frac{3}{4}$ written as a percent?

A. 34%   B. 43%
C. 60%   (D) not here

Form A • Multiple-Choice   A69   Go on. ▶

Name _____

13. What is 6% written as a decimal?

(A) 0.06   B. 0.6
C. 0.66   D. 6.0

14. What is 30% written as a ratio?

A. $\frac{3}{100}$ (B) $\frac{3}{10}$
C. $\frac{1}{3}$ D. 3:30

15. Julio spelled 18 of 20 words on a spelling test correctly. What percent did he spell correctly?

A. 18%   B. 80%
(C) 90%   D. 98%

16. Of the 50 players who tried out for the town soccer team, 22 made the team. What percent of the players made the team?

A. 22%   (B) 44%
C. 66%   D. 72%

17. What percent of the figure is shaded?

A. 12.5%   B. 25%
C. 37.5%   (D) 50%

18. What percent of the figure is shaded?

(A) 15%   B. 20%
C. 30%   D. $33\frac{1}{3}$%

19. Mr. Ippoliti's garden has 10 rows of vegetables. There are 2 rows of carrots. What percent of the rows are carrots?

(A) 20%   B. 22%
C. 25%   D. 30%

20. A restaurant divided a chocolate fudge layer cake into 12 equal pieces. If 3 pieces were sold, what percent of the cake was left?

A. 30%   B. 60%
C. 70%   (D) 75%

21. In gym class a student measures her pulse after running. Her heart beats 30 times in 15 sec. How many times does it beat in 1 min?

A. 90 times   B. 110 times
(C) 120 times   D. 150 times

22. If 6 color copies cost $2.40, how much will 9 color copies cost at the same rate?

A. $1.80   B. $2.70
C. $3.20   (D) $3.60

23. CDs are on sale at 3 for $21. How much will Lorenzo pay for 5 CDs at the same rate?

(A) $35   B. $37
C. $42   D. $49

24. Ms. Neela's van uses 20 gal of gas to go 400 mi. How much gas will she use to go 120 mi?

A. 5 gal   (B) 6 gal
C. 8 gal   D. 9 gal

Form A • Multiple-Choice   A70   ▶ Stop!

Name _____

Choose the letter of the correct answer.

For questions 1–4, solve each problem.

1. A TV music awards show was seen by 40 million viewers. Of these viewers, 60% were teenagers. How many viewers were teenagers?

A. 2.4 million
B. 16 million
(C) 24 million
D. 60 million

2. The Henry Street School is building an addition. The current building has 30,000 ft². The addition will provide 20% more space. How many square feet will the addition be?

A. 1,500 ft²   (B) 6,000 ft²
C. 12,000 ft²   D. 15,000 ft²

3. An orchard has 10,000 apple trees. Of these trees, 10% produce the Northern Spy variety of apples. How many trees produce Northern Spy apples?

A. 100 trees   B. 110 trees
C. 900 trees   (D) not here

4. A town has a budget of $10 million. The town spends 40% of the budget on education. How much does the town spend on education?

A. $1 million
B. $2 million
C. $3 million
(D) $4 million

5. What is one way to find 50% of 200?

(A) Multiply 200 by $\frac{1}{2}$.
B. Multiply 50 by 200.
C. Divide 200 by 0.50.
D. not here

6. What is 80% of 40?

A. 16   B. 24
(C) 32   D. 48

7. What is 15% of 60?

(A) 9
B. 12
C. 18
D. not here

8. What is 4% of 24?

A. 0.6   B. 0.66
(C) 0.96   D. 6.0

9. Find the sales tax.

price: $38
tax rate: 6%

A. $0.28
B. $0.63
(C) $2.28
D. $6.33

For questions 10–11, use the data in the table below for a circle graph.

CAFETERIA LUNCH SALES IN APRIL	
Lunch Choices	Percent
Hot Meal	25%
Sandwich	35%
Salad Bar	40%

10. What angle measure should you use for the Salad Bar section of the graph?

A. 40°   B. 80°
C. 120°   (D) 144°

11. What angle measure should you use for the Hot Meal section of the graph?

A. 25°   (B) 90°
C. 100°   D. 125°

Form A • Multiple-Choice   A71   Go on. ▶

Name _____

For questions 12–13, use the circle graph.

MAIN SOURCE OF NEWS

Radio 20%
Newspapers 45%
TV 35%

12. If 200 people were surveyed, how many said TV was their main source of news?

A. 35 people   (B) 70 people
C. 105 people   D. not here

13. If 1,000 people were surveyed, how many picked radio?

(A) 200 people   B. 220 people
C. 400 people   D. 440 people

14. What is the amount of discount if the regular price is $30.00 and the discount rate is 15%?

A. $1.50   B. $2.00
C. $3.50   (D) $4.50

15. What is the amount of discount if the regular price is $20.00 and the discount rate is 25%?

A. $4.00   B. $4.50
(C) $5.00   D. $15.00

16. What is the sale price if the regular price is $120 and the discount rate is 60%?

(A) $48   B. $60
C. $72   D. not here

17. What is the sale price if the regular price is $48.00 and the discount rate is 30%?

A. $14.40   B. $18.00
C. $30.00   (D) $33.60

18. CDs are on sale for 15% off the regular price of $12.00. If Jodi buys 3 CDs, what is her total discount?

A. $1.80   B. $3.60
(C) $5.40   D. $6.00

19. What is the interest for 1 year if the principal is $2,000 and the simple interest rate is 5%?

(A) $100   B. $150
C. $1,000   D. not here

20. Amir put $1,200 in the bank for 1 year. He earned simple interest at the rate of 6% a year. How much interest did he earn?

A. $60   (B) $72
C. $120   D. $200

21. What is the interest for 1 year if the principal is $800 and the simple interest rate is 6.5%?

A. $48   (B) $52
C. $123   D. $133

22. Katie put $200 in the bank and earned simple interest at the rate of 4.5% a year. How much interest did she earn in 2 years?

(A) $18.00   B. $204.50
C. $209.00   D. $218.00

Form A • Multiple-Choice   A72   ▶ Stop!

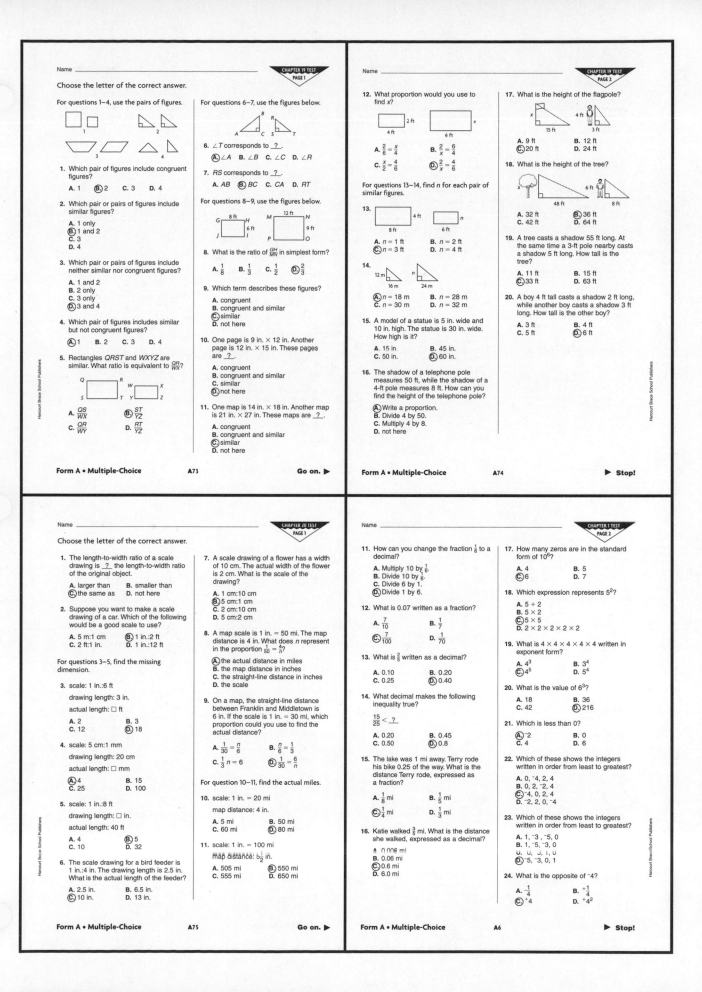

Choose the letter of the correct answer.

For questions 1–4, use the pairs of figures.

1. Which pair of figures include congruent figures?
   A. 1   **B.** 2   C. 3   D. 4

2. Which pair or pairs of figures include similar figures?
   A. 1 only   **B.** 1 and 2   C. 3   D. 4

3. Which pair or pairs of figures include neither similar nor congruent figures?
   A. 1 and 2   B. 2 only   C. 3 only   **D.** 3 and 4

4. Which pair of figures includes similar but not congruent figures?
   A. 1   B. 2   C. 3   D. 4

5. Rectangles QRST and WXYZ are similar. What ratio is equivalent to $\frac{QR}{WX}$?
   A. $\frac{QS}{WX}$ **B.** $\frac{ST}{YZ}$
   C. $\frac{QR}{WY}$ D. $\frac{RT}{YZ}$

For questions 6–7, use the figures below.

6. ∠T corresponds to ___?___ .
   A. ∠A   B. ∠B   C. ∠C   D. ∠R

7. RS corresponds to ___?___ .
   A. AB   **B.** BC   C. CA   D. RT

For questions 8–9, use the figures below.

8. What is the ratio of $\frac{GH}{MN}$ in simplest form?
   A. $\frac{1}{8}$ B. $\frac{1}{3}$ C. $\frac{1}{2}$ **D.** $\frac{2}{3}$

9. Which term describes these figures?
   A. congruent
   B. congruent and similar
   C. similar
   D. not here

10. One page is 9 in. × 12 in. Another page is 12 in. × 15 in. These pages are ___?___ .
    A. congruent
    B. congruent and similar
    C. similar
    D. not here

11. One map is 14 in. × 18 in. Another map is 21 in. × 27 in. These maps are ___?___ .
    A. congruent
    B. congruent and similar
    C. similar
    D. not here

Form A • Multiple-Choice   A73   Go on. ▶

12. What proportion would you use to find x?
    A. $\frac{2}{6} = \frac{x}{4}$ B. $\frac{2}{x} = \frac{6}{4}$
    C. $\frac{x}{2} = \frac{6}{4}$ **D.** $\frac{2}{x} = \frac{4}{6}$

For questions 13–14, find n for each pair of similar figures.

13.
    A. n = 1 ft   B. n = 2 ft
    C. n = 3 ft   D. n = 4 ft

14.
    A. n = 18 m   B. n = 28 m
    C. n = 30 m   D. n = 32 m

15. A model of a statue is 5 in. wide and 10 in. high. The statue is 30 in. wide. How high is it?
    A. 15 in.   B. 45 in.
    C. 50 in.   **D.** 60 in.

16. The shadow of a telephone pole measures 50 ft, while the shadow of a 4-ft pole measures 8 ft. How can you find the height of the telephone pole?
    A. Write a proportion.
    B. Divide 4 by 50.
    C. Multiply 4 by 8.
    D. not here

17. What is the height of the flagpole?
    A. 9 ft   B. 12 ft
    C. 20 ft   D. 24 ft

18. What is the height of the tree?
    A. 32 ft   **B.** 36 ft
    C. 42 ft   **D.** 64 ft

19. A tree casts a shadow 55 ft long. At the same time a 3-ft pole nearby casts a shadow 5 ft long. How tall is the tree?
    A. 11 ft   B. 15 ft
    C. 33 ft   D. 63 ft

20. A boy 4 ft tall casts a shadow 2 ft long, while another boy casts a shadow 3 ft long. How tall is the other boy?
    A. 3 ft   B. 4 ft
    C. 5 ft   **D.** 6 ft

Form A • Multiple-Choice   A74   ▶ Stop!

Choose the letter of the correct answer.

1. The length-to-width ratio of a scale drawing is ___?___ the length-to-width ratio of the original object.
   A. larger than   B. smaller than
   C. the same as   D. not here

2. Suppose you want to make a scale drawing of a car. Which of the following would be a good scale to use?
   A. 5 m:1 cm   **B.** 1 in.:2 ft
   C. 2 ft:1 m   D. 1 in.:12 ft

For questions 3–5, find the missing dimension.

3. scale: 1 in.:6 ft
   drawing length: 3 in.
   actual length: ☐ ft
   A. 2   B. 3
   C. 12   **D.** 18

4. scale: 5 cm:1 mm
   drawing length: 20 cm
   actual length: ☐ mm
   A. 4   B. 15
   C. 25   D. 100

5. scale: 1 in.:8 ft
   drawing length: ☐ in.
   actual length: 40 ft
   A. 4   **B.** 5
   C. 10   D. 32

6. The scale drawing for a bird feeder is 1 in.:4 in. The drawing length is 2.5 in. What is the actual length of the feeder?
   A. 2.5 in.   B. 6.5 in.
   C. 10 in.   D. 13 in.

7. A scale drawing of a flower has a width of 10 cm. The actual width of the flower is 2 cm. What is the scale of the drawing?
   A. 1 cm:10 cm
   B. 5 cm:1 cm
   C. 2 cm:10 cm
   D. 5 cm:2 cm

8. A map scale is 1 in. = 50 mi. The map distance is 4 in. What does n represent in the proportion $\frac{1}{50} = \frac{4}{n}$?
   A. the actual distance in miles
   B. the map distance in inches
   C. the straight-line distance in inches
   D. the scale

9. On a map, the straight-line distance between Franklin and Middletown is 6 in. If the scale is 1 in. = 30 mi, which proportion could you use to find the actual distance?
   A. $\frac{1}{30} = \frac{n}{6}$ B. $\frac{n}{6} = \frac{1}{3}$
   C. $\frac{1}{3}n = 6$ **D.** $\frac{1}{30} = \frac{6}{n}$

For question 10–11, find the actual miles.

10. scale: 1 in. = 20 mi
    map distance: 4 in.
    A. 5 mi   B. 50 mi
    C. 60 mi   **D.** 80 mi

11. scale: 1 in. = 100 mi
    map distance: $5\frac{1}{2}$ in.
    A. 505 mi   **B.** 550 mi
    C. 555 mi   D. 650 mi

Form A • Multiple-Choice   A75   Go on. ▶

11. How can you change the fraction $\frac{1}{6}$ to a decimal?
    A. Multiply 10 by $\frac{1}{6}$.
    B. Divide 10 by $\frac{1}{6}$.
    C. Divide 6 by 1.
    D. Divide 1 by 6.

12. What is 0.07 written as a fraction?
    A. $\frac{7}{10}$ B. $\frac{1}{7}$
    C. $\frac{7}{100}$ D. $\frac{1}{70}$

13. What is $\frac{2}{5}$ written as a decimal?
    A. 0.10   B. 0.20
    C. 0.25   **D.** 0.40

14. What decimal makes the following inequality true?
    $\frac{15}{25} < $ ___?___
    A. 0.20   B. 0.45
    C. 0.50   **D.** 0.8

15. The lake was 1 mi away. Terry rode his bike 0.25 of the way. What is the distance Terry rode, expressed as a fraction?
    A. $\frac{1}{8}$ mi   B. $\frac{1}{5}$ mi
    C. $\frac{1}{4}$ mi   D. $\frac{1}{3}$ mi

16. Katie walked $\frac{3}{5}$ mi. What is the distance she walked, expressed as a decimal?
    A. 0.008 mi
    B. 0.06 mi
    C. 0.6 mi
    D. 6.0 mi

17. How many zeros are in the standard form of 10^6?
    A. 4   B. 5
    C. 6   D. 7

18. Which expression represents 5^2?
    A. 5 + 2
    B. 5 × 2
    C. 5 × 5
    D. 2 × 2 × 2 × 2 × 2

19. What is 4 × 4 × 4 × 4 × 4 written in exponent form?
    A. 4^3 B. 3^4
    C. 4^5 D. 5^4

20. What is the value of 6^3?
    A. 18   B. 36
    C. 42   **D.** 216

21. Which is less than 0?
    A. ⁻2   B. 0
    C. 4   D. 6

22. Which of these shows the integers written in order from least to greatest?
    A. 0, ⁻4, 2, 4
    B. 0, 2, ⁻2, 4
    C. ⁻4, 0, 2, 4
    D. ⁻2, 2, 0, ⁻4

23. Which of these shows the integers written in order from least to greatest?
    A. 1, ⁻3, ⁻5, 0
    B. 1, ⁻5, ⁻3, 0
    C. 0, ⁻3, 1, 0
    D. ⁻5, ⁻3, 0, 1

24. What is the opposite of ⁻4?
    A. $-\frac{1}{4}$ B. $+\frac{1}{4}$
    C. ⁺4   D. ⁺4^2

Form A • Multiple-Choice   A6   ▶ Stop!

HarcCurt Brace School Publishers

Choose the letter of the correct answer.

1. Which of the following are two equivalent ratios that compare the number of circles to the number of squares?

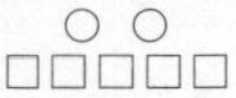

○ ○
□ □ □ □ □

A. $\frac{4}{5}, \frac{8}{10}$ B. $\frac{6}{15}, \frac{8}{20}$

C. $\frac{3}{6}, \frac{9}{18}$ D. $\frac{4}{6}, \frac{8}{12}$

17-A.1

2. What is the ratio for 125 mi in 5 gal written as a fraction?

A. $\frac{1}{25}$ B. $\frac{5}{125}$

C. $\frac{25}{5}$ D. $\frac{125}{5}$

17-A.2

3. What is $\frac{13}{20}$ written as a percent?

A. 13% B. 52%

C. 65% D. 75%

17-A.3

4. What percent of the figure is shaded?

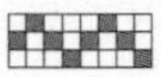

A. 8% B. 33.3%
C. 45% D. 66.6%

17-A.4

5. Wayne bought 4 tickets to the show for $26. How much would 7 tickets cost?

A. $32.50 B. $39.00
C. $45.50 D. $52.00

17-A.5

6. A music group sold 16 million copies of their newest album. Of the people who bought the album, 45% were adults. How many adults bought the group's new album?

A. 4.5 million B. 6 million
C. 7.2 million D. 45 million

18-A.1

For questions 7–8, use the data in the table below for a circle graph.

Favorite Movies of Teenagers

Movie Type	Percent
Action	45%
Comedy	25%
Drama	30%

7. What angle measure should you use for the Drama section of the graph?

A. 30° B. 60°
C. 90° D. 108°

18-A.2

8. What angle measure should you use for the Action section of the graph?

A. 45° B. 90°
C. 162° D. 198°

18-A.2

9. A clothing store had a Spring sale. All shorts were 20% off the regular price of $18. If Tamara bought 2 pairs of shorts, what would her total discount be?

A. $3.60 B. $7.20
C. $10.80 D. $14.40

18-A.3

10. What is the interest for 1 year if the principal is $1,400 and the simple interest rate is 4.5%?

A. $63 B. $75
C. $97 D. $113

18-A.4

11. Identify the pair of figures.

○ ○

A. similar B. congruent
C. circular D. neither

19-A.1

12. One picture frame is 6 in. × 8 in. Another frame is 18 in. × 24 in. The frames are __?__ .

A. congruent
B. congruent and similar
C. similar
D. not alike

19-A.2

13. Find x for the pair of similar figures.

8 cm [____] 2 cm   x [____] 3 cm

A. x = 9 cm B. x = 10 cm
C. x = 11 cm D. x = 12 cm

19-A.3

14. What is the height of the flagpole?

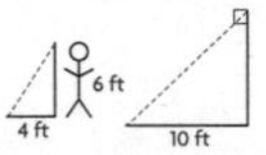

6 ft
4 ft   10 ft

A. 12 ft B. 15 ft
C. 18 ft D. 20 ft

19-A.4

15. A building casts a shadow 75 ft long. At the same time a 18 ft statue casts a shadow 30 ft long. How tall is the building?

A. 45 ft B. 60 ft
C. 90 ft D. 105 ft

19-A.4

16. Find the missing dimension.

scale: 8 m:1 cm
drawing length: 4 cm
actual length: = m

A. 12 m B. 16 m C. 24 m D. 32 m

20-A.1

17. Find the actual miles.

scale: 1 in. = 45 mi
map distance: 5 in.

A. 90 mi B. 135 mi
C. 225 mi D. 315 mi

20-A.2

For questions 18–19, use the map. Each square equals one city block.

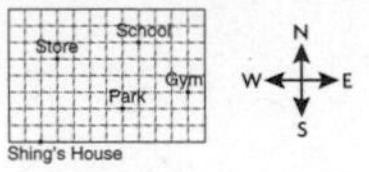

[map: Store, School, Park, Gym, Shing's House]
N W E S

18. Shing left his house and walked 2 blocks north, 6 blocks east, and 4 blocks north. Where was he?

A. park B. gym
C. school D. store

20-A.3

19. Ema left the gym and walked 3 blocks west, 2 blocks north, and 5 blocks west. Where did she go?

A. store B. school
C. Shing's house D. park

20-A.3

20. Rectangle A is 112 m × 80 m. Rectangle B is 250 m × 150 m. Which is a Golden Rectangle?

A. Rectangle A B. Rectangle B
C. both D. neither

20-A.4

Choose the letter of the correct answer.

1. What is $\frac{7}{8}$ written as a decimal?

A. 0.07 B. 0.70
C. 0.875 D. 0.0875

1-A.2

2. What is the opposite of ⁻9?

A. $\frac{-1}{9}$ B. $\frac{+1}{9}$

C. ⁺9 D. ⁻9²

1-A.4

3. Use mental math to find the sum.

8 + 47 + 12

A. 55 B. 57
C. 65 D. 67

2-A.1

4. There were 215 laser light shows held in the museum theater last year. The theater holds 280 people and was full for every show. About how many people attended the shows?

A. about 4,000 people
B. about 6,000 people
C. about 40,000 people
D. about 60,000 people

2-A.4

5. 15.5 + 1.856

A. 16.256 B. 16.356
C. 17.256 D. 17.356

3-A.1

6. 66.5 ÷ 7

A. 0.95 B. 9.5
C. 9.55 D. 95

3-A.3

7. What is the prime factorization of 40?

A. $3^2 \times 5$ B. $2^3 \times 5$
C. 3×5^2 D. $2^4 \times 5$

4-A.2

8. What is $\frac{17}{4}$ written as a mixed number?

A. $4\frac{1}{7}$ B. $4\frac{1}{4}$

C. $6\frac{1}{7}$ D. not here

4-A.5

9. Find the sum in simplest form.

$\frac{4}{9} + \frac{2}{9}$

A. $\frac{1}{3}$ B. $\frac{5}{9}$

C. $\frac{2}{3}$ D. $\frac{3}{4}$

5-A.1

For questions 10–11, find the answer in simplest form.

10. $3\frac{3}{4} - 2\frac{3}{8}$

A. $\frac{3}{8}$ B. $1\frac{3}{8}$

C. $1\frac{3}{4}$ D. $1\frac{1}{4}$

6-A.1

11. $1\frac{1}{2} \times 1\frac{3}{5}$

A. $1\frac{2}{5}$ B. $2\frac{1}{5}$

C. $2\frac{2}{5}$ D. not here

7-A.1

12. Kent has $3\frac{3}{4}$ lb of sausage. He wants to allow $\frac{1}{4}$ lb of sausage for each individual pizza he makes. How many pizzas can he make?

A. 12 pizzas B. 15 pizzas
C. 18 pizzas D. 21 pizzas

7-A.3

13. An angle that measures 120° is classified as a(n) __?__ .

A. obtuse angle B. right angle
C. acute angle D. straight angle

8-A.2

14. What construction do the figures below represent?

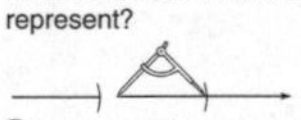

A. congruent line segments
B. bisected line segments
C. congruent angles
D. perpendicular line segments

8-A.3

15. How many lines of symmetry does this figure have?

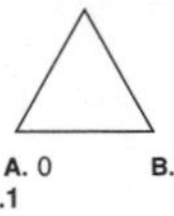

△

A. 0 B. 1 C. 3 D. 6

9-A.1

16. Which polygon will not tessellate a plane?

A. rhombus B. triangle
C. hexagon D. not here

9-A.3

17. Name this figure.

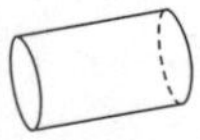

A. cone
B. triangular prism
C. cylinder
D. rectangular prism

10-A.1

18. The top and bottom views of a solid figure are triangles. The front view is a rectangle. What kind of figure is it?

A. triangular prism
B. triangular pyramid
C. rectangular prism
D. rectangular pyramid

10-A.2

19. The sixth graders at Laurel School are being surveyed to find out where they want to go on their class trip. Which question is biased?

A. Do you have a favorite on the list of suggested places?
B. Which day of the week would you prefer to have the trip?
C. Do you agree with the teacher that the museum is the best place to go?
D. Can you suggest other places to go?

11-A.3

For questions 20–21, use the graph.

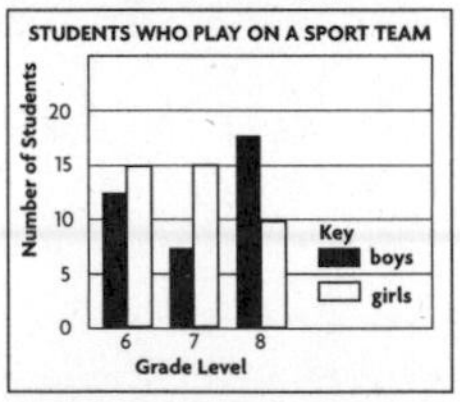

STUDENTS WHO PLAY ON A SPORT TEAM
Number of Students / Grade Level
Key: boys, girls

20. What tells you which bars represent girls and which bars represent boys?

A. the data B. the key
C. the scale D. the grade

12-A.3

21. Which statement is true?

A. There are more 6th-grade boys than 6th-grade girls who play on a sport team.
B. There are fewer 7th-grade girls than 7th-grade boys who play on a sport team.
C. There are more 8th-grade boys than 8th-grade girls who play on a sport team.
D. not here

12-A.3

Multiple-Choice Format • Test Answers   138

For questions 22–23, use the line graph.

NUMBER OF CARS SOLD

22. What has been the trend in car sales?

A. decreasing   C. increasing
B. staying the same   D. not here
13-A.1

23. Based on the graph, predict how many cars will be sold in November.

A. 10 cars   B. 20 cars
C. 30 cars   D. 40 cars
13-A.1

24. Michelle has gotten a hit in 30 of the last 100 times at bat. How many hits can she expect to get in her next 50 times at bat?

A. 10   B. 15   C. 20   D. 25
14-A.3

25. Evaluate $3 + \frac{1}{4}y$ for $y = 8$.

A. 5   B. 7   C. 11   D. not here
15-A.1

26. $10 = s + 2$

A. $s = 2$ B. $s = 8$
C. $s = 10$ D. $s = 12$
15-A.3

27. $3w = 15$

A. $w = 3$ B. $w = 5$
C. $w = 12$ D. $w = 30$
16-A.1

28. $\frac{b}{3} = 12$

A. $b = 3$ B. $b = 4$
C. $b = 24$ D. $b = 36$
16-A.1

29. What are 10 German marks worth in U.S. dollars? Use the formula $0.6200 \times M = D$. (M = marks; D = dollars)

A. $0.62   B. $6.20
C. $62.00   D. $620.00
16-A.2

30. To the nearest degree, what is 30°C in degrees Fahrenheit? Use the formula $F = (\frac{9}{5} \times C) + 32$.

A. 30°F   B. 49°F
C. 54°F   D. 86°F
16-A.3

31. Todd drove an average of 45 mi per hr from his home to the beach. He drove 2.5 hr to get there. How far does Todd live from the beach? Use the formula $d = r \times t$.

A. 11.25 mi   B. 18 mi
C. 112.5 mi   D. 180 mi
16-A.4

32. Jill weighs 38 kg. Jan weighs 98 lb. How many pounds more does Jan weigh than Jill? (1 kg = 2.2 lb)

A. 1.44 lb   B. 6.55 lb
C. 14.4 lb   D. 65.5 lb
16-A.5

33. Which is another way to write the ratio 3 to 7?

A. 7:3   B. 3:10
C. $\frac{7}{3}$ D. $\frac{3}{7}$
17-A.1

34. What is 20% written as a fraction in simplest form?

A. $\frac{1}{20}$ B. $\frac{1}{5}$
C. $\frac{1}{4}$ D. $\frac{1}{2}$
17-A.3

35. What percent of the figure is shaded?

A. 15%   B. 25%   C. 35%   D. 45%
17-A.4

36. The Brown family spent $8,000 remodeling their home. They spent 60% of this on improvements to their kitchen. How much did the Browns spend remodeling their kitchen?

A. $4,200   B. $4,800
C. $5,400   D. not here
18-A.1

37. Books are on sale for 25% off the regular price of $8.00. If Joan buys two books, what is her total discount?

A. $2   B. $4
C. $6   D. $8
18-A.3

38. Andy put $1,800 in the bank for a year. He earned interest at the rate of 5% a year. How much interest did he earn?

A. $50   B. $90
C. $150   D. $180
18-A.4

39. Use the figures below.

What is the ratio in simplest form of $\frac{AB}{EF}$?

A. $\frac{1}{6}$ B. $\frac{1}{8}$ C. $\frac{1}{2}$ D. $\frac{3}{4}$
19-A.2

40. A photograph is 3 in. wide by 4 in. long. James wants to have the photo enlarged so the length measures 12 in. How wide will the enlarged photo be?

A. 8 in.   B. 9 in.   C. 16 in.   D. 24 in.
19-A.3

41. A tree casts a shadow 48 ft long. At the same time a 3-ft pole nearby casts a shadow 4 ft long. How tall is the tree?

A. 30 ft   B. 36 ft   C. 40 ft   D. 54 ft
19-A.4

42. A scale drawing of a cabin has a scale of 1 in.:2.5 ft. The width in the drawing is 11.5 in. What is the actual width?

A. 11.5 ft   B. 23 ft
C. 28.75 ft   D. 20 ft
20-A.1

43. A map scale is 1 in. = 25 mi. The map distance is 5 in. Find the actual miles.

A. 5 mi   B. 50 mi   C. 100 mi   D. 125 mi
20-A.2

44. A rectangle is 48 in. long. It is a Golden Rectangle. What is its width?

A. 20 in.   B. 30 in.
C. 32 in.   D. 40 in.
20-A.4

Choose the letter of the correct answer.

1. To change pounds to ounces, you should __?__.

A. multiply by 10   B. multiply by 16
C. divide by 10   D. divide by 16

Change to the given unit.

2. 48 pt = □ gal

A. 6   B. 8   C. 12   D. 16

3. For the holiday meal at the Senior Center, juice glasses are filled with 4 fl oz of cranberry juice. How many glasses can be filled with 1 gal of cranberry juice?

A. 8 glasses   B. 16 glasses
C. 24 glasses   D. 32 glasses

4. To get to school, Marco walks 1 mi to the park. Then he walks 1,500 ft to the front door of the school. How many feet does he walk in all?

A. 2,028 ft   B. 3,260 ft
C. 3,500 ft   D. 6,780 ft

5. To change kilometers to meters, you multiply by __?__.

A. 10   B. 100
C. 1,000   D. 10,000

For questions 6–7, change to the given units.

6. 200 g = □ kg

A. 0.02   B. 0.2   C. 2   D. 20

7. 5 L = □ mL

A. 0.5   B. 50   C. 500   D. 5,000

8. Nadia is going to run in a 10K Fun Run. She will run 10 km. How many meters will she run?

A. 100 m   B. 1,000 m
C. 10,000 m   D. 100,000 m

9. When Jerome fills his backpack for school, it weighs 4,500 g. How many kilograms does it weigh?

A. 0.45 kg   B. 4.5 kg
C. 45 kg   D. 450 kg

10. Which is the most precise measurement for the length of a board?

A. 4 ft   B. 44 in.
C. $3\frac{1}{2}$ ft   D. 2 yd

11. Which is the most precise measurement for the height of a kitchen table?

A. 110 cm   B. 1.12 m
C. 1 m   D. 1,118 mm

12. Which is the most precise measurement for the length of a car?

A. 3 yd   B. $9\frac{1}{3}$ ft
C. $106\frac{1}{4}$ in.   D. 108 in.

13. Which is the most precise measurement for the height of a bedroom ceiling?

A. $112\frac{1}{2}$ in.
B. 8 ft
C. $8\frac{1}{2}$ ft
D. $3\frac{1}{3}$ yd

For questions 14–15, use the network below.

14. What is the length of the route TSRQ?

A. 74 km   B. 104 km
C. 111 km   D. 179 km

15. What is the length of the route QTSR?

A. 83 km   B. 104 km
C. 121 km   D. 179 km

For questions 17–18, use the network below.

L = Library
G = Grocery
S = School
M = Music Lesson

16. Mrs. Monroe has to go from the school to the grocery store and the library before going to a music lesson. How much difference is there between the routes SGLM and SLGM?

A. SLGM is 1 km shorter.
B. SLGM is 2 km shorter.
C. SGLM is 1 km shorter.
D. SGLM is 1 km shorter.

17. If Mrs. Monroe chooses the shorter route, how many kilometers will she travel?

A. 21 km   B. 23 km
C. 25 km   D. 27 km

18. What is the perimeter?

A. 5 cm
B. 5.5 cm
C. 6.5 cm
D. 7 cm

19. Find the missing length. Then find the perimeter.

A. 120 yd   B. 140 yd
C. 160 yd   D. 180 yd

20. The perimeter is 103 mi. What is the missing length?

A. 16 mi   B. 20 mi   C. 22 mi   D. 26 mi

21. The Four Corners city garden is located in the center of town. The garden is rectangular and is 1,150 ft by 820 ft. What is its perimeter?

A. 1,970 ft   B. 2,790 ft
C. 2,940 ft   D. 3,940 ft

22. A puzzle is in the shape of a regular hexagon. The perimeter of the puzzle is 48 in. What is the length of each side?

A. 6 in.   B. 8 in.
C. 12 in.   D. 16 in.

Multiple-Choice Format • Test Answers

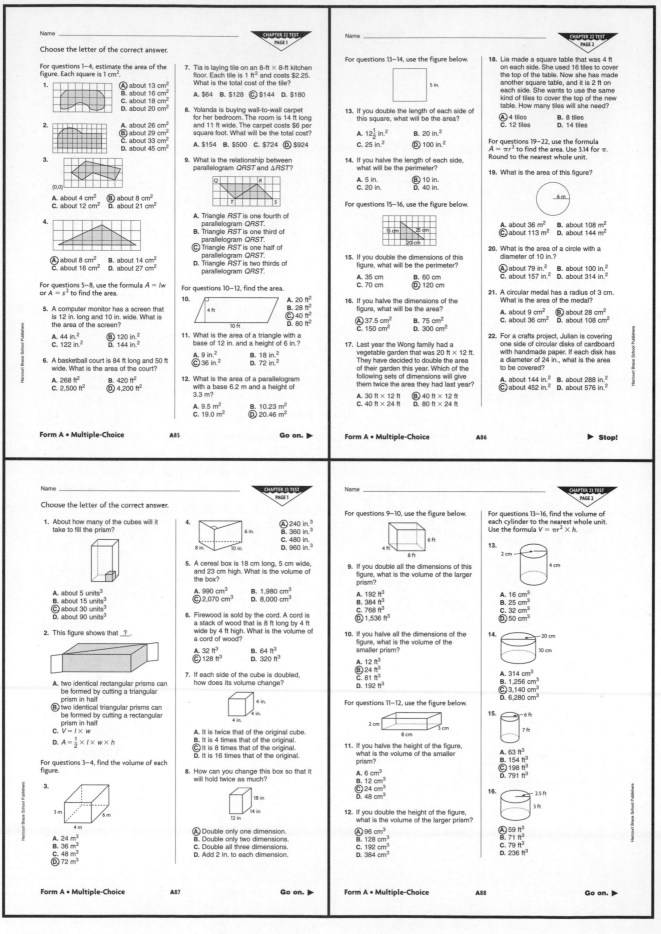

Name _____

Choose the letter of the correct answer.

For questions 1–4, estimate the area of the figure. Each square is 1 cm².

1.
- (A) about 13 cm²
- B. about 16 cm²
- C. about 18 cm²
- D. about 20 cm²

2.
- A. about 26 cm²
- (B) about 29 cm²
- C. about 33 cm²
- D. about 45 cm²

3.
(0,0)
- A. about 4 cm²
- (B) about 8 cm²
- C. about 12 cm²
- D. about 21 cm²

4.
- (A) about 8 cm²
- B. about 14 cm²
- C. about 16 cm²
- D. about 27 cm²

For questions 5–8, use the formula $A = lw$ or $A = s^2$ to find the area.

5. A computer monitor has a screen that is 12 in. long and 10 in. wide. What is the area of the screen?
- A. 44 in.²
- (B) 120 in.²
- C. 122 in.²
- D. 144 in.²

6. A basketball court is 84 ft long and 50 ft wide. What is the area of the court?
- A. 268 ft²
- B. 420 ft²
- C. 2,500 ft²
- (D) 4,200 ft²

7. Tia is laying tile on an 8-ft × 8-ft kitchen floor. Each tile is 1 ft² and costs $2.25. What is the total cost of the tile?
- A. $64
- B. $128
- (C) $144
- D. $180

8. Yolanda is buying wall-to-wall carpet for her bedroom. The room is 14 ft long and 11 ft wide. The carpet costs $6 per square foot. What will be the total cost?
- A. $154
- B. $500
- C. $724
- (D) $924

9. What is the relationship between parallelogram QRST and △RST?

- A. Triangle RST is one fourth of parallelogram QRST.
- B. Triangle RST is one third of parallelogram QRST.
- (C) Triangle RST is one half of parallelogram QRST.
- D. Triangle RST is two thirds of parallelogram QRST.

For questions 10–12, find the area.

10.
4 ft
10 ft
- A. 20 ft²
- B. 28 ft²
- (C) 40 ft²
- D. 80 ft²

11. What is the area of a triangle with a base of 12 in. and a height of 6 in.?
- A. 9 in.²
- B. 18 in.²
- (C) 36 in.²
- D. 72 in.²

12. What is the area of a parallelogram with a base 6.2 m and a height of 3.3 m?
- A. 9.5 m²
- B. 10.23 m²
- C. 19.0 m²
- (D) 20.46 m²

Name _____

For questions 13–14, use the figure below.

5 in.

13. If you double the length of each side of this square, what will be the area?
- A. 12½ in.²
- B. 20 in.²
- C. 25 in.²
- (D) 100 in.²

14. If you halve the length of each side, what will be the perimeter?
- A. 5 in.
- (B) 10 in.
- C. 20 in.
- D. 40 in.

For questions 15–16, use the figure below.

15 cm   25 cm
20 cm

15. If you double the dimensions of this figure, what will be the perimeter?
- A. 35 cm
- B. 60 cm
- C. 70 cm
- (D) 120 cm

16. If you halve the dimensions of the figure, what will be the area?
- (A) 37.5 cm²
- B. 75 cm²
- C. 150 cm²
- D. 300 cm²

17. Last year the Wong family had a vegetable garden that was 20 ft × 12 ft. They have decided to double the area of their garden this year. Which of the following sets of dimensions will give them twice the area they had last year?
- A. 30 ft × 12 ft
- (B) 40 ft × 12 ft
- C. 40 ft × 24 ft
- D. 80 ft × 24 ft

18. Lia made a square table that was 4 ft on each side. She used 16 tiles to cover the top of the table. Now she has made another square table, and it is 2 ft on each side. She wants to use the same kind of tiles to cover the top of the new table. How many tiles will she need?
- (A) 4 tiles
- B. 8 tiles
- C. 12 tiles
- D. 14 tiles

For questions 19–22, use the formula $A = \pi r^2$ to find the area. Use 3.14 for π. Round to the nearest whole unit.

19. What is the area of this figure?

6 m

- A. about 36 m²
- B. about 108 m²
- (C) about 113 m²
- D. about 144 m²

20. What is the area of a circle with a diameter of 10 in.?
- (A) about 79 in.²
- B. about 100 in.²
- C. about 157 in.²
- D. about 314 in.²

21. A circular medal has a radius of 3 cm. What is the area of the medal?
- A. about 9 cm²
- (B) about 28 cm²
- C. about 36 cm²
- D. about 108 cm²

22. For a crafts project, Julian is covering one side of circular disks of cardboard with handmade paper. If each disk has a diameter of 24 in., what is the area to be covered?
- A. about 144 in.²
- B. about 288 in.²
- (C) about 452 in.²
- D. about 576 in.²

Name _____

Choose the letter of the correct answer.

1. About how many of the cubes will it take to fill the prism?

- A. about 5 units³
- B. about 15 units³
- (C) about 30 units³
- D. about 90 units³

2. This figure shows that __?__.

- A. two identical rectangular prisms can be formed by cutting a triangular prism in half
- (B) two identical triangular prisms can be formed by cutting a rectangular prism in half
- C. $V = l \times w$
- D. $A = \frac{1}{2} \times l \times w \times h$

For questions 3–4, find the volume of each figure.

3.
3 m   6 m
4 m
- A. 24 m³
- B. 36 m³
- C. 48 m³
- (D) 72 m³

4.
6 in.
8 in.   10 in.
- (A) 240 in.³
- B. 360 in.³
- C. 480 in.³
- D. 960 in.³

5. A cereal box is 18 cm long, 5 cm wide, and 23 cm high. What is the volume of the box?
- A. 990 cm³
- B. 1,980 cm³
- (C) 2,070 cm³
- D. 8,000 cm³

6. Firewood is sold by the cord. A cord is a stack of wood that is 8 ft long by 4 ft wide by 4 ft high. What is the volume of a cord of wood?
- A. 32 ft³
- B. 64 ft³
- (C) 128 ft³
- D. 320 ft³

7. If each side of the cube is doubled, how does its volume change?

4 in.
4 in.   4 in.

- A. It is twice that of the original cube.
- B. It is 4 times that of the original.
- (C) It is 8 times that of the original.
- D. It is 16 times that of the original.

8. How can you change this box so that it will hold twice as much?

18 in
14 in
12 in

- (A) Double only one dimension.
- B. Double only two dimensions.
- C. Double all three dimensions.
- D. Add 2 in. to each dimension.

Name _____

For questions 9–10, use the figure below.

6 ft
4 ft   8 ft

9. If you double all the dimensions of this figure, what is the volume of the larger prism?
- A. 192 ft³
- B. 384 ft³
- C. 768 ft³
- (D) 1,536 ft³

10. If you halve all the dimensions of the figure, what is the volume of the smaller prism?
- A. 12 ft³
- (B) 24 ft³
- C. 81 ft³
- D. 192 ft³

For questions 11–12, use the figure below.

2 cm
8 cm   3 cm

11. If you halve the height of the figure, what is the volume of the smaller prism?
- A. 6 cm³
- B. 12 cm³
- (C) 24 cm³
- D. 48 cm³

12. If you double the height of the figure, what is the volume of the larger prism?
- (A) 96 cm³
- B. 128 cm³
- C. 192 cm³
- D. 384 cm³

For questions 13–16, find the volume of each cylinder to the nearest whole unit. Use the formula $V = \pi r^2 \times h$.

13.
2 cm
4 cm
- A. 16 cm³
- B. 25 cm³
- C. 32 cm³
- (D) 50 cm³

14.
20 cm
10 cm
- A. 314 cm³
- B. 1,256 cm³
- (C) 3,140 cm³
- D. 6,280 cm³

15.
6 ft
7 ft
- A. 63 ft³
- B. 154 ft³
- (C) 198 ft³
- D. 791 ft³

16.
2.5 ft
3 ft
- (A) 59 ft³
- B. 71 ft³
- C. 79 ft³
- D. 236 ft³

Multiple-Choice Format • Test Answers   **140**

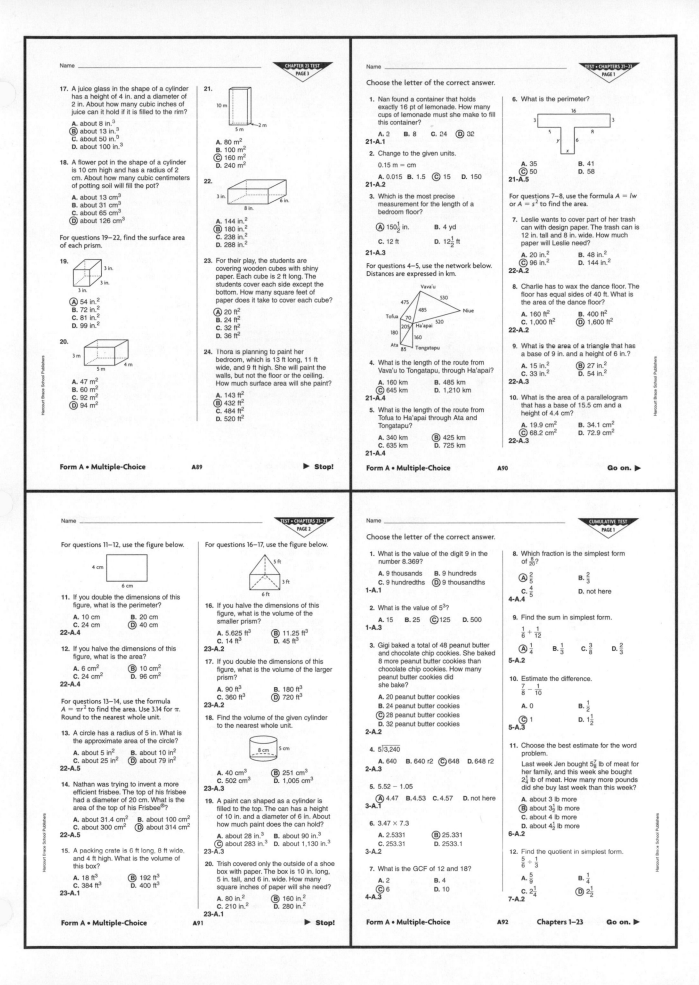

Name _____

17. A juice glass in the shape of a cylinder has a height of 4 in. and a diameter of 2 in. About how many cubic inches of juice can it hold if it is filled to the rim?

   A. about 8 in.^{3}
   B. about 13 in.^{3}
   C. about 50 in.^{9}
   D. about 100 in.^{3}

18. A flower pot in the shape of a cylinder is 10 cm high and has a radius of 2 cm. About how many cubic centimeters of potting soil will fill the pot?

   A. about 13 cm^3
   B. about 31 cm^3
   C. about 65 cm^3
   D. about 126 cm^3

For questions 19–22, find the surface area of each prism.

19.

   A. 54 in.^{2}
   B. 72 in.^{2}
   C. 81 in.^{2}
   D. 99 in.^{2}

20.

   A. 47 m^2
   B. 60 m^2
   C. 92 m^2
   D. 94 m^2

21.

   A. 80 m^2
   B. 100 m^2
   C. 160 m^2
   D. 240 m^2

22.

   A. 144 in.^{2}
   B. 180 in.^{2}
   C. 238 in.^{2}
   D. 288 in.^{2}

23. For their play, the students are covering wooden cubes with shiny paper. Each cube is 2 ft long. The students cover each side except the bottom. How many square feet of paper does it take to cover each cube?

   A. 20 ft^2
   B. 24 ft^2
   C. 32 ft^2
   D. 36 ft^2

24. Thora is planning to paint her bedroom, which is 13 ft long, 11 ft wide, and 9 ft high. She will paint the walls, but not the floor or the ceiling. How much surface area will she paint?

   A. 143 ft^2
   B. 432 ft^2
   C. 484 ft^2
   D. 520 ft^2

Form A • Multiple-Choice   A89   ▶ **Stop!**

Name _____

Choose the letter of the correct answer.

1. Nan found a container that holds exactly 16 pt of lemonade. How many cups of lemonade must she make to fill this container?

   A. 2   **B.** 8   **C.** 24   **D.** 32
21-A.1

2. Change to the given units.

0.15 m = ___ cm

   A. 0.015   **B.** 1.5   **C.** 15   **D.** 150
21-A.2

3. Which is the most precise measurement for the length of a bedroom floor?

   A. $150\frac{1}{2}$ in.   **B.** 4 yd
   C. 12 ft   **D.** $12\frac{1}{2}$ ft
21-A.3

For questions 4–5, use the network below. Distances are expressed in km.

4. What is the length of the route from Vava'u to Tongatapu, through Ha'apai?

   A. 160 km   **B.** 485 km
   C. 645 km   **D.** 1,210 km
21-A.4

5. What is the length of the route from Tofua to Ha'apai through Ata and Tongatapu?

   A. 340 km   **B.** 425 km
   C. 635 km   **D.** 725 km
21-A.4

6. What is the perimeter?

   A. 35   **B.** 41
   C. 50   **D.** 58
21-A.5

For questions 7–8, use the formula $A = lw$ or $A = s^2$ to find the area.

7. Leslie wants to cover part of her trash can with design paper. The trash can is 12 in. tall and 8 in. wide. How much paper will Leslie need?

   A. 20 in.^{2} **B.** 48 in.^{2}
   C. 96 in.^{2} **D.** 144 in.^{2}
22-A.2

8. Charlie has to wax the dance floor. The floor has equal sides of 40 ft. What is the area of the dance floor?

   A. 160 ft^2 **B.** 400 ft^2
   C. 1,000 ft^2 **D.** 1,600 ft^2
22-A.2

9. What is the area of a triangle that has a base of 9 in. and a height of 6 in.?

   A. 15 in.^{2} **B.** 27 in.^{2}
   C. 33 in.^{2} **D.** 54 in.^{2}
22-A.3

10. What is the area of a parallelogram that has a base of 15.5 cm and a height of 4.4 cm?

   A. 19.9 cm^2 **B.** 34.1 cm^2
   C. 68.2 cm^2 **D.** 72.9 cm^2
22-A.3

Form A • Multiple-Choice   A90   Go on. ▶

Name _____

For questions 11–12, use the figure below.

11. If you double the dimensions of this figure, what is the perimeter?

   A. 10 cm   **B.** 20 cm
   C. 24 cm   **D.** 40 cm
22-A.4

12. If you halve the dimensions of this figure, what is the area?

   A. 6 cm^2 **B.** 10 cm^2
   C. 24 cm^2 **D.** 96 cm^2
22-A.4

For questions 13–14, use the formula $A = \pi r^2$ to find the area. Use 3.14 for π. Round to the nearest whole unit.

13. A circle has a radius of 5 in. What is the approximate area of the circle?

   A. about 5 in^2 **B.** about 10 in^2
   C. about 25 in^2 **D.** about 79 in^2
22-A.5

14. Nathan was trying to invent a more efficient frisbee. The top of his frisbee had a diameter of 20 cm. What is the area of the top of his Frisbee®?

   A. about 31.4 cm^2 **B.** about 100 cm^2
   C. about 300 cm^2 **D.** about 314 cm^2
22-A.5

15. A packing crate is 6 ft long, 8 ft wide, and 4 ft high. What is the volume of this box?

   A. 18 ft^3 **B.** 192 ft^3
   C. 384 ft^3 **D.** 400 ft^3
23-A.1

For questions 16–17, use the figure below.

16. If you halve the dimensions of this figure, what is the volume of the smaller prism?

   A. 5.625 ft^3 **B.** 11.25 ft^3
   C. 14 ft^3 **D.** 45 ft^3
23-A.2

17. If you double the dimensions of this figure, what is the volume of the larger prism?

   A. 90 ft^3 **B.** 180 ft^3
   C. 360 ft^3 **D.** 720 ft^3
23-A.2

18. Find the volume of the given cylinder to the nearest whole unit.

   A. 40 cm^3 **B.** 251 cm^3
   C. 502 cm^3 **D.** 1,005 cm^3
23-A.3

19. A paint can shaped as a cylinder is filled to the top. The can has a height of 10 in. and a diameter of 6 in. About how much paint does the can hold?

   A. about 28 in.^{3} **B.** about 90 in.^{3}
   C. about 283 in.^{3} **D.** about 1,130 in.^{3}
23-A.3

20. Trish covered only the outside of a shoe box with paper. The box is 10 in. long, 5 in. tall, and 6 in. wide. How many square inches of paper will she need?

   A. 80 in.^{2} **B.** 160 in.^{2}
   C. 210 in.^{2} **D.** 280 in.^{2}
23-A.1

Form A • Multiple-Choice   A91   ▶ **Stop!**

Name _____

Choose the letter of the correct answer.

1. What is the value of the digit 9 in the number 8.369?

   A. 9 thousands   **B.** 9 hundreds
   C. 9 hundredths   **D.** 9 thousandths
1-A.1

2. What is the value of 5^3?

   A. 15   **B.** 25   **C.** 125   **D.** 500
1-A.3

3. Gigi baked a total of 48 peanut butter and chocolate chip cookies. She baked 8 more peanut butter cookies than chocolate chip cookies. How many peanut butter cookies did she bake?

   A. 20 peanut butter cookies
   B. 24 peanut butter cookies
   C. 28 peanut butter cookies
   D. 32 peanut butter cookies
2-A.2

4. $5)\overline{3,240}$

   A. 640   **B.** 640 r2   **C.** 648   **D.** 648 r2
2-A.3

5. $5.52 - 1.05$

   A. 4.47   **B.** 4.53   **C.** 4.57   **D.** not here
3-A.1

6. 3.47×7.3

   A. 2.5331   **B.** 25.331
   C. 253.31   **D.** 2533.1
3-A.2

7. What is the GCF of 12 and 18?

   A. 2   **B.** 4
   C. 6   **D.** 10
4-A.3

8. Which fraction is the simplest form of $\frac{8}{20}$?

   A. $\frac{2}{5}$ **B.** $\frac{2}{3}$
   C. $\frac{4}{5}$ **D.** not here
4-A.4

9. Find the sum in simplest form.

$\frac{1}{6} + \frac{1}{12}$

   A. $\frac{1}{4}$ **B.** $\frac{1}{3}$ **C.** $\frac{3}{8}$ **D.** $\frac{2}{3}$
5-A.2

10. Estimate the difference.

$\frac{7}{8} - \frac{1}{10}$

   A. 0   **B.** $\frac{1}{2}$
   C. 1   **D.** $1\frac{1}{2}$
5-A.3

11. Choose the best estimate for the word problem.

Last week Jen bought $5\frac{7}{8}$ lb of meat for her family, and this week she bought $2\frac{1}{4}$ lb of meat. How many more pounds did she buy last week than this week?

   A. about 3 lb more
   B. about $3\frac{1}{2}$ lb more
   C. about 4 lb more
   D. about $4\frac{1}{2}$ lb more
6-A.2

12. Find the quotient in simplest form.

$\frac{5}{6} \div \frac{1}{3}$

   A. $\frac{5}{9}$ **B.** $\frac{1}{4}$
   C. $2\frac{1}{4}$ **D.** $2\frac{1}{2}$
7-A.2

Form A • Multiple-Choice   A92   Chapters 1–23   Go on. ▶

Harcourt Brace School Publishers

Multiple-Choice Format • Test Answers

13. What does the symbol $\overline{AB}$ refer to?

 A. plane AB   C. line AB
 B. line segment AB   D. ray AB
8-A.1

14. How many angles does an octagon have?

 A. 5   B. 6   C. 8   D. 12
8-A.4

15. Choose the figure that is a translation of the original figure.

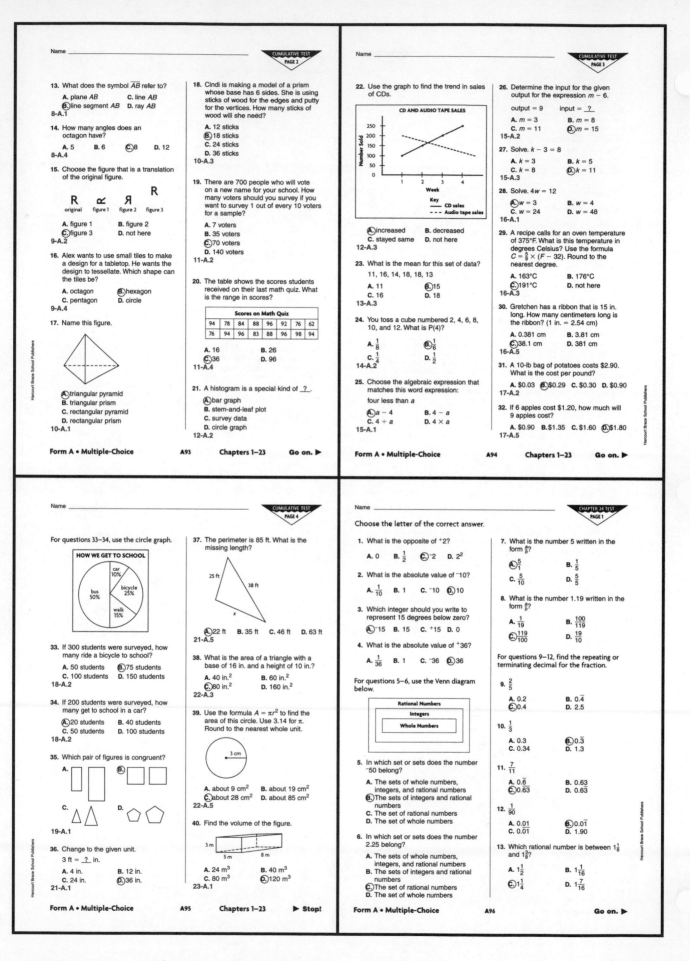

 R   ⋉   Я   R
 original   figure 1   figure 2   figure 3

 A. figure 1   B. figure 2
 C. figure 3   D. not here
9-A.2

16. Alex wants to use small tiles to make a design for a tabletop. He wants the design to tessellate. Which shape can the tiles be?

 A. octagon   B. hexagon
 C. pentagon   D. circle
9-A.4

17. Name this figure.

 A. triangular pyramid
 B. triangular prism
 C. rectangular pyramid
 D. rectangular prism
10-A.1

18. Cindi is making a model of a prism whose base has 6 sides. She is using sticks of wood for the edges and putty for the vertices. How many sticks of wood will she need?

 A. 12 sticks
 B. 18 sticks
 C. 24 sticks
 D. 36 sticks
10-A.3

19. There are 700 people who will vote on a new name for your school. How many voters should you survey if you want to survey 1 out of every 10 voters for a sample?

 A. 7 voters
 B. 35 voters
 C. 70 voters
 D. 140 voters
11-A.2

20. The table shows the scores students received on their last math quiz. What is the range in scores?

Scores on Math Quiz

| 94 | 78 | 84 | 88 | 96 | 92 | 76 | 62 |
| 76 | 94 | 96 | 83 | 88 | 96 | 98 | 94 |

 A. 16   B. 26
 C. 36   D. 96
11-A.4

21. A histogram is a special kind of __?__.

 A. bar graph
 B. stem-and-leaf plot
 C. survey data
 D. circle graph
12-A.2

Form A • Multiple-Choice   A93   Chapters 1–23   Go on. ▶

22. Use the graph to find the trend in sales of CDs.

CD AND AUDIO TAPE SALES

Key
—— CD sales
- - - Audio tape sales

 A. increased   B. decreased
 C. stayed same   D. not here
12-A.3

23. What is the mean for this set of data?

 11, 16, 14, 18, 18, 13

 A. 11   B. 15
 C. 16   D. 18
13-A.3

24. You toss a cube numbered 2, 4, 6, 8, 10, and 12. What is P(4)?

 A. $\frac{1}{8}$ B. $\frac{1}{6}$
 C. $\frac{1}{4}$ D. $\frac{1}{2}$
14-A.2

25. Choose the algebraic expression that matches this word expression:

 four less than a

 A. $a - 4$ B. $4 - a$
 C. $4 \div a$ D. $4 \times a$
15-A.1

26. Determine the input for the given output for the expression $m - 6$.

 output = 9   input = __?__

 A. $m = 3$ B. $m = 8$
 C. $m = 11$ D. $m = 15$
15-A.2

27. Solve. $k - 3 = 8$

 A. $k = 3$ B. $k = 5$
 C. $k = 8$ D. $k = 11$
15-A.3

28. Solve. $4w = 12$

 A. $w = 3$ B. $w = 4$
 C. $w = 24$ D. $w = 48$
16-A.1

29. A recipe calls for an oven temperature of 375°F. What is this temperature in degrees Celsius? Use the formula $C = \frac{5}{9} \times (F - 32)$. Round to the nearest degree.

 A. 163°C   B. 176°C
 C. 191°C   D. not here
16-A.3

30. Gretchen has a ribbon that is 15 in. long. How many centimeters long is the ribbon? (1 in. = 2.54 cm)

 A. 0.381 cm   B. 3.81 cm
 C. 38.1 cm   D. 381 cm
16-A.5

31. A 10-lb bag of potatoes costs $2.90. What is the cost per pound?

 A. $0.03   B. $0.29   C. $0.30   D. $0.90
17-A.2

32. If 6 apples cost $1.20, how much will 9 apples cost?

 A. $0.90   B. $1.35   C. $1.60   D. $1.80
17-A.5

Form A • Multiple-Choice   A94   Chapters 1–23   Go on. ▶

For questions 33–34, use the circle graph.

HOW WE GET TO SCHOOL

 car 10%
 bicycle 25%
 bus 50%
 walk 15%

33. If 300 students were surveyed, how many ride a bicycle to school?

 A. 50 students   B. 75 students
 C. 100 students   D. 150 students
18-A.2

34. If 200 students were surveyed, how many get to school in a car?

 A. 20 students   B. 40 students
 C. 50 students   D. 100 students
18-A.2

35. Which pair of figures is congruent?

 A.   B.   C.   D.
19-A.1

36. Change to the given unit.

 3 ft = __?__ in.

 A. 4 in.   B. 12 in.
 C. 24 in.   D. 36 in.
21-A.1

37. The perimeter is 85 ft. What is the missing length?

 25 ft   38 ft   x

 A. 22 ft   B. 35 ft   C. 46 ft   D. 63 ft
21-A.5

38. What is the area of a triangle with a base of 16 in. and a height of 10 in.?

 A. 40 in.²   B. 60 in.²
 C. 80 in.²   D. 160 in.²
22-A.3

39. Use the formula $A = \pi r^2$ to find the area of this circle. Use 3.14 for π. Round to the nearest whole unit.

 3 cm

 A. about 9 cm²   B. about 19 cm²
 C. about 28 cm²   D. about 85 cm²
22-A.5

40. Find the volume of the figure.

 3 m   5 m   8 m

 A. 24 m³   B. 40 m³
 C. 80 m³   D. 120 m³
23-A.1

Form A • Multiple-Choice   A95   Chapters 1–23   ▶ Stop!

Choose the letter of the correct answer.

1. What is the opposite of ⁺2?

 A. 0   B. $\frac{1}{2}$ C. ⁻2   D. 2^2

2. What is the absolute value of ⁻10?

 A. $\frac{1}{10}$ B. 1   C. ⁻10   D. 10

3. Which integer should you write to represent 15 degrees below zero?

 A. ⁻15   B. 15   C. ⁺15   D. 0

4. What is the absolute value of ⁺36?

 A. $\frac{1}{36}$ B. 1   C. ⁻36   D. 36

For questions 5–6, use the Venn diagram below.

Rational Numbers
Integers
Whole Numbers

5. In which set or sets does the number ⁻50 belong?

 A. The sets of whole numbers, integers, and rational numbers
 B. The sets of integers and rational numbers
 C. The set of rational numbers
 D. The set of whole numbers

6. In which set or sets does the number 2.25 belong?

 A. The sets of whole numbers, integers, and rational numbers
 B. The sets of integers and rational numbers
 C. The set of rational numbers
 D. The set of whole numbers

7. What is the number 5 written in the form $\frac{a}{b}$?

 A. $\frac{5}{1}$ B. $\frac{1}{5}$
 C. $\frac{5}{10}$ D. $\frac{5}{5}$

8. What is the number 1.19 written in the form $\frac{a}{b}$?

 A. $\frac{1}{19}$ B. $\frac{100}{119}$
 C. $\frac{119}{100}$ D. $\frac{19}{10}$

For questions 9–12, find the repeating or terminating decimal for the fraction.

9. $\frac{2}{5}$

 A. 0.2   B. $0.\overline{4}$
 C. 0.4   D. 2.5

10. $\frac{1}{3}$

 A. 0.3   B. $0.\overline{3}$
 C. 0.34   D. 1.3

11. $\frac{7}{11}$

 A. $0.\overline{6}$ B. 0.63
 C. $0.\overline{63}$ D. 0.63

12. $\frac{1}{90}$

 A. 0.01   B. $0.0\overline{1}$
 C. 0.01   D. 1.90

13. Which rational number is between $1\frac{1}{8}$ and $1\frac{3}{8}$?

 A. $1\frac{1}{2}$ B. $1\frac{1}{16}$
 C. $1\frac{1}{4}$ D. $1\frac{7}{16}$

Form A • Multiple-Choice   A96   Go on. ▶

Multiple-Choice Format • Test Answers

Top-left quadrant — Chapter 24 Test, Page 2:

14. Which rational number is between 0 and $-\frac{1}{2}$?

Ⓐ $\frac{-2}{10}$ B. $\frac{-5}{8}$ C. $\frac{1}{4}$ D. $\frac{-5}{10}$

15. Which rational number is between -1.5 and -1.6?

A. -1.7 B. 1.55 C. -1.65 Ⓓ -1.59

16. Which rational number is between $-2\frac{3}{4}$ and -3?

A. $2\frac{7}{8}$ Ⓑ $-2\frac{15}{16}$ C. $-2\frac{5}{8}$ D. $-3\frac{1}{16}$

17. In a race, the winner's time was 10.3 sec. The third-place finisher's time was 10.4 sec. What could have been the time for the second-place finisher?

A. 10.0 sec   B. 10.5 sec   C. 10.25 sec   Ⓓ 10.33 sec

18. At 6 P.M. a snail was at -8.5 m in a well. By 7 P.M. it was at -9.5 m. At 6:30 P.M. the snail was between these two levels. At what level could the snail have been at 6:30 P.M.?

Ⓐ -9.1 m   B. -8.4 m   C. 9.0 m   D. -10.0 m

For questions 19–20, compare the numbers. Choose <, >, or =.

19. $\frac{3}{5}$ ◯ 0.6

A. <   B. >   Ⓒ =

20. $-\frac{3}{8}$ ◯ 0.375

Ⓐ <   B. >   C. =

For questions 21–22, order the rational numbers from least to greatest.

21. $\frac{1}{2}$, $-\frac{3}{4}$, 0.3

A. $-\frac{3}{4}, \frac{1}{2}$, 0.3   Ⓑ $-\frac{3}{4}$, 0.3, $\frac{1}{2}$

C. 0.3, $\frac{1}{2}, -\frac{3}{4}$ D. $\frac{1}{2}$, 0.3, $-\frac{3}{4}$

22. $-\frac{2}{3}$, -1, -1.4

A. $-\frac{2}{3}, -1, -1.4$ B. $-1, -\frac{2}{3}, -1.4$

C. $-1.4, -\frac{2}{3}, -1$ Ⓓ $-1.4, -1, -\frac{2}{3}$

23. Nora, Harry, Jinn, and Tamika each have a solo at the concert. Nora's solo lasts $1\frac{1}{2}$ min, Harry's lasts 1.2 min, Jinn's lasts $1\frac{4}{5}$ min, and Tamika's lasts 1.85 min. Who has the longest solo?

A. Nora   B. Harry   C. Jinn   Ⓓ Tamika

24. LeeAnne recorded the time it took her to walk a mile on four different days. The times were $12\frac{4}{5}$ min on Monday, 11.3 min on Tuesday, $12\frac{1}{4}$ min on Wednesday, and $11\frac{5}{8}$ min on Thursday. On which day did she walk the fastest?

A. Monday   Ⓑ Tuesday   C. Wednesday   D. Thursday

Form A • Multiple-Choice   A97   ▶ Stop!

Top-right quadrant — Chapter 25 Test, Page 1:

Choose the letter of the correct answer.

1. Which addition equation is modeled on the number line below?

(number line from -9 to $+2$)

A. $+3 + -2 = +1$ Ⓑ $-3 + -2 = -5$ C. $+3 + +2 = +5$ D. $-3 + +2 = -1$

For questions 2–4, find the sum.

2. $-10 + +5$

A. -15 Ⓑ -5 C. $+5$ D. $+10$

3. $-7 + +9$

A. -16 B. -2 Ⓒ $+2$ D. $+16$

4. $-21 + -11$

Ⓐ -32 B. -10 C. $+10$ D. $+32$

5. The day's low temperature was $-5°F$. The high temperature was 25° greater. What was the high temperature?

A. $-30°F$ B. $-20°F$ Ⓒ $+20°F$ D. $+30°F$

6. On its first play, a football team lost 3 yd. On its second play, it lost 2 yd. Which integer shows the total gain or loss on the two plays?

Ⓐ -5 yd   B. -1 yd   C. $+1$ yd   D. $+5$ yd

7. Which of the following problems has the same solution as $+4 - +6$?

A. $-4 + +6$ B. $-4 + -6$ C. $+4 + +6$ Ⓓ $+4 + -6$

For questions 8–10, find the difference.

8. $+8 - +12$

A. -20 Ⓑ -4 C. $+4$ D. $+20$

9. $-5 + +15$

Ⓐ -20 B. -10 C. $+10$ D. $+20$

10. $+20 - -15$

A. -35 B. -5 C. $+5$ Ⓓ $+35$

11. At dinnertime the temperature was 2°F. By midnight the temperature was 10° less. What was the temperature at midnight?

A. $+8°F$ B. $+12°F$ Ⓒ $-8°F$ D. $-12°F$

12. On a winter day in Maine, the high temperature was $-3°F$. The low temperature was 13° less. What was the low temperature?

Ⓐ $-16°F$ B. $-10°F$ C. $+10°F$ D. $+16°F$

Form A • Multiple-Choice   A98   Go on. ▶

Bottom-left quadrant — Chapter 25 Test, Page 2:

13. The product of a positive integer and a negative integer is __?__.

A. a positive integer   Ⓑ a negative integer   C. zero   D. the same sign as the larger integer

For questions 14–16, find the product.

14. -12×-3

A. -36 B. -4 C. $+4$ Ⓓ $+36$

15. $-8 \times +2$

Ⓐ -16 B. -6 C. $+6$ D. $+16$

16. -10×-5

A. -50 B. -2 C. $+2$ Ⓓ $+50$

17. A medical textbook suggests that a safe weight loss is 3 lb per month. Mrs. Hudson lost weight at that rate for 6 months. How do you express the change in her weight as a negative number?

Ⓐ -18 lb   B. -9 lb   C. -3 lb   D. -2 lb

18. A container filled with water at a temperature of 70°F was put in a refrigerator. The water temperature fell 5° each hour for the next 4 hr. What was the temperature then?

A. $-20°F$ B. $+20°F$ Ⓒ $+50°F$ D. $-65°F$

19. If you divide a negative integer by a negative integer, the quotient __?__.

Ⓐ is a positive integer   B. is a negative integer   C. is zero   D. has the same sign of the larger integer

For questions 20–22, find the quotient.

20. $-15 \div -5$

A. -10 B. -3 Ⓒ $+3$ D. $+10$

21. $-24 \div +4$

A. -20 Ⓑ -6 C. $+6$ D. $+20$

22. $-12 \div -3$

A. -9 B. -4 Ⓒ $+4$ D. $+9$

23. Which of the following problems has the greatest quotient?

A. $+12 \div -4$ B. $+60 \div -10$ C. $-36 \div -9$ Ⓓ $-20 \div -4$

24. In 8 hr the temperature fell 24°. If it fell the same number of degrees every hour, how many degrees did it change every hour?

A. $-16°F$ Ⓑ $-3°F$ C. $+3°F$ D. $+16°F$

Form A • Multiple-Choice   A99   ▶ Stop!

Bottom-right quadrant — Chapter 26 Test, Page 1:

Choose the letter of the correct answer.

1. Evaluate $20 - 10 \div -2$.

A. -5 B. 5   C. 15   Ⓓ 25

2. Evaluate $y - 10$ for $y = 2$.

A. -12 Ⓑ -8 C. 8   D. 12

3. Evaluate $4x$ for $x = -3$.

Ⓐ -12 B. -7 C. 7   D. 12

4. Evaluate $t^2 + 2$ for $t = -1$.

A. -3 B. -1 C. 1   Ⓓ 3

For questions 5–8, solve the equation.

5. $4p = -16$

A. $p = -20$ B. $p = -12$ Ⓒ $p = -4$ D. $p = 4$

6. $m + 5 = 2$

Ⓐ $m = -3$ B. $m = \frac{2}{5}$ C. $m = 3$ D. $m = 7$

7. $\frac{x}{-2} = -6$

A. $x = -12$ B. $x = -3$ C. $x = 3$ Ⓓ $x - 12$

8. $10 = y + 25$

A. $y = -35$ Ⓑ $y = -15$ C. $y = 15$ D. $y = 35$

9. Which equation should you write for this word sentence?

Six less than a number, y, is negative twenty-four.

A. $6y = -24$ B. $y + 6 = -24$ Ⓒ $y - 6 = -24$ D. $\frac{y}{6} = -24$

10. This morning the temperature increased 4°F to the current temperature of $-16°F$. Which equation shows how to find the original temperature, t?

A. $t = -16$ B. $t + 4 = -16$ Ⓒ $t - 4 = -16$ D. $4t = -16$

11. What are the whole-number solutions of $x < 4$?

A. 0, 1, 2, 3, 4   B. 1, 2, 3, 4   C. 1, 2, 3   Ⓓ 0, 1, 2, 3

12. What are the whole-number solutions of $a \leq 1$?

A. 0   B. 1   Ⓒ 0 and 1   D. all whole numbers except 0

13. Which algebraic inequality is represented by this number line?

(number line from -5 to 5)

Ⓐ $x > 2$ B. $x < 2$ C. $x \geq 2$ D. $x \leq 2$

Form A • Multiple-Choice   A100   Go on. ▶

Multiple-Choice Format • Test Answers   **143**

14. Which graph represents the algebraic inequality $x < ^-1$?

A.
B.
C.
D.

15. Which algebraic inequality represents this word sentence?

All numbers y are greater than or equal to eight.

A. $y < 8$ B. $y \geq 8$
C. $y \leq 8$ D. $y > 8$

16. The speed limit in front of a school is 20 mi per hour. Which inequality represents the speeds that a driver can legally go?

A. $x < 20$ B. $x \leq 20$
C. $x \geq 20$ D. $x > 20$

Use the coordinate plane to answer questions 17–20.

17. Which point is located by the ordered pair $(^-2,3)$?

A. point L B. point M
C. point N D. point P

18. Which point is located by the ordered pair $(2,^-3)$?

A. point L B. point M
C. point N D. point P

19. What is the ordered pair for point W?

A. $(^-4,^-3)$ B. $(^-3,^-4)$
C. $(^-4,3)$ D. $(3,^-4)$

20. What is the ordered pair for point T?

A. $(^-4,1)$ B. $(4,^-1)$
C. $(1,^-4)$ D. $(^-1,4)$

For questions 21–22, use the table.

x	-3	-2	-1	0	1	2	3
y	-4	-3	-2	-1	0	1	

21. Which number completes the table?

A. $^-4$ B. 2   C. 3   D. 4

22. Which expression gives each value of y?

A. $x - 1$ B. $x + 1$
C. $2x$ D. $\frac{x}{2}$

For questions 23–24, use the table.

x	2	1	0	-1
y	6	3	0	

23. Which number completes the table?

A. $^-3$ B. $^-1$ C. 1   D. 3

24. Which expression gives each value of y?

A. $x - 3$ B. $x + 4$
C. $3x$ D. $3 - x$

Form A • Multiple-Choice   A101   ▶ **Stop!**

Choose the letter of the correct answer.

1. What is the opposite of $^-6$?

A. 0   B. $^+\frac{1}{6}$
C. $^+6$ D. 6^2
24-A.1

2. What is the number 8 written in the form $\frac{a}{b}$?

A. $\frac{1}{8}$ B. $\frac{8}{1}$
C. $\frac{8}{10}$ D. $\frac{8}{8}$
24-A.2

For questions 3–4, find the repeating or terminating decimal for the fraction.

3. $\frac{6}{11}$

A. 0.54   B. 0.58   C. 0.60   D. 0.61
24-A.3

4. $\frac{5}{8}$

A. 0.56   B. 0.625   C. 0.80   D. 0.83
24-A.3

5. Which rational number is between $2\frac{1}{6}$ and $2\frac{1}{3}$?

A. $1\frac{1}{4}$ B. $2\frac{1}{4}$
C. $2\frac{3}{4}$ D. $3\frac{1}{4}$
24-A.4

6. A campsite is located 8.43 mi from parking Lot B. A picnic area is 8.48 mi from parking lot B. A waterfall is between the campsite and the picnic area. How far from parking lot B could the waterfall be?

A. 4.24 mi   B. 8.40 mi
C. 8.47 mi   D. 16.91 mi
24-A.4

7. Compare the numbers. Choose $<$, $>$, or $=$.

$\frac{3}{8}$ ● 0.365

A. $<$ B. $>$ C. $=$
24-A.5

8. Kane, Aaron, Leon, and Keith had a juggling contest. Kane juggled for $8\frac{3}{8}$ sec, Aaron for 8.45 sec, Leon for $8\frac{1}{8}$ sec, and Keith for 8.08 sec. Who juggled the longest?

A. Kane   B. Aaron
C. Leon   D. Keith
24-A.5

For questions 9–10, find each sum.

9. $^-6 + ^+4$

A. $^-2$ B. $^+2$
C. $^+4$ D. $^+10$
25-A.1

10. $^-11 + ^-4$

A. $^-15$ B. $^-7$
C. $^+11$ D. $^+15$
25-A.1

11. Find the difference.

$^+6 - ^-5$

A. $^-11$ B. $^-1$
C. $^+1$ D. $^+11$
25-A.1

12. When Yoshi went to bed, it was $^-5°F$. In the morning it was 20° warmer. What was the temperature in the morning?

A. $^-15°F$ B. $^-5°F$
C. $^+15°F$ D. $^+25°F$
25-A.1

Form A • Multiple-Choice   A102   **Go on.** ▶

---

13. The product of a negative integer and a negative integer is ___?___ .

A. a positive integer
B. a negative integer
C. zero
D. the same sign as the larger integer
25-A.2

14. Find the product.

$^-5 \times ^+3$

A. $^-15$ B. $^-\frac{3}{5}$
C. $\frac{3}{5}$ D. 15
25-A.2

15. Find the quotient.

$^+24 \div ^-3$

A. $^-21$ B. $^-8$
C. $^-\frac{1}{8}$ D. 8
25-A.2

16. At 4:00 P.M. the temperature dropped by 21°. If the temperature was 15°F at noon, what was the temperature at 4:00 P.M.?

A. $^-20°F$ B. $^-14°F$
C. $^-6°F$ D. $^-4°F$
25-A.2

17. Evaluate $t + 12$ for $t = ^-3$.

A. $^-15$ B. $^-9$
C. 9   D. 15
26-A.1

18. Evaluate $7y$ for $y = ^-2$.

A. $^-14$ B. $^-3\frac{1}{2}$
C. 9   D. 14
26-A.1

19. Solve the equation.

$a + 3 = ^-9$

A. $a = ^-15$ B. $a = ^-12$
C. $a = ^-6$ D. $a = ^+12$
26-A.2

20. Which equation should you write for this word sentence?

3 more than a number, c, is negative 18.

A. $c - 3 = ^-18$ B. $3 - c = 18$
C. $3 - c = ^-18$ D. $c + 3 = ^-18$
26-A.2

21. What are the whole-number solutions to the inequality $x \leq 5$?

A. 0, 1, 2, 3, 4   B. 0, 1, 2, 3, 4, 5
C. 1, 2, 3, 4, 5   D. 1, 2, 3, 4
26-A.3

22. A roller coaster can travel at speeds up to and including, but not greater than, 35 mi per hr. Which inequality represents the speeds that the roller coaster can travel?

A. $x < 35$ B. $x > 35$
C. $x \geq 35$ D. $x \leq 35$
26-A.3

For questions 23–24, use the table.

x	-2	-1	0	1	2
y	-1	0	1	2	

23. Which number completes the table?

A. $^-2$ B. $^-1$
C. 0   D. 3
26-A.5

24. Which expression, using x, gives the value of y?

A. $x - 1$ B. $^-\frac{1}{2}x + 1$
C. $x + 1$ D. $2x - 1$
26-A.5

Form A • Multiple-Choice   A103   ▶ **Stop!**

Choose the letter of the correct answer.

1. What is 0.2 written as a fraction?

A. $\frac{1}{20}$ B. $\frac{2}{100}$
C. $\frac{1}{2}$ D. $\frac{2}{10}$
1-A.2

2. Which of these shows the integers written in order from least to greatest?

A. 0, $^-1$, 3, 2   B. 0, 2, $^-1$, 3
C. $^-1$, 0, 2, 3   D. $^-1$, 2, 0, $^-3$
1-A.4

3. Use mental math to find the difference.

$62 - 19$

A. 41   B. 42   C. 43   D. 44
2-A.1

4. Choose the best estimate of the sum.

$\begin{array}{r} 4,188 \\ 2,204 \\ + 3,829 \end{array}$

A. 9,000   B. 10,000
C. 11,000   D. 12,000
2-A.4

5. $27.26 \div 0.58$

A. 0.047   B. 0.47
C. 4.7   D. 47
3-A.3

6. Which of these numbers is a composite number?

A. 7   B. 11   C. 15   D. 17
4-A.1

7. What is $2\frac{3}{8}$ written as an improper fraction?

A. $\frac{5}{8}$ B. $\frac{17}{8}$ C. $\frac{19}{8}$ D. $\frac{21}{8}$
4-A.5

8. Find the difference in simplest form.

$\frac{11}{12} - \frac{1}{12}$

A. $\frac{4}{5}$ B. $\frac{5}{6}$
C. $\frac{7}{8}$ D. not here
5-A.1

9. Find the sum in simplest form.

$1\frac{1}{4} + 2\frac{5}{12}$

A. $3\frac{5}{8}$ B. $3\frac{2}{3}$
C. $4\frac{5}{8}$ D. not here
6-A.1

10. Find the product in simplest form.

$\frac{1}{4} \times 2\frac{2}{3}$

A. $\frac{1}{3}$ B. $\frac{2}{3}$ C. 1   D. 2
7-A.1

11. Which of these statements about pairs of lines is true?

A. Parallel lines sometimes intersect.
B. Parallel lines form right angles.
C. All intersecting lines are parallel.
D. Some intersecting lines are perpendicular.
8-A.2

12. What construction do the figures below represent?

A. congruent line segments
B. bisected line segments
C. congruent angles
D. perpendicular line segments
8-A.3

Form A • Multiple-Choice   A104   Chapters 1–26   **Go on.** ▶

Multiple-Choice Format • Test Answers

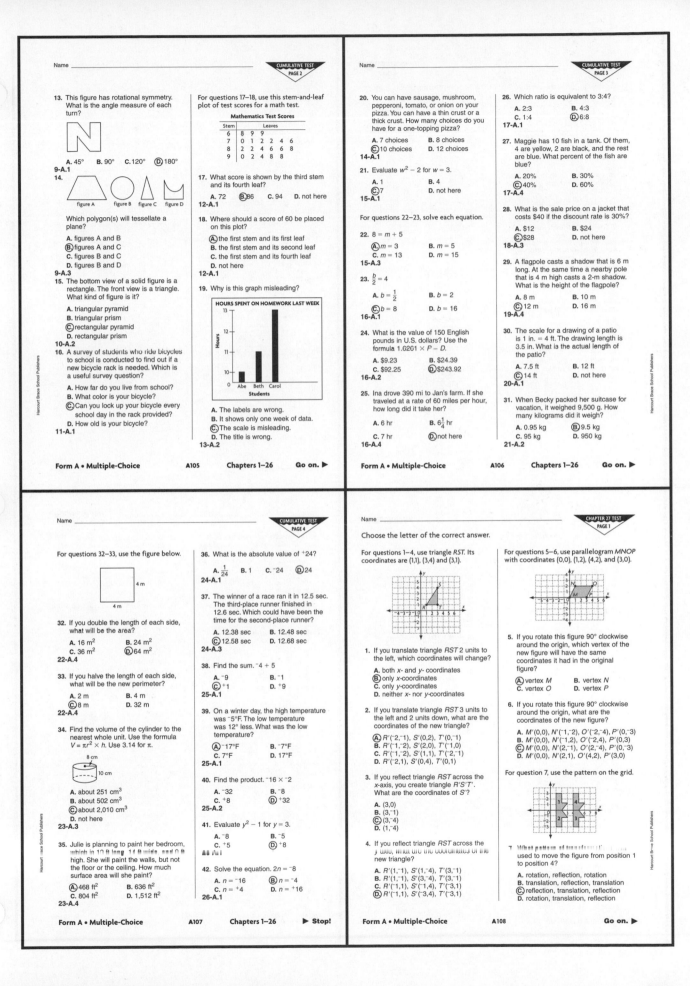

CUMULATIVE TEST PAGE 2

13. This figure has rotational symmetry. What is the angle measure of each turn?

N

A. 45°   B. 90°   C. 120°   D. 180°
9-A.1

14.

figure A   figure B   figure C   figure D

Which polygon(s) will tessellate a plane?

A. figures A and B
B. figures A and C
C. figures B and C
D. figures B and D
9-A.3

15. The bottom view of a solid figure is a rectangle. The front view is a triangle. What kind of figure is it?

A. triangular pyramid
B. triangular prism
C. rectangular pyramid
D. rectangular prism
10-A.2

16. A survey of students who ride bicycles to school is conducted to find out if a new bicycle rack is needed. Which is a useful survey question?

A. How far do you live from school?
B. What color is your bicycle?
C. Can you lock up your bicycle every school day in the rack provided?
D. How old is your bicycle?
11-A.1

For questions 17–18, use this stem-and-leaf plot of test scores for a math test.

Mathematics Test Scores

Stem	Leaves
6	8 9 9
7	0 1 2 2 4 6
8	2 2 4 6 6 8
9	0 2 4 8 8

17. What score is shown by the third stem and its fourth leaf?

A. 72   B. 86   C. 94   D. not here
12-A.1

18. Where should a score of 60 be placed on this plot?

A. the first stem and its first leaf
B. the first stem and its second leaf
C. the first stem and its fourth leaf
D. not here
12-A.1

19. Why is this graph misleading?

HOURS SPENT ON HOMEWORK LAST WEEK

A. The labels are wrong.
B. It shows only one week of data.
C. The scale is misleading.
D. The title is wrong.
13-A.2

Form A • Multiple-Choice   A105   Chapters 1–26   Go on. ▶

Name _____

CUMULATIVE TEST PAGE 3

20. You can have sausage, mushroom, pepperoni, tomato, or onion on your pizza. You can have a thin crust or a thick crust. How many choices do you have for a one-topping pizza?

A. 7 choices   B. 8 choices
C. 10 choices   D. 12 choices
14-A.1

21. Evaluate $w^2 - 2$ for $w = 3$.

A. 1   B. 4
C. 7   D. not here
15-A.1

For questions 22–23, solve each equation.

22. $8 = m + 5$

A. $m = 3$ B. $m = 5$
C. $m = 13$ D. $m = 15$
15-A.3

23. $\frac{b}{2} = 4$

A. $b = \frac{1}{2}$ B. $b = 2$
C. $b = 8$ D. $b = 16$
16-A.1

24. What is the value of 150 English pounds in U.S. dollars? Use the formula $1.6201 \times P - D$.

A. $9.23   B. $24.39
C. $92.25   D. $243.92
16-A.2

25. Ina drove 390 mi to Jan's farm. If she traveled at a rate of 60 miles per hour, how long did it take her?

A. 6 hr   B. $6\frac{1}{4}$ hr
C. 7 hr   D. not here
16-A.4

26. Which ratio is equivalent to 3:4?

A. 2:3   B. 4:3
C. 1:4   D. 6:8
17-A.1

27. Maggie has 10 fish in a tank. Of them, 4 are yellow, 2 are black, and the rest are blue. What percent of the fish are blue?

A. 20%   B. 30%
C. 40%   D. 60%
17-A.4

28. What is the sale price on a jacket that costs $40 if the discount rate is 30%?

A. $12   B. $24
C. $28   D. not here
18-A.3

29. A flagpole casts a shadow that is 6 m long. At the same time a nearby pole that is 4 m high casts a 2-m shadow. What is the height of the flagpole?

A. 8 m   B. 10 m
C. 12 m   D. 16 m
19-A.4

30. The scale for a drawing of a patio is 1 in. = 4 ft. The drawing length is 3.5 in. What is the actual length of the patio?

A. 7.5 ft   B. 12 ft
C. 14 ft   D. not here
20-A.1

31. When Becky packed her suitcase for vacation, it weighed 9,500 g. How many kilograms did it weigh?

A. 0.95 kg   B. 9.5 kg
C. 95 kg   D. 950 kg
21-A.2

Form A • Multiple-Choice   A106   Chapters 1–26   Go on. ▶

Name _____

CUMULATIVE TEST PAGE 4

For questions 32–33, use the figure below.

4 m
4 m

32. If you double the length of each side, what will be the area?

A. 16 m²   B. 24 m²
C. 36 m²   D. 64 m²
22-A.4

33. If you halve the length of each side, what will be the new perimeter?

A. 2 m   B. 4 m
C. 8 m   D. 32 m
22-A.4

34. Find the volume of the cylinder to the nearest whole unit. Use the formula $V = \pi r^2 \times h$. Use 3.14 for π.

8 cm
10 cm

A. about 251 cm³
B. about 502 cm³
C. about 2,010 cm³
D. not here
23-A.3

35. Julie is planning to paint her bedroom, which is 12 ft long, 14 ft wide, and 8 ft high. She will paint the walls, but not the floor or the ceiling. How much surface area will she paint?

A. 468 ft²   B. 636 ft²
C. 804 ft²   D. 1,512 ft²
23-A.4

36. What is the absolute value of ⁺24?

A. $\frac{1}{24}$ B. 1   C. ⁻24   D. 24
24-A.1

37. The winner of a race ran it in 12.5 sec. The third-place runner finished in 12.6 sec. Which could have been the time for the second-place runner?

A. 12.38 sec   B. 12.48 sec
C. 12.58 sec   D. 12.68 sec
24-A.3

38. Find the sum. ⁻4 + 5

A. ⁻9   B. ⁻1
C. ⁺1   D. ⁺9
25-A.1

39. On a winter day, the high temperature was ⁻5°F. The low temperature was 12° less. What was the low temperature?

A. ⁻17°F   B. ⁻7°F
C. 7°F   D. 17°F
25-A.1

40. Find the product. ⁻16 × ⁻2

A. ⁻32   B. ⁻8
C. ⁺8   D. ⁺32
25-A.2

41. Evaluate $y^2 - 1$ for $y = 3$.

A. ⁻8   B. ⁻5
C. ⁺5   D. ⁺8
26-A.1

42. Solve the equation. $2n = ⁻8$

A. $n = ⁻16$ B. $n = ⁻4$
C. $n = ⁺4$ D. $n = ⁺16$
26-A.1

Form A • Multiple-Choice   A107   Chapters 1–26   ▶ Stop!

Name _____

CHAPTER 27 TEST PAGE 1

Choose the letter of the correct answer.

For questions 1–4, use triangle RST. Its coordinates are (1,1), (3,4) and (3,1).

1. If you translate triangle RST 2 units to the left, which coordinates will change?

A. both x- and y- coordinates
B. only x-coordinates
C. only y-coordinates
D. neither x- nor y-coordinates

2. If you translate triangle RST 3 units to the left and 2 units down, what are the coordinates of the new triangle?

A. R'(⁻2,⁻1), S'(0,2), T'(0,⁻1)
B. R'(⁻1,⁻2), S'(2,0), T'(⁻1,0)
C. R'(⁻1,⁻2), S'(1,1), T'(⁻2,⁻1)
D. R'(2,1), S'(0,4), T'(0,1)

3. If you reflect triangle RST across the x-axis, you create triangle R'S'T'. What are the coordinates of S'?

A. (3,0)
B. (3,⁻1)
C. (3,⁻4)
D. (1,⁻4)

4. If you reflect triangle RST across the y-axis, what are the coordinates of the new triangle?

A. R'(1,⁻1), S'(1,⁻4), T'(3,⁻1)
B. R'(1,⁻1), S'(3,⁻4), T'(3,⁻1)
C. R'(1,1), S'(⁻1,4), T'(⁻3,1)
D. R'(⁻1,1), S'(⁻3,4), T'(⁻3,1)

For questions 5–6, use parallelogram MNOP with coordinates (0,0), (1,2), (4,2), and (3,0).

5. If you rotate this figure 90° clockwise around the origin, which vertex of the new figure will have the same coordinates it had in the original figure?

A. vertex M   B. vertex N
C. vertex O   D. vertex P

6. If you rotate this figure 90° clockwise around the origin, what are the coordinates of the new figure?

A. M'(0,0), N'(⁻1,2), O'(⁻2,⁻4), P'(0,⁻3)
B. M'(0,0), N'(1,2), O'(2,4), P'(0,3)
C. M'(0,0), N'(2,⁻1), O'(2,⁻4), P'(0,⁻3)
D. M'(0,0), N'(2,1), O'(4,2), P'(3,0)

For question 7, use the pattern on the grid.

7. What pattern of transformation is used to move the figure from position 1 to position 4?

A. rotation, reflection, rotation
B. translation, reflection, translation
C. reflection, translation, reflection
D. rotation, translation, reflection

Form A • Multiple-Choice   A108   Go on. ▶

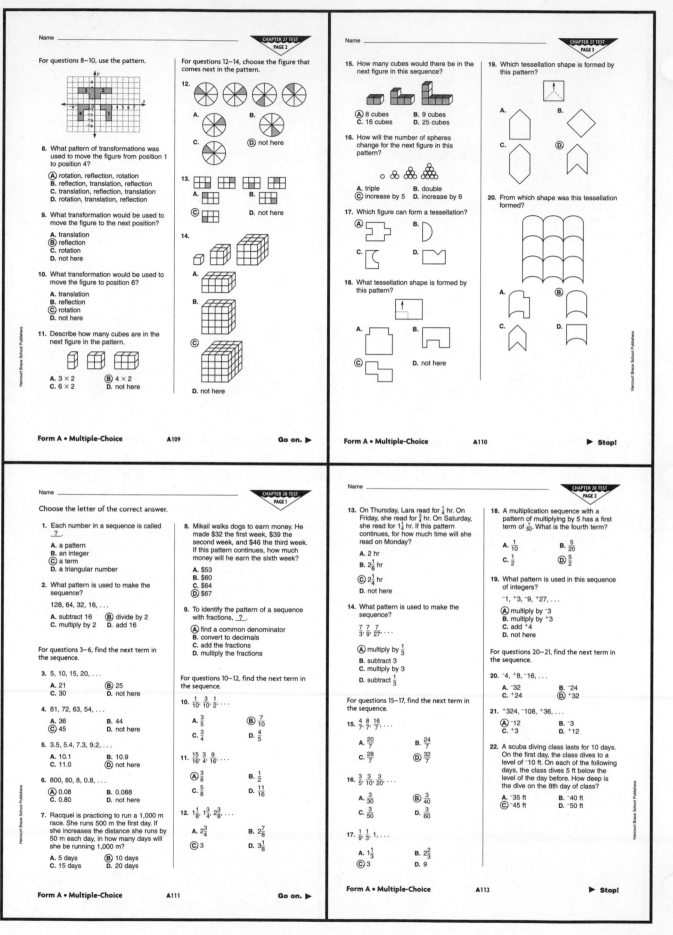

For questions 8–10, use the pattern.

8. What pattern of transformations was used to move the figure from position 1 to position 4?

(A) rotation, reflection, rotation
B. reflection, translation, reflection
C. translation, reflection, translation
D. rotation, translation, reflection

9. What transformation would be used to move the figure to the next position?

A. translation
(B) reflection
C. rotation
D. not here

10. What transformation would be used to move the figure to position 6?

A. translation
B. reflection
(C) rotation
D. not here

11. Describe how many cubes are in the next figure in the pattern.

A. 3 × 2   (B) 4 × 2
C. 6 × 2   D. not here

For questions 12–14, choose the figure that comes next in the pattern.

12.
A.   B.
C.   (D) not here

13.
A.   B.
(C)   D. not here

14.
A.
B.
(C)
D. not here

15. How many cubes would there be in the next figure in this sequence?

(A) 8 cubes   B. 9 cubes
C. 16 cubes   D. 25 cubes

16. How will the number of spheres change for the next figure in this pattern?

A. triple   B. double
(C) increase by 5   D. increase by 6

17. Which figure can form a tessellation?

(A)   B.
C.   D.

18. What tessellation shape is formed by this pattern?

A.   B.
(C)   D. not here

19. Which tessellation shape is formed by this pattern?

A.   B.
C.   (D)

20. From which shape was this tessellation formed?

A.   (B)
C.   D.

Choose the letter of the correct answer.

1. Each number in a sequence is called __?__.

A. a pattern
B. an integer
(C) a term
D. a triangular number

2. What pattern is used to make the sequence?

128, 64, 32, 16, . . .

A. subtract 16   (B) divide by 2
C. multiply by 2   D. add 16

For questions 3–6, find the next term in the sequence.

3. 5, 10, 15, 20, . . .

A. 21   (B) 25
C. 30   D. not here

4. 81, 72, 63, 54, . . .

A. 36   B. 44
(C) 45   D. not here

5. 3.5, 5.4, 7.3, 9.2, . . .

A. 10.1   B. 10.9
C. 11.0   (D) not here

6. 800, 80, 8, 0.8, . . .

(A) 0.08   B. 0.088
C. 0.80   D. not here

7. Racquel is practicing to run a 1,000 m race. She runs 500 m the first day. If she increases the distance she runs by 50 m each day, in how many days will she be running 1,000 m?

A. 5 days   (B) 10 days
C. 15 days   D. 20 days

8. Mikail walks dogs to earn money. He made $32 the first week, $39 the second week, and $46 the third week. If this pattern continues, how much money will he earn the sixth week?

A. $53
B. $60
C. $64
(D) $67

9. To identify the pattern of a sequence with fractions, __?__.

(A) find a common denominator
B. convert to decimals
C. add the fractions
D. multiply the fractions

For questions 10–12, find the next term in the sequence.

10. $\frac{1}{10}$, $\frac{3}{10}$, $\frac{1}{2}$, . . .

A. $\frac{3}{5}$ (B) $\frac{7}{10}$
C. $\frac{3}{4}$ D. $\frac{4}{5}$

11. $\frac{15}{16}$, $\frac{3}{4}$, $\frac{9}{16}$, . . .

(A) $\frac{3}{8}$ B. $\frac{1}{2}$
C. $\frac{5}{8}$ D. $\frac{11}{16}$

12. $1\frac{1}{8}$, $1\frac{3}{4}$, $2\frac{3}{8}$, . . .

A. $2\frac{3}{4}$ B. $2\frac{7}{8}$
(C) 3   D. $3\frac{1}{8}$

13. On Thursday, Lara read for $\frac{1}{4}$ hr. On Friday, she read for $\frac{3}{4}$ hr. On Saturday, she read for $1\frac{1}{4}$ hr. If this pattern continues, for how much time will she read on Monday?

A. 2 hr
B. $2\frac{1}{8}$ hr
(C) $2\frac{1}{4}$ hr
D. not here

14. What pattern is used to make the sequence?

$\frac{7}{3}$, $\frac{7}{9}$, $\frac{7}{27}$, . . .

(A) multiply by $\frac{1}{3}$
B. subtract 3
C. multiply by 3
D. subtract $\frac{1}{3}$

For questions 15–17, find the next term in the sequence.

15. $\frac{4}{7}$, $\frac{8}{7}$, $\frac{16}{7}$, . . .

A. $\frac{20}{7}$ B. $\frac{24}{7}$
C. $\frac{28}{7}$ (D) $\frac{32}{7}$

16. $\frac{3}{5}$, $\frac{3}{10}$, $\frac{3}{20}$, . . .

A. $\frac{3}{30}$ (B) $\frac{3}{40}$
C. $\frac{3}{50}$ D. $\frac{3}{60}$

17. $\frac{1}{9}$, $\frac{1}{3}$, 1, . . .

A. $1\frac{1}{3}$ B. $2\frac{2}{3}$
(C) 3   D. 9

18. A multiplication sequence with a pattern of multiplying by 5 has a first term of $\frac{1}{50}$. What is the fourth term?

A. $\frac{1}{10}$ B. $\frac{5}{20}$
C. $\frac{1}{2}$ (D) $\frac{5}{2}$

19. What pattern is used in this sequence of integers?

$^-1$, $^+3$, $^-9$, $^+27$, . . .

(A) multiply by $^-3$
B. multiply by $^+3$
C. add $^+4$
D. not here

For questions 20–21, find the next term in the sequence.

20. $^-4$, $^+8$, $^-16$, . . .

A. $^-32$ B. $^-24$
C. $^+24$ (D) $^+32$

21. $^+324$, $^-108$, $^+36$, . . .

(A) $^-12$ B. $^-3$
C. $^+3$ D. $^+12$

22. A scuba diving class lasts for 10 days. On the first day, the class dives to a level of $^-10$ ft. On each of the following days, the class dives 5 ft below the level of the day before. How deep is the dive on the 8th day of class?

A. $^-35$ ft   B. $^-40$ ft
(C) $^-45$ ft   D. $^-50$ ft

Multiple-Choice Format • Test Answers

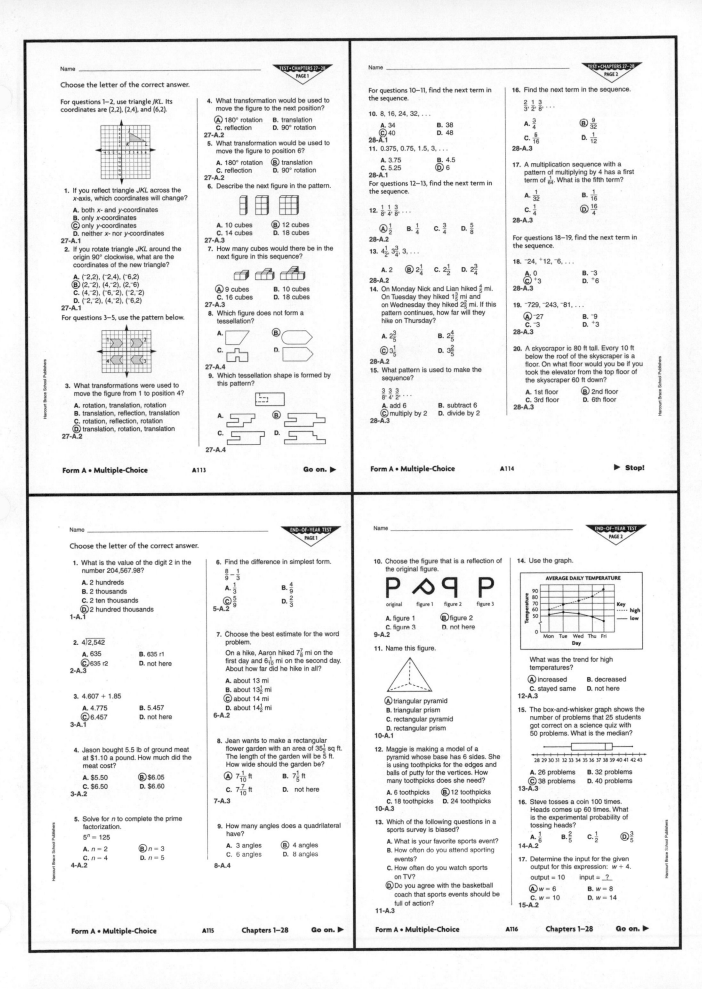

Name _____

Choose the letter of the correct answer.

For questions 1–2, use triangle *JKL*. Its coordinates are (2,2), (2,4), and (6,2).

1. If you reflect triangle *JKL* across the *x*-axis, which coordinates will change?

   A. both *x*- and *y*-coordinates
   B. only *x*-coordinates
   C. only *y*-coordinates
   D. neither *x*- nor *y*-coordinates
   27-A.1

2. If you rotate triangle *JKL* around the origin 90° clockwise, what are the coordinates of the new triangle?

   A. (⁻2,2), (⁻2,4), (⁻6,2)
   B. (2,⁻2), (4,⁻2), (2,⁻6)
   C. (4,⁻2), (⁻6,2), (⁻2,⁻2)
   D. (⁻2,⁻2), (4,⁻2), (⁻6,2)
   27-A.1

For questions 3–5, use the pattern below.

3. What transformations were used to move the figure from 1 to position 4?

   A. rotation, translation, rotation
   B. translation, reflection, translation
   C. rotation, reflection, rotation
   D. translation, rotation, translation
   27-A.2

4. What transformation would be used to move the figure to the next position?

   A. 180° rotation   B. translation
   C. reflection   D. 90° rotation
   27-A.2

5. What transformation would be used to move the figure to position 6?

   A. 180° rotation   B. translation
   C. reflection   D. 90° rotation
   27-A.2

6. Describe the next figure in the pattern.

   A. 10 cubes   B. 12 cubes
   C. 14 cubes   D. 18 cubes
   27-A.3

7. How many cubes would there be in the next figure in this sequence?

   A. 9 cubes   B. 10 cubes
   C. 16 cubes   D. 18 cubes
   27-A.3

8. Which figure does not form a tessellation?

   A.   B.
   C.   D.
   27-A.4

9. Which tessellation shape is formed by this pattern?

   A.   B.
   C.   D.
   27-A.4

Form A • Multiple-Choice   A113   **Go on. ▶**

Name _____

For questions 10–11, find the next term in the sequence.

10. 8, 16, 24, 32, . . .

    A. 34   B. 38
    C. 40   D. 48
    28-A.1

11. 0.375, 0.75, 1.5, 3, . . .

    A. 3.75   B. 4.5
    C. 5.25   D. 6
    28-A.1

For questions 12–13, find the next term in the sequence.

12. $\frac{1}{8}, \frac{1}{4}, \frac{3}{8}, \ldots$

    A. $\frac{1}{2}$ B. $\frac{1}{4}$ C. $\frac{3}{4}$ D. $\frac{5}{8}$
    28-A.2

13. $4\frac{1}{2}, 3\frac{3}{4}, 3, \ldots$

    A. 2   B. $2\frac{1}{4}$ C. $2\frac{1}{2}$ D. $2\frac{3}{4}$
    28-A.2

14. On Monday Nick and Lian hiked $\frac{4}{5}$ mi. On Tuesday they hiked $1\frac{3}{5}$ mi and on Wednesday they hiked $2\frac{2}{5}$ mi. If this pattern continues, how far will they hike on Thursday?

    A. $2\frac{3}{5}$ B. $2\frac{4}{5}$
    C. $3\frac{1}{5}$ D. $3\frac{2}{5}$
    28-A.2

15. What pattern is used to make the sequence?

    $\frac{3}{8}, \frac{3}{4}, \frac{3}{2}, \ldots$

    A. add 6   B. subtract 6
    C. multiply by 2 D. divide by 2
    28-A.3

16. Find the next term in the sequence.

    $\frac{2}{3}, \frac{1}{2}, \frac{3}{8}, \ldots$

    A. $\frac{3}{4}$ B. $\frac{9}{32}$
    C. $\frac{5}{16}$ D. $\frac{1}{12}$
    28-A.3

17. A multiplication sequence with a pattern of multiplying by 4 has a first term of $\frac{1}{64}$. What is the fifth term?

    A. $\frac{1}{32}$ B. $\frac{1}{16}$
    C. $\frac{1}{4}$ D. $\frac{16}{4}$
    28-A.3

For questions 18–19, find the next term in the sequence.

18. ⁻24, ⁺12, ⁻6, . . .

    A. 0   B. ⁻3
    C. ⁺3   D. ⁺6
    28-A.3

19. ⁻729, ⁻243, ⁻81, . . .

    A. ⁻27   B. ⁻9
    C. ⁻3   D. ⁺3
    28-A.3

20. A skyscraper is 80 ft tall. Every 10 ft below the roof of the skyscraper is a floor. On what floor would you be if you took the elevator from the top floor of the skyscraper 60 ft down?

    A. 1st floor   B. 2nd floor
    C. 3rd floor   D. 6th floor
    28-A.3

Form A • Multiple-Choice   A114   **▶ Stop!**

Name _____

Choose the letter of the correct answer.

1. What is the value of the digit 2 in the number 204,567.98?

   A. 2 hundreds
   B. 2 thousands
   C. 2 ten thousands
   D. 2 hundred thousands
   1-A.1

2. 4)2,542

   A. 635   B. 635 r1
   C. 635 r2   D. not here
   2-A.3

3. 4.607 + 1.85

   A. 4.775   B. 5.457
   C. 6.457   D. not here
   3-A.1

4. Jason bought 5.5 lb of ground meat at $1.10 a pound. How much did the meat cost?

   A. $5.50   B. $6.05
   C. $6.50   D. $6.60
   3-A.2

5. Solve for *n* to complete the prime factorization.

   $5^n = 125$

   A. *n* = 2   B. *n* = 3
   C. *n* = 4   D. *n* = 5
   4-A.2

6. Find the difference in simplest form.

   $\frac{8}{9} - \frac{1}{3}$

   A. $\frac{1}{3}$ B. $\frac{4}{9}$
   C. $\frac{5}{9}$ D. $\frac{2}{3}$
   5-A.2

7. Choose the best estimate for the word problem.

   On a hike, Aaron hiked $7\frac{7}{8}$ mi on the first day and $6\frac{1}{10}$ mi on the second day. About how far did he hike in all?

   A. about 13 mi
   B. about $13\frac{1}{2}$ mi
   C. about 14 mi
   D. about $14\frac{1}{2}$ mi
   6-A.2

8. Jean wants to make a rectangular flower garden with an area of $35\frac{1}{2}$ sq ft. The length of the garden will be 5 ft. How wide should the garden be?

   A. $7\frac{1}{10}$ ft   B. $7\frac{1}{5}$ ft
   C. $7\frac{7}{10}$ ft   D. not here
   7-A.3

9. How many angles does a quadrilateral have?

   A. 3 angles   B. 4 angles
   C. 6 angles   D. 8 angles
   8-A.4

Form A • Multiple-Choice   A115   Chapters 1–28   **Go on. ▶**

Name _____

10. Choose the figure that is a reflection of the original figure.

    original   figure 1   figure 2   figure 3

    A. figure 1   B. figure 2
    C. figure 3   D. not here
    9-A.2

11. Name this figure.

    A. triangular pyramid
    B. triangular prism
    C. rectangular pyramid
    D. rectangular prism
    10-A.1

12. Maggie is making a model of a pyramid whose base has 6 sides. She is using toothpicks for the edges and balls of putty for the vertices. How many toothpicks does she need?

    A. 6 toothpicks   B. 12 toothpicks
    C. 18 toothpicks   D. 24 toothpicks
    10-A.3

13. Which of the following questions in a sports survey is biased?

    A. What is your favorite sports event?
    B. How often do you attend sporting events?
    C. How often do you watch sports on TV?
    D. Do you agree with the basketball coach that sports events should be full of action?
    11-A.3

14. Use the graph.

    AVERAGE DAILY TEMPERATURE

    Key
    · · · · high
    —— low

    What was the trend for high temperatures?

    A. increased   B. decreased
    C. stayed same   D. not here
    12-A.3

15. The box-and-whisker graph shows the number of problems that 25 students got correct on a science quiz with 50 problems. What is the median?

    28 29 30 31 32 33 34 35 36 37 38 39 40 41 42 43

    A. 26 problems   B. 32 problems
    C. 38 problems   D. 40 problems
    13-A.3

16. Steve tosses a coin 100 times. Heads comes up 60 times. What is the experimental probability of tossing heads?

    A. $\frac{1}{6}$ B. $\frac{2}{5}$ C. $\frac{1}{2}$ D. $\frac{3}{5}$
    14-A.2

17. Determine the input for the given output for this expression: *w* + 4.

    output = 10   input = _?_

    A. *w* = 6   B. *w* = 8
    C. *w* = 10   D. *w* = 14
    15-A.2

Form A • Multiple-Choice   A116   Chapters 1–28   **Go on. ▶**

Harcourt Brace School Publishers

Multiple-Choice Format • Test Answers   **147**

18. $b - 2 = 6$
- **A.** $b = 4$
- **B.** $b = 6$
- **Ⓒ** $b = 8$
- **D.** $b = 12$

15-A.3

19. $2m = 8$
- **Ⓐ** $m = 4$
- **B.** $m = 6$
- **C.** $m = 10$
- **D.** $m = 16$

16-A.1

20. What is 23°C converted to degrees Fahrenheit? Use the formula $F = (\frac{9}{5} \times C) + 32$. Round to the nearest degree.
- **A.** 41°F
- **B.** 45°F
- **C.** 65°F
- **Ⓓ** 73°F

16-A.3

21. Mike is in a 20-mi bike race. How long is this ride in kilometers? (1 mi = 1.609 km)
- **A.** 12.43 km
- **Ⓑ** 32.18 km
- **C.** 123.4 km
- **D.** 321.8 km

16-A.5

22. Paulo answered 45 of the 50 problems on his math test correctly. What percent did he answer correctly?
- **A.** 45%
- **B.** 80%
- **Ⓒ** 90%
- **D.** 95%

17-A.3

23. What is 60% of 80?
- **A.** 40
- **B.** 60
- **C.** 80
- **Ⓓ** not here

18-A.1

24. Beatrice had $200 that earned 5% simple interest a year in a bank. After 2 years, she withdrew her money. How much did she withdraw?
- **A.** $10
- **B.** $20
- **C.** $210
- **Ⓓ** $220

18-A.4

25. Find n in this pair of similar triangles.

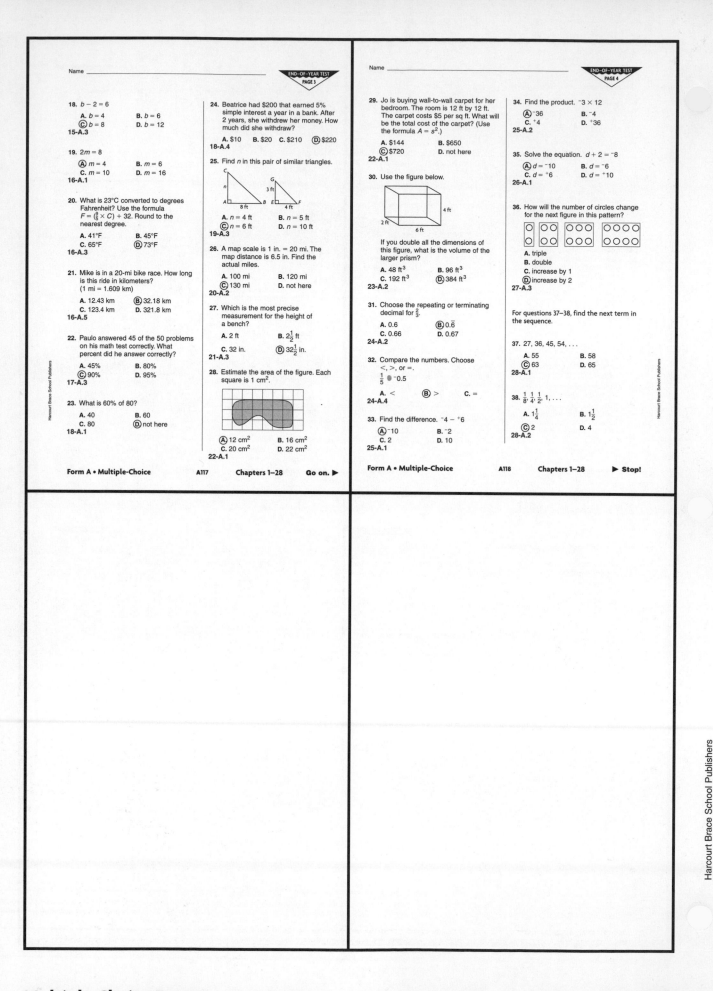

- **A.** $n = 4$ ft
- **B.** $n = 5$ ft
- **Ⓒ** $n = 6$ ft
- **D.** $n = 10$ ft

19-A.3

26. A map scale is 1 in. = 20 mi. The map distance is 6.5 in. Find the actual miles.
- **A.** 100 mi
- **B.** 120 mi
- **Ⓒ** 130 mi
- **D.** not here

20-A.2

27. Which is the most precise measurement for the height of a bench?
- **A.** 2 ft
- **B.** $2\frac{1}{2}$ ft
- **C.** 32 in.
- **Ⓓ** $32\frac{1}{2}$ in.

21-A.3

28. Estimate the area of the figure. Each square is 1 cm².

- **Ⓐ** 12 cm²
- **B.** 16 cm²
- **C.** 20 cm²
- **D.** 22 cm²

22-A.1

29. Jo is buying wall-to-wall carpet for her bedroom. The room is 12 ft by 12 ft. The carpet costs $5 per sq ft. What will be the total cost of the carpet? (Use the formula $A = s^2$.)
- **A.** $144
- **B.** $650
- **Ⓒ** $720
- **D.** not here

22-A.1

30. Use the figure below.

If you double all the dimensions of this figure, what is the volume of the larger prism?
- **A.** 48 ft³
- **B.** 96 ft³
- **C.** 192 ft³
- **Ⓓ** 384 ft³

23-A.2

31. Choose the repeating or terminating decimal for $\frac{2}{3}$.
- **A.** 0.6
- **Ⓑ** $0.\overline{6}$
- **C.** 0.66
- **D.** 0.67

24-A.2

32. Compare the numbers. Choose <, >, or =.
$\frac{1}{5}$ ● ⁻0.5
- **A.** <
- **Ⓑ** >
- **C.** =

24-A.4

33. Find the difference. ⁻4 − ⁺6
- **Ⓐ** ⁻10
- **B.** ⁻2
- **C.** 2
- **D.** 10

25-A.1

34. Find the product. ⁻3 × 12
- **Ⓐ** ⁻36
- **B.** ⁻4
- **C.** ⁺4
- **D.** ⁺36

25-A.2

35. Solve the equation. $d + 2 = ⁻8$
- **Ⓐ** $d = ⁻10$
- **B.** $d = ⁻6$
- **C.** $d = ⁺6$
- **D.** $d = ⁺10$

26-A.1

36. How will the number of circles change for the next figure in this pattern?

- **A.** triple
- **B.** double
- **C.** increase by 1
- **Ⓓ** increase by 2

27-A.3

For questions 37–38, find the next term in the sequence.

37. 27, 36, 45, 54, . . .
- **A.** 55
- **B.** 58
- **Ⓒ** 63
- **D.** 65

28-A.1

38. $\frac{1}{8}, \frac{1}{4}, \frac{1}{2}, 1, \ldots$
- **A.** $1\frac{1}{4}$
- **B.** $1\frac{1}{2}$
- **Ⓒ** 2
- **D.** 4

28-A.2

Multiple-Choice Format • Test Answers

Free-Response Format Tests

The free-response format tests are useful as diagnostic tools. The work the student performs provides information about what the student understands about the concepts and/or procedures so that appropriate reteaching can be chosen from the many options in the program.

There is an Inventory Test which tests the learning goals from the previous grade level. This can be used at the beginning of the year or as a placement test when a new student enters your class.

There is a Chapter Test for each chapter and a Multi-Chapter Test to be used as review after several chapters in a content cluster. Also, there are Cumulative Tests at the same point as the Multi-Chapter Tests. The Cumulative Test reviews content from Chapter 1 through the current chapter.

Math Advantage also provides multiple-choice format tests that parallel the free-response format tests. You may wish to use one form as a pretest and one form as a posttest.

Harcourt Brace School Publishers

Write the correct answer.

1. What is the value of the digit 7 in the number 140,785,632?

_____

2. Order these numbers from least to greatest.

   20,480; 20,084; 20,408

_____

3. Mark has 1,500 baseball cards. His sister has 625 baseball cards. How many more cards does Mark have than his sister?

_____

4. What is $5,000 + 700 + 0 + 5 + 0 + 0.03 + 0.004$ in standard form?

_____

5. $6.5 - 0.145 = n$

_____

6. Estimate the sum to the nearest tenth.

   $\begin{array}{r} 4.23 \\ +3.86 \\ \hline \end{array}$

_____

7. Find the area of the rectangle.

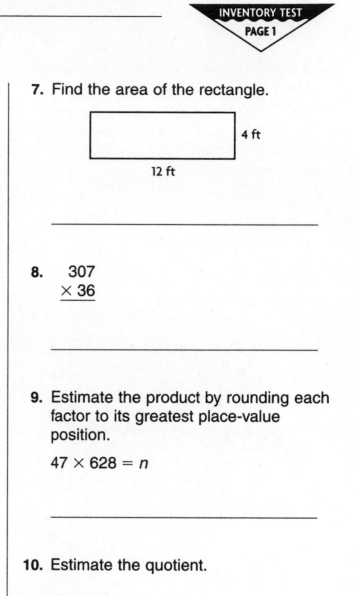

   4 ft

   12 ft

_____

8. $\begin{array}{r} 307 \\ \times\ 36 \\ \hline \end{array}$

_____

9. Estimate the product by rounding each factor to its greatest place-value position.

   $47 \times 628 = n$

_____

10. Estimate the quotient.

    $6\overline{)193}$

_____

11. $32\overline{)285}$

_____

Name _____

12. Write the number sentence that can be used to solve the word problem.

Joe bought a new CD player that cost $1,470. He paid for it in 24 monthly payments. How much was each payment?

_____

13. What is the mean for the set of data?

18, 25, 15, 18, 32, 18

_____

14. Use the graph.

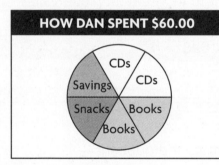

HOW DAN SPENT $60.00

What fraction of his money did Dan spend on CDs?

_____

15. Is it *likely, unlikely, impossible,* or *certain* that you would pull a black marble from a bag that has 9 blue marbles and 2 red marbles?

_____

16. Use the spinner.

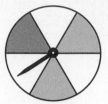

What is the probability the pointer will stop on a white section?

_____

17. 4.37
    $\times$ 3.6

_____

18. $4\overline{)18.32}$

_____

19. What is the most reasonable metric unit you might use for finding the length of your classroom?

_____

20. In an 8-person relay race, each person on the relay team must run 500 m. How many kilometers long is the whole race?

_____

21. Write the fraction to tell what part of the strip is white.

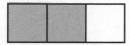

_____

22. Use $<$, $>$, or $=$ to compare the fractions.

$\frac{2}{3} \bigcirc \frac{1}{4}$

_____

23. Use division to write an equivalent fraction for $\frac{7}{28}$.

_____

24. Mike made some bread. He used 4 c of whole wheat flour. He used 12 c of flour in all. In simplest terms, what fraction of the flour was whole wheat flour?

_____

For questions 25–26, use fraction strips to find the sum or difference expressed in simplest form.

25. $\frac{2}{3} + \frac{1}{12} = \underline{\ ?\ }$

_____

26. $\frac{3}{4} - \frac{1}{12} = \underline{\ ?\ }$

_____

27. Estimate the sum. $\quad \frac{1}{8} + \frac{4}{5}$

_____

28. Find the answer in simplest form.

$$1\frac{2}{3}$$
$$+4\frac{5}{6}$$

_____

29. Book reports are due on April 20. Barry will work on his report for 2 weeks. When should he begin working on the report?

_____

30. Find the product in simplest form.

$\frac{2}{5} \times 3\frac{1}{2} = n$

_____

Name _____

31. Use this figure.

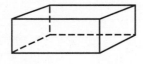

Name an obtuse angle found in this figure.

_____

32. Name a quadrilateral that has 2 pairs of congruent sides and 4 right angles.

_____

33. A cake pan has a diameter of 8 in. What is the radius of the pan?

_____

34. Identify the solid figure.

_____

35. Write a ratio that is equivalent to 3:21?.

_____

36. Find the length of the missing side in the similar triangles.

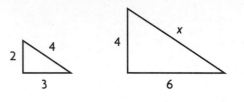

_____

37. What is 36% written as a decimal?

_____

38. What is $\frac{2}{5}$ written as a percent?

_____

▶ **Stop!**

Write the correct answer.

For questions 1–2, use the place-value chart.

PLACE VALUE									
9	6	4	5	8	2	7	.1	0	3

1. What is the value of the digit 6?

_____

2. What is the value of the digit 3?

_____

3. What is the value of the digit 5 in the number 147,250.68?

_____

4. What is the value of the digit 2 in the number 3.02719?

_____

5. Write the standard form of six million, five hundred eighty thousand, twelve.

_____

6. Write the standard form of thirteen hundredths.

_____

7. Is 8.528 greater than, equal to, or less than 8.534?

8.528 is _____ 8.534.

8. Write the following numbers in order from greatest to least.

593.7; 539.75; 593.73

_____

9. The snowfall was 6.3 in. during December, 9.9 in. during January, 6.6 in. during February, and 7.5 in. during March. Write the numbers in order from the greatest to the least snowfall.

_____

10. At the swim meet, the four fastest swimmers in a race were Scott, Theo, Jesse, and Paul. Scott finished the race in 34.56 sec, Theo finished in 33.65 sec, Jesse finished in 34.78 sec, and Paul in 33.92 sec. Who finished in third place?

_____

11. When changing 0.7 to a fraction, what number would you use in the denominator?

_____

12. The way to change a fraction to a decimal is to __?__ the numerator by the denominator.

_____

13. What is $\frac{3}{8}$ written as a decimal?

_____

14. What sign will make the following inequality true?

$\frac{13}{20}$ ● 0.70

_____

15. Mrs. Gordon's stock went up $0.625 yesterday. What fraction did the stock go up?

_____

16. Nina swam $\frac{9}{20}$ mi. What is the distance she swam, expressed as a decimal?

_____

17. How many zeros are in the standard form of 10^{13}?

_____

18. What is $15 \times 15 \times 15 \times 15 \times 15$ written in exponent form?

_____

19. What is the value of 12^2?

_____

20. What is the value of 3^4?

_____

21. Is $^{+}8$ greater than, equal to, or less than $^{-}9$?

_____

For questions 22–23, write the integers in order from least to greatest.

22. $^{-}5$, $^{+}3$, $^{+}6$, $^{-}4$

_____

23. $^{-}8$, $^{+}1$, $^{-}7$, 0

_____

24. What is the opposite of $^{+}74$?

_____

Write the correct answer.

For questions 1–2, use mental math.

1. $14 + 9 + 26$

_____

2. $37 + 18 + 22 + 13$

_____

For questions 3–4, use compensation.

3. $44 - 28$

_____

4. $65 - 39$

_____

5. The piñata was filled with 83 jelly beans, some red and some black. There were 15 more red jelly beans than black ones. How many red jelly beans were there?

_____

6. Iris recycled a total of 48 newspapers and magazines. She recycled 10 more newspapers than magazines. How many newspapers did she recycle?

_____

7. During a 30-day period, there were 6 more rainy days than dry days. How many rainy days were there?

_____

8. The perimeter of the class garden is 52 ft. The length is 8 ft longer than the width. What is the length of the garden?

_____

9. Which property is being used in the multiplication problem below?

$5 \times 3 = 3 \times 5$

_____Property

For questions 10–11, use mental math to find the product.

10. $2 \times 6 \times 7$

_____

11. $6 \times 15 \times 4$

_____

12. Find the missing factor.

$52 \times 16 = (52 \times \square) + (52 \times 6)$

_____

13. Rhonda is solving the multiplication problem below. What mistake, if any, has Rhonda made?

$$\begin{array}{r} 105 \\ \times\ 24 \\ \hline 420 \\ 210 \end{array}$$

_____

14. In this division problem, where would you place the first digit of the quotient?

$6\overline{)452}$

in the _____ place, or over the ___

15.   280
       $\times$ 42

16.   4,327
       $\times$ 156

17. $14\overline{)882}$

18. $20\overline{)3,054}$

19. The football stadium holds 2,500 people. All 7 games held at the stadium were sold out. How many people attended games at the stadium?

_____

20. The Hudson family drove 1,248 mi on their vacation. They used 48 gal of gas. How many miles per gallon did they get?

_____

21. Estimate the difference to the nearest hundred.

     7,385
    $-4,712$

22. Estimate the product to the nearest hundred.

      621
     $\times 569$

23. On Monday 312 students visited the museum. On Tuesday 273 students visited the museum, and on Wednesday, 341. About how many students visited the museum in all? Round to the nearest hundred students.

_____

24. For the upcoming concert, 5,589 tickets were sold in 73 min. About how many tickets were sold per minute? Round to the nearest ten tickets.

_____

Harcourt Brace School Publishers

Write the correct answer.

For questions 1–2, estimate the sum to the nearest whole number.

1. 3.28 + 1.71 + 0.65

   _____

2. 5.05 + 1.38 + 13.53

   _____

For questions 3–4, find the sum.

3. 8.63 + 0.74

   _____

4. $42.38 + $8.89 + $112.76

   _____

5. Jill needs to buy some camping equipment. A sleeping bag costs $21.75, a compass costs $5.38, and a water jug costs $2.98. How much money does Jill need to buy the equipment?

   _____

6. It rained 3.4 in. in April, 2.7 in. in May, 0.8 in. in June, and 1.5 in. in July. How much did it rain during the four months?

   _____

7. 4.7 − 2.3

   _____

8. 8.571 − 6.729

   _____

9. $53.12 − $7.25

   _____

10. 27.65 − 13.0389

    _____

11. The basketball team has a 0.47 shooting average this year. Last year it had a 0.39 shooting average. What is the difference between the two averages?

    _____

12. Ray earned $78.50 last week mowing lawns. This week he earned $112.25. How much more did he earn this week?

    _____

Form B • Free-Response

Go on. ▶

Name _____

13. Use the decimal square to find
4 × 0.12.

0.12 0.12 0.12 0.12

_____

14. How many decimal places are there in
the product 1.48 × 0.093?

_____

15. 2.4 × 3

_____

16. 0.81 × 0.27

_____

17. $6.15 × 5

_____

18. 36.79 × 8

_____

19. Mrs. Velarde put 12.8 gal of gas in her
car. Gas costs $1.35 per gal. How
much did the gas cost?

_____

20. A 2-liter soft drink bottle costs $1.79.
Mr. Durand's class bought six 2-liter
bottles for their class picnic. How much
did they spend on soft drinks?

_____

21. By what number should you multiply to
make the divisor a whole number?

0.4)‾8.132

_____

22. 21.32 ÷ 8.2

_____

23. 54.6 ÷ 3.5

_____

24. 7.5)‾4.125

_____

Form B • Free-Response   B160   ▶ **Stop!**

Harcourt Brace School Publishers

Write the correct answer.

1. Write all the prime numbers that are between 10 and 20.

_____

2. What is the next multiple of 9?

9, 18, 27, 36, _____

3. Write all the factors of 35.

_____

4. List all the composite numbers from 40 through 50.

_____

5. In September, Bo worked every fourth day at the store. He started on September 5. How many days did Bo work in September?

_____

6. Joe skated with Wendy every fifth day in May, beginning on May 3. How many times did Joe and Wendy skate in May?

_____

7. What is the missing factor?

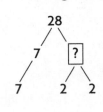

_____

8. What is the missing factor?

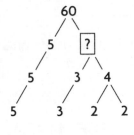

_____

9. What is the prime factorization of 45?

_____

10. Solve for *n* to complete the prime factorization.

$2^n \times 3 = 48$

_____

11. What is the least common multiple of 5 and 6?

5:	5	10	15	20	25	30	35	40
6:	6	12	18	24	30	36	42	48

_____

Name _____

12. Use the factor trees to find the greatest common factor of 18 and 27.

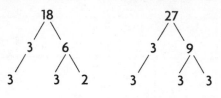

_____

13. What is the LCM of 8 and 12?

_____

14. What is the LCM of 10 and 25?

_____

15. What is the GCF of 24 and 32?

_____

16. Wanda has 51 party favors and 34 balloons for her party. What is the greatest number of people Wanda can have at her party so that each person receives the same number of party favors and the same number of balloons?

_____

For questions 17–20, write the fraction in simplest form.

17. $\frac{6}{36} =$ _____

18. $\frac{36}{60} =$ _____

19. $\frac{24}{56} =$ _____

20. $\frac{36}{81} =$ _____

21. The model shows 4 whole pizzas and $\frac{3}{4}$ of another pizza. Write a fraction to show this.

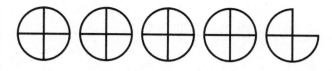

_____

22. What is $3\frac{1}{3}$ written as a fraction?

_____

23. What is $\frac{32}{5}$ written as a mixed number?

_____

24. What is the missing number?

$7\frac{7}{8} = \frac{\blacksquare}{8}$

_____

Harcourt Brace School Publishers

Form B • Free-Response   **B168**   ▶ **Stop!**

Name 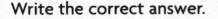 _____

Write the correct answer.

Give answers in simplest form.

1. Use the model to find the difference.

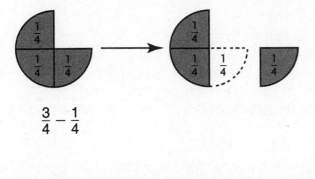

$$\frac{3}{4} - \frac{1}{4}$$

_____

2. $\frac{3}{12} + \frac{7}{12}$

_____

3. $\frac{15}{16} - \frac{7}{16}$

_____

4. $\frac{5}{8}$ of Gail's rock collection consists of quartz. How much of her collection is not quartz?

_____

5. Use the diagram to find the sum.

$\frac{1}{2}$		$\frac{1}{4}$
$\frac{1}{4}$	$\frac{1}{4}$	$\frac{1}{4}$

$$\frac{1}{2} + \frac{1}{4}$$

_____

6. Use the diagram to find the difference.

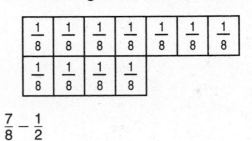

$$\frac{7}{8} - \frac{1}{2}$$

_____

For questions 7–8, find the sum or difference.

7. $\frac{3}{4} - \frac{7}{12}$

_____

8. $\frac{2}{3} + \frac{1}{9}$

_____

9. What is the LCM of the denominators of $\frac{3}{4} + \frac{7}{10}$?

_____

10. What LCM would you use to rewrite the problem with equivalent fractions?

$$\frac{4}{5} + \frac{1}{3}$$

_____

Form B • Free-Response   B169   **Go on.** ▶

Name _____

For questions 11–12, find each sum.

11. $\frac{3}{8} + \frac{5}{12}$

_____

12. $\frac{7}{10} + \frac{3}{15}$

_____

13. The math class spent $\frac{1}{6}$ hr reviewing for the test, $\frac{2}{3}$ hr taking the test, and $\frac{1}{4}$ hr discussing the test. How many hours was this in all?

_____

14. Mr. Olson drank $\frac{2}{3}$ c of soda at lunch and $\frac{3}{4}$ c of soda at dinner. How much soda did Mr. Olson drink?

_____

15. $\frac{2}{3} - \frac{5}{8}$

_____

16. $\frac{3}{4} - \frac{3}{10}$

_____

17. Ross spent $\frac{3}{4}$ hr on science homework and $\frac{7}{12}$ hr on social studies homework. How much more time did he spend on science homework?

_____

18. Donna has $\frac{7}{8}$ bag of sugar for cooking. While baking desserts she uses $\frac{5}{6}$ bag of sugar. How much sugar is remaining?

_____

For questions 19–20, use the number line.

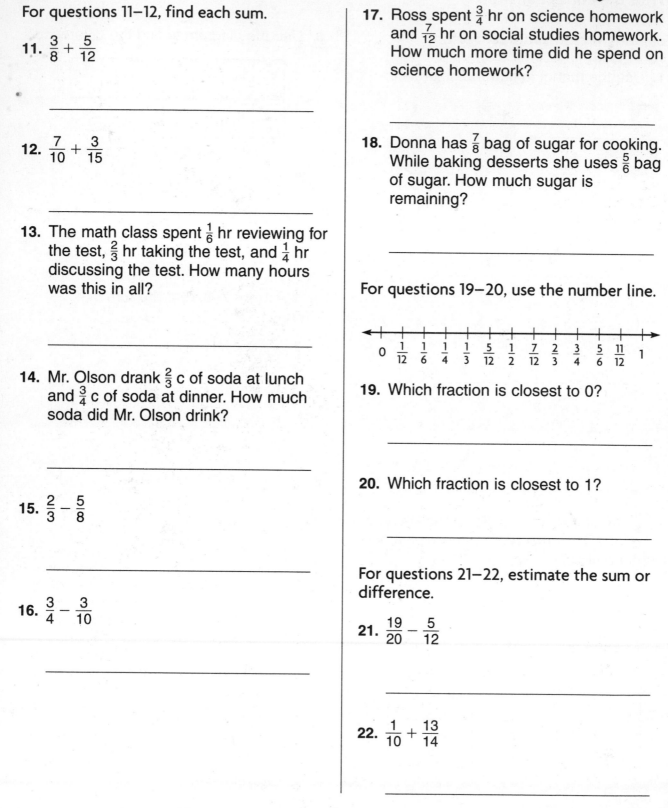

19. Which fraction is closest to 0?

_____

20. Which fraction is closest to 1?

_____

For questions 21–22, estimate the sum or difference.

21. $\frac{19}{20} - \frac{5}{12}$

_____

22. $\frac{1}{10} + \frac{13}{14}$

_____

Harcourt Brace School Publishers

Name _____

Write the correct answer.

1. Write the standard form of forty-two million, six hundred three thousand, seven hundred twelve.

   _____

2. What is the value of the digit 8 in the number 3.078?

   _____

3. Write $\frac{2}{5}$ as a decimal.

   _____

4. What is $3 \times 3 \times 3 \times 3$ written in exponent form?

   _____

5. Write the integers in order from greatest to least.

   $^-7, 1, 7, 0, 6$

   _____

6. Use mental math to find the sum.

   $45 + 8 + 25 + 12$

   _____

7. Jack has a total of 36 red and blue pencils. He has 4 more red pencils than blue pencils. How many blue pencils does Jack have?

   _____

8. $\begin{array}{r} 380 \\ \times\ 46 \\ \hline \end{array}$

   _____

9. $8\overline{)4{,}576}$

   _____

10. Write the best estimate of the product.

    $\begin{array}{r} 66 \\ \times 19 \\ \hline \end{array}$

   _____

11. The diving competition was held once a day for 18 days. There were 4,237 people who attended the competitions. About how many people attended each of the competitions?

   _____

12. $85.63 - 18.9$

_____

13. Cody bought 6.8 lb of oranges at $0.70 a pound. How much did the oranges cost?

_____

14. $37.58 \div 0.05$

_____

15. Which of these numbers is a composite number?

31, 21, 17, 23

_____

16. What is the prime factorization of 80?

_____

17. What is the GCF of 18 and 30?

_____

18. Write $\frac{18}{24}$ in simplest form.

_____

19. Write $\frac{27}{8}$ as a mixed number.

_____

20. What is the missing number?

$7\frac{1}{5} = \frac{?}{5}$

_____

For questions 21–22, find the sum or difference. Answers are in simplest form.

21. $\frac{9}{12} - \frac{7}{12}$

_____

22. $\frac{7}{9} + \frac{2}{3}$

_____

23. Estimate the difference.

$\frac{8}{9} - \frac{1}{11}$

_____

For questions 24–25, find the sum or difference. Answers are in simplest form.

24. $3\frac{3}{4} + 2\frac{5}{8}$

_____

25. $3\frac{2}{3} - 1\frac{5}{12}$

_____

26. Write the best estimate for the word problem.

Timmy bought $3\frac{9}{10}$ lb of bananas on Wednesday and $1\frac{1}{8}$ lb of bananas on Friday. About how many pounds of bananas did he buy?

_____

For questions 27–28, find the product or quotient. Answers are in simplest form.

27. $3\frac{3}{7} \times \frac{5}{8}$

_____

28. $\frac{5}{12} \div \frac{2}{3}$

_____

29. Jocelyn wants to make a rectangular garden with an area of $27\frac{1}{2}$ sq ft. The length of the garden will be 8 ft. How wide should the garden be?

_____

30. An angle that measures 85° is classified as a(n) __?__.

_____

31. Could the measure of the angle shown below be 120°?

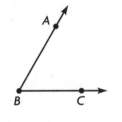

_____

32. Does the construction below show congruent line segments?

_____

33. How many angles does a pentagon have?

_____

34. This figure has rotational symmetry. What is the angle measure of each turn?

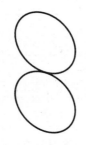

_____

35. Which figure is a translation of the original figure?

Original   Figure 1   Figure 2   Figure 3

_____

36. Ted wants to make a design that will tessellate a plane. Can he use a hexagon?

_____

37. Mike built a pyramid using toothpicks for edges and miniature marshmallows for vertices. He used 8 toothpicks and 5 marshmallows What kind of pyramid did he build?

_____

38. What solid figure has these views?

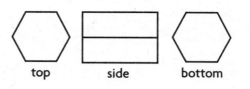

top   side   bottom

_____

39. The bottom view of a solid figure is a circle. The front view is a triangle. What kind of figure is it?

_____

40. Tanya wants to make a paperweight by covering each face of a pentagonal pyramid with a separate piece of paper. How many pieces of paper will she use?

_____

Write the correct answer.

1. The Kindergarten teachers plan to have 1 sixth-grade student accompany every 2 kindergarten students on a trip to the zoo. What information do they need to figure out how many sixth-grade students are needed?

_____

2. If you survey 1 out of every 15 voters exiting the polling place, how many people should you survey from a sample of 4,500 voters?

_____

3. Is the following question in a customer survey about the service provided by the clerks in a well-known chain store biased or not biased?

Why do you think our staff is well-trained and courteous?

_____

For questions 4–5, use the data showing the ages of listeners to a local radio station who took part in a survey.

Ages of Listeners					
19	50	42	38	52	21
61	34	47	36	34	71
42	59	22	17	39	67

4. What is the range?

_____

5. If you want to arrange the data into 6 age intervals, how many ages should be put into each interval?

_____

6. Mr. Ryan has scored 31 science tests that he gave to his sixth-grade class. What type of graph would be most useful for displaying this data?

_____

7. What type of graph would be most appropriate to display the data below?

ABC Company Car and Truck Sales						
Month	Jan.	Feb.	Mar.	Apr.	May	June
Cars	5	8	14	15	14	23
Trucks	10	15	10	10	11	8

_____

For questions 8–9, use the following data.

Lisi wants to make a circle graph showing how she spends her weekly allowance. She spends $5 for school lunches, $4 for the movies, $3.50 for personal needs, and $2.50 for treats.

8. In the circle graph, what does the circle represent?

_____

9. What angle measure should Lisi use for the Movies section of the graph?

_____

Form B • Free-Response

Go on. ▶

Name _____

For questions 10–11, use the graph.

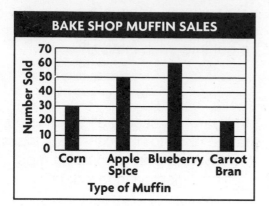

BAKE SHOP MUFFIN SALES

10. Which type of muffin was least popular with the customers?

_____

11. How does the number of corn muffins sold compare with the number of blueberry muffins sold?

_____

12. A used car was priced at $5,200 the first month it was on the lot. After 3 months it was priced at $4,900. After 6 months the price was reduced to $4,600. What will the price probably be at the end of 12 months if the car has not been sold?

_____

For questions 13–14, use the table below.

Points Dan Scored During Basketball Season				
14	21	17	25	17
18	16	22	17	23

13. What is the mean number of points Dan scored?

_____

14. What is the median of Dan's scores?

_____

15. Marie has signed up for ballet lessons. She can take lessons on Monday, Tuesday, Thursday or Friday at 3:00, 4:00, or 5:00. How many choices does she have?

_____

16. You toss a cube labeled 1, 2, 3, 4, 5, 6. What is P(2, 4, or 6)?

_____

17. Carla collects T-shirts. In her drawer there are 3 red shirts, 2 black shirts, 4 blue shirts, 5 green shirts, and 6 yellow shirts. If she chooses a shirt without looking, what is the probability of choosing a blue T-shirt?

_____

18. Margaret hit the bullseye on the dart board in 18 of her last 45 tries. How many bullseyes can she expect to make in 100 tries?

_____

Name _____

Write the correct answer.

1. The rainfall averages for three months are 0.470, 0.474, 0.407. Write these averages in order from greatest to least.

   _____

2. Write 0.08 as a fraction.

   _____

3. What is the value of 3^4?

   _____

4. What is the opposite of $^+6$?

   _____

5. Use mental math to find the difference.
   $92 - 37$

   _____

6. Martha sold a total of 57 blue or yellow pennants at the soccer game. She sold 11 more yellow pennants than blue pennants. How many yellow pennants did she sell?

   _____

7.   368
   $\times\ 537$

   _____

8. Write the best estimate of the difference.
   $958 - 461$

   _____

9. A hiking path has three sections. The lengths of the sections are 3.6 km, 2.7 km, and 4.7 km. How many kilometers long is the hiking path?

   _____

10. 4.73×6.8

   _____

11. $0.296 \div 3.7$

   _____

12. Solve for n to complete the prime factorization.
   $6^n = 216$

   _____

13. What is the LCM of 6 and 9?

_____

14. What is $6\frac{2}{3}$ written as a fraction?

_____

For questions 15–16, find the sum or difference. Answers are in simplest form.

15. $\frac{2}{15} + \frac{3}{15}$

_____

16. $\frac{4}{6} - \frac{4}{9}$

_____

17. Estimate the sum.

$\frac{8}{9} + \frac{4}{7}$

_____

18. Find the sum in simplest form.

$6\frac{7}{12} + 1\frac{2}{3}$

_____

19. Write the best estimate for the word problem.

Todd used $2\frac{4}{5}$ c of pecans and $1\frac{1}{10}$ c of cheese crackers to make a snack mix. About how many more cups of pecans than crackers did he use?

_____

For questions 20–21, find the product or quotient. Answers are in simplest form.

20. $\frac{3}{5} \times \frac{4}{9}$

_____

21. $\frac{1}{3} \div \frac{4}{9}$

_____

22. Rachel bought a piece of pipe $8\frac{3}{4}$ ft long. It is 5 times the length she needs to repair her watering system. How long is the piece she needs to repair the watering system?

_____

23. Write *true* or *false*. Perpendicular lines are always the same distance apart.

_____

Name _____

24. Write *true* or *false.* The construction below shows congruent angles.

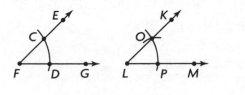

_____

25. What is the name for this polygon?

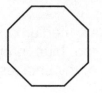

_____

26. How many lines of symmetry does this figure have?

_____

27. Choose the figure that is a reflection of the original figure.

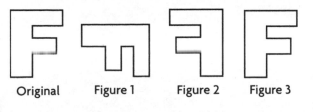

Original   Figure 1   Figure 2   Figure 3

_____

28. What is the measure of each angle that surrounds the circled vertex?

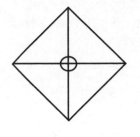

_____

29. Sharon is planning a design that will tessellate a plane. Could she use an octagon? Write *yes* or *no.*

_____

30. Fred built a rectangular prism, using toothpicks for edges and miniature marshmallows for vertices. How many toothpicks did he use?

_____

31. The bottom view of a solid figure is a circle. The front view is a rectangle. What kind of figure is it?

_____

32. Sally is making a model of a prism whose base has 8 sides. She is using toothpicks for the edges and balls of clay for the vertices. How many balls of clay does she need?

_____

33. There are 900 students at Highlander School. How many students should you survey if you want to survey 2 out of every 10 students for a sample?

_____

34. Is this question biased or not biased? What is your favorite kind of dessert?

_____

35. The table shows the ages of the players on Leslie's hockey team. What is the range in age?

Ages of Soccer Players							
12	14	12	15	12	14	15	14
13	14	12	15	16	13	15	15

_____

36. Sara wants to show the number of CDs 30 students have. Which is the best way to display the data?

_____

37. Ms. Johns wants to display the 250 scores students received on a history quiz. Which is the best way to display the data?

_____

38. What is the mode for this set of data?

22, 56, 32, 16, 22, 33

_____

39. Swimsuits come in small, medium, or large. They come with red, blue, gray, or white designs. How many choices for swimsuits are there?

_____

40. Jackie tosses a number cube 200 times. The number 4 comes up 30 times. What is the experimental probability of tossing a 4?

_____

Name _____

Write the correct answer.

1. A mathematical phrase that contains only numbers and operation symbols is called a_?_ expression.

_____

2. What is the algebraic expression that matches this word expression?

27 less than y

_____

3. At the birthday party, after each person got one piece of cake, 12 pieces were left. If c represents the total number of pieces into which the cake was cut, what algebraic expression represents how many people were at the party?

_____

4. Evaluate this numerical expression.

$9 - 27 \div 3$

_____

5. Evaluate this algebraic expression for $z = 11$.

$z \times 3$

_____

For questions 6–7, use the input-output table.

Input	Algebraic Expression	Output
q	$36 \div q$	
18	$36 \div 18$	2
?	?	4
?	$36 \div ?$	6

6. What is the input when the output is 6?

_____

7. What is the algebraic expression when the output is 4?

_____

For questions 8–9, find the value of the variable.

8. $s - 9 = 81$

_____

9. $50 = t + 12$

_____

For questions 10–11, write the equation that represents each statement.

10. Seven less than a number, w, is 15.

_____

11. A number, y, is 27 more than 12.

_____

12. What is the inverse of the operation in the equation $\frac{m}{8} = 11$?

_____

13. Solve the equation.

$\frac{n}{4} = 16$

_____

Harcourt Brace School Publishers

14. How many dimes are there in $9.80?

_____

15. What is 24°C converted to degrees Fahrenheit? Use the formula

$F = (\frac{9}{5} \times C) + 32$. Round to the nearest degree.

_____

16. What is 32°F converted to degrees Celsius? Use the formula

$C = \frac{5}{9} \times (F - 32)$. Round to the nearest degree.

_____

17. Normal body temperature in a human is 98.6°F. What is this temperature on the Celsius scale?

_____

For questions 18–19, use the formula $d = r \times t$.

18. $d = 12$ miles

$r = 3$ miles per hour

$t = ?$

_____

19. $d = 3000$ km

$r = ?$

$t = 12$ minutes

_____

20. An orbiting satellite travels at about 17,500 mi per hour. At that rate, how long would it take for it to travel 140,000 miles?

_____

21. The speedometer on a bicycle measures only in miles. If it shows that the rider is traveling at a speed of 17 miles per hour, how fast is this in kilometers per hour? (1 mi = 1.6 km)

_____

22. June's potato salad recipe called for 11 pounds of potatoes. At the market, potatoes were sold in kilograms. How many kilograms of potatoes should June buy? (1 kg = 2.2 lb)

_____

Form B • Free-Response B214 ▶ **Stop!**

Harcourt Brace School Publishers

Write the correct answer.

1. Write 4 thousandths in standard form.

   _____

2. Write 3^4 in product form.

   _____

3. Write the integers in order from least to greatest.

   $^-5, 0, 6, 2, ^-1$

   _____

4. A baker baked 22 pies for his Saturday customers. He baked 9 apple pies and 5 more blueberry than peach pies. How many peach pies did he bake?

   _____

5. $32\overline{)1,856}$

   _____

6. $84.15 - 16.52$

   _____

7. Elizabeth earns $4.50 per hour baby-sitting. Last week Elizabeth worked 3.5 hr. How much did she earn baby-sitting last week?

   _____

8. $40.8 \div 6$

   _____

9. List all the prime numbers between 10 and 20.

   _____

10. Write $\frac{42}{56}$ in simplest form.

    _____

11. Find the difference in simplest form.

    $\frac{5}{6} - \frac{1}{6}$

    _____

12. Estimate the sum.

    $\frac{3}{8} + \frac{2}{3}$

    _____

13. Write the sum in simplest form.

    $7\frac{1}{6} + 2\frac{7}{18}$

    _____

14. Alejandro's recipe for punch uses $6\frac{1}{4}$ quarts of fruit juice and $4\frac{7}{8}$ quarts of ginger ale. Estimate how many quarts of punch the recipe makes.

    _____

15. Write the product in simplest form.

$1\frac{3}{5} \times 4\frac{3}{8}$

_____

16. Write the quotient in simplest form.

$\frac{5}{12} \div \frac{3}{4}$

_____

17. A flat surface that goes on forever in all directions is called a __?__ .

_____

18. What is the measure of an obtuse angle?

_____

_____

19. How many angles does an octagon have?

_____

20. This figure has rotational symmetry. What is the fraction of each turn?

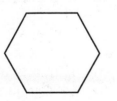

_____

21. Describe the rotation of the figure from position 1 to position 2.

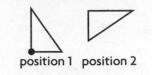

position 1   position 2

_____

22. Risa wants to make a wallpaper design using one shape to tessellate a plane. Name three different shapes she could consider using.

_____

_____

_____

_____

23. A crystal paperweight is in the shape of a square pyramid. How many faces does the paperweight have?

_____

24. Gordon made a model of a pyramid with 16 edges. How many sides did the base of his pyramid have?

_____

25. The sixth grade is planning a car wash. Which of these decisions can the students NOT make?

A. where the car wash will be held

B. who will wash the cars

C. how much to charge

D. whose cars they will wash

_____

_____

26. The principal at Central School wants to find out which teacher is the favorite among students. How can she get a random sample?

_____

_____

_____

_____

_____

For questions 27–28, use the frequency table.

FAVORITE PETS	
Animal	**Frequency**
Dog	14
Cat	16
Fish	9
Bird	4
Rabbit	1
Reptile	4

27. Why is a bar graph the most appropriate graph for this set of data?

_____

_____

28. If one axis of the graph is labeled *Number of People,* what should the other axis be labeled?

_____

29. Anya says this graph is misleading. Bill says it is not. Who is correct and why?

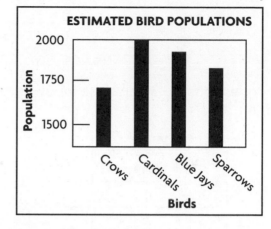

ESTIMATED BIRD POPULATIONS

_____

_____

30. What is the median for this set of data?

29, 31, 24, 31, 26

_____

31. Vests come in green, blue, or brown. They come with brass buttons or wooden buttons. How many choices of vests are there?

_____

32. There are 12 girls and 16 boys in class. The teacher puts everyone's name in a bag and draws one name without looking. What is the probability of choosing a girl's name?

_____

33. Write the algebraic expression that matches the word expression.

ninety less than k

_____

34. Evaluate $x^2 + 6$ for $x = 4$.

_____

For questions 35–36, use the input-output table.

Input	Algebraic Expression	Output
n	$n + 4$	
3	$3 + 4$	7
4	$4 + 4$	8
5	$5 + 4$	?
6	?	?

35. When the output is 9, what is the input?

_____

36. What is the output when the input is 6?

_____

For questions 37–40, solve each equation.

37. $k - 9 = 14$

_____

38. $13 = m + 6$

_____

39. $4a = 24$

_____

40. $\frac{b}{3} = 12$

_____

41. What is 1,000 English pounds in U.S. dollars? Use the formula $1.6261 \times P = D$.

_____

42. What is 40°C converted to degrees Fahrenheit? Use the formula $F = (\frac{9}{5} \times C) + 32$. Round to the nearest degree.

_____

43. A recipe calls for an oven temperature of 450°F. What is this temperature in degrees Celsius? Use the formula $C = \frac{5}{9} \times (F - 32)$. Round to the nearest degree.

_____

44. Use the formula $d = r \times t$.

$d = 405$ mi
$r = 45$ mi per hr
$t = \underline{\quad?\quad}$

_____

45. The Kinder family went on a trip and traveled 4 hr at an average speed of 52 mi per hr. How far did they travel on their trip?

_____

46. Bethany's car holds 16 gal of gas. If she buys gas in liters, how many liters of gas would Bethany need to fill her car? (1 gal = 3.785 liters)

_____

Name _____

Write the correct answer.

1. If the exact length-to-width ratio of an object is also used to make a drawing of the object, it is a _?_ drawing.

   _____

2. If you want to make a scale drawing of a sailboat that is 40 ft long and 60 ft tall on an 11 in. × 17 in. piece of paper, would the scale 1 in.:2 ft allow you to do this?

   _____

For questions 3–5, determine the missing dimension.

3. scale: 1 in.:5 ft

   drawing height: 6 in.

   actual height: _?_

   _____

4. scale: 3 cm:25 cm

   drawing length: 30 cm

   actual length: _?_

   _____

5. scale: 1 in.:4 ft

   drawing length: _?_

   actual length: 20 ft

   _____

6. The scale drawing of a tree house is 1 in.:6 in. The drawing height is 12 in. What is the actual height of the tree house?

   _____

7. A scale drawing of a beetle has a length of 12 cm. The actual length of the beetle is 3 cm. What is the scale of the drawing?

   _____

8. A map scale is 1 in. = 25 mi. The actual distance is 125 mi. What does n represent in the proportion $\frac{1}{25} = \frac{n}{125}$?

   _____

9. On a map, the straight-line distance between Denver and Fort Collins is 5 in. If the scale is 1 in. = 25 mi, what is the proportion you could use to find the actual distance?

   _____

For questions 10–11, determine the actual miles.

10. scale: 1 in. = 50 mi

    map distance: 4.5 in.

    actual distance: _?_

    _____

11. scale: 1 in. = 3 mi

    map distance: 7 in.

    actual distance: _?_

    _____

Form B • Free-Response   **Go on.** ▶

Name _____

12. Find the actual miles.

scale: 1 in. = 25 mi

map distance: $1\frac{1}{2}$ in.

actual distance: __?__

_____

For questions 13 and 14, use the scale
1 in. = 5 mi.

13. Sara and Shirley hiked a mountain trail. The map distance for the trail was 3.5 in. How far did they hike?

_____

14. For a field trip to the science museum, the map distance the bus traveled one way was 4.5 in. What was the actual round-trip distance?

_____

For questions 15–18, use the map. Each square equals one city block.

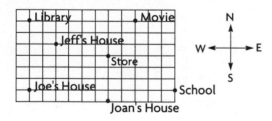

15. Joe left his house and walked 2 blocks east. Where would he go from there to get to Jeff's house?

_____

16. Calvin left the school and went 5 blocks west and 3 blocks north. Where was he?

_____

17. Joan left her house and walked 3 blocks north, 2 blocks east and 4 blocks north. Where did she go?

_____

18. The librarian left school and drove by the shortest route to the store and then to the library. How many blocks did she drive?

_____

19. The value of the Golden Ratio is about __?__ .

_____

20. A Golden Rectangle is 100 mm high. What is its length?

_____

21. Which rectangle is a Golden Rectangle?

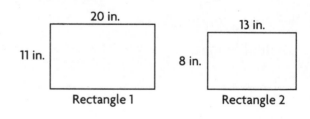

_____

22. Rectangle S is 800 cm × 667 cm. Rectangle T is 480 cm × 300 cm. Which is a Golden Rectangle?

_____

Form B • Free-Response   B226   ▶ **Stop!**

Name _____

Write the correct answer.

1. What are two equivalent ratios that compare the number of triangles to the number of squares?

_____

2. What is the ratio for $12 for each 100 persons written as a fraction?

_____

3. What is $\frac{14}{56}$ written as a percent?

_____

4. What percent of this figure is shaded?

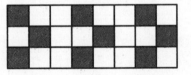

_____

5. Julie sold 12 greeting cards for $18.00. At that rate, what would 50 cards sell for?

_____

6. A manufacturer of computer chips sold 4.4 million chips last year. Of these sales, 25% were to foreign companies. How many computer chips were sold to foreign companies?

_____

For questions 7–8, use the data in the table below for a circle graph.

Bookstore Sales	
Type of Book	Percent
Fiction	45%
Non-fiction	25%
Reference	15%
Other	15%

7. What angle measure should you use for the Non-fiction section of the graph?

_____

8. What angle measure should you use for each of the sections labeled Reference and Other?

_____

9. The Garden Center advertised a spring special on petunias. They are giving 30% off the regular price of $1.50 per plant. If Mr. Chan buys 12 petunia plants, what will his total discount be?

_____

10. With a simple interest rate of 7.75%, what will the interest be on a loan of $2,200 for 1 year?

_____

Harcourt Brace School Publishers

11. Are the figures below similar, congruent, or, both similar and congruent?

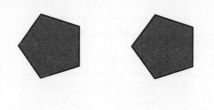

_____

12. One photograph is 9 cm × 18 cm. Another is 18 cm × 17 cm. Are the photos similar, congruent, both similar and congruent, or neither similar nor congruent?

_____

13. Find c for this pair of similar figures.

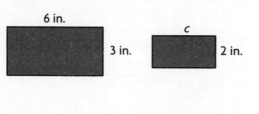

6 in.

3 in.

c

2 in.

_____

14. What is the height of the building?

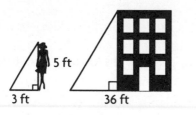

5 ft

3 ft   36 ft

_____

15. A monument known to be 90 m tall casts a shadow 81 m long. At the same time a nearby tree casts a shadow 18 m long. How tall is the tree?

_____

16. Find the missing dimension.

scale: 0.5 in.:3 ft

drawing length: 3.5 in.

actual length: _?_ ft

_____

17. Find the actual distance.

scale: 1 cm:25 km

map distance: 9 cm

_____

For questions 18–19, use the map. Each square equals one city block.

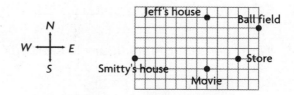

18. Smitty left his house and rode 10 blocks east, 4 blocks north and 3 blocks west. Where did he end up?

_____

19. Sara left the ball field and went to the store. Then she went to the movie. How many blocks did she walk?

_____

20. The short side of a Golden Rectangle is 27 mm long. How long is the other side?

_____

Form B • Free-Response   B228   ▶ **Stop!**

Harcourt Brace School Publishers

Name _____

Write the correct answer.

1. Write $\frac{5}{8}$ as a decimal.

_____

2. Write the opposite of $^{+}4$.

_____

3. Use mental math to find the sum.

$91 + 24 + 9$

_____

4. There were 32 bus tours in Kokito Bay City last week. The most each bus can hold is 28 people, not counting the bus driver. Every bus was full last week. About how many people toured Kokito Bay City?

_____

5. $36.4 + 8.725$

_____

6. $49.6 \div 8$

_____

7. Write the prime factorization of 45.

_____

8. Write $\frac{23}{5}$ as a mixed number.

_____

9. Find the sum in simplest form.

$\frac{5}{12} + \frac{1}{12}$

_____

For questions 10–11, find the answer in simplest form.

10. $5\frac{7}{8} - 1\frac{3}{4}$

_____

11. $1\frac{1}{3} \times 1\frac{4}{5}$

_____

12. Kent bought $6\frac{1}{4}$ lb of sliced turkey. He wants to allow $\frac{1}{4}$ lb of sliced turkey for each submarine sandwich he makes. How many sandwiches can he make?

_____

13. An angle that measures 85° is classified as a(n) _?_ angle.

_____

Name _____

14. What construction do the figures below represent?

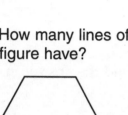

_____

15. How many lines of symmetry does this figure have?

_____

16. Name a polygon that will tessellate a plane.

_____

_____

_____

17. Name this figure.

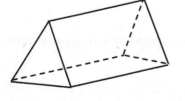

_____

18. The top and bottom views of a solid figure are squares. The front view is a rectangle. What kind of figure is it?

_____

19. The sixth graders are being surveyed to find out their choice for a class trip. Is the following question biased?

What is your first choice from the suggested places on the list?

_____

For questions 20–21, use the graph.

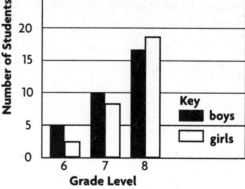

20. What tells you which bars represent girls and which bars represent boys?

_____

21. In which grade are there more girls than boys who play chess?

_____

For questions 22–23, use the line graph.

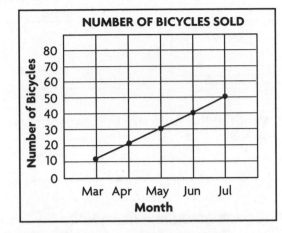

NUMBER OF BICYCLES SOLD

22. What has been the trend in bicycle sales?

_____

23. Use the graph to predict how many bicycles will be sold in August.

_____

24. Karen has gotten a hit in 60 of the last 100 times she has been up to bat. How many hits can she expect to get in her next 50 times at bat?

_____

25. Evaluate $6 + \frac{1}{3}y$ for $y = 12$.

_____

26. Solve for m. $8 = m + 6$

_____

27. Solve for k. $5k = 20$

_____

28. Solve for a. $\frac{a}{3} = 15$

_____

29. What are 100 German marks worth in U.S. dollars? Use the formula $0.6200 \times M = D$. (M = marks; D = dollars)

_____

30. What is 20°C converted to degrees Fahrenheit? Use the formula $F = (\frac{9}{5} \times C) + 32$.

_____

31. Paul drove an average of 40 mi per hr from his home to the beach. He drove 3.5 hr to get there. How far does Paul live from the beach? Use the formula $d = r \times t$.

_____

32. Kevin weighs 42 kg. Christopher weighs 104 lb. How many more pounds than Kevin does Christopher weigh? (1 kg = 2.2 lb)

_____

33. Write the ratio 3 to 7 in another form.

_____

34. Write 40% as a fraction in simplest form.

_____

35. What percent of the figure is shaded?

36. The Maxwell family spent $9,000 remodeling their home. They spent 20% of this on bathroom and kitchen tiling. How much did the Maxwells spend on tile?

_____

37. Scarves are on sale for 30% off the regular price of $18.00. If Samantha buys 5 scarves, what is her total discount?

_____

38. Andrianna put $2,500 in the bank for one year. She earned interest at the rate of 4% a year. How much interest did she earn?

_____

39. Use the figures below.

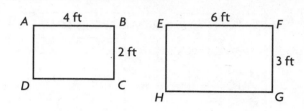

What is the ratio in simplest form of $\frac{AB}{EF}$?

_____

40. A photograph is 4 in. wide by 5 in. long. Tammy wants to have the photo enlarged so the width measures 20 in. How long will the enlarged photo be?

_____

41. A tree casts a shadow 36 ft long. At the same time a 6-ft pole nearby casts a shadow 18 ft long. How tall is the tree?

_____

42. The scale drawing of a dog house is 1 in.:1.5 ft. The length in the drawing is 6.5 in. What is the actual length of the dog house?

_____

43. The scale on a map is 1 in. = 40 mi. The map shows 8 in. between Diamond Lake Village and Chesterville. Find the actual miles between the two towns.

_____

44. A rectangle is 24 in. long. It is a Golden Rectangle. What is its width?

_____

Name _____

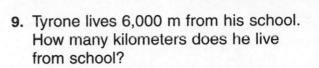

Write the correct answer.

1. To change fluid ounces to cups, you should _?_.

   _____

For questions 2 and 3, change to the given units.

2. 15 ft = ☐ yd

   _____

3. 7 qt = ☐ pt

   _____

4. Tammy walked 20 feet from the restaurant to the parking lot. Then she walked 90 yd to her car. How many feet did she walk?

   _____

5. Tom poured orange juice into 32 glasses which each held 8 ounces of juice. How many gallons of orange juice did he use?

   _____

6. To change grams to kilograms, you should divide by _?_.

   _____

For questions 7 and 8, change to the given units.

7. 72 cm = ☐ mm

   _____

8. 1,200 mL = ☐ L

   _____

9. Tyrone lives 6,000 m from his school. How many kilometers does he live from school?

   _____

10. Mackenzie's sports equipment bag weighs 3.8 kg. How many grams does it weigh?

    _____

11. Which measurement is more precise for measuring the height of a chair, 3 yd or 38 in.?

    _____

12. If Mandy was measuring the length of a paper clip in metric units, which unit would give the most precise measurement?

    _____

13. Which measurement is more precise for measuring distance, 987 m or 1 km?

    _____

For question 14, answer yes or no.

14. If you need a precise measure of a section of wallpaper would you use feet?

    _____

Name _____

For questions 15 and 16, use the network below.

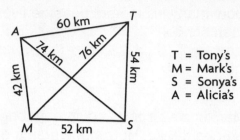

T = Tony's
M = Mark's
S = Sonya's
A = Alicia's

15. Tony left his house and went to Mark's. Mark and he then picked up Sonya and drove to Alicia's house. How long was this route?

_____

16. If Tony had picked up Sonya first, then Mark and then driven to Alicia's house, how many kilometers shorter would his route have been?

_____

For questions 17 and 18, use the network below.

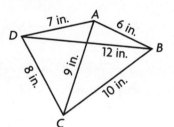

17. What is the length of the route ABDC?

_____

18. What is the length of the route ABCD?

_____

19. What is the perimeter?

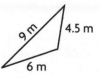

_____

20. Find the missing length. Then find the perimeter.

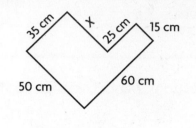

_____

21. What is the perimeter?

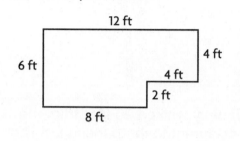

_____

22. The perimeter is 60 km. What is the missing length?

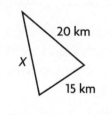

_____

23. A city parking lot is 120 yd long and 90 yd wide. What is its perimeter?

_____

24. A fencing company just installed a fence around a regular octagonal garden. If the fence was 112 ft long, what was the length of each side of the octagon?

_____

Form B • Free-Response   B234   ▶ **Stop!**

Name _____

Write the correct answer.

For questions 1–4, estimate the area of the figure. Each square is 1 cm².

1.

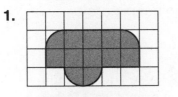

_____

2.

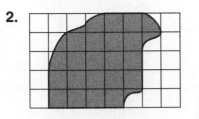

_____

3.

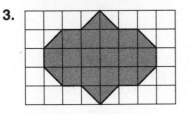

_____

4.

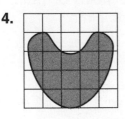

_____

For questions 5–8, use the formula $A = lw$ or $A = s^2$ to find the area.

5. A sports poster is 30 in. long and 24 in. wide. What is the area of the poster?

_____

6. The Jeffersons bought a quilt that is 210 cm long and 90 cm wide. What is the area of the quilt?

_____

7. Craig is installing red bricks to construct a 12-ft × 3-ft walkway that leads to the house. Each brick is 1 ft² and costs $3.50. What is the total cost of the bricks?

_____

8. Wanda plans to buy carpet for a room in her house. The room is 8 ft long and 8 ft wide. The carpet costs $9 per square foot. What will be the total cost?

_____

9. What is the relationship between parallelogram *ABCD* and △*BCD*?

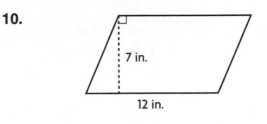

_____

For questions 10–12, find the area.

10.

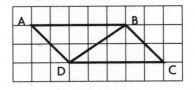

7 in.

12 in.

_____

11. What is the area of a triangle with a base of 13 cm and a height of 8 cm? Use $A = \frac{1}{2} \times b \times h$.

_____

12. What is the area of a parallelogram with a base of 8.6 m and a height of 4.9 m? Use $A = b \times h$.

_____

Harcourt Brace School Publishers

Form B • Free-Response

Go on. ▶

Name _____

For questions 13–14, use the figure below.

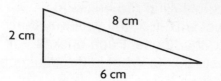

13. If you halve the length of each side of the triangle, what will be the perimeter?

_____

14. If you double the length of each side, what will be the area?

_____

For questions 15–16, use the figure below.

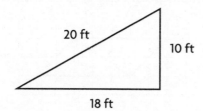

15. If you double the length of each side of the figure, what will be the perimeter?

_____

16. If you halve the length of each side of the figure, what will be the area?

_____

17. A restaurant had a parking area of 100 ft × 50 ft. What dimensions would double the area of the parking lot?

_____

18. Sam has a picture that is 2 ft by 4 ft. He wants to reduce it to fit a space that is half the area of the original picture. What dimensions will halve the area of the original picture?

_____

For questions 19–22, use the formula $A = \pi r^2$ to find the area. Use 3.14 for π. Round to the nearest whole unit.

19. What is the area of this figure?

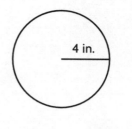

_____

20. What is the area of a circle with a diameter of 60 ft?

_____

21. A circular plate has a radius of 12 in. What is the area of the plate?

_____

22. Will a cake baked in a 9 in. cake pan fit on a circular plate with an area of 80 in.^{2}? Explain your answer.

_____

Form B • Free-Response   B236   ▶ **Stop!**

Name _____

Write the correct answer.

1. About how many of the cubes will it take to fill the prism?

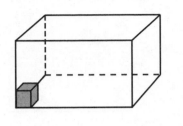

_____

2. When a rectangular prism is cut diagonally in half, what two figures are formed?

_____

For questions 3–4, find the volume of each figure.

3.

3 in.
5 in.
7 in.

_____

4. Use $V = \frac{1}{2} \times l \times w \times h$.

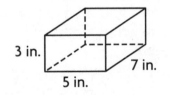

5 m
4 m
8 m

_____

5. The department store has a sale on glass vases that measure 2 in. wide, 6 in. long, and 15 in. high. What is the volume of the vase?

_____

6. Tara has a box that measures 3 cm wide, 10 cm long, and 20 cm high. What is the volume of the box?

_____

7. If each side of the cube is doubled, how does its volume change?

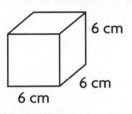

6 cm
6 cm
6 cm

_____

8. How can you change any box so that it will hold twice as much?

_____

For questions 9–10, use the figure below.

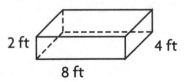

2 ft
4 ft
8 ft

9. If you double all the dimensions of this figure, what is the volume of the larger prism?

_____

10. If you halve all the dimensions of the figure, what is the volume of the smaller prism?

_____

Form B • Free-Response   B237   **Go on.** ▶

For questions 11–12, use the figure below.

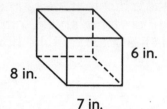

8 in. 6 in. 7 in.

11. If you halve the height of the figure, what is the volume of the smaller prism?

_____

12. If you double the height of the figure, what is the volume of the larger prism?

_____

For questions 13–16, find the volume of each cylinder to the nearest whole unit. Use the formula $V = \pi r^2 \times h$.

13.

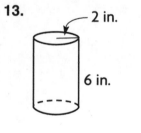

2 in.

6 in.

_____

14.

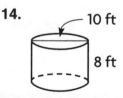

10 ft

8 ft

_____

15.

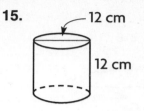

12 cm

12 cm

_____

16.

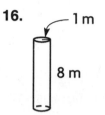

1 m

8 m

_____

17. A vat that processes juice is in the shape of a cylinder and has a diameter of 30 feet and a height of 8 feet. About how many cubic feet of juice can the vat hold?

_____

18. A plastic container in the shape of a cylinder is 10 in. high and has a radius of 20 in. About how many cubic in. of flour will fill the container?

_____

For questions 19–22, find the surface area of each prism.

19.
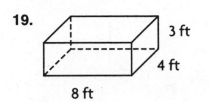
3 ft
4 ft
8 ft

_____

20.
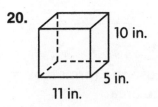
10 in.
5 in.
11 in.

_____

21.
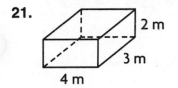
2 m
3 m
4 m

_____

22.
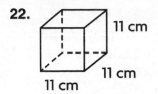
11 cm
11 cm
11 cm

_____

23. Theresa plans to paint storage cubes for her room. Each cube is 3 ft long. She will paint each side except the front. How many square feet of paint will it take to cover each cube?

_____

24. Miguel is covering the walls of his room with wallpaper. His room is 11 ft wide, 10 ft long, and 7 ft high. He will not cover the floor or the ceiling. How much surface area will he cover?

_____

Form B • Free-Response

▶ **Stop!**

Name _____

Write the correct answer.

1. Sal wants to transfer 24 pint containers of juice into gallon jugs. How many gallon jugs will he use?

   _____

2. Change to the given units.

   15 cm = __?__ mm

   _____

3. Is the most precise measurement of the height of a desk 1 yd, $2\frac{1}{2}$ ft, or $29\frac{1}{2}$ in.?

   _____

For questions 4 and 5, use the network below. Distances are expressed in mi.

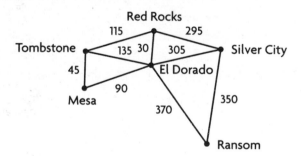

4. What is the length of the route from Red Rocks to Ransom through El Dorado?

   _____

5. What is the length of the route from Tombstone to Silver City by way of El Dorado and Ransom?

   _____

6. What is the perimeter?

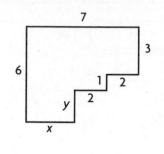

   _____

For questions 7 and 8, use the formula $A = lw$ or $A = s^2$ to find the area.

7. Mrs. King is buying new carpet for a room that is 14 ft long and 11 ft wide. How much carpet does she need?

   _____

8. A computer monitor has a screen that is 10 in. long and 8 in. wide. What is the area of the computer screen?

   _____

9. What is the area of a parallelogram that has a base of 12 in. and a height of 7 in.? Use the formula $A = bh$.

   _____

10. What is the area of a triangle that has a base of 6.5 cm and a height of 8.4 cm? Use the formula $A = \frac{1}{2}bh$.

   _____

Form B • Free-Response   B240   **Go on.** ▶

For questions 11 and 12, use the figure below.

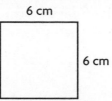

6 cm

6 cm

11. If you halve the dimensions of this figure, what is the perimeter?

_____

12. If you double the dimensions of this figure, what is the area?

_____

For questions 13 and 14, use the formula $A = \pi r^2$. Use 3.14 for π and round to the nearest whole number.

13. A circle has a diameter of 14 cm. What is the approximate area of the circle?

_____

14. The head of a bongo drum has a radius of 11 in. What is the area of the drumhead?

_____

15. A triangular prism has a right triangle as its base, with legs 3m and 4m. The height of the prism is 6m. What is its volume? Use $V = \frac{1}{2} l \times w \times h$.

_____

For questions 16 and 17, use the figure below.

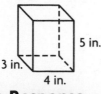

5 in.

3 in.

4 in.

16. If you double the dimensions of this figure, what is the volume of the larger prism?

_____

17. If you halve the dimensions of this figure, what is the volume of the smaller figure?

_____

18. Find the volume of the cylinder to the nearest whole unit.

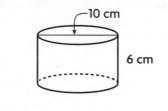

10 cm

6 cm

_____

19. An individual serving of tomato juice comes in a can that is 4 in. high and has a diameter of 2 in. About how many cubic inches of juice does the can hold when it is completely filled?

_____

20. Andy wants to cover the outside of an old box with fabric. The box is 12 in. long, 3 in. high, and 6 in. wide. How many square inches of fabric does he need?

_____

Form B • Free-Response   B241   ▶ **Stop!**

Name _____

Write the correct answer.

1. What is the place value of the digit 7 in the number 4.271?

_____

2. What is the value of 4^3?

_____

3. Carmen baked a total of 102 peanut butter and chocolate chip cookies. She baked 42 more peanut butter cookies than chocolate chip cookies. How many peanut butter cookies did she bake?

_____

4. $6\overline{)2{,}610}$

_____

5. $6.43 - 1.07$

_____

6. 4.13×6.4

_____

7. What is the GCF of 12 and 27?

_____

8. Write $\frac{12}{18}$ in simplest form.

_____

9. Write the sum in simplest form.
$\frac{2}{5} + \frac{4}{15}$

_____

10. Estimate the difference.
$\frac{11}{12} - \frac{1}{20}$

_____

11. Find the best estimate for the word problem.

Last week Brenda bought $8\frac{7}{8}$ lb of meat for her family, and this week she bought $5\frac{1}{2}$ lb of meat. How many more pounds did she buy last week than this week?

_____

12. Find the quotient in simplest form.
$\frac{7}{12} \div \frac{1}{4}$

_____

13. What does the symbol $\overleftrightarrow{MN}$ refer to?

_____

14. How many angles does a hexagon have?

_____

15. Draw the figure that is a rotation of the original figure.

original
figure

16. Tremane wants to use small tiles to make a design for a tabletop. He wants the design to tessellate. What shape can he use?

_____

_____

_____

_____

17. Name this figure.

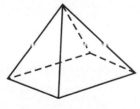

_____

18. Ronita is making a model of a prism whose base has 5 sides. She is using sticks of wood for the edges and putty for the vertices. How many sticks of wood will she need?

_____

19. There are 600 people who will vote on a new name for your school. How many voters should you survey if you want to survey 1 out of every 10 voters for a sample?

_____

20. The table shows the scores students received on their last math quiz. What is the range in scores?

Scores on Math Quiz							
91	58	87	88	97	100	96	98
89	80	64	79	99	82	98	90

_____

21. What kind of graph is this?

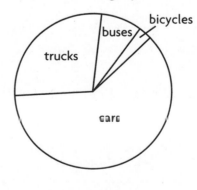

_____

22. Use the graph to find the trend for sales of audio tapes.

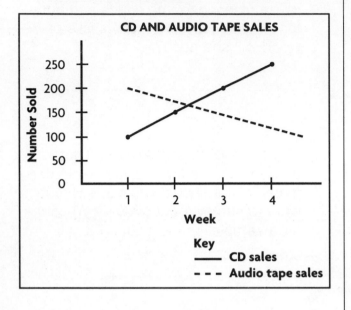

23. What is the mean for this set of data?

10, 19, 22, 13, 9, 11

_____

24. You toss a cube numbered 3, 6, 9, 12, 15, and 18. What is P(even)?

_____

25. Write the algebraic expression that matches this word expression:

k more than 7

_____

26. Determine the input for the given output for this expression: $w - 4$

output = 10   input = ___?___

_____

27. Solve. $n - 5 = 7$

_____

28. Solve. $3a = 18$

_____

29. A recipe calls for an oven temperature of 250°F. What is this temperature in degrees Celsius? Use the formula $C = \frac{5}{9} \times (F - 32)$. Round to the nearest degree.

_____

30. Jacqueline has a ribbon that is 21 in. long. How many centimeters long is the ribbon? (1 in. = 2.54 cm)

_____

31. A 10-lb bag of potatoes costs $3.10. What is the cost per pound?

_____

32. If 4 melons cost $5.00, how much will 6 melons cost?

_____

Name _____

For questions 33–34, use the circle graph.

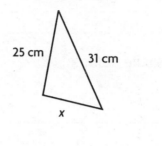

HOW WE GET TO SCHOOL

walk
15%

bicycle
5%

bus
60%

car
20%

33. If 80 students were surveyed, how many ride a bicycle to school?

_____

34. If 300 students were surveyed, how many get to school in a car?

_____

35. How can you tell when two figures are congruent?

_____

_____

36. Change to the given unit.

6 ft = _?_ in.

_____

37. The perimeter is 75 cm. What is the missing length?

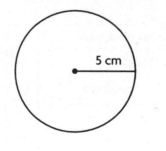

25 cm   31 cm

x

_____

38. What is the area of a triangle with a base of 22 in. and a height of 9 in.?

_____

39. Use the formula $A = \pi r^2$ to find the area of this circle. Use 3.14 for π. Round to the nearest whole unit.

5 cm

_____

40. Find the volume of the figure.

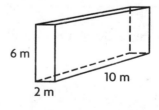

6 m

10 m

2 m

_____

Name _____

Write the correct answer.

1. What is the opposite of ⁺5?

_____

2. What is the absolute value of ⁻25?

_____

3. What integer represents 74 degrees above zero?

_____

4. What is the absolute value of ⁺41?

_____

For questions 5 and 6, use the Venn diagram.

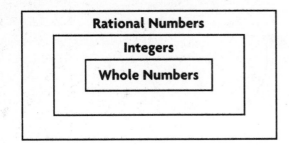

5. In which set or sets does the number 0 belong?

_____

6. In which set or sets does the number 15.75 belong?

_____

7. What is the number 13 in the form $\frac{a}{b}$?

_____

8. What is the number 0.75 in the form $\frac{a}{b}$?

_____

For questions 9–12, write the repeating or terminating decimal for the fraction.

9. $\frac{5}{8}$

_____

10. $\frac{2}{3}$

_____

11. $\frac{1}{5}$

_____

12. $1\frac{1}{3}$

_____

13. Write a rational number between $3\frac{3}{4}$ and 4.

_____

14. Write a rational number between 0 and $\frac{1}{4}$.

_____

15. Write a rational number between 4.5 and 4.51.

_____

16. Write a rational number between $^-13\frac{3}{4}$ and $^-14\frac{1}{4}$.

_____

17. The winning tomato was 4.8 lb. The third-place tomato was 4.7 lb. What is a possible weight of the second-place tomato?

_____

18. The baby's length at birth was 19.8 in. At 2 days, the baby had already grown to 20.2 in. What is a possible length to which the baby might have grown at 1 day?

_____

For questions 19 and 20, compare the numbers. Use $<$, $>$, or $=$.

19. $\frac{7}{8}$ $\bigcirc$ 0.9

_____

20. $\frac{1}{4}$ $\bigcirc$ $^-.25$

_____

For questions 21 and 22, order the rational numbers from greatest to least.

21. $\frac{^-1}{4}$, 0.375, $\frac{1}{3}$

_____

22. $^-0.875$, $\frac{^-5}{6}$, $\frac{^-1}{8}$

_____

23. Marty ran the quarter-mile track on each of 4 days while the gym teacher timed him. On Monday, his time was 60.75 sec, on Tuesday it was $60\frac{3}{8}$ sec, on Wednesday it was $60\frac{1}{3}$ sec, and on Thursday it was $60\frac{7}{8}$ sec. On which day was his time the fastest?

_____

24. Calvin, Mark, Sara, and Tamika each picked a bushel of apples at the orchard. Calvin's bushel weighed 25.6 lb, Mark's weighed $25\frac{1}{4}$ lb, Sara's weighed $25\frac{6}{8}$ lb, and Tamika's weighed 25.65 lb. Whose bushel of apples weighed the most?

_____

Form B • Free-Response   B247   ▶ **Stop!**

Name _____

Write the correct answer.

1. Write an addition equation modeled on this number line.

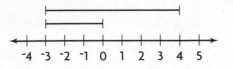

_____

For questions 2–4, find the sum.

2. $^-13 + {}^+7$

_____

3. $^+28 + {}^-9$

_____

4. $^-101 + {}^-24$

_____

5. The day's high temperature was $^-8°C$. The low temperature was $15°$ less. What was the low temperature?

_____

6. On the first play of the down, Bill threw a pass for a gain of 8 yd. On the next play, he was tackled for a loss of 10 yd. Write the integer that shows the total gain or loss on the two plays.

_____

7. Do these two problems have the same solution?

$^+12 - {}^+5$ and $^+12 + {}^-5$

_____

For questions 8–10, find the difference.

8. $^+15 - {}^+8$

_____

9. $^-25 - {}^-12$

_____

10. $^+1 - {}^-18$

_____

11. When we went to bed, the temperature was $^+1°C$. When we woke up it was $^-7°C$. What was the overnight temperature change?

_____

12. At the top of Mt. Washington, the low temperature for the day was $^-28°F$. The high temperature was $32°$ greater. What was the high temperature?

_____

Form B • Free-Response   **Go on.** ▶

13. The product of a negative integer and a negative integer will be a __?__ integer.

_____

For questions 14–16, find the product.

14. $^+13 \times {}^-3$

_____

15. $^-5 \times {}^-7$

_____

16. $^-4 \times {}^+4$

_____

17. The cold snap caused the temperature to fall at the rate of 2.5°F per hour. This trend continued for 10 hours. Express the change in temperature as a negative number.

_____

18. Bud had a savings account balance of $75. He withdrew $6 a week for 7 weeks to pay for guitar lessons. What was his balance then?

_____

19. If you divide a negative integer by a positive integer, the quotient will be a __?__ integer.

_____

For questions 20–22, determine the quotient.

20. $^-27 \div {}^+3$

_____

21. $^-35 \div {}^-7$

_____

22. $^+22 \div {}^+2$

_____

23. Which of the following problems has the greater quotient?

$^+3 \div {}^+1$ or $^-33 \div {}^+11$

_____

24. Jerry gained the same amount of weight in each of 4 years. His total weight gain over the 4 years was 36 pounds. By how many pounds did his weight change each year?

_____

Name _____

Write the correct answer.

1. Evaluate $6 + {}^-9 \div 3$.

_____

2. Evaluate $y \times {}^-2$ for $y = {}^-7$.

_____

3. Evaluate $t \div 3 + 5$ for $t = 24$.

_____

4. Evaluate m^2 for $m = {}^-5$.

_____

For questions 5–8, solve the equation.

5. $t - 50 = {}^-12$

_____

6. $z + 15 = 45$

_____

7. ${}^-5b = 15$

_____

8. $\frac{a}{3} = {}^-48$

_____

9. Write an equation for this word sentence. Eight less than a number, m, is negative 2.

_____

10. Abby stood on a boat deck and lowered a thermometer 15 feet to a depth of 7 feet below sea level. Write an equation to show how to find the height, h, at which she lowered the thermometer.

_____

11. What are the whole-number solutions of $s < 7$?

_____

12. What are the whole-number solutions of $m \leq 3$?

_____

13. What algebraic inequality is represented by the integers graphed on the number line?

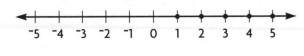

_____

14. What algebraic inequality is represented by the integers graphed on the number line?

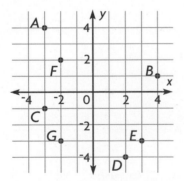

_____

15. Write an algebraic inequality to represent this word sentence.

All numbers *t* are less than or equal to ⁻7.

_____

16. To ride the roller coaster, a person, *p*, must be taller than 48 in. Write an algebraic inequality to represent this.

_____

Use the coordinate plane to answer questions 17–20.

17. Which point is located by the ordered pair (2,⁻4)?

_____

18. Which point is located by the ordered pair (⁻3,4)?

_____

19. What is the ordered pair for point *F*?

_____

20. What is the ordered pair for point *C*?

_____

For questions 21 and 22, use the table.

x	⁻3	⁻2	⁻1	0	1	2	3
y	⁻5	⁻4	⁻3	⁻2	⁻1	0	?

21. Which number completes the table?

_____

22. Which expression gives each value of *y*?

_____

For questions 23 and 24, use the table.

x	⁻3	⁻2	⁻1	0	1	2	3
y	12	8	4	0	⁻4	⁻8	?

23. Which number completes the table?

_____

24. Which expression gives each value of *y*?

_____

Form B • Free-Response

▶ **Stop!**

Write the correct answer.

1. What is the opposite of $^+15$?

_____

2. What is the number 3 written in the form $\frac{a}{b}$?

_____

For questions 3–4, find the repeating or terminating decimal for the fraction.

3. $\frac{11}{9}$

_____

4. $\frac{15}{16}$

_____

5. Name a rational number between $7\frac{1}{2}$ and $7\frac{1}{3}$.

_____

6. From the starting point of a road rally, a driver passes the fire station at 6.25 mi, the library at 6.26 mi, the gas station at 6.31 mi and the monument at 7.28 mi. The first left-turn in the race was supposed to be at 6.28 mi. Between what two landmarks should the driver have made a left turn?

_____

7. Compare the numbers. Choose $<$, $>$, or $=$.

$\frac{13}{16}$ O .8125

_____

8. In a contest to see who could stand on their head the longest Angel lasted $17\frac{1}{3}$ sec, Juanita lasted $17\frac{3}{8}$ sec, Joan lasted 17.32 sec, and Shirley lasted $17\frac{1}{4}$ sec. Who won the contest?

_____

For questions 9–10, find each sum.

9. $^-7 + {}^-4$

_____

10. $^+17 + {}^-8$

_____

11. Find the difference.

$^-9 - {}^+16$

_____

12. At 7:00 A.M. it was 15°F. A cold wave caused the temperature to fall about 22° by noon. What was the temperature then?

_____

13. The quotient of a positive integer and a negative integer is a __?__

_____

14. Find the product.

$^+17 \times {}^-3$

_____

15. Find the quotient.

$^-8 \div {}^-32$

_____

16. The temperature of the water in the pot on the stove increased 92°F in four minutes. If it increased the same amount each minute, how many degrees did it change every minute?

_____

17. Evaluate $k + 19$ for $k = {}^-6$.

_____

18. Evaluate $13r$ for $r = {}^-3$.

_____

19. Solve this equation:

$x - 98 = {}^-2$

_____

20. Write the equation for this word sentence.

14 less than a number, m, is negative 25.

_____

21. Write the whole number solutions to the inequality $i < 6$.

_____

22. A hummingbird's wings beat as fast as 80 beats per second. Write the inequality that represents how fast its wings can beat.

_____

For questions 23–24, use the table.

p	$^-3$	$^-2$	$^-1$	0	$^+1$
q	$^-8$	$^-5$	?	$^+1$	$^+4$

23. What number completes the table?

_____

24. Write the expression, using p, that gets the value of q.

_____

Form B • Free-Response

▶ **Stop!**

Name _____

Write the correct answer.

1. Write 0.9 as a fraction.

_____

2. List the integers in order from least to greatest.

4, ⁻3, 0, 1, ⁻5, 2

_____

3. Use mental math to find the difference.

52 − 29

_____

4. Estimate the sum.

5,122
9,372
+ 8,910

_____

5. 12.18 ÷ 0.42

_____

6. Why is the number 12 called a composite number?

_____

_____

_____

7. Write $6\frac{5}{8}$ as an improper fraction.

_____

8. Write the difference in simplest form.

$\frac{7}{15} - \frac{2}{15}$

_____

9. Find the sum in simplest form.

$4\frac{2}{3} + 3\frac{1}{12}$

_____

10. Write the product in simplest form.

$3\frac{1}{5} \times \frac{1}{8}$

_____

11. Write a true statement about parallel lines.

_____

12. Construct an angle congruent to the angle below.

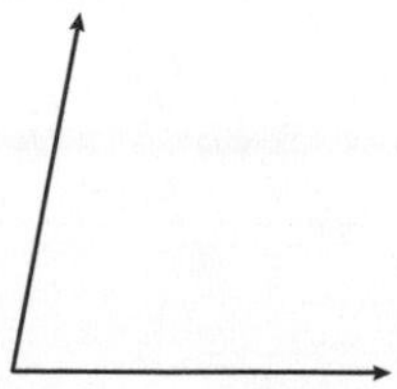

Harcourt Brace School Publishers

Form B • Free-Response   **B254**   **Chapters 1–26**   **Go on.** ▶

13. This figure has rotational symmetry. What is the angle measure of each turn?

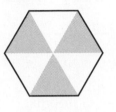

_____

14. Name a polygon that will NOT tessellate a plane.

_____

_____

_____

15. The bottom view of a solid figure is a rectangle. The front view is a rectangle. What kind of figure is it?

_____

16. Andersonville Park District is considering building an indoor ice-skating rink. A survey is conducted to find out if the citizens of Andersonville would use the rink once it is constructed. What is a useful survey question to ask?

_____

_____

_____

_____

_____

_____

For questions 17–18, use this stem-and-leaf plot of test scores for a math test.

Mathematics Test Scores

Stem	Leaves					
6	8					
7	1	1	1	3	8	
8	2	2	5	7	7	8
9	1	4	6	9	9	

17. What score is shown by the fourth stem and its third leaf?

_____

18. Where should a score of 80 be placed on this plot?

_____

19. Why is this graph misleading?

_____

20. Carlotta's Ice Cream Parlor offers chocolate, vanilla, strawberry, mint, fudge swirl, black cherry, and butter pecan ice cream. For ice cream cones, the parlor offers a waffle cone or a sugar cone. How many choices for a one-scoop ice cream cone are there?

_____

21. Evaluate $a^2 - 4$ for $a = 6$.

_____

22. Solve. $6 = w + 2$

_____

23. Solve. $\frac{n}{3} = 9$

_____

24. What is the value of 455 English pounds in U.S. dollars? Use the formula $1.6261 \times P = D$.

_____

25. Mrs. Cassin drove 270 miles on the first day of her trip. If she traveled at a rate of 60 miles per hour, how long did it take her?

_____

26. Write a ratio equivalent to 12:18.

_____

_____

27. A pizza was divided into 10 slices. Of these slices, 5 had mushrooms, 3 had onions, and the rest had only cheese. What percent of the pizza had only cheese?

_____

28. What is the sale price on a sweater that costs $60 if the discount rate is 20%?

_____

29. A tree casts a shadow that is 40 m long. At the same time a nearby bush that is 2 m high casts a 10-m shadow. What is the height of the tree?

_____

30. The scale for a drawing of a brick walkway is 1 in. = 6 ft. The drawing length is 18.5 in. What is the actual length of the walkway?

_____

31. When Richard packed his suitcase for vacation, it weighed 8,400 g. How many kilograms did it weigh?

_____

Harcourt Brace School Publishers

For questions 32–33, use the figure below.

6 ft

6 ft

32. If you double the length of each side, what will be the area?

_____

33. If you halve the length of each side, what will be the perimeter?

_____

34. Find the volume of the cylinder to the nearest whole unit. Use the formula $V = \pi r^2 \times h$. Use 3.14 for π.

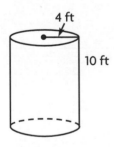

4 ft

10 ft

_____

35. Kimberly is planning to paint her bedroom, which is 11 ft long, 15 ft wide, and 8 ft high. She will paint the walls, but not the floor or the ceiling. How much surface area will she paint?

_____

36. What is the absolute value of $^{+}51$?

_____

37. The winner of a race ran it in 36.4 sec. The third-place runner finished in 36.5 sec. Write a number that could be the time for the second-place runner.

_____

_____

38. Find the sum. $^{-}8 + 3$

_____

39. On a winter day, the high temperature was $^{-}10°$F. The low temperature was 15° less. What was the low temperature?

_____

40. Find the product. $^{-}21 \times {}^{-}3$

_____

41. Evaluate $x^2 - 4$ for $x = 5$.

_____

42. Solve the equation. $5m = {}^{-}45$

_____

Name _____

Write or draw the correct answer.

For questions 1–4, use triangle *ABC*. Its coordinates are ($^-$4,2), ($^-$1,2), and ($^-$4,4).

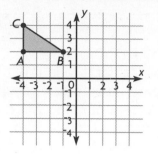

1. If you translate triangle *ABC* 4 units to the right, which coordinates will change?

   _____

2. If you translate triangle *ABC* 2 units down and 3 units to the right, what are the coordinates of the new triangle?

   _____

3. If you reflect triangle *ABC* across the *y*-axis, you create triangle *A'B'C'*. What are the coordinates of *A'*?

   _____

4. If you reflect triangle *ABC* across the *x*-axis, what are the coordinates of the new triangle?

   _____

For questions 5 and 6, use trapezoid *RSTU* with coordinates (0,3), (2,2), (2,1), and (0,0).

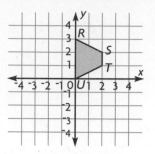

5. If you rotate this figure 90° counterclockwise around the origin, which vertex is the point of rotation?

   _____

6. If you rotate this figure 90° clockwise around the origin, what are the coordinates of the new figure?

   _____

For question 7, use the pattern on the grid.

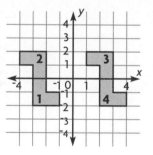

7. What pattern of transformations was used to move the figure from position 1 to position 4?

   _____

Harcourt Brace School Publishers

For questions 8–10, use the pattern.

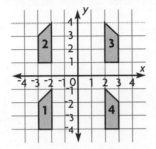

8. What pattern of transformations was used to move the figure from position 1 to position 4?

_____

9. What transformation would be used to move the figure to position 5?

_____

10. What transformation would be used to move the figure to position 6?

_____

11. How many cubes are in the next figure in the pattern?

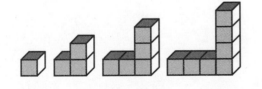

_____

For questions 12–14, draw the figure that comes next in the pattern.

12.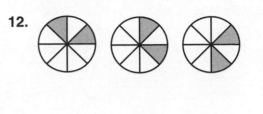

_____

13.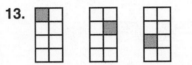

_____

14.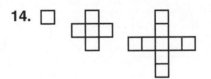

_____

15. How many dots will be in the next figure in the pattern?

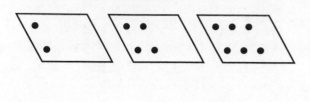

_____

16. How will the number of circles change for the next figure in this pattern?

_____

17. Can this figure be used to form a tessellation? Write *yes* or *no*.

_____

For questions 18–19, draw the tessellation shape described by the pattern.

18.

_____

19.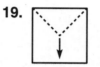

_____

20. Draw the shape that was used to form this tessellation.

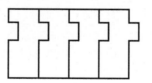

_____

Name _____

Write the correct answer.

1. An ordered set of numbers is a __?__.

_____

2. What rule is used to make this sequence?

3, 9, 27, 81

_____

For questions 3–6, find the next term in the sequence.

3. 7, 14, 21, 28, . . .

_____

4. 96, 72, 48, 24, . . .

_____

5. 0.7, 1.4, 2.8, 5.6, . . .

_____

6. 0.003, 0.3, 30, 3,000, . . .

_____

7. Sam wants to be able to lift a 200-lb weight. His training starts at 75 lb and increases 12.5 lb per day. In how many days will he reach his goal?

_____

8. Angel weeds gardens during the summer to make money. She earned $8 the first week, $17 the second week, and $26 the third week. If this pattern continues, how much money will she earn the sixth week?

_____

9. What should you do first to find the pattern of a sequence of fractions with different denominators?

_____

For questions 10–12, find the next term in the sequence.

10. $\frac{1}{6}, \frac{1}{3}, \frac{1}{2}, \ldots$

_____

11. $1, \frac{7}{8}, \frac{3}{4}, \ldots$

_____

12. $2\frac{3}{16}, 3\frac{1}{4}, 4\frac{5}{16}, \ldots$

_____

Harcourt Brace School Publishers

13. On the first day, Serena walked $\frac{1}{12}$ mi. On the next day, she walked $\frac{1}{3}$ mi. On the third day, she walked $\frac{7}{12}$ mi. To maintain this pattern, how far does she need to walk on the fourth day?

_____

14. What rule is used to make this sequence?

$\frac{3}{7}$, $1\frac{2}{7}$, $3\frac{6}{7}$, . . .

_____

For questions 15–17, find the next term in the sequence.

15. $\frac{17}{7}$, $\frac{12}{7}$, 1, . . .

_____

16. $\frac{1}{12}$, $\frac{1}{6}$, $\frac{1}{3}$, . . .

_____

17. 1, $\frac{1}{5}$, $\frac{1}{25}$, . . .

_____

18. A division sequence with a pattern of dividing by 3 has a first term of $\frac{1}{3}$. What is the fifth term?

_____

19. What rule is used in this sequence of integers?

$^+48$, $^-24$, $^+12$, $^-6$

_____

For questions 20–21, find the next term in the sequence.

20. $^-3$, $^+15$, $^-75$, . . .

_____

21. $^+512$, $^-64$, $^+8$, . . .

_____

22. Juan found a frog and wanted to see how far it could jump. On the first day it jumped $2\frac{1}{2}$ ft. On each of the following days, the frog jumped $\frac{1}{3}$ ft farther than the day before. How far did it jump on the seventh day?

_____

Name  _____

Write the correct answer.

For questions 1 and 2, use triangle *ABC*. Its coordinates are (1,2), (1,5), and (3,2).

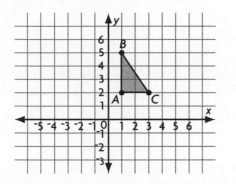

1. If you translate triangle *ABC* 3 units to the left, which of the coordinates will change?

_____

2. If you reflect triangle *ABC* across the *x* axis, what are the coordinates of the new triangle?

_____

For questions 3–5, use the pattern on the grid.

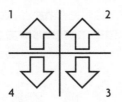

3. What pattern of transformations was used to move the figure from position 1 to position 4?

_____

4. What transformation would be used to move the figure to the next position?

_____

5. What transformation would be used to move the figure to position 6?

_____

6. How many spheres will there be in the next figure in the pattern?

_____

7. How many cubes will there be in the next figure in this sequence?

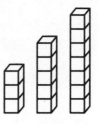

_____

8. Tell whether the shape shown below will form a tessellation.

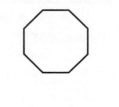

_____

9. Draw the tessellation shape that is formed by this pattern.

Form B • Free-Response   B263   **Go on.** ▶

For questions 10 and 11, find the next term in the sequence.

10. 54, 42, 30, 18, . . .

_____

11. 12, 6, 3, 1.5, . . .

_____

For questions 12 and 13, find the next term in the sequence.

12. $\frac{5}{8}, \frac{1}{2}, \frac{3}{8}, \frac{1}{4}, \ldots$

_____

13. $1\frac{4}{5}, 2\frac{1}{5}, 2\frac{3}{5}, 3, \ldots$

_____

14. Lea babysat for $1\frac{1}{2}$ hr on Monday, $2\frac{1}{4}$ hr on Tuesday, and 3 hr on Wednesday. If this pattern continues, how many hours will she babysit on Thursday?

_____

15. What pattern is used to make the sequence?

$\frac{1}{8}, \frac{5}{8}, 3\frac{1}{8}, \ldots$

_____

16. Find the next term in the sequence.

$\frac{3}{10}, \frac{6}{10}, 1\frac{1}{5}, \ldots$

_____

17. A multiplication sequence with a pattern of multiplying by 3 has a first term of $\frac{1}{6}$. What is the fourth term?

_____

For questions 18 and 19, find the next term in the sequence.

18. $^{+}36, ^{-}18, ^{+}9, \ldots$

_____

19. $^{-}24, ^{-}21, ^{-}18, \ldots$

_____

20. The temperature on Monday was 20°F. The forecast was for the temperature to fall 6° a day for the next 4 days. What was the probable temperature on Friday?

_____

Name _____

Write the correct answer.

1. What is the value of the digit 4 in the number 347,560.21?

_____

2. $7\overline{)5{,}422}$

_____

3. $3.076 + 2.73$

_____

4. Cheryl bought 2.5 lb of chicken at $2.82 a pound. How much did the chicken cost?

_____

5. Solve for n to complete the prime factorization.

$3^n = 243$

_____

6. Find the difference in simplest form.

$\dfrac{2}{3} - \dfrac{5}{12}$

_____

7. Stephanie jogged $9\frac{5}{8}$ mi on the first day and $6\frac{9}{10}$ mi on the second day. About how far did she jog in all?

_____

8. Jocelyn wants to make a rectangular patio with an area of $48\frac{1}{2}$ sq ft. The width of the patio will be 8 ft. How long should the patio be?

_____

9. How many angles does a hexagon have?

_____

10. Choose the figure that is a rotation of the original figure.

original   figure 1   figure 2   figure 3

_____

11. Name this figure.

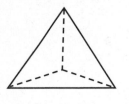

_____

12. Dan is making a model of a pyramid whose base has 8 sides. He is using toothpicks for the edges and balls of putty for the vertices. How many balls of putty does he need?

_____

13. Is the following question from a sports survey biased or not biased?

How often do you attend sporting events?

_____

14. Use the graph.

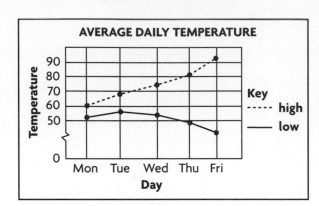

What was the trend for low temperatures?

_____

15. The box-and-whisker graph shows the number of problems that 18 students got correct on a history quiz with 45 problems. What is the median?

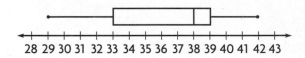

28 29 30 31 32 33 34 35 36 37 38 39 40 41 42 43

_____

16. Erin tosses a coin 150 times. Heads comes up 70 times. What is the experimental probability of tossing heads?

_____

17. Determine the input for the given output for this expression: $w + 14$.

output = 32   input = _?_

_____

18. Solve for *c*. $c - 7 = 8$

_____

19. Solve for *m*. $4m = 52$

_____

20. What is 18°C converted to degrees Fahrenheit? Use the formula $F = (\frac{9}{5} \times C) + 32$. Round to the nearest degree.

_____

21. Barbara is in a 30-mi bike race. How long is this ride in kilometers? (1 mi = 1.609 km)

_____

22. Keri answered 28 of the 40 problems on her science test correctly. What percent did she answer correctly?

_____

23. What is 20% of 90?

_____

24. Barry had $100 that earned 6% simple interest a year in a bank. After 3 years, he withdrew his money. How much did he withdraw?

_____

25. Find *n* in this pair of similar triangles.

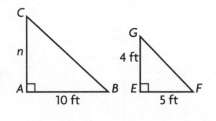

_____

26. A map scale is 1 in. = 15 mi. The map distance is 7.3 in. Find the actual miles.

_____

27. Which is the more precise measurement for the length of a table—3 ft or 37 in.?

_____

28. Estimate the area of the figure. Each square is 2 cm^2.

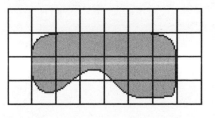

_____

29. Byron is installing wallpaper in his bedroom on one wall. The wall is 13 ft by 9 ft. The wallpaper costs $6 per sq ft. What will be the total cost of the wallpaper? (Use the formula $A = l \times w$.)

_____

30. Use the figure below.

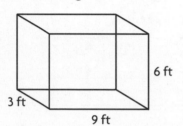

If you double all the dimensions of this figure, what is the volume of the larger prism?

_____

31. Write the repeating or terminating decimal for $\frac{1}{6}$.

_____

32. Compare the numbers. Choose $<$, $>$, or $=$.

$\frac{4}{5}$ ● $^-0.80$

_____

33. Find the difference. $^+9 - {^-6}$

_____

34. Find the product. $^-6 \times 29$

_____

35. Solve the equation. $f + 7 = {^-5}$

_____

36. How will the number of circles change for the next figure in this pattern?

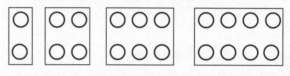

_____

For questions 37–38, find the next term in the sequence.

37. 18, 27, 36, 45, . . .

_____

38. 2, 1, $\frac{1}{2}$, $\frac{1}{4}$, $\frac{1}{8}$, . . .

_____

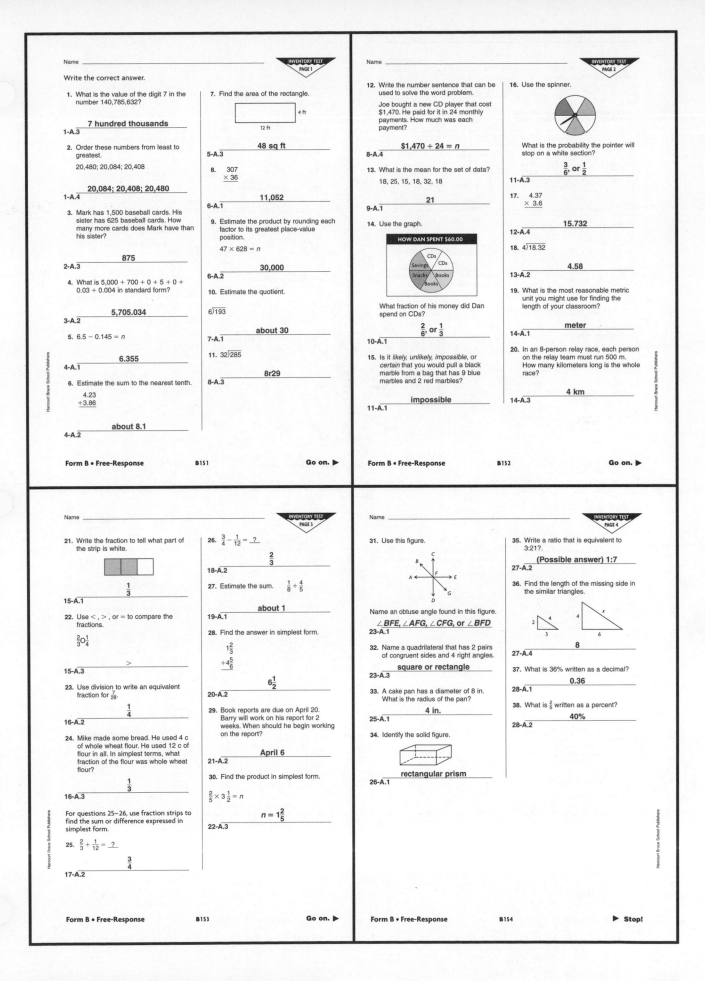

Name _____

Write the correct answer.

1. What is the value of the digit 7 in the number 140,785,632?

7 hundred thousands
1-A.3

2. Order these numbers from least to greatest.

20,480; 20,084; 20,408

20,084; 20,408; 20,480
1-A.4

3. Mark has 1,500 baseball cards. His sister has 625 baseball cards. How many more cards does Mark have than his sister?

875
2-A.3

4. What is 5,000 + 700 + 0 + 5 + 0 + 0.03 + 0.004 in standard form?

5,705.034
3-A.2

5. 6.5 − 0.145 = n

6.355
4-A.1

6. Estimate the sum to the nearest tenth.

4.23
+3.86

about 8.1
4-A.2

7. Find the area of the rectangle.

4 ft
12 ft

48 sq ft
5-A.3

8. 307
× 36

11,052
6-A.1

9. Estimate the product by rounding each factor to its greatest place-value position.

47 × 628 = n

30,000
6-A.2

10. Estimate the quotient.

6)193

about 30
7-A.1

11. 32)285

8r29
8-A.3

Form B • Free-Response   B151   **Go on. ▶**

Name _____

12. Write the number sentence that can be used to solve the word problem.

Joe bought a new CD player that cost $1,470. He paid for it in 24 monthly payments. How much was each payment?

$1,470 ÷ 24 = n
8-A.4

13. What is the mean for the set of data?

18, 25, 15, 18, 32, 18

21
9-A.1

14. Use the graph.

HOW DAN SPENT $60.00

CDs
CDs
Savings
Snacks
Books
Books

What fraction of his money did Dan spend on CDs?

$\frac{2}{6}$, or $\frac{1}{3}$
10-A.1

15. Is it likely, unlikely, impossible, or certain that you would pull a black marble from a bag that has 9 blue marbles and 2 red marbles?

impossible
11-A.1

16. Use the spinner.

What is the probability the pointer will stop on a white section?

$\frac{3}{6}$, or $\frac{1}{2}$
11-A.3

17. 4.37
× 3.6

15.732
12-A.4

18. 4)18.32

4.58
13-A.2

19. What is the most reasonable metric unit you might use for finding the length of your classroom?

meter
14-A.1

20. In an 8-person relay race, each person on the relay team must run 500 m. How many kilometers long is the whole race?

4 km
14-A.3

Form B • Free-Response   B152   **Go on. ▶**

Name _____

21. Write the fraction to tell what part of the strip is white.

$\frac{1}{3}$
15-A.1

22. Use <, >, or = to compare the fractions.

$\frac{2}{3}$ ◯ $\frac{1}{4}$

>
15-A.3

23. Use division to write an equivalent fraction for $\frac{7}{28}$.

$\frac{1}{4}$
16-A.2

24. Mike made some bread. He used 4 c of whole wheat flour. He used 12 c of flour in all. In simplest terms, what fraction of the flour was whole wheat flour?

$\frac{1}{3}$
16-A.3

For questions 25–26, use fraction strips to find the sum or difference expressed in simplest form.

25. $\frac{2}{3} + \frac{1}{12} = $?

$\frac{3}{4}$
17-A.2

26. $\frac{3}{4} - \frac{1}{12} = $?

$\frac{2}{3}$
18-A.2

27. Estimate the sum. $\frac{1}{8} + \frac{4}{5}$

about 1
19-A.1

28. Find the answer in simplest form.

$1\frac{2}{3}$
$+4\frac{5}{6}$

$6\frac{1}{2}$
20-A.2

29. Book reports are due on April 20. Barry will work on his report for 2 weeks. When should he begin working on the report?

April 6
21-A.2

30. Find the product in simplest form.

$\frac{2}{5} \times 3\frac{1}{2} = n$

$n = 1\frac{2}{5}$
22-A.3

Form B • Free-Response   B153   **Go on. ▶**

Name _____

31. Use this figure.

Name an obtuse angle found in this figure.

∠BFE, ∠AFG, ∠CFG, or ∠BFD
23-A.1

32. Name a quadrilateral that has 2 pairs of congruent sides and 4 right angles.

square or rectangle
23-A.3

33. A cake pan has a diameter of 8 in. What is the radius of the pan?

4 in.
25-A.1

34. Identify the solid figure.

rectangular prism
26-A.1

35. Write a ratio that is equivalent to 3:21?.

(Possible answer) 1:7
27-A.2

36. Find the length of the missing side in the similar triangles.

8
27-A.4

37. What is 36% written as a decimal?

0.36
28-A.1

38. What is $\frac{2}{5}$ written as a percent?

40%
28-A.2

Form B • Free-Response   B154   **▶ Stop!**

Harcourt Brace School Publishers

Free-Response Format • Test Answers

Name

Write the correct answer.

For questions 1–2, use the place-value chart.

PLACE VALUE									
9	6	4	5	8	2	7	.1	0	3

1. What is the value of the digit 6?

6 hundred thousands

2. What is the value of the digit 3?

3 thousandths

3. What is the value of the digit 5 in the number 147,250.68?

5 tens

4. What is the value of the digit 2 in the number 3.02719?

2 hundredths

5. Write the standard form of six million, five hundred eighty thousand, twelve.

6,580,012

6. Write the standard form of thirteen hundredths.

0.13

7. Is 8.528 greater than, equal to, or less than 8.534?

8.528 is **less than** 8.534.

8. Write the following numbers in order from greatest to least.
593.7; 539.75; 593.73

593.73, 593.7, 539.75

9. The snowfall was 6.3 in. during December, 9.9 in. during January, 6.6 in. during February, and 7.5 in. during March. Write the numbers in order from the greatest to the least snowfall.

9.9 in., 7.5 in., 6.6 in., 6.3 in.

10. At the swim meet, the four fastest swimmers in a race were Scott, Theo, Jesse, and Paul. Scott finished the race in 34.56 sec, Theo finished in 33.65 sec, Jesse finished in 34.78 sec, and Paul in 33.92 sec. Who finished in third place?

Scott

Form B • Free-Response   B155   Go on. ▶

Name

11. When changing 0.7 to a fraction, what number would you use in the denominator?

10

12. The way to change a fraction to a decimal is to _?_ the numerator by the denominator.

divide

13. What is $\frac{3}{8}$ written as a decimal?

0.375

14. What sign will make the following inequality true?

$\frac{13}{20}$ ● 0.70

<

15. Mrs. Gordon's stock went up $0.625 yesterday. What fraction did the stock go up?

$\frac{625}{1,000}$

16. Nina swam $\frac{9}{20}$ mi. What is the distance she swam, expressed as a decimal?

0.45 mi

17. How many zeros are in the standard form of 10^{13}?

13

18. What is $15 \times 15 \times 15 \times 15 \times 15$ written in exponent form?

15^5

19. What is the value of 12^2?

144

20. What is the value of 3^4?

81

21. Is $^+8$ greater than, equal to, or less than $^-9$?

greater than

For questions 22–23, write the integers in order from least to greatest.

22. $^-5, {}^+3, {}^+6, {}^-4$

$^-5, {}^-4, {}^+3, {}^+6$

23. $^-8, {}^+1, {}^-7, 0$

$^-8, {}^-7, 0, {}^+1$

24. What is the opposite of $^+74$?

$^-74$

Form B • Free-Response   B156   ▶ Stop!

Name

Write the correct answer.

For questions 1–2, use mental math.

1. $14 + 9 + 26$

49

2. $37 + 18 + 22 + 13$

90

For questions 3–4, use compensation.

3. $44 - 28$

16

4. $65 - 39$

26

5. The piñata was filled with 83 jelly beans, some red and some black. There were 15 more red jelly beans than black ones. How many red jelly beans were there?

49 red jelly beans

6. Iris recycled a total of 48 newspapers and magazines. She recycled 10 more newspapers than magazines. How many newspapers did she recycle?

29 newspapers

7. During a 30-day period, there were 6 more rainy days than dry days. How many rainy days were there?

18 days

8. The perimeter of the class garden is 52 ft. The length is 8 ft longer than the width. What is the length of the garden?

17 ft

9. Which property is being used in the multiplication problem below?

$5 \times 3 = 3 \times 5$

Commutative Property

For questions 10–11, use mental math to find the product.

10. $2 \times 6 \times 7$

84

11. $6 \times 15 \times 4$

360

12. Find the missing factor.

$52 \times 16 = (52 \times \square) + (52 \times 6)$

10

13. Rhonda is solving the multiplication problem below. What mistake, if any, has Rhonda made?

$\begin{array}{r} 105 \\ \times\ 24 \\ \hline 420 \\ 210 \end{array}$

Possible answer: She multiplied by 2 instead of 20.

Form B • Free-Response   B157   Go on. ▶

Name

14. In this division problem, where would you place the first digit of the quotient?

$6\overline{)452}$

in the **tens** place, or over the **5**

15. $\begin{array}{r} 280 \\ \times\ 42 \\ \hline 11,760 \end{array}$

16. $\begin{array}{r} 4,327 \\ \times\ 156 \\ \hline 675,012 \end{array}$

17. $14\overline{)882}$ → **63**

18. $20\overline{)3,054}$ → **152 r14**

19. The football stadium holds 2,500 people. All 7 games held at the stadium were sold out. How many people attended games at the stadium?

17,500 people

20. The Hudson family drove 1,248 mi on their vacation. They used 48 gal of gas. How many miles per gallon did they get?

26 mi per gallon

21. Estimate the difference to the nearest hundred.

$\begin{array}{r} 7,385 \\ -4,712 \\ \hline 2,700 \end{array}$

22. Estimate the product to the nearest hundred.

$\begin{array}{r} 621 \\ \times 569 \\ \hline 360,000 \end{array}$

23. On Monday 312 students visited the museum. On Tuesday 273 students visited the museum, and on Wednesday, 341. About how many students visited the museum in all? Round to the nearest hundred students.

900 students

24. For the upcoming concert, 5,589 tickets were sold in 73 min. About how many tickets were sold per minute? Round to the nearest ten tickets.

80 tickets per minute

Form B • Free-Response   B158   ▶ Stop!

Free-Response Format • Test Answers

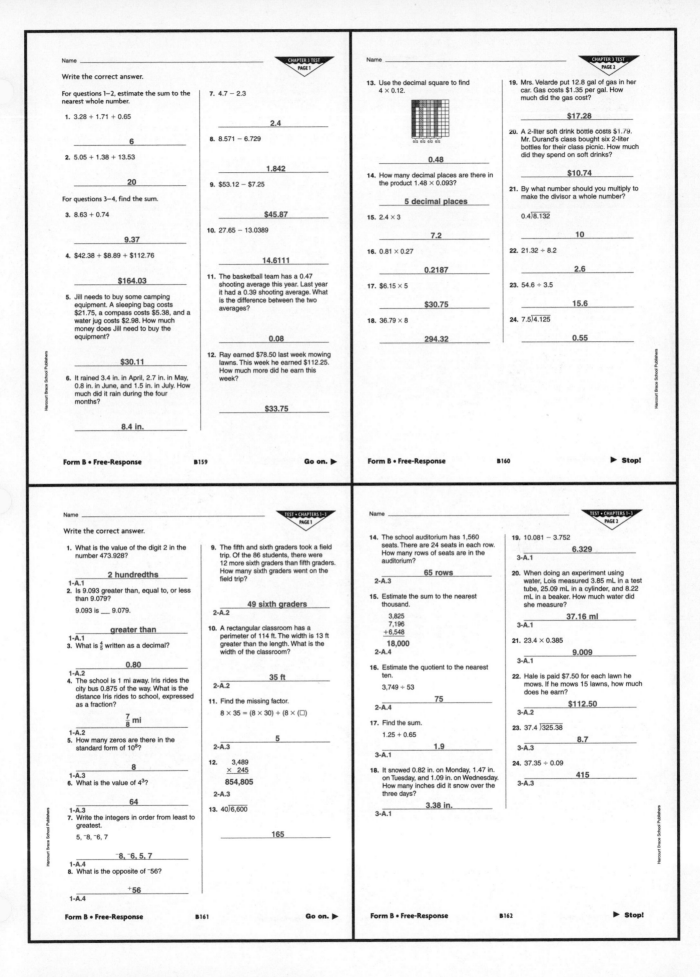

Write the correct answer.

For questions 1–2, estimate the sum to the nearest whole number.

1. 3.28 + 1.71 + 0.65

_____ 6

2. 5.05 + 1.38 + 13.53

_____ 20

For questions 3–4, find the sum.

3. 8.63 + 0.74

_____ 9.37

4. $42.38 + $8.89 + $112.76

_____ $164.03

5. Jill needs to buy some camping equipment. A sleeping bag costs $21.75, a compass costs $5.38, and a water jug costs $2.98. How much money does Jill need to buy the equipment?

_____ $30.11

6. It rained 3.4 in. in April, 2.7 in. in May, 0.8 in. in June, and 1.5 in. in July. How much did it rain during the four months?

_____ 8.4 in.

7. 4.7 − 2.3

_____ 2.4

8. 8.571 − 6.729

_____ 1.842

9. $53.12 − $7.25

_____ $45.87

10. 27.65 − 13.0389

_____ 14.6111

11. The basketball team has a 0.47 shooting average this year. Last year it had a 0.39 shooting average. What is the difference between the two averages?

_____ 0.08

12. Ray earned $78.50 last week mowing lawns. This week he earned $112.25. How much more did he earn this week?

_____ $33.75

Form B • Free-Response   B159   **Go on. ▶**

---

13. Use the decimal square to find 4 × 0.12.

_____ 0.48

14. How many decimal places are there in the product 1.48 × 0.093?

_____ 5 decimal places

15. 2.4 × 3

_____ 7.2

16. 0.81 × 0.27

_____ 0.2187

17. $6.15 × 5

_____ $30.75

18. 36.79 × 8

_____ 294.32

19. Mrs. Velarde put 12.8 gal of gas in her car. Gas costs $1.35 per gal. How much did the gas cost?

_____ $17.28

20. A 2-liter soft drink bottle costs $1.79. Mr. Durand's class bought six 2-liter bottles for their class picnic. How much did they spend on soft drinks?

_____ $10.74

21. By what number should you multiply to make the divisor a whole number?

0.4)8.132

_____ 10

22. 21.32 ÷ 8.2

_____ 2.6

23. 54.6 ÷ 3.5

_____ 15.6

24. 7.5)4.125

_____ 0.55

Form B • Free-Response   B160   **▶ Stop!**

Write the correct answer.

1. What is the value of the digit 2 in the number 473.928?

_____ 2 hundredths
1-A.1

2. Is 9.093 greater than, equal to, or less than 9.079?

9.093 is ___ 9.079.

_____ greater than
1-A.1

3. What is $\frac{4}{5}$ written as a decimal?

_____ 0.80
1-A.2

4. The school is 1 mi away. Iris rides the city bus 0.875 of the way. What is the distance Iris rides to school, expressed as a fraction?

_____ $\frac{7}{8}$ mi
1-A.2

5. How many zeros are there in the standard form of 10^8?

_____ 8
1-A.3

6. What is the value of 4^3?

_____ 64
1-A.3

7. Write the integers in order from least to greatest.

5, ⁻8, ⁻6, 7

_____ ⁻8, ⁻6, 5, 7
1-A.4

8. What is the opposite of ⁻56?

_____ ⁺56
1-A.4

9. The fifth and sixth graders took a field trip. Of the 86 students, there were 12 more sixth graders than fifth graders. How many sixth graders went on the field trip?

_____ 49 sixth graders
2-A.2

10. A rectangular classroom has a perimeter of 114 ft. The width is 13 ft greater than the length. What is the width of the classroom?

_____ 35 ft
2-A.2

11. Find the missing factor.

8 × 35 = (8 × 30) + (8 × (□))

_____ 5
2-A.3

12. 3,489
   × 245
   _____
   854,805
2-A.3

13. 40)6,600

_____ 165

Form B • Free-Response   B161   **Go on. ▶**

---

14. The school auditorium has 1,560 seats. There are 24 seats in each row. How many rows of seats are in the auditorium?

_____ 65 rows
2-A.3

15. Estimate the sum to the nearest thousand.

   3,825
   7,196
   +6,548
   _____
   18,000
2-A.4

16. Estimate the quotient to the nearest ten.

3,749 ÷ 53

_____ 75
2-A.4

17. Find the sum.

1.25 + 0.65

_____ 1.9
3-A.1

18. It snowed 0.82 in. on Monday, 1.47 in. on Tuesday, and 1.09 in. on Wednesday. How many inches did it snow over the three days?

_____ 3.38 in.
3-A.1

19. 10.081 − 3.752

_____ 6.329
3-A.1

20. When doing an experiment using water, Lois measured 3.85 mL in a test tube, 25.09 mL in a cylinder, and 8.22 mL in a beaker. How much water did she measure?

_____ 37.16 ml
3-A.1

21. 23.4 × 0.385

_____ 9.009
3-A.1

22. Hale is paid $7.50 for each lawn he mows. If he mows 15 lawns, how much does he earn?

_____ $112.50
3-A.2

23. 37.4)325.38

_____ 8.7
3-A.3

24. 37.35 ÷ 0.09

_____ 415
3-A.3

Form B • Free-Response   B162   **▶ Stop!**

Free-Response Format • Test Answers

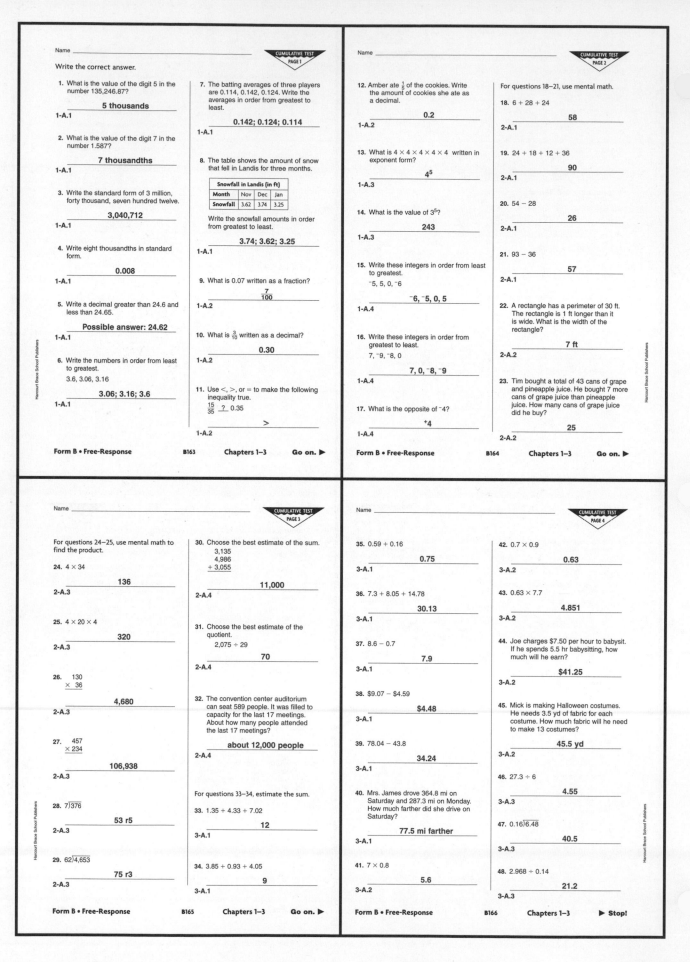

Write the correct answer.

1. What is the value of the digit 5 in the number 135,246.87?

5 thousands

1-A.1

2. What is the value of the digit 7 in the number 1.587?

7 thousandths

1-A.1

3. Write the standard form of 3 million, forty thousand, seven hundred twelve.

3,040,712

1-A.1

4. Write eight thousandths in standard form.

0.008

1-A.1

5. Write a decimal greater than 24.6 and less than 24.65.

Possible answer: 24.62

1-A.1

6. Write the numbers in order from least to greatest.

3.6, 3.06, 3.16

3.06; 3.16; 3.6

1-A.1

7. The batting averages of three players are 0.114, 0.142, 0.124. Write the averages in order from greatest to least.

0.142; 0.124; 0.114

1-A.1

8. The table shows the amount of snow that fell in Landis for three months.

Snowfall in Landis (in ft)			
Month	Nov	Dec	Jan
Snowfall	3.62	3.74	3.25

Write the snowfall amounts in order from greatest to least.

3.74; 3.62; 3.25

1-A.1

9. What is 0.07 written as a fraction?

$\frac{7}{100}$

1-A.2

10. What is $\frac{3}{10}$ written as a decimal?

0.30

1-A.2

11. Use <, >, or = to make the following inequality true.

$\frac{15}{35}$ __?__ 0.35

>

1-A.2

Form B • Free-Response　　B163　　**Chapters 1–3**　　Go on. ▶

12. Amber ate $\frac{1}{5}$ of the cookies. Write the amount of cookies she ate as a decimal.

0.2

1-A.2

13. What is $4 \times 4 \times 4 \times 4 \times 4$ written in exponent form?

4^5

1-A.3

14. What is the value of 3^5?

243

1-A.3

15. Write these integers in order from least to greatest.

$^-5$, 5, 0, $^-6$

$^-6, ^-5, 0, 5$

1-A.4

16. Write these integers in order from greatest to least.

7, $^-9$, $^-8$, 0

$7, 0, ^-8, ^-9$

1-A.4

17. What is the opposite of $^-4$?

$^+4$

1-A.4

For questions 18–21, use mental math.

18. $6 + 28 + 24$

58

2-A.1

19. $24 + 18 + 12 + 36$

90

2-A.1

20. $54 - 28$

26

2-A.1

21. $93 - 36$

57

2-A.1

22. A rectangle has a perimeter of 30 ft. The rectangle is 1 ft longer than it is wide. What is the width of the rectangle?

7 ft

2-A.2

23. Tim bought a total of 43 cans of grape and pineapple juice. He bought 7 more cans of grape juice than pineapple juice. How many cans of grape juice did he buy?

25

2-A.2

Form B • Free-Response　　B164　　**Chapters 1–3**　　Go on. ▶

For questions 24–25, use mental math to find the product.

24. 4×34

136

2-A.3

25. $4 \times 20 \times 4$

320

2-A.3

26. 130
　× 36

4,680

2-A.3

27. 457
　× 234

106,938

2-A.3

28. $7)\overline{376}$

53 r5

2-A.3

29. $62)\overline{4,653}$

75 r3

2-A.3

30. Choose the best estimate of the sum.

3,135
4,986
+ 3,055

11,000

2-A.4

31. Choose the best estimate of the quotient.

$2,075 \div 29$

70

2-A.4

32. The convention center auditorium can seat 589 people. It was filled to capacity for the last 17 meetings. About how many people attended the last 17 meetings?

about 12,000 people

2-A.4

For questions 33–34, estimate the sum.

33. $1.35 + 4.33 + 7.02$

12

3-A.1

34. $3.85 + 0.93 + 4.05$

9

3-A.1

Form B • Free-Response　　B165　　**Chapters 1–3**　　Go on. ▶

35. $0.59 + 0.16$

0.75

3-A.1

36. $7.3 + 8.05 + 14.78$

30.13

3-A.1

37. $8.6 - 0.7$

7.9

3-A.1

38. $\$9.07 - \$4.59$

$4.48

3-A.1

39. $78.04 - 43.8$

34.24

3-A.1

40. Mrs. James drove 364.8 mi on Saturday and 287.3 mi on Monday. How much farther did she drive on Saturday?

77.5 mi farther

3-A.1

41. 7×0.8

5.6

3-A.2

42. 0.7×0.9

0.63

3-A.2

43. 0.63×7.7

4.851

3-A.2

44. Joe charges $7.50 per hour to babysit. If he spends 5.5 hr babysitting, how much will he earn?

$41.25

3-A.2

45. Mick is making Halloween costumes. He needs 3.5 yd of fabric for each costume. How much fabric will he need to make 13 costumes?

45.5 yd

3-A.2

46. $27.3 \div 6$

4.55

3-A.3

47. $0.16)\overline{6.48}$

40.5

3-A.3

48. $2.968 \div 0.14$

21.2

3-A.3

Form B • Free-Response　　B166　　**Chapters 1–3**　　▶ Stop!

Free-Response Format • Test Answers

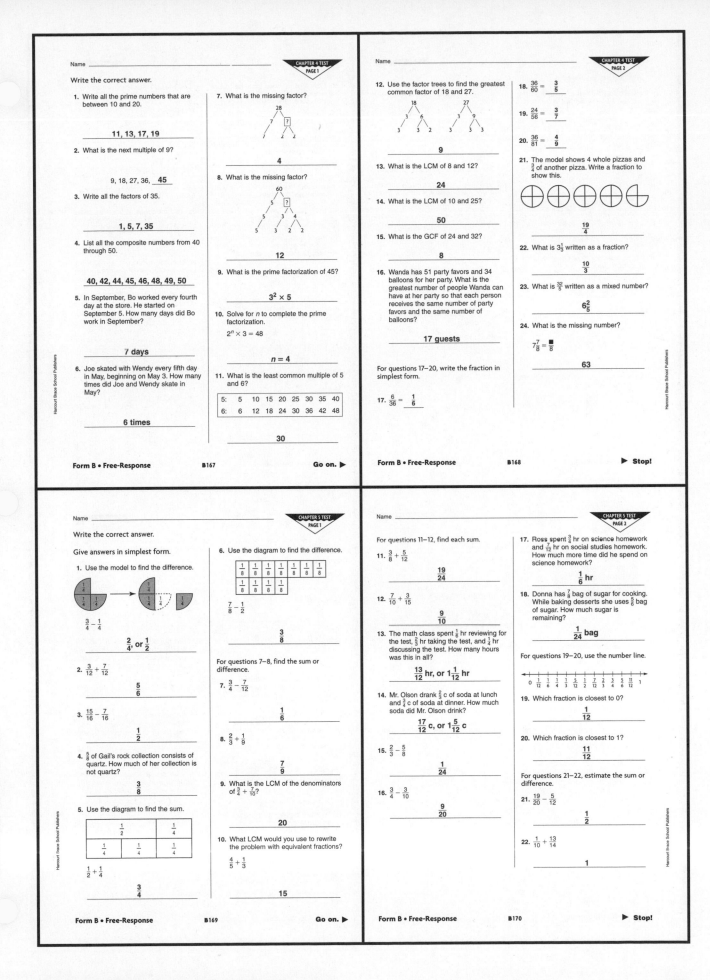

Name _____

Write the correct answer.

1. Write all the prime numbers that are between 10 and 20.

11, 13, 17, 19

2. What is the next multiple of 9?

9, 18, 27, 36, **45**

3. Write all the factors of 35.

1, 5, 7, 35

4. List all the composite numbers from 40 through 50.

40, 42, 44, 45, 46, 48, 49, 50

5. In September, Bo worked every fourth day at the store. He started on September 5. How many days did Bo work in September?

7 days

6. Joe skated with Wendy every fifth day in May, beginning on May 3. How many times did Joe and Wendy skate in May?

6 times

7. What is the missing factor?

4

8. What is the missing factor?

12

9. What is the prime factorization of 45?

$3^2 \times 5$

10. Solve for n to complete the prime factorization.

$2^n \times 3 = 48$

$n = 4$

11. What is the least common multiple of 5 and 6?

| 5: | 5 | 10 | 15 | 20 | 25 | 30 | 35 | 40 |
| 6: | 6 | 12 | 18 | 24 | 30 | 36 | 42 | 48 |

30

Form B • Free-Response   B167   Go on. ▶

Name _____

12. Use the factor trees to find the greatest common factor of 18 and 27.

9

13. What is the LCM of 8 and 12?

24

14. What is the LCM of 10 and 25?

50

15. What is the GCF of 24 and 32?

8

16. Wanda has 51 party favors and 34 balloons for her party. What is the greatest number of people Wanda can have at her party so that each person receives the same number of party favors and the same number of balloons?

17 guests

For questions 17–20, write the fraction in simplest form.

17. $\frac{6}{36} = \frac{1}{6}$

18. $\frac{36}{60} = \frac{3}{5}$

19. $\frac{24}{56} = \frac{3}{7}$

20. $\frac{36}{81} = \frac{4}{9}$

21. The model shows 4 whole pizzas and $\frac{3}{4}$ of another pizza. Write a fraction to show this.

$\frac{19}{4}$

22. What is $3\frac{1}{3}$ written as a fraction?

$\frac{10}{3}$

23. What is $\frac{32}{5}$ written as a mixed number?

$6\frac{2}{5}$

24. What is the missing number?

$7\frac{7}{8} = \frac{\blacksquare}{8}$

63

Form B • Free-Response   B168   ▶ Stop!

Name _____

Write the correct answer.

Give answers in simplest form.

1. Use the model to find the difference.

$\frac{3}{4} - \frac{1}{4}$

$\frac{2}{4}$, or $\frac{1}{2}$

2. $\frac{3}{12} + \frac{7}{12}$

$\frac{5}{6}$

3. $\frac{15}{16} - \frac{7}{16}$

$\frac{1}{2}$

4. $\frac{5}{8}$ of Gail's rock collection consists of quartz. How much of her collection is not quartz?

$\frac{3}{8}$

5. Use the diagram to find the sum.

| $\frac{1}{2}$ | | $\frac{1}{4}$ |
| $\frac{1}{4}$ | $\frac{1}{4}$ | $\frac{1}{4}$ |

$\frac{1}{2} + \frac{1}{4}$

$\frac{3}{4}$

6. Use the diagram to find the difference.

$\frac{7}{8} - \frac{1}{2}$

$\frac{3}{8}$

For questions 7–8, find the sum or difference.

7. $\frac{3}{4} - \frac{7}{12}$

$\frac{1}{6}$

8. $\frac{2}{3} + \frac{1}{9}$

$\frac{7}{9}$

9. What is the LCM of the denominators of $\frac{3}{4} + \frac{7}{10}$?

20

10. What LCM would you use to rewrite the problem with equivalent fractions?

$\frac{4}{5} + \frac{1}{3}$

15

Form B • Free-Response   B169   Go on. ▶

Name _____

For questions 11–12, find each sum.

11. $\frac{3}{8} + \frac{5}{12}$

$\frac{19}{24}$

12. $\frac{7}{10} + \frac{3}{15}$

$\frac{9}{10}$

13. The math class spent $\frac{1}{8}$ hr reviewing for the test, $\frac{2}{3}$ hr taking the test, and $\frac{1}{4}$ hr discussing the test. How many hours was this in all?

$\frac{13}{12}$ hr, or $1\frac{1}{12}$ hr

14. Mr. Olson drank $\frac{2}{3}$ c of soda at lunch and $\frac{3}{4}$ c of soda at dinner. How much soda did Mr. Olson drink?

$\frac{17}{12}$ c, or $1\frac{5}{12}$ c

15. $\frac{2}{3} - \frac{5}{8}$

$\frac{1}{24}$

16. $\frac{3}{4} - \frac{3}{10}$

$\frac{9}{20}$

17. Ross spent $\frac{3}{4}$ hr on science homework and $\frac{7}{12}$ hr on social studies homework. How much more time did he spend on science homework?

$\frac{1}{6}$ hr

18. Donna has $\frac{7}{8}$ bag of sugar for cooking. While baking desserts she uses $\frac{5}{6}$ bag of sugar. How much sugar is remaining?

$\frac{1}{24}$ bag

For questions 19–20, use the number line.

19. Which fraction is closest to 0?

$\frac{1}{12}$

20. Which fraction is closest to 1?

$\frac{11}{12}$

For questions 21–22, estimate the sum or difference.

21. $\frac{19}{20} - \frac{5}{12}$

$\frac{1}{2}$

22. $\frac{1}{10} + \frac{13}{14}$

1

Form B • Free-Response   B170   ▶ Stop!

Free-Response Format • Test Answers

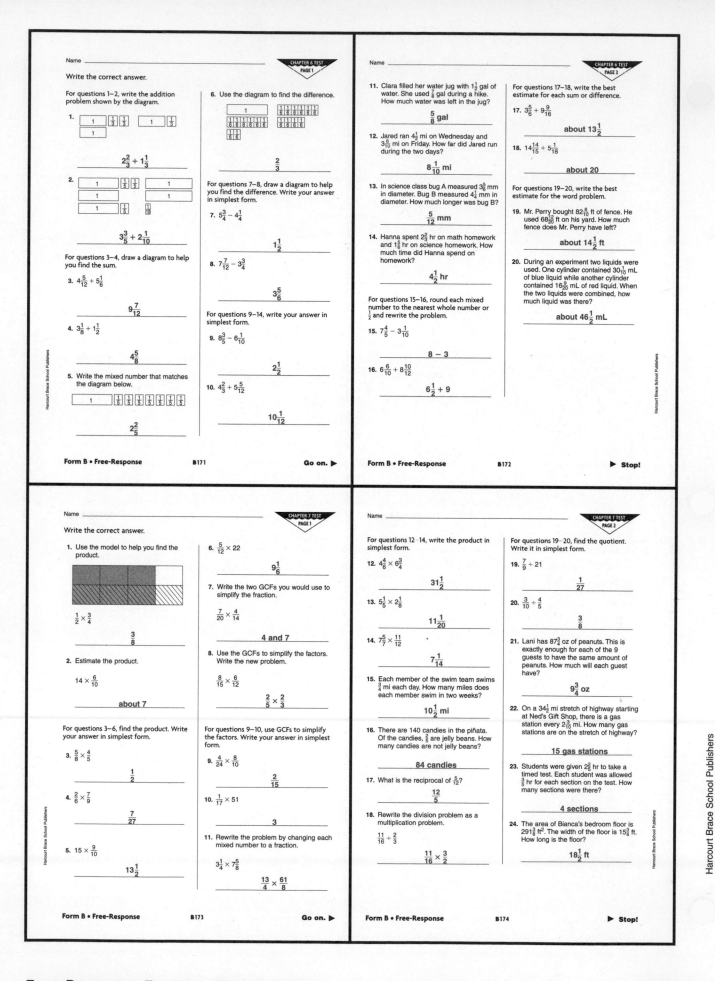

Chapter 6 Test — Page 1

Name _____

Write the correct answer.

For questions 1–2, write the addition problem shown by the diagram.

1. [diagram]

$2\frac{2}{3} + 1\frac{1}{3}$

2. [diagram]

$3\frac{3}{5} + 2\frac{1}{10}$

For questions 3–4, draw a diagram to help you find the sum.

3. $4\frac{5}{12} + 5\frac{1}{6}$

$9\frac{7}{12}$

4. $3\frac{1}{8} + 1\frac{1}{2}$

$4\frac{5}{8}$

5. Write the mixed number that matches the diagram below.

[diagram]

$2\frac{2}{5}$

6. Use the diagram to find the difference.

[diagram]

$\frac{2}{3}$

For questions 7–8, draw a diagram to help you find the difference. Write your answer in simplest form.

7. $5\frac{3}{4} - 4\frac{1}{4}$

$1\frac{1}{2}$

8. $7\frac{7}{12} - 3\frac{3}{4}$

$3\frac{5}{6}$

For questions 9–14, write your answer in simplest form.

9. $8\frac{3}{5} - 6\frac{1}{10}$

$2\frac{1}{2}$

10. $4\frac{2}{3} + 5\frac{5}{12}$

$10\frac{1}{12}$

Form B • Free-Response   B171   Go on. ▶

Chapter 6 Test — Page 2

Name _____

11. Clara filled her water jug with $1\frac{1}{2}$ gal of water. She used $\frac{6}{8}$ gal during a hike. How much water was left in the jug?

$\frac{5}{8}$ gal

12. Jared ran $4\frac{1}{2}$ mi on Wednesday and $3\frac{6}{10}$ mi on Friday. How far did Jared run during the two days?

$8\frac{1}{10}$ mi

13. In science class bug A measured $3\frac{5}{8}$ mm in diameter. Bug B measured $4\frac{1}{4}$ mm in diameter. How much longer was bug B?

$\frac{5}{12}$ mm

14. Hanna spent $2\frac{5}{8}$ hr on math homework and $1\frac{5}{8}$ hr on science homework. How much time did Hanna spend on homework?

$4\frac{1}{2}$ hr

For questions 15–16, round each mixed number to the nearest whole number or $\frac{1}{2}$ and rewrite the problem.

15. $7\frac{4}{5} - 3\frac{1}{10}$

$8 - 3$

16. $6\frac{6}{10} + 8\frac{10}{12}$

$6\frac{1}{2} + 9$

For questions 17–18, write the best estimate for each sum or difference.

17. $3\frac{5}{6} + 9\frac{9}{16}$

about $13\frac{1}{2}$

18. $14\frac{14}{15} + 5\frac{1}{18}$

about 20

For questions 19–20, write the best estimate for the word problem.

19. Mr. Perry bought $82\frac{8}{10}$ ft of fence. He used $68\frac{12}{20}$ ft on his yard. How much fence does Mr. Perry have left?

about $14\frac{1}{2}$ ft

20. During an experiment two liquids were used. One cylinder contained $30\frac{1}{10}$ mL of blue liquid while another cylinder contained $16\frac{8}{20}$ mL of red liquid. When the two liquids were combined, how much liquid was there?

about $46\frac{1}{2}$ mL

Form B • Free-Response   B172   ▶ Stop!

Chapter 7 Test — Page 1

Name _____

Write the correct answer.

1. Use the model to help you find the product.

[model]

$\frac{1}{2} \times \frac{3}{4}$

$\frac{3}{8}$

2. Estimate the product.

$14 \times \frac{6}{10}$

about 7

For questions 3–6, find the product. Write your answer in simplest form.

3. $\frac{5}{8} \times \frac{4}{5}$

$\frac{1}{2}$

4. $\frac{2}{6} \times \frac{7}{9}$

$\frac{7}{27}$

5. $15 \times \frac{9}{10}$

$13\frac{1}{2}$

6. $\frac{5}{12} \times 22$

$9\frac{1}{6}$

7. Write the two GCFs you would use to simplify the fraction.

$\frac{7}{20} \times \frac{4}{14}$

4 and 7

8. Use the GCFs to simplify the factors. Write the new problem.

$\frac{8}{15} \times \frac{6}{12}$

$\frac{2}{5} \times \frac{2}{3}$

For questions 9–10, use GCFs to simplify the factors. Write your answer in simplest form.

9. $\frac{4}{24} \times \frac{8}{10}$

$\frac{2}{15}$

10. $\frac{1}{17} \times 51$

3

11. Rewrite the problem by changing each mixed number to a fraction.

$3\frac{1}{4} \times 7\frac{5}{8}$

$\frac{13}{4} \times \frac{61}{8}$

Form B • Free-Response   B173   Go on. ▶

Chapter 7 Test — Page 2

Name _____

For questions 12–14, write the product in simplest form.

12. $4\frac{4}{6} \times 6\frac{3}{4}$

$31\frac{1}{2}$

13. $5\frac{1}{5} \times 2\frac{1}{8}$

$11\frac{1}{20}$

14. $7\frac{5}{7} \times \frac{11}{12}$

$7\frac{1}{14}$

15. Each member of the swim team swims $\frac{3}{4}$ mi each day. How many miles does each member swim in two weeks?

$10\frac{1}{2}$ mi

16. There are 140 candies in the piñata. Of the candies, $\frac{2}{5}$ are jelly beans. How many candies are not jelly beans?

84 candies

17. What is the reciprocal of $\frac{5}{12}$?

$\frac{12}{5}$

18. Rewrite the division problem as a multiplication problem.

$\frac{11}{16} \div \frac{2}{3}$

$\frac{11}{16} \times \frac{3}{2}$

For questions 19–20, find the quotient. Write it in simplest form.

19. $\frac{7}{9} \div 21$

$\frac{1}{27}$

20. $\frac{3}{10} \div \frac{4}{5}$

$\frac{3}{8}$

21. Lani has $87\frac{3}{4}$ oz of peanuts. This is exactly enough for each of the 9 guests to have the same amount of peanuts. How much will each guest have?

$9\frac{3}{4}$ oz

22. On a $34\frac{1}{2}$ mi stretch of highway starting at Ned's Gift Shop, there is a gas station every $2\frac{3}{10}$ mi. How many gas stations are on the stretch of highway?

15 gas stations

23. Students were given $2\frac{5}{8}$ hr to take a timed test. Each student was allowed $\frac{5}{8}$ hr for each section on the test. How many sections were there?

4 sections

24. The area of Bianca's bedroom floor is $291\frac{3}{8}$ ft². The width of the floor is $15\frac{3}{4}$ ft. How long is the floor?

$18\frac{1}{2}$ ft

Form B • Free-Response   B174   ▶ Stop!

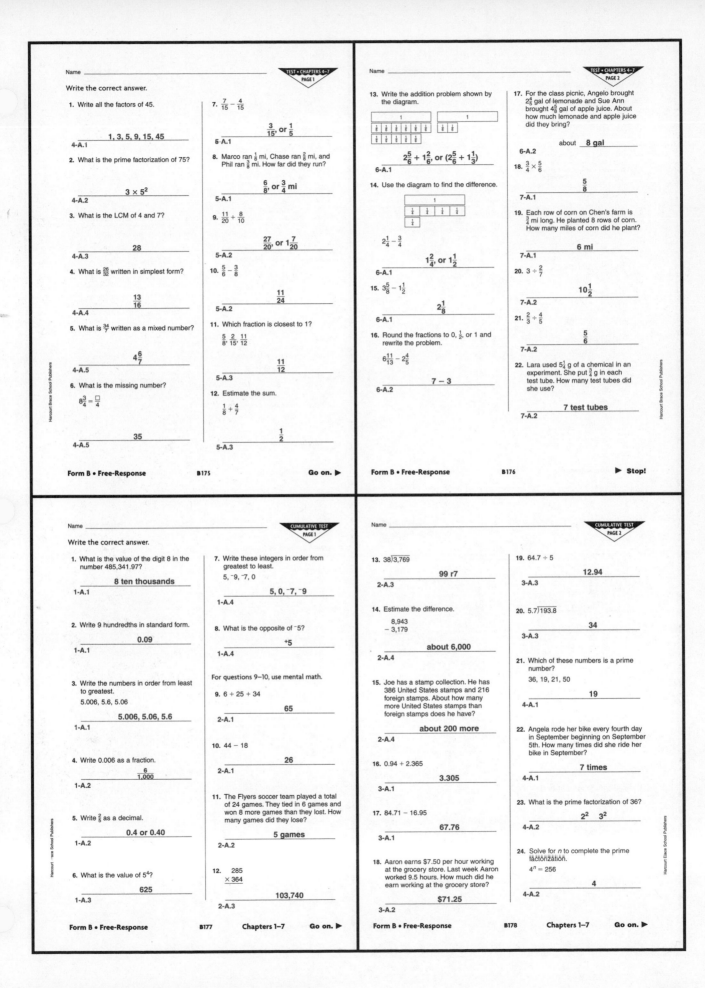

Name _____

Write the correct answer.

1. Write all the factors of 45.

__1, 3, 5, 9, 15, 45__
4-A.1

2. What is the prime factorization of 75?

__3×5^2__
4-A.2

3. What is the LCM of 4 and 7?

__28__
4-A.3

4. What is $\frac{26}{32}$ written in simplest form?

__$\frac{13}{16}$__
4-A.4

5. What is $\frac{34}{7}$ written as a mixed number?

__$4\frac{6}{7}$__
4-A.5

6. What is the missing number?

$8\frac{3}{4} = \frac{\square}{4}$

__35__
4-A.5

7. $\frac{7}{15} - \frac{4}{15}$

__$\frac{3}{15}$, or $\frac{1}{5}$__
5-A.1

8. Marco ran $\frac{1}{8}$ mi, Chase ran $\frac{2}{8}$ mi, and Phil ran $\frac{3}{8}$ mi. How far did they run?

__$\frac{6}{8}$, or $\frac{3}{4}$ mi__
5-A.1

9. $\frac{11}{20} + \frac{8}{10}$

__$\frac{27}{20}$, or $1\frac{7}{20}$__
5-A.2

10. $\frac{5}{6} - \frac{3}{8}$

__$\frac{11}{24}$__
5-A.2

11. Which fraction is closest to 1?

$\frac{5}{8}, \frac{2}{15}, \frac{11}{12}$

__$\frac{11}{12}$__
5-A.3

12. Estimate the sum.

$\frac{1}{8} + \frac{4}{7}$

__$\frac{1}{2}$__
5-A.3

Form B • Free-Response   B175   Go on. ▶

Name _____

13. Write the addition problem shown by the diagram.

__$2\frac{5}{6} + 1\frac{2}{6}$, or $(2\frac{5}{6} + 1\frac{1}{3})$__
6-A.1

14. Use the diagram to find the difference.

$2\frac{1}{4} - \frac{3}{4}$

__$1\frac{2}{4}$, or $1\frac{1}{2}$__
6-A.1

15. $3\frac{5}{8} - 1\frac{1}{2}$

__$2\frac{1}{8}$__
6-A.1

16. Round the fractions to 0, $\frac{1}{2}$, or 1 and rewrite the problem.

$6\frac{11}{13} - 2\frac{4}{5}$

__$7 - 3$__
6-A.2

17. For the class picnic, Angelo brought $2\frac{4}{8}$ gal of lemonade and Sue Ann brought $4\frac{5}{8}$ gal of apple juice. About how much lemonade and apple juice did they bring?

about __8 gal__
6-A.2

18. $\frac{3}{4} \times \frac{5}{6}$

__$\frac{5}{8}$__
7-A.1

19. Each row of corn on Chen's farm is $\frac{3}{4}$ mi long. He planted 8 rows of corn. How many miles of corn did he plant?

__6 mi__
7-A.1

20. $3 \div \frac{2}{7}$

__$10\frac{1}{2}$__
7-A.2

21. $\frac{2}{3} \div \frac{4}{5}$

__$\frac{5}{6}$__
7-A.2

22. Lara used $5\frac{1}{4}$ g of a chemical in an experiment. She put $\frac{3}{4}$ g in each test tube. How many test tubes did she use?

__7 test tubes__
7-A.2

Form B • Free-Response   B176   ▶ Stop!

Name _____

Write the correct answer.

1. What is the value of the digit 8 in the number 485,341.97?

__8 ten thousands__
1-A.1

2. Write 9 hundredths in standard form.

__0.09__
1-A.1

3. Write the numbers in order from least to greatest.

5.006, 5.6, 5.06

__5.006, 5.06, 5.6__
1-A.1

4. Write 0.006 as a fraction.

__$\frac{6}{1,000}$__
1-A.2

5. Write $\frac{2}{5}$ as a decimal.

__0.4 or 0.40__
1-A.2

6. What is the value of 5^4?

__625__
1-A.3

7. Write these integers in order from greatest to least.

5, ⁻9, ⁻7, 0

__5, 0, ⁻7, ⁻9__
1-A.4

8. What is the opposite of ⁻5?

__⁺5__
1-A.4

For questions 9-10, use mental math.

9. $6 + 25 + 34$

__65__
2-A.1

10. $44 - 18$

__26__
2-A.1

11. The Flyers soccer team played a total of 24 games. They tied in 6 games and won 8 more games than they lost. How many games did they lose?

__5 games__
2-A.2

12. $\begin{array}{r} 285 \\ \times 364 \\ \hline \end{array}$

__103,740__
2-A.3

Form B • Free-Response   B177   Chapters 1-7   Go on. ▶

Name _____

13. $38)\overline{3,769}$

__99 r7__
2-A.3

14. Estimate the difference.

$\begin{array}{r} 8,943 \\ - 3,179 \\ \hline \end{array}$

__about 6,000__
2-A.4

15. Joe has a stamp collection. He has 386 United States stamps and 216 foreign stamps. About how many more United States stamps than foreign stamps does he have?

__about 200 more__
2-A.4

16. $0.94 + 2.365$

__3.305__
3-A.1

17. $84.71 - 16.95$

__67.76__
3-A.1

18. Aaron earns $7.50 per hour working at the grocery store. Last week Aaron worked 9.5 hours. How much did he earn working at the grocery store?

__$71.25__
3-A.2

19. $64.7 \div 5$

__12.94__
3-A.3

20. $5.7)\overline{193.8}$

__34__
3-A.3

21. Which of these numbers is a prime number?

36, 19, 21, 50

__19__
4-A.1

22. Angela rode her bike every fourth day in September beginning on September 5th. How many times did she ride her bike in September?

__7 times__
4-A.1

23. What is the prime factorization of 36?

__$2^2 \quad 3^2$__
4-A.2

24. Solve for n to complete the prime factorization.

$4^n = 256$

__4__
4-A.2

Form B • Free-Response   B178   Chapters 1-7   Go on. ▶

Free-Response Format • Test Answers

275

25. What is the LCM of 6 and 15?

30

4-A.3

26. Jeremy has 18 erasers and 36 pencils to put in packages. All the packages will contain the same number of erasers and pencils. What is the greatest number of packages he can make?

18

4-A.3

27. Write $\frac{21}{27}$ in simplest form.

$\frac{7}{9}$

4-A.4

28. The model shows 2 whole pizzas and $\frac{1}{4}$ of another pizza. What fraction could you use to show this?

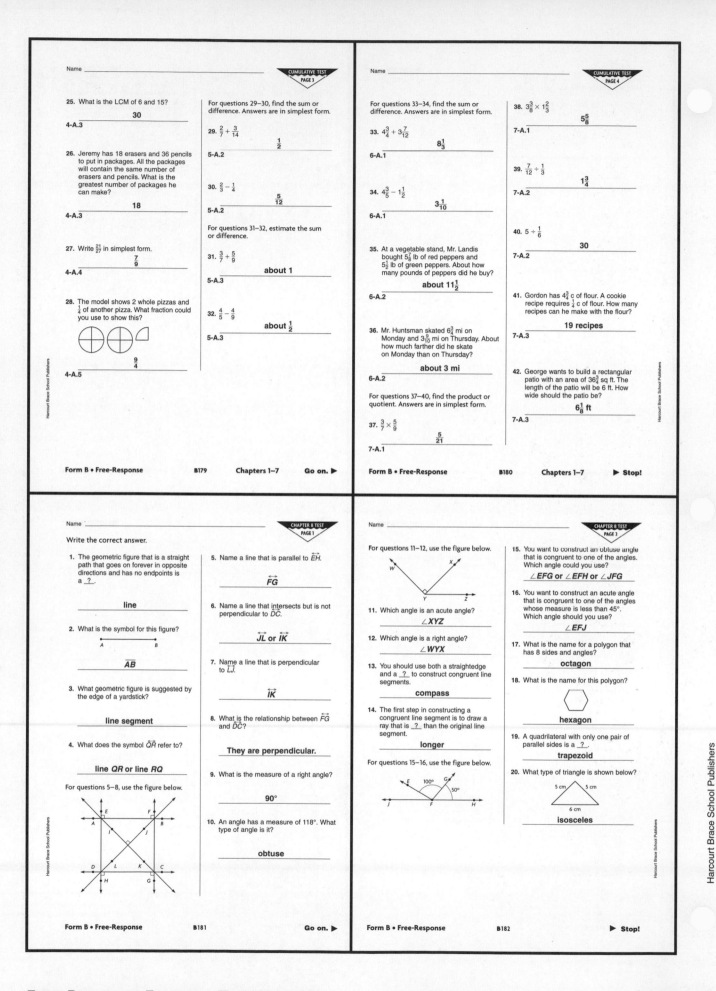

$\frac{9}{4}$

4-A.5

For questions 29–30, find the sum or difference. Answers are in simplest form.

29. $\frac{2}{7} + \frac{3}{14}$

$\frac{1}{2}$

5-A.2

30. $\frac{2}{3} - \frac{1}{4}$

$\frac{5}{12}$

5-A.2

For questions 31–32, estimate the sum or difference.

31. $\frac{3}{7} + \frac{5}{9}$

about 1

5-A.3

32. $\frac{4}{5} - \frac{4}{9}$

about $\frac{1}{2}$

5-A.3

Form B • Free-Response   B179   **Chapters 1–7**   **Go on.** ▶

For questions 33–34, find the sum or difference. Answers are in simplest form.

33. $4\frac{3}{4} + 3\frac{7}{12}$

$8\frac{1}{3}$

6-A.1

34. $4\frac{3}{5} - 1\frac{1}{2}$

$3\frac{1}{10}$

6-A.1

35. At a vegetable stand, Mr. Landis bought $5\frac{7}{8}$ lb of red peppers and $5\frac{1}{2}$ lb of green peppers. About how many pounds of peppers did he buy?

about $11\frac{1}{2}$

6-A.2

36. Mr. Huntsman skated $6\frac{9}{4}$ mi on Monday and $3\frac{9}{10}$ mi on Thursday. About how much farther did he skate on Monday than on Thursday?

about 3 mi

6-A.2

For questions 37–40, find the product or quotient. Answers are in simplest form.

37. $\frac{3}{7} \times \frac{5}{9}$

$\frac{5}{21}$

7-A.1

38. $3\frac{3}{8} \times 1\frac{2}{3}$

$5\frac{5}{8}$

7-A.1

39. $\frac{7}{12} \div \frac{1}{3}$

$1\frac{3}{4}$

7-A.2

40. $5 \div \frac{1}{6}$

30

7-A.2

41. Gordon has $4\frac{3}{4}$ c of flour. A cookie recipe requires $\frac{1}{4}$ c of flour. How many recipes can he make with the flour?

19 recipes

7-A.3

42. George wants to build a rectangular patio with an area of $36\frac{3}{4}$ sq ft. The length of the patio will be 6 ft. How wide should the patio be?

$6\frac{1}{8}$ ft

7-A.3

Form B • Free-Response   B180   **Chapters 1–7**   ▶ **Stop!**

Write the correct answer.

1. The geometric figure that is a straight path that goes on forever in opposite directions and has no endpoints is a _?_.

line

2. What is the symbol for this figure?

A ————— B

$\overline{AB}$

3. What geometric figure is suggested by the edge of a yardstick?

line segment

4. What does the symbol $\overleftrightarrow{QR}$ refer to?

line QR or line RQ

For questions 5–8, use the figure below.

5. Name a line that is parallel to $\overleftrightarrow{EH}$.

$\overleftrightarrow{FG}$

6. Name a line that intersects but is not perpendicular to $\overleftrightarrow{DC}$.

$\overleftrightarrow{JL}$ or $\overleftrightarrow{IK}$

7. Name a line that is perpendicular to $\overleftrightarrow{LJ}$.

$\overleftrightarrow{IK}$

8. What is the relationship between $\overleftrightarrow{FG}$ and $\overleftrightarrow{DC}$?

They are perpendicular.

9. What is the measure of a right angle?

90°

10. An angle has a measure of 118°. What type of angle is it?

obtuse

Form B • Free-Response   B181   **Go on.** ▶

For questions 11–12, use the figure below.

11. Which angle is an acute angle?

∠XYZ

12. Which angle is a right angle?

∠WYX

13. You should use both a straightedge and a _?_ to construct congruent line segments.

compass

14. The first step in constructing a congruent line segment is to draw a ray that is _?_ than the original line segment.

longer

For questions 15–16, use the figure below.

15. You want to construct an obtuse angle that is congruent to one of the angles. Which angle could you use?

∠EFG or ∠EFH or ∠JFG

16. You want to construct an acute angle that is congruent to one of the angles whose measure is less than 45°. Which angle should you use?

∠EFJ

17. What is the name for a polygon that has 8 sides and angles?

octagon

18. What is the name for this polygon?

hexagon

19. A quadrilateral with only one pair of parallel sides is a _?_.

trapezoid

20. What type of triangle is shown below?

isosceles

Form B • Free-Response   B182   ▶ **Stop!**

Free-Response Format • Test Answers

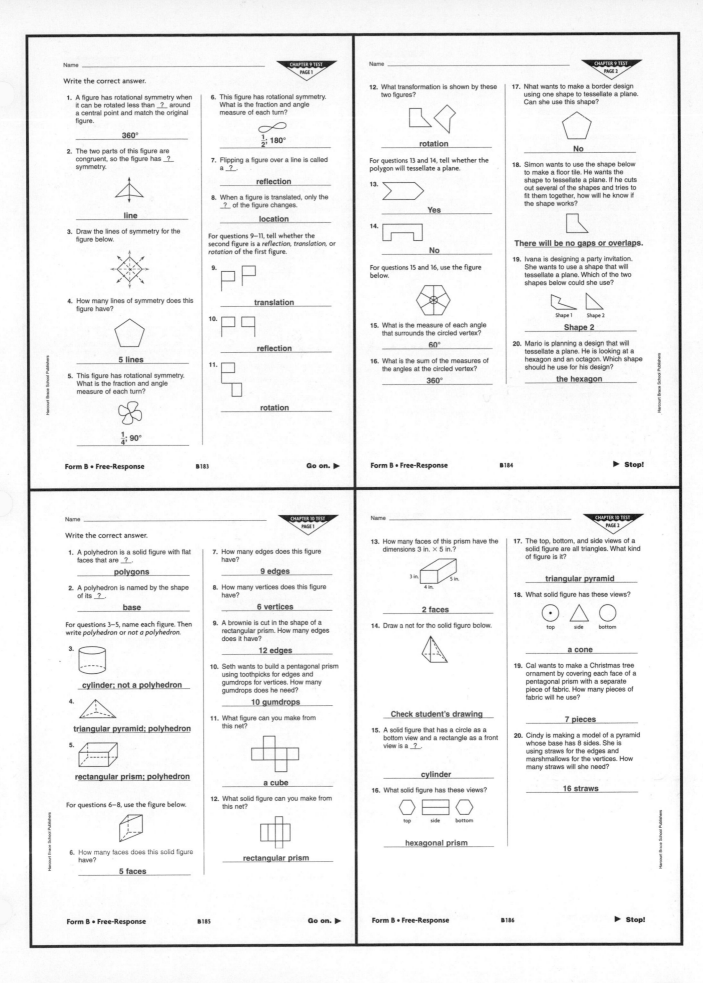

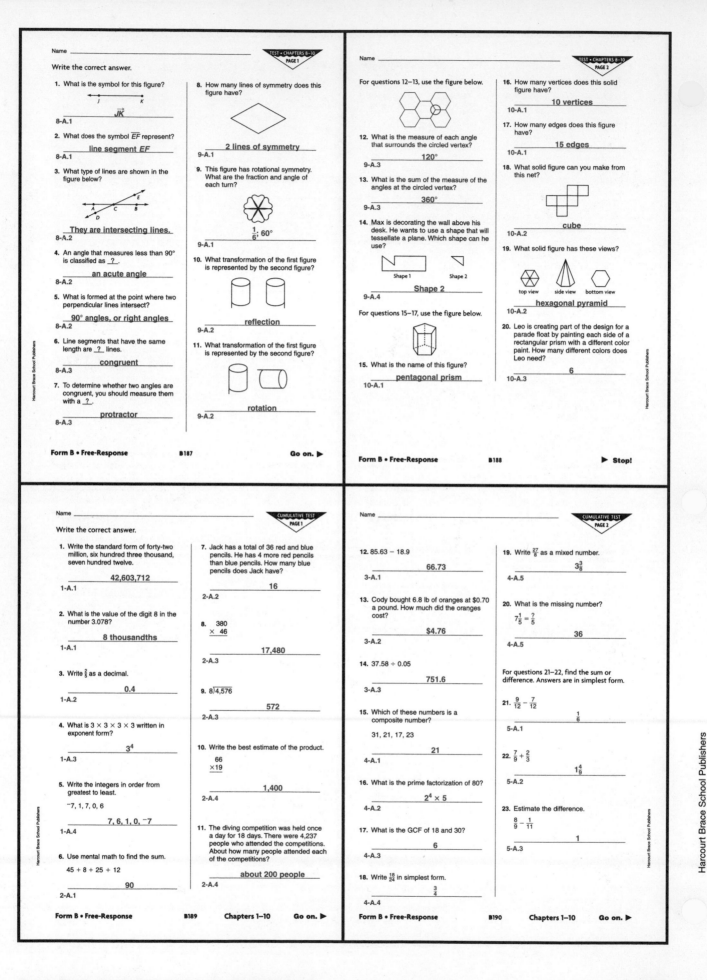

Name _____

Write the correct answer.

1. What is the symbol for this figure?

$\overrightarrow{JK}$

8-A.1

2. What does the symbol $\overline{EF}$ represent?

line segment EF

8-A.1

3. What type of lines are shown in the figure below?

They are intersecting lines.

8-A.2

4. An angle that measures less than 90° is classified as _?_.

an acute angle

8-A.2

5. What is formed at the point where two perpendicular lines intersect?

90° angles, or right angles

8-A.2

6. Line segments that have the same length are _?_ lines.

congruent

8-A.3

7. To determine whether two angles are congruent, you should measure them with a _?_.

protractor

8-A.3

8. How many lines of symmetry does this figure have?

2 lines of symmetry

9-A.1

9. This figure has rotational symmetry. What are the fraction and angle of each turn?

$\frac{1}{6}$; 60°

9-A.1

10. What transformation of the first figure is represented by the second figure?

reflection

9-A.2

11. What transformation of the first figure is represented by the second figure?

rotation

9-A.2

Form B • Free-Response   B187   Go on. ▶

Name _____

For questions 12–13, use the figure below.

12. What is the measure of each angle that surrounds the circled vertex?

120°

9-A.3

13. What is the sum of the measure of the angles at the circled vertex?

360°

9-A.3

14. Max is decorating the wall above his desk. He wants to use a shape that will tessellate a plane. Which shape can he use?

Shape 1   Shape 2

Shape 2

9-A.4

For questions 15–17, use the figure below.

15. What is the name of this figure?

pentagonal prism

10-A.1

16. How many vertices does this solid figure have?

10 vertices

10-A.1

17. How many edges does this figure have?

15 edges

10-A.1

18. What solid figure can you make from this net?

cube

10-A.2

19. What solid figure has these views?

top view   side view   bottom view

hexagonal pyramid

10-A.2

20. Leo is creating part of the design for a parade float by painting each side of a rectangular prism with a different color paint. How many different colors does Leo need?

6

10-A.3

Form B • Free-Response   B188   ▶ Stop!

Name _____

Write the correct answer.

1. Write the standard form of forty-two million, six hundred three thousand, seven hundred twelve.

42,603,712

1-A.1

2. What is the value of the digit 8 in the number 3.078?

8 thousandths

1-A.1

3. Write $\frac{2}{5}$ as a decimal.

0.4

1-A.2

4. What is $3 \times 3 \times 3 \times 3$ written in exponent form?

3^4

1-A.3

5. Write the integers in order from greatest to least.

$^-7, 1, 7, 0, 6$

$7, 6, 1, 0, ^-7$

1-A.4

6. Use mental math to find the sum.

$45 + 8 + 25 + 12$

90

2-A.1

7. Jack has a total of 36 red and blue pencils. He has 4 more red pencils than blue pencils. How many blue pencils does Jack have?

16

2-A.2

8.
$$\begin{array}{r} 380 \\ \times\ 46 \\ \hline 17{,}480 \end{array}$$

2-A.3

9. $8)\overline{4{,}576}$

572

2-A.3

10. Write the best estimate of the product.

$$\begin{array}{r} 66 \\ \times 19 \\ \hline 1{,}400 \end{array}$$

2-A.4

11. The diving competition was held once a day for 18 days. There were 4,237 people who attended the competitions. About how many people attended each of the competitions?

about 200 people

2-A.4

Form B • Free-Response   B189   Chapters 1–10   Go on. ▶

Name _____

12. $85.63 - 18.9$

66.73

3-A.1

13. Cody bought 6.8 lb of oranges at $0.70 a pound. How much did the oranges cost?

$4.76

3-A.2

14. $37.58 \div 0.05$

751.6

3-A.3

15. Which of these numbers is a composite number?

31, 21, 17, 23

21

4-A.1

16. What is the prime factorization of 80?

$2^4 \times 5$

4-A.2

17. What is the GCF of 18 and 30?

6

4-A.3

18. Write $\frac{18}{24}$ in simplest form.

$\frac{3}{4}$

4-A.4

19. Write $\frac{27}{8}$ as a mixed number.

$3\frac{3}{8}$

4-A.5

20. What is the missing number?

$7\frac{1}{5} = \frac{?}{5}$

36

4-A.5

For questions 21–22, find the sum or difference. Answers are in simplest form.

21. $\frac{9}{12} - \frac{7}{12}$

$\frac{1}{6}$

5-A.1

22. $\frac{7}{9} + \frac{2}{3}$

$1\frac{4}{9}$

5-A.2

23. Estimate the difference.

$\frac{8}{9} - \frac{1}{11}$

1

5-A.3

Form B • Free-Response   B190   Chapters 1–10   Go on. ▶

Free-Response Format • Test Answers

For questions 24–25, find the sum or difference. Answers are in simplest form.

24. $3\frac{3}{4} + 2\frac{5}{8}$

$6\frac{3}{8}$

6-A.1

25. $3\frac{2}{3} - 1\frac{5}{12}$

$2\frac{1}{4}$

6-A.1

26. Write the best estimate for the word problem.

Timmy bought $3\frac{9}{10}$ lb of bananas on Wednesday and $1\frac{1}{8}$ lb of bananas on Friday. About how many pounds of bananas did he buy?

about 5 lb

6-A.2

For questions 27–28, find the product or quotient. Answers are in simplest form.

27. $3\frac{3}{7} \times \frac{5}{8}$

$2\frac{1}{7}$

7-A.1

28. $\frac{5}{12} \div \frac{2}{3}$

$\frac{5}{8}$

7-A.2

29. Jocelyn wants to make a rectangular garden with an area of $27\frac{1}{2}$ sq ft. The length of the garden will be 8 ft. How wide should the garden be?

$3\frac{7}{16}$ ft

7-A.3

30. An angle that measures 85° is classified as a(n) _?_ .

acute angle

8-A.1

31. Could the measure of the angle shown below be 120°?

no

8-A.2

32. Does the construction below show congruent line segments?

yes

8-A.3

---

33. How many angles does a pentagon have?

5 angles

8-A.4

34. This figure has rotational symmetry. What is the angle measure of each turn?

180°

9-A.1

35. Which figure is a translation of the original figure?

Figure 3

10-A.2

36. Ted wants to make a design that will tessellate a plane. Can he use a hexagon?

yes

9-A.4

37. Mike built a pyramid using toothpicks for edges and miniature marshmallows for vertices. He used 8 toothpicks and 5 marshmallows. What kind of pyramid did he build?

rectangular

10-A.1

38. What solid figure has these views?

top   side   bottom

hexagonal prism

10-A.2

39. The bottom view of a solid figure is a circle. The front view is a triangle. What kind of figure is it?

cone

10-A.2

40. Tanya wants to make a paperweight by covering each face of a pentagonal pyramid with a separate piece of paper. How many pieces of paper will she use?

6 pieces of paper

10-A.3

Write the correct answer.

1. Jon's class is selling chocolate chip cookies. What is a decision about the sale that the students can make?

Possible answer: How much will each cookie cost?

2. For the class trip, two buses are available. One seats 30 students and the other seats 45 students. What information do you need to find out which bus to use?

How many students are going on the trip?

3. The scouts are ready to work on a new badge. What information might be useful to know before they choose a new badge?

Possible answer: What badges have already been earned?

4. The city council would like to build a new community center and have several drawings of new buildings. Before they choose a building, what information might be helpful in their decision?

Possible answer: What activities will be performed in the new building?

For questions 5–6, find the number of people you should survey if you survey 1 out of every 10 people for a sample.

5. 430 shoppers

43

6. 270 teachers

27

7. The video store in the mall wants to survey shoppers to see what videos they prefer. How can they get a random sample?

Randomly survey shoppers as they enter the mall.

8. A vaccination day was held for dog and cat owners. A dog food manufacturer prepared a survey for dog owners. They surveyed 1 out of every 10 pet owners entering the clinic. Is this a good sample? Explain why or why not.

No; the right population would not be surveyed if cat owners were also included.

For questions 9–10, use the table. As students entered the school, 1 out of every 10 students was asked whether there should be a picnic at the end of the school year.

School Picnic	Number of Votes
Yes	45
No	30

9. How many students voted?

75

10. Suppose 150 students were surveyed. How many would you expect to have voted *no*?

60

---

11. A movie critic randomly surveys 1 out of every 100 moviegoers about a new movie. Is this sample biased? Explain why or why not.

Yes; the sample is not large enough.

12. Shoppers are asked whether they prefer Brand *A* or Brand *B* dish detergent. Is this question biased?

Not biased

For questions 13–14, 300 students at Pine Middle School are being surveyed to find out their choice of a school mascot.

13. How could a random sample be chosen?

Possible answer: Use the computer to randomly choose 30 students.

14. Is this question biased?

Do you agree with us that a lion would be the best mascot?

Biased

For questions 15–16, use the data showing the ages of musicians in a community orchestra.

Ages of Musicians in Community Orchestra							
20	53	42	59	46	48	64	36
21	40	14	45	38	29	34	39
35	61	19	27	26	18	52	57

15. What is the range?

50

16. If you want to arrange the data into 5 age intervals, how many ages should be put in each interval?

10

For questions 17–18, use the table.

Jodi surveyed scouts in her troop.

Favorite Activities	Tally
Sports	卌 卌 l
Computer Games	卌 lll
Reading	卌 l

17. What is the size of the sample?

25 scouts

18. If Jodi adds a new column to the table that shows the numerical value for the tally marks, what would she label the new column?

Frequency

Free-Response Format • Test Answers   279

Harcourt Brace School Publishers

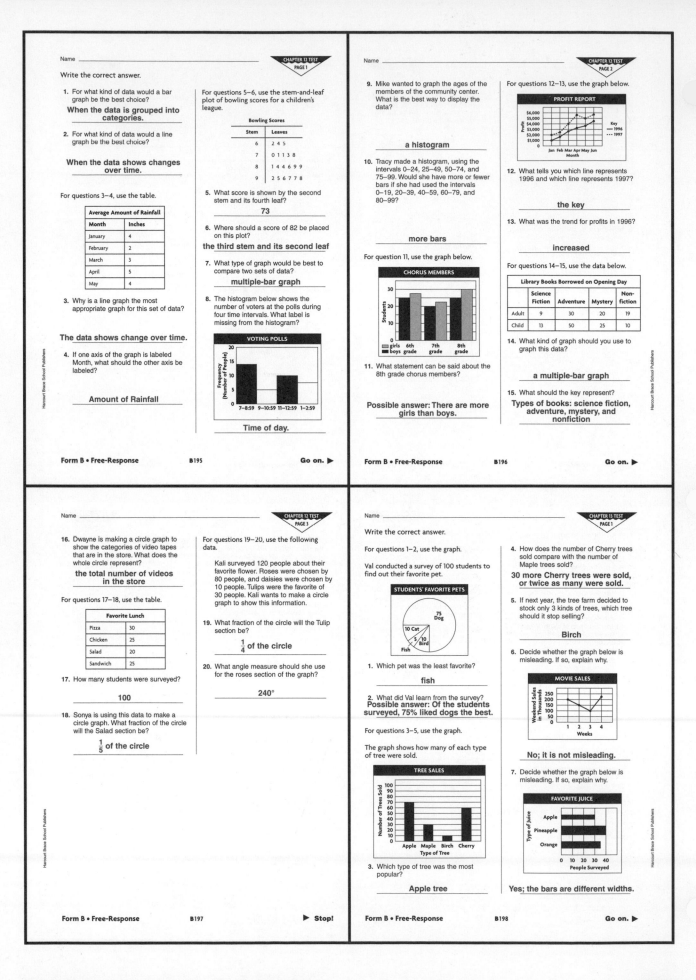

Write the correct answer.

1. For what kind of data would a bar graph be the best choice?

When the data is grouped into categories.

2. For what kind of data would a line graph be the best choice?

When the data shows changes over time.

For questions 3–4, use the table.

Average Amount of Rainfall	
Month	Inches
January	4
February	2
March	3
April	5
May	4

3. Why is a line graph the most appropriate graph for this set of data?

The data shows change over time.

4. If one axis of the graph is labeled Month, what should the other axis be labeled?

Amount of Rainfall

For questions 5–6, use the stem-and-leaf plot of bowling scores for a children's league.

Bowling Scores	
Stem	Leaves
6	2 4 5
7	0 1 1 3 8
8	1 4 4 6 9 9
9	2 5 6 7 7 8

5. What score is shown by the second stem and its fourth leaf?

73

6. Where should a score of 82 be placed on this plot?

the third stem and its second leaf

7. What type of graph would be best to compare two sets of data?

multiple-bar graph

8. The histogram below shows the number of voters at the polls during four time intervals. What label is missing from the histogram?

VOTING POLLS

Time of day.

9. Mike wanted to graph the ages of the members of the community center. What is the best way to display the data?

a histogram

10. Tracy made a histogram, using the intervals 0–24, 25–49, 50–74, and 75–99. Would she have more or fewer bars if she had used the intervals 0–19, 20–39, 40–59, 60–79, and 80–99?

more bars

For question 11, use the graph below.

CHORUS MEMBERS

11. What statement can be said about the 8th grade chorus members?

Possible answer: There are more girls than boys.

For questions 12–13, use the graph below.

PROFIT REPORT

12. What tells you which line represents 1996 and which line represents 1997?

the key

13. What was the trend for profits in 1996?

increased

For questions 14–15, use the data below.

Library Books Borrowed on Opening Day				
	Science Fiction	Adventure	Mystery	Non-fiction
Adult	9	30	20	19
Child	13	50	25	10

14. What kind of graph should you use to graph this data?

a multiple-bar graph

15. What should the key represent?

Types of books: science fiction, adventure, mystery, and nonfiction

16. Dwayne is making a circle graph to show the categories of video tapes that are in the store. What does the whole circle represent?

the total number of videos in the store

For questions 17–18, use the table.

Favorite Lunch	
Pizza	30
Chicken	25
Salad	20
Sandwich	25

17. How many students were surveyed?

100

18. Sonya is using this data to make a circle graph. What fraction of the circle will the Salad section be?

$\frac{1}{5}$ **of the circle**

For questions 19–20, use the following data.

Kali surveyed 120 people about their favorite flower. Roses were chosen by 80 people, and daisies were chosen by 10 people. Tulips were the favorite of 30 people. Kali wants to make a circle graph to show this information.

19. What fraction of the circle will the Tulip section be?

$\frac{1}{4}$ **of the circle**

20. What angle measure should she use for the roses section of the graph?

240°

Write the correct answer.

For questions 1–2, use the graph.

Val conducted a survey of 100 students to find out their favorite pet.

STUDENTS' FAVORITE PETS

1. Which pet was the least favorite?

fish

2. What did Val learn from the survey?
Possible answer: Of the students surveyed, 75% liked dogs the best.

For questions 3–5, use the graph.

The graph shows how many of each type of tree were sold.

TREE SALES

3. Which type of tree was the most popular?

Apple tree

4. How does the number of Cherry trees sold compare with the number of Maple trees sold?

30 more Cherry trees were sold, or twice as many were sold.

5. If next year, the tree farm decided to stock only 3 kinds of trees, which tree should it stop selling?

Birch

6. Decide whether the graph below is misleading. If so, explain why.

MOVIE SALES

No; it is not misleading.

7. Decide whether the graph below is misleading. If so, explain why.

FAVORITE JUICE

Yes; the bars are different widths.

Free-Response Format • Test Answers

Harcourt Brace School Publishers

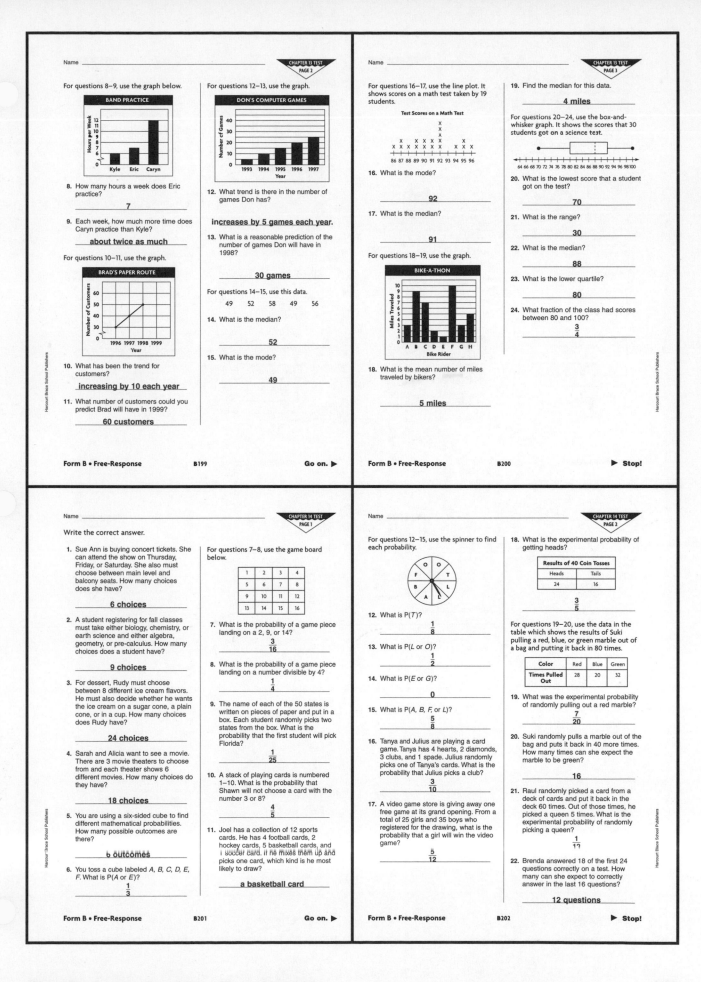

Name _____

For questions 8–9, use the graph below.

BAND PRACTICE

8. How many hours a week does Eric practice?

   7

9. Each week, how much more time does Caryn practice than Kyle?

   about twice as much

For questions 10–11, use the graph.

BRAD'S PAPER ROUTE

10. What has been the trend for customers?

    increasing by 10 each year

11. What number of customers could you predict Brad will have in 1999?

    60 customers

For questions 12–13, use the graph.

DON'S COMPUTER GAMES

12. What trend is there in the number of games Don has?

    increases by 5 games each year.

13. What is a reasonable prediction of the number of games Don will have in 1998?

    30 games

For questions 14–15, use this data.

   49   52   58   49   56

14. What is the median?

    52

15. What is the mode?

    49

Form B • Free-Response   B199   **Go on. ▶**

Name _____

For questions 16–17, use the line plot. It shows scores on a math test taken by 19 students.

Test Scores on a Math Test

86 87 88 89 90 91 92 93 94 95 96

16. What is the mode?

    92

17. What is the median?

    91

For questions 18–19, use the graph.

BIKE-A-THON

18. What is the mean number of miles traveled by bikers?

    5 miles

19. Find the median for this data.

    4 miles

For questions 20–24, use the box-and-whisker graph. It shows the scores that 30 students got on a science test.

64 66 68 70 72 74 76 78 80 82 84 86 88 90 92 94 96 98 100

20. What is the lowest score that a student got on the test?

    70

21. What is the range?

    30

22. What is the median?

    88

23. What is the lower quartile?

    80

24. What fraction of the class had scores between 80 and 100?

    3/4

Form B • Free-Response   B200   **▶ Stop!**

Name _____

Write the correct answer.

1. Sue Ann is buying concert tickets. She can attend the show on Thursday, Friday, or Saturday. She also must choose between main level and balcony seats. How many choices does she have?

   6 choices

2. A student registering for fall classes must take either biology, chemistry, or earth science and either algebra, geometry, or pre-calculus. How many choices does a student have?

   9 choices

3. For dessert, Rudy must choose between 8 different ice cream flavors. He must also decide whether he wants the ice cream on a sugar cone, a plain cone, or in a cup. How many choices does Rudy have?

   24 choices

4. Sarah and Alicia want to see a movie. There are 3 movie theaters to choose from and each theater shows 6 different movies. How many choices do they have?

   18 choices

5. You are using a six-sided cube to find different mathematical probabilities. How many possible outcomes are there?

   6 outcomes

6. You toss a cube labeled A, B, C, D, E, F. What is P(A or E)?

   1/3

For questions 7–8, use the game board below.

1	2	3	4
5	6	7	8
9	10	11	12
13	14	15	16

7. What is the probability of a game piece landing on a 2, 9, or 14?

   3/16

8. What is the probability of a game piece landing on a number divisible by 4?

   1/4

9. The name of each of the 50 states is written on pieces of paper and put in a box. Each student randomly picks two states from the box. What is the probability that the first student will pick Florida?

   1/25

10. A stack of playing cards is numbered 1–10. What is the probability that Shawn will not choose a card with the number 3 or 8?

    4/5

11. Joel has a collection of 12 sports cards. He has 4 football cards, 2 hockey cards, 5 basketball cards, and 1 soccer card. If he mixes them up and picks one card, which kind is he most likely to draw?

    a basketball card

Form B • Free-Response   B201   **Go on. ▶**

Name _____

For questions 12–15, use the spinner to find each probability.

12. What is P(T)?

    1/8

13. What is P(L or O)?

    1/2

14. What is P(E or G)?

    0

15. What is P(A, B, F, or L)?

    5/8

16. Tanya and Julius are playing a card game. Tanya has 4 hearts, 2 diamonds, 3 clubs, and 1 spade. Julius randomly picks one of Tanya's cards. What is the probability that Julius picks a club?

    3/10

17. A video game store is giving away one free game at its grand opening. From a total of 25 girls and 35 boys who registered for the drawing, what is the probability that a girl will win the video game?

    5/12

18. What is the experimental probability of getting heads?

Results of 40 Coin Tosses	
Heads	Tails
24	16

   3/5

For questions 19–20, use the data in the table which shows the results of Suki pulling a red, blue, or green marble out of a bag and putting it back in 80 times.

| Color | Red | Blue | Green |
| Times Pulled Out | 28 | 20 | 32 |

19. What was the experimental probability of randomly pulling out a red marble?

    7/20

20. Suki randomly pulls a marble out of the bag and puts it back in 40 more times. How many times can she expect the marble to be green?

    16

21. Raul randomly picked a card from a deck of cards and put it back in the deck 60 times. Out of those times, he picked a queen 5 times. What is the experimental probability of randomly picking a queen?

    1/12

22. Brenda answered 18 of the first 24 questions correctly on a test. How many can she expect to correctly answer in the last 16 questions?

    12 questions

Form B • Free-Response   B202   **▶ Stop!**

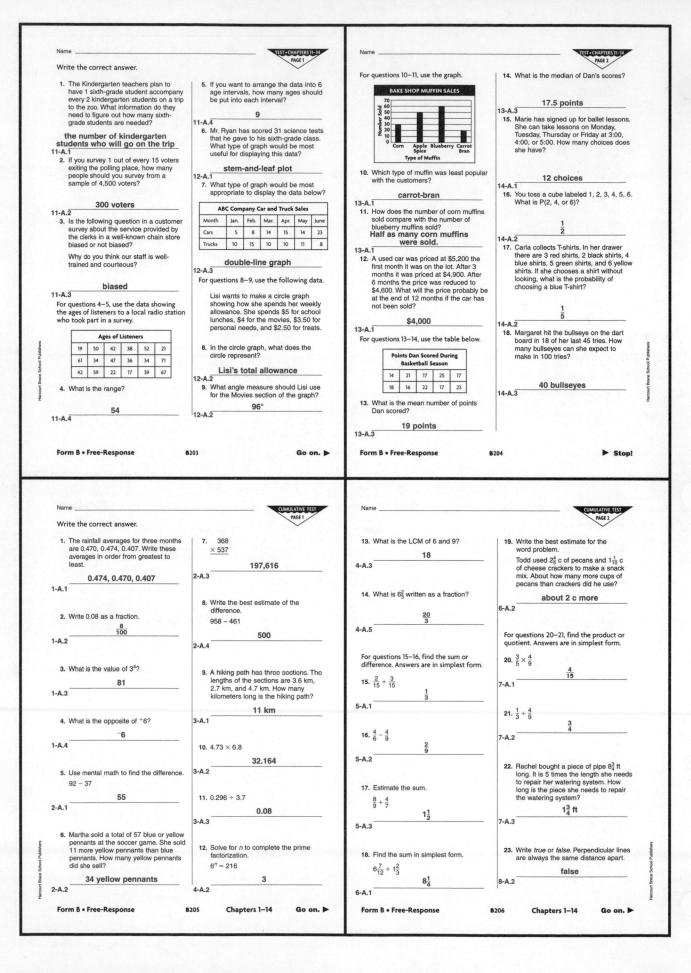

Write the correct answer.

1. The Kindergarten teachers plan to have 1 sixth-grade student accompany every 2 kindergarten students on a trip to the zoo. What information do they need to figure out how many sixth-grade students are needed?

the number of kindergarten students who will go on the trip

11-A.1

2. If you survey 1 out of every 15 voters exiting the polling place, how many people should you survey from a sample of 4,500 voters?

300 voters

11-A.2

3. Is the following question in a customer survey about the service provided by the clerks in a well-known chain store biased or not biased?

Why do you think our staff is well-trained and courteous?

biased

11-A.3

For questions 4–5, use the data showing the ages of listeners to a local radio station who took part in a survey.

Ages of Listeners					
19	50	42	38	52	21
61	34	47	36	34	71
42	59	22	17	39	67

4. What is the range?

54

11-A.4

5. If you want to arrange the data into 6 age intervals, how many ages should be put into each interval?

9

11-A.4

6. Mr. Ryan has scored 31 science tests that he gave to his sixth-grade class. What type of graph would be most useful for displaying this data?

stem-and-leaf plot

12-A.1

7. What type of graph would be most appropriate to display the data below?

ABC Company Car and Truck Sales						
Month	Jan.	Feb.	Mar.	Apr.	May	June
Cars	5	8	14	15	14	23
Trucks	10	15	10	10	11	8

double-line graph

12-A.1

For questions 8–9, use the following data.

Lisi wants to make a circle graph showing how she spends her weekly allowance. She spends $5 for school lunches, $4 for the movies, $3.50 for personal needs, and $2.50 for treats.

8. In the circle graph, what does the circle represent?

Lisi's total allowance

12-A.2

9. What angle measure should Lisi use for the Movies section of the graph?

96°

12-A.2

Form B • Free-Response   B203   Go on. ▶

For questions 10–11, use the graph.

BAKE SHOP MUFFIN SALES

10. Which type of muffin was least popular with the customers?

carrot-bran

13-A.1

11. How does the number of corn muffins sold compare with the number of blueberry muffins sold?

Half as many corn muffins were sold.

13-A.1

12. A used car was priced at $5,200 the first month it was on the lot. After 3 months it was priced at $4,900. After 6 months the price was reduced to $4,600. What will the price probably be at the end of 12 months if the car has not been sold?

$4,000

13-A.1

For questions 13–14, use the table below.

Points Dan Scored During Basketball Season				
14	21	17	25	17
18	16	22	17	23

13. What is the mean number of points Dan scored?

19 points

13-A.3

14. What is the median of Dan's scores?

17.5 points

13-A.3

15. Marie has signed up for ballet lessons. She can take lessons on Monday, Tuesday, Thursday or Friday at 3:00, 4:00, or 5:00. How many choices does she have?

12 choices

14-A.1

16. You toss a cube labeled 1, 2, 3, 4, 5, 6. What is P(2, 4, or 6)?

$\frac{1}{2}$

14-A.2

17. Carla collects T-shirts. In her drawer there are 3 red shirts, 2 black shirts, 4 blue shirts, 5 green shirts, and 6 yellow shirts. If she chooses a shirt without looking, what is the probability of choosing a blue T-shirt?

$\frac{1}{5}$

14-A.2

18. Margaret hit the bullseye on the dart board in 18 of her last 45 tries. How many bullseyes can she expect to make in 100 tries?

40 bullseyes

14-A.3

Form B • Free-Response   B204   ▶ Stop!

Write the correct answer.

1. The rainfall averages for three months are 0.470, 0.474, 0.407. Write these averages in order from greatest to least.

0.474, 0.470, 0.407

1-A.1

2. Write 0.08 as a fraction.

$\frac{8}{100}$

1-A.2

3. What is the value of 3^4?

81

1-A.3

4. What is the opposite of $^+6$?

$^-6$

1-A.4

5. Use mental math to find the difference.

92 – 37

55

2-A.1

6. Martha sold a total of 57 blue or yellow pennants at the soccer game. She sold 11 more yellow pennants than blue pennants. How many yellow pennants did she sell?

34 yellow pennants

2-A.2

7.   368
   × 537

197,616

2-A.3

8. Write the best estimate of the difference.

958 – 461

500

2-A.4

9. A hiking path has three sections. The lengths of the sections are 3.6 km, 2.7 km, and 4.7 km. How many kilometers long is the hiking path?

11 km

3-A.1

10. 4.73 × 6.8

32.164

3-A.2

11. 0.296 ÷ 3.7

0.08

3-A.3

12. Solve for n to complete the prime factorization.

$6^n = 216$

3

4-A.2

Form B • Free-Response   B205   Chapters 1–14   Go on. ▶

13. What is the LCM of 6 and 9?

18

4-A.3

14. What is $6\frac{2}{3}$ written as a fraction?

$\frac{20}{3}$

4-A.5

For questions 15–16, find the sum or difference. Answers are in simplest form.

15. $\frac{2}{15} + \frac{3}{15}$

$\frac{1}{3}$

5-A.1

16. $\frac{4}{6} - \frac{4}{9}$

$\frac{2}{9}$

5-A.2

17. Estimate the sum.

$\frac{8}{9} + \frac{4}{7}$

$1\frac{1}{2}$

5-A.3

18. Find the sum in simplest form.

$6\frac{7}{12} + 1\frac{2}{3}$

$8\frac{1}{4}$

6-A.1

19. Write the best estimate for the word problem.

Todd used $2\frac{4}{5}$ c of pecans and $1\frac{1}{10}$ c of cheese crackers to make a snack mix. About how many more cups of pecans than crackers did he use?

about 2 c more

6-A.2

For questions 20–21, find the product or quotient. Answers are in simplest form.

20. $\frac{3}{5} \times \frac{4}{9}$

$\frac{4}{15}$

7-A.1

21. $\frac{1}{3} \div \frac{4}{9}$

$\frac{3}{4}$

7-A.2

22. Rachel bought a piece of pipe $8\frac{3}{4}$ ft long. It is 5 times the length she needs to repair her watering system. How long is the piece she needs to repair the watering system?

$1\frac{3}{4}$ ft

7-A.3

23. Write *true* or *false*. Perpendicular lines are always the same distance apart.

false

8-A.2

Form B • Free-Response   B206   Chapters 1–14   Go on. ▶

24. Write *true* or *false*. The construction below shows congruent angles.

true

8-A.3

25. What is the name for this polygon?

octagon

8-A.4

26. How many lines of symmetry does this figure have?

2 lines

9-A.1

27. Choose the figure that is a reflection of the original figure.

Original   Figure 1   Figure 2   Figure 3

Figure 2

9-A.2

28. What is the measure of each angle that surrounds the circled vertex?

90°

9-A.3

29. Sharon is planning a design that will tessellate a plane. Could she use an octagon? Write *yes* or *no*.

no

9-A.4

30. Fred built a rectangular prism, using toothpicks for edges and miniature marshmallows for vertices. How many toothpicks did he use?

12

10-A.1

31. The bottom view of a solid figure is a circle. The front view is a rectangle. What kind of figure is it?

cylinder

10-A.2

Form B • Free-Response   B207   Chapters 1–14   **Go on.** ▶

---

32. Sally is making a model of a prism whose base has 8 sides. She is using toothpicks for the edges and balls of clay for the vertices. How many balls of clay does she need?

16

10-A.3

33. There are 900 students at Highlander School. How many students should you survey if you want to survey 2 out of every 10 students for a sample?

180

11-A.2

34. Is this question biased or not biased? What is your favorite kind of dessert?

not biased

11-A.3

35. The table shows the ages of the players on Leslie's hockey team. What is the range in age?

Ages of Soccer Players							
12	14	12	15	12	14	15	14
13	14	12	15	16	13	15	15

4 years

11-A.4

36. Sara wants to show the number of CDs 30 students have. Which is the best way to display the data?

bar graph

12-A.1

37. Ms. Johns wants to display the 250 scores students received on a history quiz. Which is the best way to display the data?

Possible answer: histogram

12-A.2

38. What is the mode for this set of data? 22, 56, 32, 16, 22, 33

22

13-A.3

39. Swimsuits come in small, medium, or large. They come with red, blue, gray, or white designs. How many choices for swimsuits are there?

12 choices

14-A.1

40. Jackie tosses a number cube 200 times. The number 4 comes up 30 times. What is the experimental probability of tossing a 4?

$\frac{3}{20}$

14-A.3

Form B • Free-Response   B208   Chapters 1–14   ▶ **Stop!**

Write the correct answer.

1. An expression that contains only numbers and operation symbols is called a __?__ expression.

numerical

For questions 2–4, write an algebraic or a numerical expression that matches the word expression.

2. six less than seventeen

17 − 6

3. twenty-two more than *d*

d + 22 or 22 + d

4. eight times a number, *n*

8 × n or 8n

5. Calvin rode his bike 15 miles. Bill rode 6 miles less than Calvin. Write a numerical expression that represents how far Bill rode.

15 − 6

6. Seven friends shared some apples equally. If *a* represents the total number of apples, write the algebraic expression that represents how many apples each person got.

a ÷ 7

7. Evaluate this numerical expression.

14 + 9 × 2

32

For questions 8–10, evaluate each algebraic expression for $y = 6$.

8. 29 − y

23

9. $y^2 + 3$

39

10. $7 \times \frac{1}{3}y$

14

11. A recipe calls for $1\frac{1}{2}$ cups of chopped celery. Sara wants to double the recipe. Write a numerical expression that represents the amount of chopped celery she will need.

$2 \times 1\frac{1}{2}$

12. Juan is planning a trip. He plans to go 220 miles the first day, and 220 + x miles the second day. If x = 75, how far does he plan to go the second day?

295 miles

Form B • Free-Response   B209   **Go on.** ▶

For questions 13 and 14, use the input-output table.

INPUT	ALGEBRAIC EXPRESSION	OUTPUT
x	x − 5	
11	11 − 5	6
12	12 − 5	7
13	13 − 5	?
14	?	?

13. When the output is 8, what is the input?

13

14. What is the output when the input is 14?

9

For questions 15 and 16, determine the input for the given output.

15. y ÷ 5

output = 5   input = __?__

25

16. t + 12

output = 36   input = __?__

24

For questions 17–20, solve each equation.

17. m − 6 = 13

19

18. d + 4 = 30

26

19. 38 = t − 12

50

20. 47 + p = 60

13

For questions 21 and 22, write an equation that represents each statement.

21. Fifteen more than a number, *n*, is thirty-five.

n + 15 = 35 OR 15 + n = 35

22. Six less than a number, *b*, is three.

b − 6 = 3

23. Mark is younger than Cindy by 3 years. Mark is 15 years old. If *c* = Cindy's age, what equation would you use to find her age?

c − 3 = 15 OR c = 15 + 3

24. Today at the bakery, 25 pies were sold and 6 pies were left. If *p* = the total number of pies, what equation would you use to find the total?

p − 25 = 6 OR p = 25 + 6

Form B • Free-Response   B210   ▶ **Stop!**

Free-Response Format • Test Answers   **283**

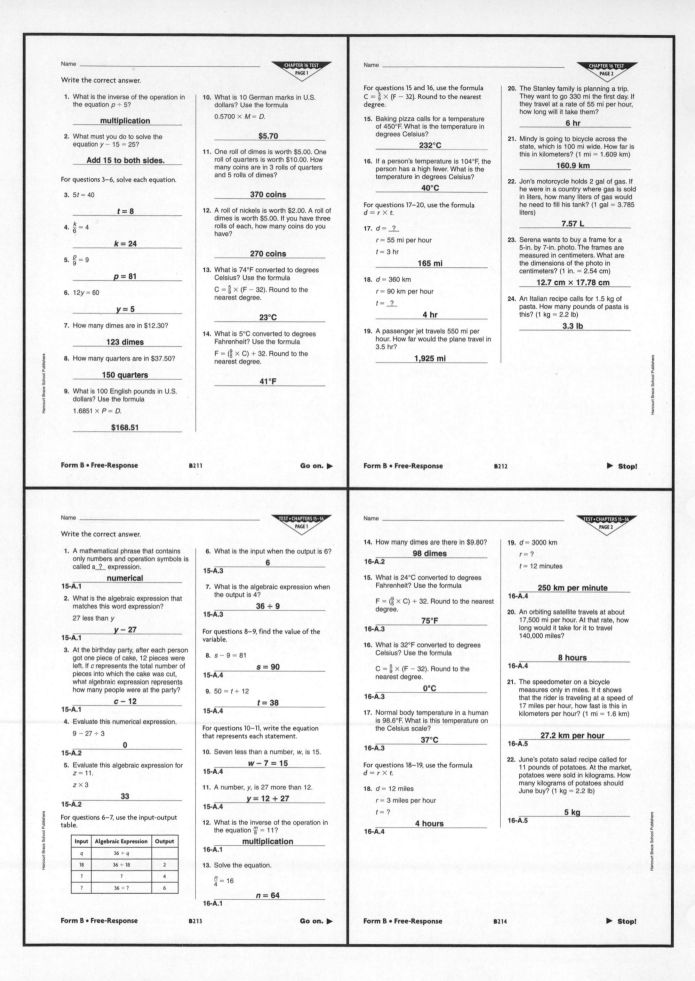

Write the correct answer.

1. What is the inverse of the operation in the equation $p \div 5$?

   multiplication

2. What must you do to solve the equation $y - 15 = 25$?

   Add 15 to both sides.

For questions 3–6, solve each equation.

3. $5t = 40$

   $t = 8$

4. $\frac{k}{6} = 4$

   $k = 24$

5. $\frac{p}{9} = 9$

   $p = 81$

6. $12y = 60$

   $y = 5$

7. How many dimes are in $12.30?

   123 dimes

8. How many quarters are in $37.50?

   150 quarters

9. What is 100 English pounds in U.S. dollars? Use the formula
   $1.6851 \times P = D$.

   $168.51

10. What is 10 German marks in U.S. dollars? Use the formula
    $0.5700 \times M = D$.

    $5.70

11. One roll of dimes is worth $5.00. One roll of quarters is worth $10.00. How many coins are in 3 rolls of quarters and 5 rolls of dimes?

    370 coins

12. A roll of nickels is worth $2.00. A roll of dimes is worth $5.00. If you have three rolls of each, how many coins do you have?

    270 coins

13. What is 74°F converted to degrees Celsius? Use the formula
    $C = \frac{5}{9} \times (F - 32)$. Round to the nearest degree.

    23°C

14. What is 5°C converted to degrees Fahrenheit? Use the formula
    $F = (\frac{9}{5} \times C) + 32$. Round to the nearest degree.

    41°F

For questions 15 and 16, use the formula $C = \frac{5}{9} \times (F - 32)$. Round to the nearest degree.

15. Baking pizza calls for a temperature of 450°F. What is the temperature in degrees Celsius?

    232°C

16. If a person's temperature is 104°F, the person has a high fever. What is the temperature in degrees Celsius?

    40°C

For questions 17–20, use the formula $d = r \times t$.

17. $d = $ _?_
    $r = 55$ mi per hour
    $t = 3$ hr

    165 mi

18. $d = 360$ km
    $r = 90$ km per hour
    $t = $ _?_

    4 hr

19. A passenger jet travels 550 mi per hour. How far would the plane travel in 3.5 hr?

    1,925 mi

20. The Stanley family is planning a trip. They want to go 330 mi the first day. If they travel at a rate of 55 mi per hour, how long will it take them?

    6 hr

21. Mindy is going to bicycle across the state, which is 100 mi wide. How far is this in kilometers? (1 mi = 1.609 km)

    160.9 km

22. Jon's motorcycle holds 2 gal of gas. If he were in a country where gas is sold in liters, how many liters of gas would he need to fill his tank? (1 gal = 3.785 liters)

    7.57 L

23. Serena wants to buy a frame for a 5-in. by 7-in. photo. The frames are measured in centimeters. What are the dimensions of the photo in centimeters? (1 in. = 2.54 cm)

    12.7 cm × 17.78 cm

24. An Italian recipe calls for 1.5 kg of pasta. How many pounds of pasta is this? (1 kg = 2.2 lb)

    3.3 lb

Write the correct answer.

1. A mathematical phrase that contains only numbers and operation symbols is called a _?_ expression.

   numerical
   15-A.1

2. What is the algebraic expression that matches this word expression?
   27 less than y

   $y - 27$
   15-A.1

3. At the birthday party, after each person got one piece of cake, 12 pieces were left. If c represents the total number of pieces into which the cake was cut, what algebraic expression represents how many people were at the party?

   $c - 12$
   15-A.1

4. Evaluate this numerical expression.
   $9 - 27 \div 3$

   0
   15-A.2

5. Evaluate this algebraic expression for $z = 11$.
   $z \times 3$

   33
   15-A.2

For questions 6–7, use the input-output table.

Input	Algebraic Expression	Output
q	$36 \div q$	
18	$36 \div 18$	2
?	?	4
?	$36 \div ?$	6

6. What is the input when the output is 6?

   6
   15-A.3

7. What is the algebraic expression when the output is 4?

   $36 \div 9$
   15-A.3

For questions 8–9, find the value of the variable.

8. $s - 9 = 81$

   $s = 90$
   15-A.4

9. $50 = t + 12$

   $t = 38$
   15-A.4

For questions 10–11, write the equation that represents each statement.

10. Seven less than a number, w, is 15.

    $w - 7 = 15$
    15-A.4

11. A number, y, is 27 more than 12.

    $y = 12 + 27$
    15-A.4

12. What is the inverse of the operation in the equation $\frac{m}{7} = 11$?

    multiplication
    16-A.1

13. Solve the equation.
    $\frac{n}{4} = 16$

    $n = 64$
    16-A.1

14. How many dimes are there in $9.80?

    98 dimes
    16-A.2

15. What is 24°C converted to degrees Fahrenheit? Use the formula
    $F = (\frac{9}{5} \times C) + 32$. Round to the nearest degree.

    75°F
    16-A.3

16. What is 32°F converted to degrees Celsius? Use the formula
    $C = \frac{5}{9} \times (F - 32)$. Round to the nearest degree.

    0°C
    16-A.3

17. Normal body temperature in a human is 98.6°F. What is this temperature on the Celsius scale?

    37°C
    16-A.3

For questions 18–19, use the formula $d = r \times t$.

18. $d = 12$ miles
    $r = 3$ miles per hour
    $t = $?

    4 hours
    16-A.4

19. $d = 3000$ km
    $r = $?
    $t = 12$ minutes

    250 km per minute
    16-A.4

20. An orbiting satellite travels at about 17,500 mi per hour. At that rate, how long would it take for it to travel 140,000 miles?

    8 hours
    16-A.4

21. The speedometer on a bicycle measures only in miles. If it shows that the rider is traveling at a speed of 17 miles per hour, how fast is this in kilometers per hour? (1 mi = 1.6 km)

    27.2 km per hour
    16-A.5

22. June's potato salad recipe called for 11 pounds of potatoes. At the market, potatoes were sold in kilograms. How many kilograms of potatoes should June buy? (1 kg = 2.2 lb)

    5 kg
    16-A.5

Free-Response Format • Test Answers   **284**

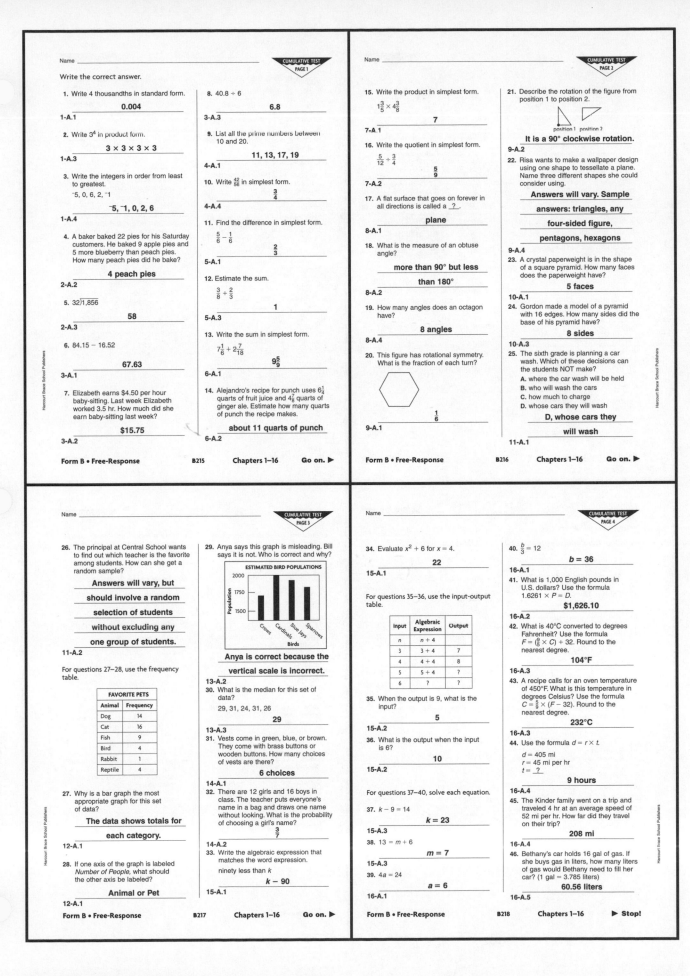

Name _____

Write the correct answer.

1. Write 4 thousandths in standard form.

0.004

1-A.1

2. Write 3^4 in product form.

3 × 3 × 3 × 3

1-A.3

3. Write the integers in order from least to greatest.

$^{-}5, 0, 6, 2, ^{-}1$

$^{-}5, ^{-}1, 0, 2, 6$

1-A.4

4. A baker baked 22 pies for his Saturday customers. He baked 9 apple pies and 5 more blueberry than peach pies. How many peach pies did he bake?

4 peach pies

2-A.2

5. $32)\overline{1,856}$

58

2-A.3

6. $84.15 - 16.52$

67.63

3-A.1

7. Elizabeth earns $4.50 per hour baby-sitting. Last week Elizabeth worked 3.5 hr. How much did she earn baby-sitting last week?

$15.75

3-A.2

8. $40.8 \div 6$

6.8

3-A.3

9. List all the prime numbers between 10 and 20.

11, 13, 17, 19

4-A.1

10. Write $\frac{42}{56}$ in simplest form.

$\frac{3}{4}$

4-A.4

11. Find the difference in simplest form.

$\frac{5}{6} - \frac{1}{6}$

$\frac{2}{3}$

5-A.1

12. Estimate the sum.

$\frac{3}{8} + \frac{2}{3}$

1

5-A.3

13. Write the sum in simplest form.

$7\frac{1}{6} + 2\frac{7}{18}$

$9\frac{5}{9}$

6-A.1

14. Alejandro's recipe for punch uses $6\frac{1}{4}$ quarts of fruit juice and $4\frac{7}{8}$ quarts of ginger ale. Estimate how many quarts of punch the recipe makes.

about 11 quarts of punch

6-A.2

Form B • Free-Response   B215   Chapters 1–16   Go on. ▶

Name _____

15. Write the product in simplest form.

$1\frac{3}{5} \times 4\frac{3}{8}$

7

7-A.1

16. Write the quotient in simplest form.

$\frac{5}{12} \div \frac{3}{4}$

$\frac{5}{9}$

7-A.2

17. A flat surface that goes on forever in all directions is called a _?_ .

plane

8-A.1

18. What is the measure of an obtuse angle?

more than 90° but less than 180°

8-A.2

19. How many angles does an octagon have?

8 angles

8-A.4

20. This figure has rotational symmetry. What is the fraction of each turn?

$\frac{1}{6}$

9-A.1

21. Describe the rotation of the figure from position 1 to position 2.

position 1   position 2

It is a 90° clockwise rotation.

9-A.2

22. Risa wants to make a wallpaper design using one shape to tessellate a plane. Name three different shapes she could consider using.

Answers will vary. Sample answers: triangles, any four-sided figure, pentagons, hexagons

9-A.4

23. A crystal paperweight is in the shape of a square pyramid. How many faces does the paperweight have?

5 faces

10-A.1

24. Gordon made a model of a pyramid with 16 edges. How many sides did the base of his pyramid have?

8 sides

10-A.3

25. The sixth grade is planning a car wash. Which of these decisions can the students NOT make?

A. where the car wash will be held
B. who will wash the cars
C. how much to charge
D. whose cars they will wash

D, whose cars they will wash

11-A.1

Form B • Free-Response   B216   Chapters 1–16   Go on. ▶

Name _____

26. The principal at Central School wants to find out which teacher is the favorite among students. How can she get a random sample?

Answers will vary, but should involve a random selection of students without excluding any one group of students.

11-A.2

For questions 27–28, use the frequency table.

FAVORITE PETS	
Animal	Frequency
Dog	14
Cat	16
Fish	9
Bird	4
Rabbit	1
Reptile	4

27. Why is a bar graph the most appropriate graph for this set of data?

The data shows totals for each category.

12-A.1

28. If one axis of the graph is labeled *Number of People*, what should the other axis be labeled?

Animal or Pet

12-A.1

29. Anya says this graph is misleading. Bill says it is not. Who is correct and why?

ESTIMATED BIRD POPULATIONS

Population: 2000, 1750, 1500
Birds: Crows, Cardinals, Blue Jays, Sparrows

Anya is correct because the vertical scale is incorrect.

13-A.2

30. What is the median for this set of data?

29, 31, 24, 31, 26

29

13-A.3

31. Vests come in green, blue, or brown. They come with brass buttons or wooden buttons. How many choices of vests are there?

6 choices

14-A.1

32. There are 12 girls and 16 boys in class. The teacher puts everyone's name in a bag and draws one name without looking. What is the probability of choosing a girl's name?

$\frac{3}{7}$

14-A.2

33. Write the algebraic expression that matches the word expression.

ninety less than k

$k - 90$

15-A.1

Form B • Free-Response   B217   Chapters 1–16   Go on. ▶

Name _____

34. Evaluate $x^2 + 6$ for $x = 4$.

22

15-A.1

For questions 35–36, use the input-output table.

Input	Algebraic Expression	Output
n	$n + 4$	
3	$3 + 4$	7
4	$4 + 4$	8
5	$5 + 4$	?
6	?	?

35. When the output is 9, what is the input?

5

15-A.2

36. What is the output when the input is 6?

10

15-A.2

For questions 37–40, solve each equation.

37. $k - 9 = 14$

$k = 23$

15-A.3

38. $13 = m + 6$

$m = 7$

15-A.3

39. $4a = 24$

$a = 6$

16-A.1

40. $\frac{b}{3} = 12$

$b = 36$

16-A.1

41. What is 1,000 English pounds in U.S. dollars? Use the formula $1.6261 \times P = D$.

$1,626.10

16-A.2

42. What is 40°C converted to degrees Fahrenheit? Use the formula $F = (\frac{9}{5} \times C) + 32$. Round to the nearest degree.

104°F

16-A.3

43. A recipe calls for an oven temperature of 450°F. What is this temperature in degrees Celsius? Use the formula $C = \frac{5}{9} \times (F - 32)$. Round to the nearest degree.

232°C

16-A.3

44. Use the formula $d = r \times t$.

$d = 405$ mi
$r = 45$ mi per hr
$t = \_?\_$

9 hours

16-A.4

45. The Kinder family went on a trip and traveled 4 hr at an average speed of 52 mi per hr. How far did they travel on their trip?

208 mi

16-A.4

46. Bethany's car holds 16 gal of gas. If she buys gas in liters, how many liters of gas would Bethany need to fill her car? (1 gal = 3.785 liters)

60.56 liters

16-A.5

Form B • Free-Response   B218   Chapters 1–16   ▶ Stop!

Harcourt Brace School Publishers

Free-Response Format • Test Answers

285

Write the correct answer.

1. A chemical solution contains 2 mL of water and 5 mL of acid. What is the ratio of mL of acid to total mL of solution?

$$\frac{5}{7}$$

2. Write two equivalent ratios that compare the number of circles to the number of hexagons.

any two:

$$\frac{4}{5}, \frac{8}{10}, \frac{12}{15}, \frac{16}{20}, \frac{20}{25}, \frac{24}{30}, \frac{28}{35}, \frac{32}{40}, \frac{36}{45}, \frac{40}{50}$$

3. Write the ratio twelve to seven in two different ways.

any two:

$$12 \text{ to } 7, 12{:}7, \frac{12}{7}$$

4. What is the missing term that makes the ratios equivalent?

16:6, □:15

40

5. In fraction form, write the ratio for the rate 3 T-shirts for $12.

$$\frac{3 \text{ T-shirts}}{\$12}$$

6. What is the unit rate for $50 for 4 tickets?

$$\frac{\$12.50}{1 \text{ ticket}}$$

7. Kip typed 400 words in 8 min. How long will it take Kip to type 1,500 words?

30 min

8. A box of football cards costs $42. There are 25 packs of cards in the box. How much does each pack of cards cost?

$1.68

9. What percent of the squares in the figure below are shaded?

66%

10. Write 0.24 as a percent.

24%

11. What is 80% written as a ratio in simplest form?

$$\frac{4}{5}$$

12. What is $\frac{5}{8}$ written as a percent?

62.5%

---

13. What is 41% written as a decimal?

0.41

14. What is $\frac{3}{25}$ written as a percent?

12%

15. Sheila plays softball. She had 11 hits in her last 25 at bats. What percentage is she hitting?

44%, or 0.440

16. Hank saves $\frac{2}{5}$ of the money that he earns. He earned $84 last week. How much did Hank save?

$33.60

17. What percent of the figure is shaded?

64%

18. What percent of the figure is shaded?

37.5%

19. There were 52 contestants in the geography bee. Of the contestants, 39 were sixth graders. What percent of the contestants were sixth graders?

75%

20. The junior high soccer team played 16 games last year. It won 14 games. What percent of the games did it lose?

12.5%

21. Three cartons of juice cost $8.67. How much do 5 cartons of juice cost?

$14.45

22. Rebecca finished 15 homework problems in 45 min. How many homework problems can Rebecca finish in 3 hr?

60 problems

23. It cost Dave $26.25 to use the Internet for 15 hr. How much will it cost Dave for 25 hr of Internet use at the same rate?

$43.75

24. The bus made 7 stops in 40 min. How many stops will it make in 2 hr if it continues at the same rate?

21 stops

Write the correct answer.

For questions 1–4, solve each problem.

1. A TV music awards show was seen by 50 million viewers. Of these viewers, 60% were teenagers. How many viewers were teenagers?

30 million

2. The Charles Street Recreation Center is building an addition. The current building has 20,000 ft^2. The addition will provide 30% more space. How many square feet will the addition have?

6,000 ft^2

3. An orchard has 10,000 pear trees. Of these trees, 20% produce the Bartlett variety of pears. How many trees produce Bartlett pears?

2,000 trees

4. A town has a budget of $20 million. The town spends 40% of the budget on education. How much does the town spend on education?

$8 million

5. One way to find 50% of 300 is to ___?___ 300 by $\frac{1}{2}$.

multiply

6. What is 70% of 50?

35

7. What is 15% of 80?

12

8. What is 3% of 25?

0.75

9. Find the sales tax.

price: $47

tax rate: 8%

$3.76

For questions 10 and 11, use the data in the table below for a circle graph.

Frozen Yogurt Sales in June	
Flavor Choices	**Percent**
Strawberry	25%
Chocolate	35%
Vanilla	40%

10. What angle measure should you use for the Chocolate section of the graph?

126°

11. What angle measure should you use for the Strawberry section of the graph?

90°

For questions 12 and 13, use the circle graph.

Main Source of News

Radio 20%
Newspapers 45%
TV 35%

12. If 300 people were surveyed, how many said TV was their main source of news?

105 people

13. If 1,200 people were surveyed, how many picked radio?

240 people

14. What is the amount of discount if the regular price is $40.00 and the discount rate is 25%?

$10.00

15. What is the amount of discount if the regular price is $20.00 and the discount rate is 15%?

$3.00

16. What is the sale price if the regular price is $120 and the discount rate is 30%?

$84

17. What is the sale price if the regular price is $58.00 and the discount rate is 20%?

$46.40

18. CDs are on sale for 15% off the regular price of $15.00. If Sandy buys 3 CDs, what is her total discount?

$6.75

19. What is the interest for 1 year if the principal is $3,000 and the simple interest rate is 6%?

$180

20. Jamal put $1,200 in the bank for 1 year. He earned simple interest at the rate of 5% a year. How much interest did he earn?

$60

21. What is the interest for 1 year if the principal is $800 and the simple interest rate is 5.5%?

$44

22. Todd put $300 in the bank. It earned simple interest at the rate of 4.5% a year. How much money did he have after 2 years?

$327

Free-Response Format • Test Answers

Name _____

Write the correct answer.

For questions 1–4, identify each pair of shapes as similar, congruent, both, or neither.

1.

similar

2.

neither

3.

both

4.

neither

5. Rectangles QRST and WXYZ are similar. What ratio is equivalent to $\frac{RT}{XZ}$?

$\frac{QS}{WY}$

For questions 6 and 7, use the figures below.

6. P corresponds to __?__ .

X

7. MN corresponds to __?__ .

YZ

For questions 8 and 9, use the figures below.

8. What is the ratio of $\frac{GH}{MN}$ in simplest form?

$\frac{3}{5}$

9. These two rectangles are similar because the ratio of $\frac{GH}{MN}$ is the same as the ratio of __?__ .

$\frac{HI}{NO}$

10. One photograph is 5 in. × 7 in. Another photograph is 9 in. × 12 in. Are the two photographs similar?

No

11. Mr. Ji bought two carpets for his home. One carpet is 4 ft × 6 ft. The other carpet is 12 ft × 18 ft. Are the two carpets similar?

Yes

Form B • Free-Response   B223   Go on. ▶

Name _____

12. What proportion would you use to find X?

$\frac{4}{x} = \frac{6}{9}$

For questions 13 and 14, find n for each pair of similar figures.

13.

n = 2 ft

14.

n = 21m

15. A model of a statue is 7 in. wide and 14 in. high. The statue is 21 in. wide. How high is it?

42 in.

16. A building casts a shadow that is 60 ft long, while a person 5 ft tall casts a shadow that measures 12 ft. What should you do first to find the height of the building?

write a proportion

17. What is the height of the tree?

16 ft

18. What is the height of the flagpole?

20 ft

19. A radio tower casts a shadow 75 ft long. At the same time a 3 ft pole nearby casts a shadow 5 ft long. How high is the radio tower?

45 ft

20. A 6 ft tall man casts a shadow 3 ft long while his son casts a shadow 2 ft long. How tall is the son?

4 ft

Form B • Free-Response   B224   ▶ Stop!

Name _____

Write the correct answer.

1. If the exact length-to-width ratio of an object is also used to make a drawing of the object, it is a __?__ drawing.

scale

2. If you want to make a scale drawing of a sailboat that is 40 ft long and 60 ft tall on an 11 in. × 17 in. piece of paper, would the scale 1 in.:2 ft allow you to do this?

no

For questions 3–5, determine the missing dimension.

3. scale: 1 in.:5 ft
drawing height: 6 in.
actual height: __?__

30 feet

4. scale: 3 cm:25 cm
drawing length: 30 cm
actual length: __?__

250 cm

5. scale: 1 in.:4 ft
drawing length: __?__
actual length: 20 ft

5 inches

6. The scale drawing of a tree house is 1 in.:6 in. The drawing height is 12 in. What is the actual height of the tree house?

72 in. or 6 ft

7. A scale drawing of a beetle has a length of 12 cm. The actual length of the beetle is 3 cm. What is the scale of the drawing?

4 cm:1 cm

8. A map scale is 1 in. = 25 mi. The actual distance is 125 mi. What does n represent in the proportion $\frac{1}{25} = \frac{n}{125}$?

the map distance in inches

9. On a map, the straight-line distance between Denver and Fort Collins is 5 in. If the scale is 1 in. = 25 mi, what is the proportion you could use to find the actual distance?

$\frac{1}{25} = \frac{5}{n}$

For questions 10–11, determine the actual miles.

10. scale: 1 in. = 50 mi
map distance: 4.5 in.
actual distance: __?__

225 mi

11. scale: 1 in. = 3 mi
map distance: 7 in.
actual distance: __?__

21 mi

Form B • Free-Response   B225   Go on. ▶

Name _____

12. Find the actual miles.
scale: 1 in. = 25 mi
map distance: $1\frac{1}{2}$ in.
actual distance: __?__

$37\frac{1}{2}$

For questions 13 and 14, use the scale 1 in. = 5 mi.

13. Sara and Shirley hiked a mountain trail. The map distance for the trail was 3.5 in. How far did they hike?

17.5 miles

14. For a field trip to the science museum, the map distance the bus traveled one way was 4.5 in. What was the actual round-trip distance?

45 mi

For questions 15–18, use the map. Each square equals one city block.

15. Joe left his house and walked 2 blocks east. Where would he go from there to get to Jeff's house?

4 blocks north

16. Calvin left the school and went 5 blocks west and 3 blocks north. Where was he?

at the store

17. Joan left her house and walked 3 blocks north, 2 blocks east and 4 blocks north. Where did she go?

to the movie

18. The librarian left school and drove by the shortest route to the store and then to the library. How many blocks did she drive?

17 blocks

19. The value of the Golden Ratio is about __?__ .

1.6 or 1.6:1

20. A Golden Rectangle is 100 mm high. What is its length?

160 mm

21. Which rectangle is a Golden Rectangle?

Rectangle 2

22. Rectangle S is 800 cm × 667 cm. Rectangle T is 480 cm × 300 cm. Which is a Golden Rectangle?

Rectangle T

Form B • Free-Response   B226   ▶ Stop!

Free-Response Format • Test Answers

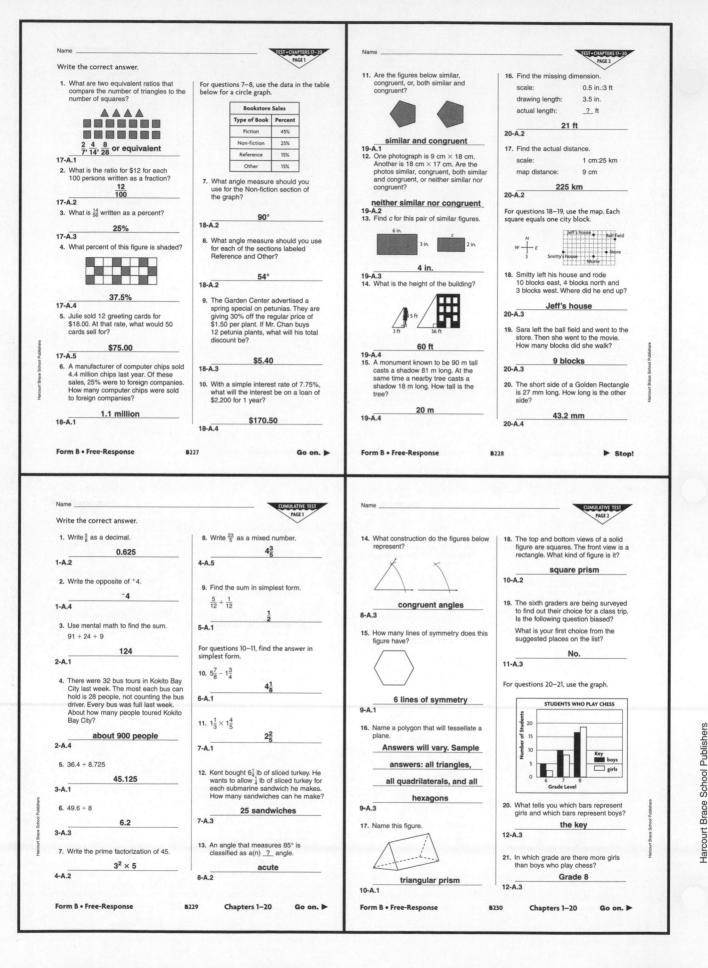

Write the correct answer.

1. What are two equivalent ratios that compare the number of triangles to the number of squares?

$\dfrac{2}{7}, \dfrac{4}{14}, \dfrac{8}{28}$ **or equivalent**

17-A.1

2. What is the ratio for $12 for each 100 persons written as a fraction?

$\dfrac{12}{100}$

17-A.2

3. What is $\frac{14}{56}$ written as a percent?

25%

17-A.3

4. What percent of this figure is shaded?

37.5%

17-A.4

5. Julie sold 12 greeting cards for $18.00. At that rate, what would 50 cards sell for?

$75.00

17-A.5

6. A manufacturer of computer chips sold 4.4 million chips last year. Of these sales, 25% were to foreign companies. How many computer chips were sold to foreign companies?

1.1 million

18-A.1

For questions 7–8, use the data in the table below for a circle graph.

Bookstore Sales	
Type of Book	**Percent**
Fiction	45%
Non-fiction	25%
Reference	15%
Other	15%

7. What angle measure should you use for the Non-fiction section of the graph?

90°

18-A.2

8. What angle measure should you use for each of the sections labeled Reference and Other?

54°

18-A.2

9. The Garden Center advertised a spring special on petunias. They are giving 30% off the regular price of $1.50 per plant. If Mr. Chan buys 12 petunia plants, what will his total discount be?

$5.40

18-A.3

10. With a simple interest rate of 7.75%, what will the interest be on a loan of $2,200 for 1 year?

$170.50

18-A.4

Form B • Free-Response   B227   **Go on.** ▶

---

11. Are the figures below similar, congruent, or, both similar and congruent?

similar and congruent

19-A.1

12. One photograph is 9 cm × 18 cm. Another is 18 cm × 17 cm. Are the photos similar, congruent, both similar and congruent, or neither similar nor congruent?

neither similar nor congruent

19-A.2

13. Find c for this pair of similar figures.

6 in.   3 in.   c   2 in.

4 in.

19-A.3

14. What is the height of the building?

5 ft
3 ft   36 ft

60 ft

19-A.4

15. A monument known to be 90 m tall casts a shadow 81 m long. At the same time a nearby tree casts a shadow 18 m long. How tall is the tree?

20 m

19-A.4

16. Find the missing dimension.

scale: 0.5 in.:3 ft
drawing length: 3.5 in.
actual length: _?_ ft

21 ft

20-A.2

17. Find the actual distance.

scale: 1 cm:25 km
map distance: 9 cm

225 km

20-A.2

For questions 18–19, use the map. Each square equals one city block.

18. Smitty left his house and rode 10 blocks east, 4 blocks north and 3 blocks west. Where did he end up?

Jeff's house

20-A.3

19. Sara left the ball field and went to the store. Then she went to the movie. How many blocks did she walk?

9 blocks

20-A.3

20. The short side of a Golden Rectangle is 27 mm long. How long is the other side?

43.2 mm

20-A.4

Form B • Free-Response   B228   ▶ **Stop!**

Write the correct answer.

1. Write $\frac{5}{8}$ as a decimal.

0.625

1-A.2

2. Write the opposite of $^+4$.

$^-4$

1-A.4

3. Use mental math to find the sum.
$91 + 24 + 9$

124

2-A.1

4. There were 32 bus tours in Kokito Bay City last week. The most each bus can hold is 28 people, not counting the bus driver. Every bus was full last week. About how many people toured Kokito Bay City?

about 900 people

2-A.4

5. $36.4 + 8.725$

45.125

3-A.1

6. $49.6 \div 8$

6.2

3-A.3

7. Write the prime factorization of 45.

$3^2 \times 5$

4-A.2

8. Write $\frac{23}{5}$ as a mixed number.

$4\frac{3}{5}$

4-A.5

9. Find the sum in simplest form.

$\dfrac{5}{12} + \dfrac{1}{12}$

$\dfrac{1}{2}$

5-A.1

For questions 10–11, find the answer in simplest form.

10. $5\frac{7}{8} - 1\frac{3}{4}$

$4\frac{1}{8}$

6-A.1

11. $1\frac{1}{3} \times 1\frac{4}{5}$

$2\frac{2}{5}$

7-A.1

12. Kent bought $6\frac{1}{4}$ lb of sliced turkey. He wants to allow $\frac{1}{4}$ lb of sliced turkey for each submarine sandwich he makes. How many sandwiches can he make?

25 sandwiches

7-A.3

13. An angle that measures 85° is classified as a(n) _?_ angle.

acute

8-A.2

Form B • Free-Response   B229   **Chapters 1–20**   **Go on.** ▶

---

14. What construction do the figures below represent?

congruent angles

8-A.3

15. How many lines of symmetry does this figure have?

6 lines of symmetry

9-A.1

16. Name a polygon that will tessellate a plane.

Answers will vary. Sample answers: all triangles, all quadrilaterals, and all hexagons

9-A.3

17. Name this figure.

triangular prism

10-A.1

18. The top and bottom views of a solid figure are squares. The front view is a rectangle. What kind of figure is it?

square prism

10-A.2

19. The sixth graders are being surveyed to find out their choice for a class trip. Is the following question biased?

What is your first choice from the suggested places on the list?

No.

11-A.3

For questions 20–21, use the graph.

STUDENTS WHO PLAY CHESS

Key: boys, girls

20. What tells you which bars represent girls and which bars represent boys?

the key

12-A.3

21. In which grade are there more girls than boys who play chess?

Grade 8

12-A.3

Form B • Free-Response   B230   **Chapters 1–20**   **Go on.** ▶

Free-Response Format • Test Answers

For questions 22–23, use the line graph.

NUMBER OF BICYCLES SOLD

22. What has been the trend in bicycle sales?

increasing

13-A.1

23. Use the graph to predict how many bicycles will be sold in August.

60 bicycles

13-A.1

24. Karen has gotten a hit in 60 of the last 100 times she has been up to bat. How many hits can she expect to get in her next 50 times at bat?

30 hits

14-A.3

25. Evaluate $6 + \frac{1}{3}y$ for $y = 12$.

10

15-A.1

26. Solve for m. $8 = m + 6$

$m = 2$

15-A.3

27. Solve for k. $5k = 20$

$k = 4$

16-A.1

28. Solve for a. $\frac{a}{3} = 15$

$a = 45$

16-A.1

29. What are 100 German marks worth in U.S. dollars? Use the formula $0.6200 \times M = D$. (M = marks; D = dollars)

$62.00

16-A.2

30. What is 20°C converted to degrees Fahrenheit? Use the formula $F = (\frac{9}{5} \times C) + 32$.

68°F

16-A.3

31. Paul drove an average of 40 mi per hr from his home to the beach. He drove 3.5 hr to get there. How far does Paul live from the beach? Use the formula $d = r \times t$.

140 mi

16-A.4

32. Kevin weighs 42 kg. Christopher weighs 104 lb. How many more pounds than Kevin does Christopher weigh? (1 kg = 2.2 lb)

11.6 lb

16-A.5

33. Write the ratio 3 to 7 in another form.

Sample answers: $\frac{3}{7}$; 3:7

17-A.1

Form B • Free-Response　　B231　　Chapters 1–20　　**Go on. ▶**

---

34. Write 40% as a fraction in simplest form.

$\frac{2}{5}$

17-A.3

35. What percent of the figure is shaded?

20%

17-A.4

36. The Maxwell family spent $9,000 remodeling their home. They spent 20% of this on bathroom and kitchen tiling. How much did the Maxwells spend on tile?

$1,800

18-A.1

37. Scarves are on sale for 30% off the regular price of $18.00. If Samantha buys 5 scarves, what is her total discount?

$27.00

18-A.3

38. Andrianna put $2,500 in the bank for one year. She earned interest at the rate of 4% a year. How much interest did she earn?

$100

18-A.4

39. Use the figures below.

What is the ratio in simplest form of $\frac{AB}{EF}$?

$\frac{2}{3}$

19-A.2

40. A photograph is 4 in. wide by 5 in. long. Tammy wants to have the photo enlarged so the width measures 20 in. How long will the enlarged photo be?

25 in.

19-A.3

41. A tree casts a shadow 36 ft long. At the same time a 6-ft pole nearby casts a shadow 18 ft long. How tall is the tree?

12 ft tall

19-A.4

42. The scale drawing of a dog house is 1 in.:1.5 ft. The length in the drawing is 6.5 in. What is the actual length of the dog house?

9.75 ft

20-A.1

43. The scale on a map is 1 in. = 40 mi. The map shows 8 in. between Diamond Lake Village and Chesterville. Find the actual miles between the two towns.

320 miles

20-A.2

44. A rectangle is 24 in. long. It is a Golden Rectangle. What is its width?

15 in.

20-A.4

Form B • Free-Response　　B232　　Chapters 1–20　　**▶ Stop!**

Write the correct answer.

1. To change fluid ounces to cups, you should ___?___.

divide by 8

For questions 2 and 3, change to the given units.

2. 15 ft = ☐ yd

5

3. 7 qt = ☐ pt

14

4. Tammy walked 20 feet from the restaurant to the parking lot. Then she walked 90 yd to her car. How many feet did she walk?

290 ft

5. Tom poured orange juice into 32 glasses which each held 8 ounces of juice. How many gallons of orange juice did he use?

2 gallons

6. To change grams to kilograms, you should divide by ___?___.

1,000

For questions 7 and 8, change to the given units.

7. 72 cm = ☐ mm

720

8. 1,200 mL = ☐ L

1.2

9. Tyrone lives 6,000 m from his school. How many kilometers does he live from school?

6 km

10. Mackenzie's sports equipment bag weighs 3.8 kg. How many grams does it weigh?

3,800 g

11. Which measurement is more precise for measuring the height of a chair, 3 yd or 38 in.?

38 in.

12. If Mandy was measuring the length of a paper clip in metric units, which unit would give the most precise measurement?

mm

13. Which measurement is more precise for measuring distance, 987 m or 1 km?

987 m

For question 14, answer yes or no.

14. If you need a precise measure of a section of wallpaper would you use feet?

no

Form B • Free-Response　　B233　　**Go on. ▶**

For questions 15 and 16, use the network below.

T = Tony's
M = Mark's
S = Sonya's
A = Alicia's

15. Tony left his house and went to Mark's. Mark he then picked up Sonya and drove to Alicia's house. How long was this route?

202 km

16. If Tony had picked up Sonya first, then Mark and then driven to Alicia's house, how many kilometers shorter would his route have been?

54 km shorter

For questions 17 and 18, use the network below.

17. What is the length of the route ABDC?

26 in.

18. What is the length of the route ABCD?

24 in.

19. What is the perimeter?

19.5 m

20. Find the missing length. Then find the perimeter.

$x = 35$, 220 cm

21. What is the perimeter?

36 ft

22. The perimeter is 60 km. What is the missing length?

25 km

23. A city parking lot is 120 yd long and 90 yd wide. What is its perimeter?

420 yd

24. A fencing company just installed a fence around a regular octagonal garden. If the fence was 112 ft long, what was the length of each side of the octagon?

14 ft

Form B • Free-Response　　B234　　**▶ Stop!**

Free-Response Format • Test Answers

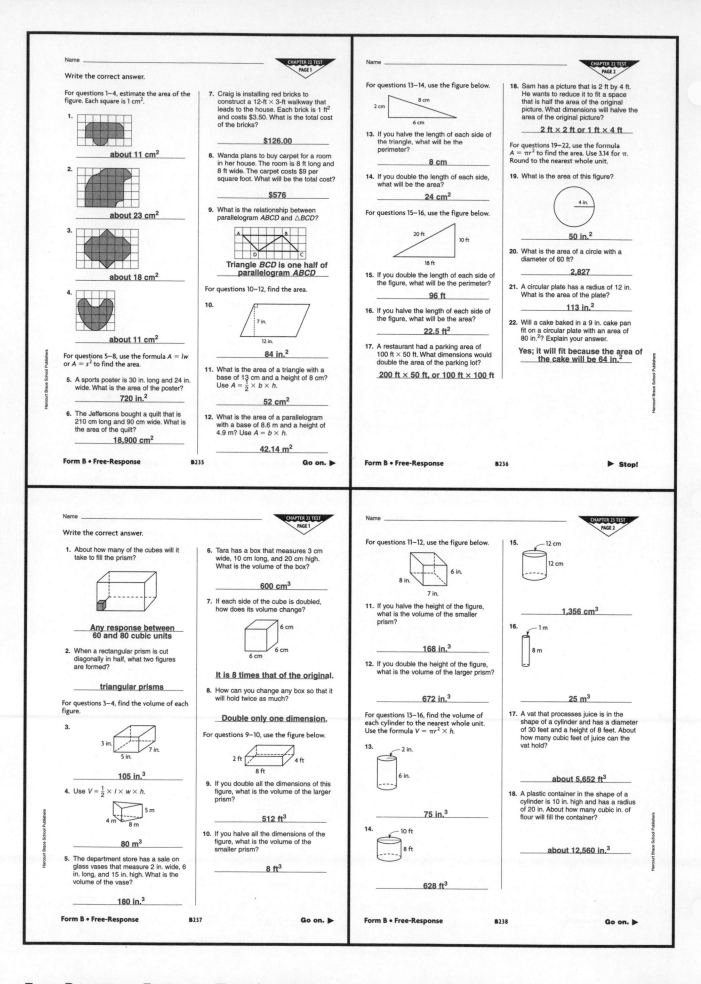

Name _____

Write the correct answer.

For questions 1–4, estimate the area of the figure. Each square is 1 cm².

1.

about 11 cm²

2.

about 23 cm²

3.

about 18 cm²

4.

about 11 cm²

For questions 5–8, use the formula $A = lw$ or $A = s^2$ to find the area.

5. A sports poster is 30 in. long and 24 in. wide. What is the area of the poster?

720 in.²

6. The Jeffersons bought a quilt that is 210 cm long and 90 cm wide. What is the area of the quilt?

18,900 cm²

7. Craig is installing red bricks to construct a 12-ft × 3-ft walkway that leads to the house. Each brick is 1 ft² and costs $3.50. What is the total cost of the bricks?

$126.00

8. Wanda plans to buy carpet for a room in her house. The room is 8 ft long and 8 ft wide. The carpet costs $9 per square foot. What will be the total cost?

$576

9. What is the relationship between parallelogram *ABCD* and △*BCD*?

Triangle *BCD* is one half of parallelogram *ABCD*

For questions 10–12, find the area.

10.

7 in.

12 in.

84 in.²

11. What is the area of a triangle with a base of 13 cm and a height of 8 cm? Use $A = \frac{1}{2} \times b \times h$.

52 cm²

12. What is the area of a parallelogram with a base of 8.6 m and a height of 4.9 m? Use $A = b \times h$.

42.14 m²

Form B • Free-Response   B235   **Go on. ▶**

Name _____

For questions 13–14, use the figure below.

2 cm   8 cm   6 cm

13. If you halve the length of each side of the triangle, what will be the perimeter?

8 cm

14. If you double the length of each side, what will be the area?

24 cm²

For questions 15–16, use the figure below.

20 ft   10 ft   18 ft

15. If you double the length of each side of the figure, what will be the perimeter?

96 ft

16. If you halve the length of each side of the figure, what will be the area?

22.5 ft²

17. A restaurant had a parking area of 100 ft × 50 ft. What dimensions would double the area of the parking lot?

200 ft × 50 ft, or 100 ft × 100 ft

18. Sam has a picture that is 2 ft by 4 ft. He wants to reduce it to fit a space that is half the area of the original picture. What dimensions will halve the area of the original picture?

2 ft × 2 ft or 1 ft × 4 ft

For questions 19–22, use the formula $A = \pi r^2$ to find the area. Use 3.14 for π. Round to the nearest whole unit.

19. What is the area of this figure?

4 in.

50 in.²

20. What is the area of a circle with a diameter of 60 ft?

2,827

21. A circular plate has a radius of 12 in. What is the area of the plate?

113 in.²

22. Will a cake baked in a 9 in. cake pan fit on a circular plate with an area of 80 in.²? Explain your answer.

Yes; it will fit because the area of the cake will be 64 in.²

Form B • Free-Response   B236   **▶ Stop!**

Name _____

Write the correct answer.

1. About how many of the cubes will it take to fill the prism?

Any response between 60 and 80 cubic units

2. When a rectangular prism is cut diagonally in half, what two figures are formed?

triangular prisms

For questions 3–4, find the volume of each figure.

3.

3 in.   5 in.   7 in.

105 in.³

4. Use $V = \frac{1}{2} \times l \times w \times h$.

5 m   4 m   8 m

80 m³

5. The department store has a sale on glass vases that measure 2 in. wide, 6 in. long, and 15 in. high. What is the volume of the vase?

180 in.³

6. Tara has a box that measures 3 cm wide, 10 cm long, and 20 cm high. What is the volume of the box?

600 cm³

7. If each side of the cube is doubled, how does its volume change?

6 cm   6 cm   6 cm

It is 8 times that of the original.

8. How can you change any box so that it will hold twice as much?

Double only one dimension.

For questions 9–10, use the figure below.

2 ft   4 ft

9. If you double all the dimensions of this figure, what is the volume of the larger prism?

512 ft³

10. If you halve all the dimensions of the figure, what is the volume of the smaller prism?

8 ft³

Form B • Free-Response   B237   **Go on. ▶**

Name _____

For questions 11–12, use the figure below.

8 in.   6 in.   7 in.

11. If you halve the height of the figure, what is the volume of the smaller prism?

168 in.³

12. If you double the height of the figure, what is the volume of the larger prism?

672 in.³

For questions 13–16, find the volume of each cylinder to the nearest whole unit. Use the formula $V = \pi r^2 \times h$.

13.

2 in.   6 in.

75 in.³

14.

10 ft   8 ft

628 ft³

15.

12 cm   12 cm

1,356 cm³

16.

1 m   8 m

25 m³

17. A vat that processes juice is in the shape of a cylinder and has a diameter of 30 feet and a height of 8 feet. About how many cubic feet of juice can the vat hold?

about 5,652 ft³

18. A plastic container in the shape of a cylinder is 10 in. high and has a radius of 20 in. About how many cubic in. of flour will fill the container?

about 12,560 in.³

Form B • Free-Response   B238   **Go on. ▶**

Harcourt Brace School Publishers

Free-Response Format • Test Answers

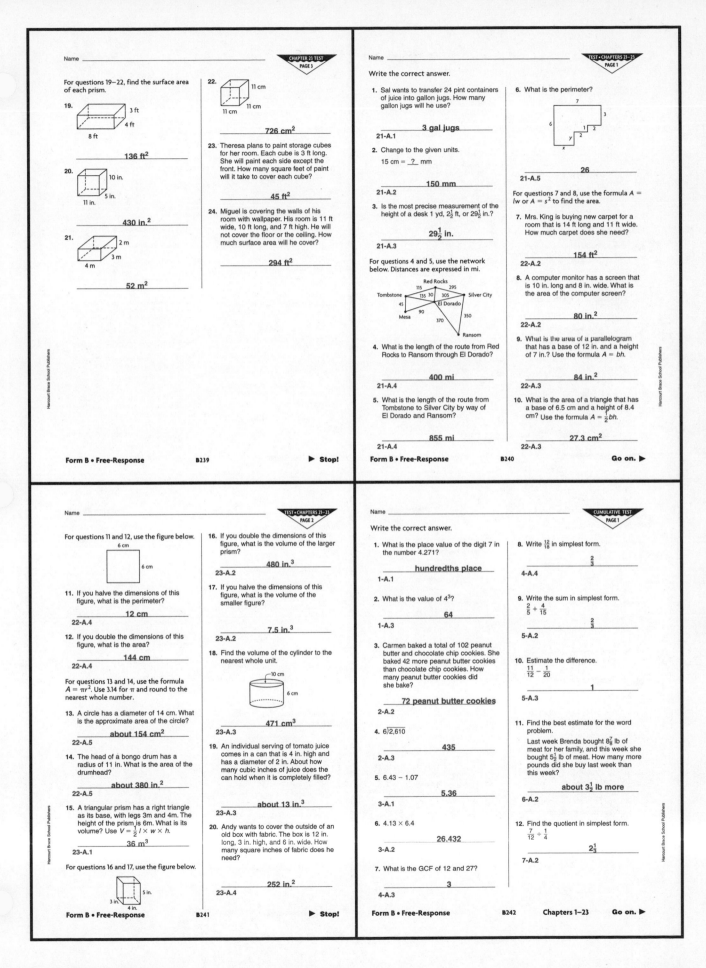

Name _____

For questions 19–22, find the surface area of each prism.

19.

3 ft
4 ft
8 ft

_____ **136 ft²**

20.

10 in.
5 in.
11 in.

_____ **430 in.²**

21.

2 m
3 m
4 m

_____ **52 m²**

22.

11 cm
11 cm
11 cm

_____ **726 cm²**

23. Theresa plans to paint storage cubes for her room. Each cube is 3 ft long. She will paint each side except the front. How many square feet of paint will it take to cover each cube?

_____ **45 ft²**

24. Miguel is covering the walls of his room with wallpaper. His room is 11 ft wide, 10 ft long, and 7 ft high. He will not cover the floor or the ceiling. How much surface area will he cover?

_____ **294 ft²**

Form B • Free-Response   B239   ▶ **Stop!**

Name _____

Write the correct answer.

1. Sal wants to transfer 24 pint containers of juice into gallon jugs. How many gallon jugs will he use?

_____ **3 gal jugs**
21-A.1

2. Change to the given units.

15 cm = _?_ mm

_____ **150 mm**
21-A.2

3. Is the most precise measurement of the height of a desk 1 yd, $2\frac{1}{2}$ ft, or $29\frac{1}{2}$ in.?

_____ **$29\frac{1}{2}$ in.**
21-A.3

For questions 4 and 5, use the network below. Distances are expressed in mi.

Red Rocks
115   295
Tombstone   135   30   305   Silver City
45   El Dorado
Mesa   90   370   350
Ransom

4. What is the length of the route from Red Rocks to Ransom through El Dorado?

_____ **400 mi**
21-A.4

5. What is the length of the route from Tombstone to Silver City by way of El Dorado and Ransom?

_____ **855 mi**
21-A.4

6. What is the perimeter?

7
3
6
1
y   2
x

_____ **26**
21-A.5

For questions 7 and 8, use the formula $A = lw$ or $A = s^2$ to find the area.

7. Mrs. King is buying new carpet for a room that is 14 ft long and 11 ft wide. How much carpet does she need?

_____ **154 ft²**
22-A.2

8. A computer monitor has a screen that is 10 in. long and 8 in. wide. What is the area of the computer screen?

_____ **80 in.²**
22-A.2

9. What is the area of a parallelogram that has a base of 12 in. and a height of 7 in.? Use the formula $A = bh$.

_____ **84 in.²**
22-A.3

10. What is the area of a triangle that has a base of 6.5 cm and a height of 8.4 cm? Use the formula $A = \frac{1}{2}bh$.

_____ **27.3 cm²**
22-A.3

Form B • Free-Response   B240   **Go on.** ▶

Name _____

For questions 11 and 12, use the figure below.

6 cm
6 cm

11. If you halve the dimensions of this figure, what is the perimeter?

_____ **12 cm**
22-A.4

12. If you double the dimensions of this figure, what is the area?

_____ **144 cm**
22-A.4

For questions 13 and 14, use the formula $A = \pi r^2$. Use 3.14 for π and round to the nearest whole number.

13. A circle has a diameter of 14 cm. What is the approximate area of the circle?

_____ **about 154 cm²**
22-A.5

14. The head of a bongo drum has a radius of 11 in. What is the area of the drumhead?

_____ **about 380 in.²**
22-A.5

15. A triangular prism has a right triangle as its base, with legs 3m and 4m. The height of the prism is 6m. What is its volume? Use $V = \frac{1}{2} l \times w \times h$.

_____ **36 m³**
23-A.1

For questions 16 and 17, use the figure below.

3 in.   5 in.
4 in.

16. If you double the dimensions of this figure, what is the volume of the larger prism?

_____ **480 in.³**
23-A.2

17. If you halve the dimensions of this figure, what is the volume of the smaller figure?

_____ **7.5 in.³**
23-A.2

18. Find the volume of the cylinder to the nearest whole unit.

10 cm
6 cm

_____ **471 cm³**
23-A.3

19. An individual serving of tomato juice comes in a can that is 4 in. high and has a diameter of 2 in. About how many cubic inches of juice does the can hold when it is completely filled?

_____ **about 13 in.³**
23-A.3

20. Andy wants to cover the outside of an old box with fabric. The box is 12 in. long, 3 in. high, and 6 in. wide. How many square inches of fabric does he need?

_____ **252 in.²**
23-A.4

Form B • Free-Response   B241   ▶ **Stop!**

Name _____

Write the correct answer.

1. What is the place value of the digit 7 in the number 4.271?

_____ **hundredths place**
1-A.1

2. What is the value of 4^3?

_____ **64**
1-A.3

3. Carmen baked a total of 102 peanut butter and chocolate chip cookies. She baked 42 more peanut butter cookies than chocolate chip cookies. How many peanut butter cookies did she bake?

_____ **72 peanut butter cookies**
2-A.2

4. $6)\overline{2,610}$

_____ **435**
2-A.3

5. 6.43 − 1.07

_____ **5.36**
3-A.1

6. 4.13 × 6.4

_____ **26.432**
3-A.2

7. What is the GCF of 12 and 27?

_____ **3**
4-A.3

8. Write $\frac{12}{18}$ in simplest form.

_____ **$\frac{2}{3}$**
4-A.4

9. Write the sum in simplest form.

$\frac{2}{5} + \frac{4}{15}$

_____ **$\frac{2}{3}$**
5-A.2

10. Estimate the difference.

$\frac{11}{12} - \frac{1}{20}$

_____ **1**
5-A.3

11. Find the best estimate for the word problem.

Last week Brenda bought $8\frac{7}{8}$ lb of meat for her family, and this week she bought $5\frac{1}{2}$ lb of meat. How many more pounds did she buy last week than this week?

_____ **about $3\frac{1}{2}$ lb more**
6-A.2

12. Find the quotient in simplest form.

$\frac{7}{12} \div \frac{1}{4}$

_____ **$2\frac{1}{3}$**
7-A.2

Form B • Free-Response   B242   Chapters 1–23   **Go on.** ▶

Harcourt Brace School Publishers

Free-Response Format • Test Answers

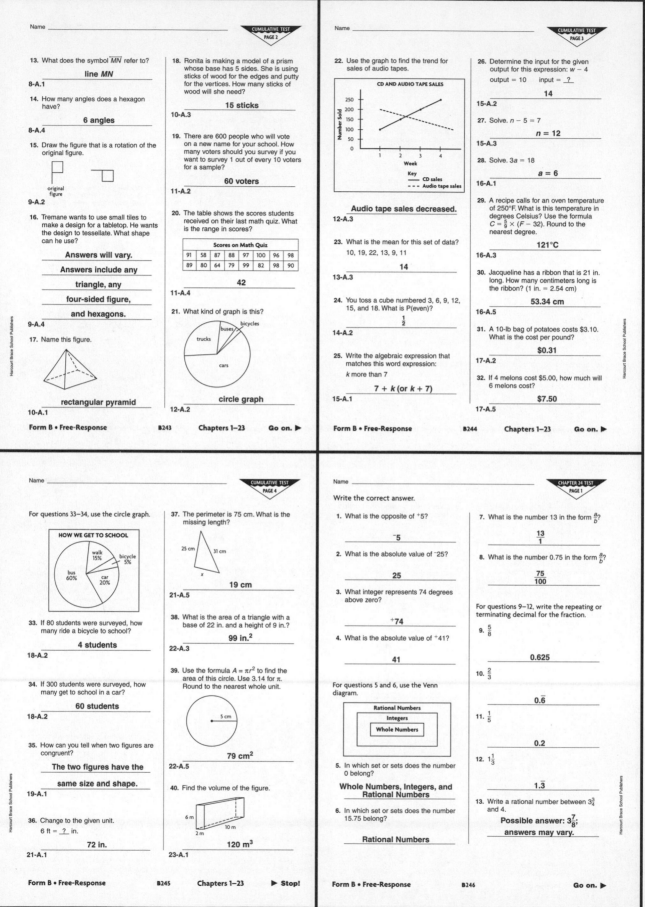

14. Write a rational number between 0 and $\frac{1}{4}$.

Possible answer: $\frac{1}{8}$; answers may vary.

15. Write a rational number between 4.5 and 4.51.

Possible answer: 4.505; answers may vary.

16. Write a rational number between $^-13\frac{3}{4}$ and $^-14\frac{1}{4}$.

Possible answer: $^-14$; answers may vary.

17. The winning tomato was 4.8 lb. The third-place tomato was 4.7 lb. What is a possible weight of the second-place tomato?

Possible answer: 4.75 lb; answers may vary.

18. The baby's length at birth was 19.8 in. At 2 days, the baby had already grown to 20.2 in. What is a possible length to which the baby might have grown at 1 day?

Possible answer: 20 in.; answers may vary.

For questions 19 and 20, compare the numbers. Use <, >, or =.

19. $\frac{7}{8}$ ○ 0.9

___<___

20. $\frac{1}{4}$ ○ $^-.25$

___>___

For questions 21 and 22, order the rational numbers from greatest to least.

21. $\frac{-1}{4}$, 0.375, $\frac{1}{3}$

___0.375, $\frac{1}{4}$, $\frac{-1}{4}$___

22. $^-0.875$, $\frac{-5}{6}$, $\frac{-1}{8}$

___$\frac{-1}{8}$, $\frac{-5}{6}$, $^-0.875$___

23. Marty ran the quarter-mile track on each of 4 days while the gym teacher timed him. On Monday, his time was 60.75 sec, on Tuesday it was $60\frac{8}{9}$ sec, on Wednesday it was $60\frac{1}{3}$ sec, and on Thursday it was $60\frac{7}{8}$ sec. On which day was his time the fastest?

___**Wednesday**___

24. Calvin, Mark, Sara, and Tamika each picked a bushel of apples at the orchard. Calvin's bushel weighed 25.6 lb, Mark's weighed $25\frac{1}{4}$ lb, Sara's weighed $25\frac{5}{8}$ lb, and Tamika's weighed 25.65 lb. Whose bushel of apples weighed the most?

___**Sara's**___

Write the correct answer.

1. Write an addition equation modeled on this number line.

___$^-3 + {}^+7 = {}^+4$___

For questions 2–4, find the sum.

2. $^-13 + {}^+7$

___$^-6$___

3. $^+28 + {}^-9$

___$^+19$___

4. $^-101 + {}^-24$

___$^-125$___

5. The day's high temperature was $^-8°C$. The low temperature was 15° less. What was the low temperature?

___$^-23°C$___

6. On the first play of the down, Bill threw a pass for a gain of 8 yd. On the next play, he was tackled for a loss of 10 yd. Write the integer that shows the total gain or loss on the two plays.

___$^-2$ yd___

7. Do these two problems have the same solution?

$^+12 - {}^+5$ and $^+12 + {}^-5$

___**yes**___

For questions 8–10, find the difference.

8. $^-15 - {}^-8$

___$^+7$___

9. $^-25 - {}^-12$

___$^-13$___

10. $^+1 - {}^-18$

___$^+19$___

11. When we went to bed, the temperature was $^+1°C$. When we woke up it was $^-7°C$. What was the overnight temperature change?

___$^-8°C$___

12. At the top of Mt. Washington, the low temperature for the day was $^-28°F$. The high temperature was 32° greater. What was the high temperature?

___$^+4°F$___

---

13. The product of a negative integer and a negative integer will be a __?__ integer.

___**positive**___

For questions 14–16, find the product.

14. $^+13 \times {}^-3$

___$^-39$___

15. $^-5 \times {}^-7$

___$^+35$___

16. $^-4 \times {}^+4$

___$^-16$___

17. The cold snap caused the temperature to fall at the rate of 2.5°F per hour. This trend continued for 10 hours. Express the change in temperature as a negative number.

___$^-25°F$___

18. Bud had a savings account balance of $75. He withdrew $6 a week for 7 weeks to pay for guitar lessons. What was his balance then?

___$33___

19. If you divide a negative integer by a positive integer, the quotient will be a __?__ integer.

___**negative**___

For questions 20–22, determine the quotient.

20. $^-27 \div {}^+3$

___$^-9$___

21. $^-35 \div {}^-7$

___$^+5$___

22. $^+22 \div {}^+2$

___$^+11$___

23. Which of the following problems has the greater quotient?

$^+3 \div {}^+1$ or $^-33 \div {}^+11$

___$^+3 \div {}^+1$___

24. Jerry gained the same amount of weight in each of 4 years. His total weight gain over the 4 years was 36 pounds. By how many pounds did his weight change each year?

___$^+9$ pounds___

Write the correct answer.

1. Evaluate $6 + {}^-9 \div 3$.

___3___

2. Evaluate $y \times {}^-2$ for $y = {}^-7$.

___14___

3. Evaluate $t \div 3 + 5$ for $t = 24$.

___13___

4. Evaluate m^2 for $m = {}^-5$.

___25___

For questions 5–8, solve the equation.

5. $t - 50 = {}^-12$

___$t = 38$___

6. $z + 15 = 45$

___$z = 30$___

7. $^-5b = 15$

___$b = {}^-3$___

8. $\frac{a}{3} = {}^-48$

___$a = {}^-144$___

9. Write an equation for this word sentence. Eight less than a number, m, is negative 2.

___$m - 8 = {}^-2$___

10. Abby stood on a boat deck and lowered a thermometer 15 feet to a depth of 7 feet below sea level. Write an equation to show how to find the height, h, at which she lowered the thermometer.

___$h - 15 = {}^-7$___

11. What are the whole-number solutions of $s < 7$?

___**0, 1, 2, 3, 4, 5, 6**___

12. What are the whole-number solutions of $m \le 3$?

___**0, 1, 2, 3**___

13. What algebraic inequality is represented by the integers graphed on the number line?

___$x > 0$___

Free-Response Format • Test Answers   **293**

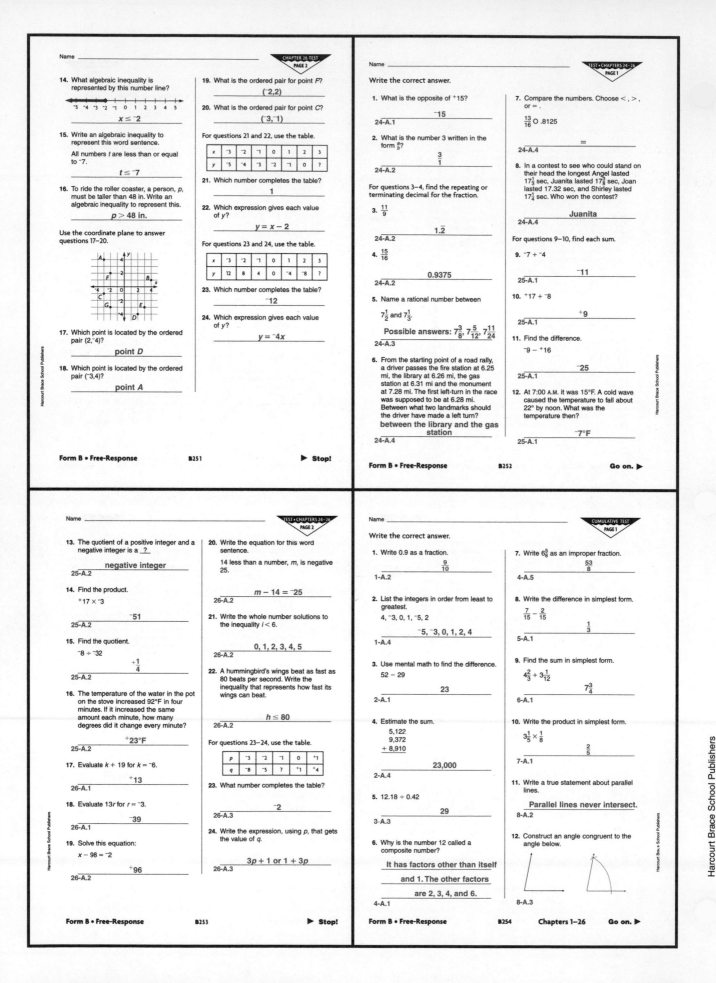

14. What algebraic inequality is represented by this number line?

-5 -4 -3 -2 -1 0 1 2 3 4 5

$x \le -2$

15. Write an algebraic inequality to represent this word sentence.

All numbers t are less than or equal to -7.

$t \le -7$

16. To ride the roller coaster, a person, p, must be taller than 48 in. Write an algebraic inequality to represent this.

$p > 48$ in.

Use the coordinate plane to answer questions 17–20.

17. Which point is located by the ordered pair (2,-4)?

point D

18. Which point is located by the ordered pair (-3,4)?

point A

19. What is the ordered pair for point F?

(-2,2)

20. What is the ordered pair for point C?

(-3,-1)

For questions 21 and 22, use the table.

x	-3	-2	-1	0	1	2	3
y	-5	-4	-3	-2	-1	0	

21. Which number completes the table?

1

22. Which expression gives each value of y?

$y = x - 2$

For questions 23 and 24, use the table.

x	-3	-2	-1	0	1	2	3
y	12	8	4	0	-4	-8	

23. Which number completes the table?

-12

24. Which expression gives each value of y?

$y = -4x$

Form B • Free-Response   B251   ▶ **Stop!**

Write the correct answer.

1. What is the opposite of +15?

-15

24-A.1

2. What is the number 3 written in the form $\frac{a}{b}$?

$\frac{3}{1}$

24-A.2

For questions 3–4, find the repeating or terminating decimal for the fraction.

3. $\frac{11}{9}$

$1.\overline{2}$

24-A.2

4. $\frac{15}{16}$

0.9375

24-A.2

5. Name a rational number between $7\frac{1}{2}$ and $7\frac{1}{3}$.

Possible answers: $7\frac{3}{8}$, $7\frac{5}{12}$, $7\frac{11}{24}$

24-A.3

6. From the starting point of a road rally, a driver passes the fire station at 6.25 mi, the library at 6.26 mi, the gas station at 6.31 mi and the monument at 7.28 mi. The first left-turn in the race was supposed to be at 6.28 mi. Between what two landmarks should the driver have made a left turn?

between the library and the gas station

24-A.4

7. Compare the numbers. Choose < , > , or = .

$\frac{13}{16}$ ○ .8125

=

24-A.4

8. In a contest to see who could stand on their head the longest Angel lasted $17\frac{3}{8}$ sec, Juanita lasted $17\frac{3}{8}$ sec, Joan lasted 17.32 sec, and Shirley lasted $17\frac{1}{4}$ sec. Who won the contest?

Juanita

24-A.4

For questions 9–10, find each sum.

9. -7 + -4

-11

25-A.1

10. +17 + -8

+9

25-A.1

11. Find the difference.

-9 - +16

-25

25-A.1

12. At 7:00 A.M. it was 15°F. A cold wave caused the temperature to fall about 22° by noon. What was the temperature then?

-7°F

25-A.1

Form B • Free-Response   B252   **Go on.** ▶

---

13. The quotient of a positive integer and a negative integer is a _?_

negative integer

25-A.2

14. Find the product.

+17 × -3

-51

25-A.2

15. Find the quotient.

-8 ÷ -32

$+\frac{1}{4}$

25-A.2

16. The temperature of the water in the pot on the stove increased 92°F in four minutes. If it increased the same amount each minute, how many degrees did it change every minute?

+23°F

25-A.2

17. Evaluate $k + 19$ for $k = -6$.

+13

26-A.1

18. Evaluate $13r$ for $r = -3$.

-39

26-A.1

19. Solve this equation:

$x - 98 = -2$

+96

26-A.2

20. Write the equation for this word sentence.

14 less than a number, m, is negative 25.

$m - 14 = -25$

26-A.2

21. Write the whole number solutions to the inequality $i < 6$.

0, 1, 2, 3, 4, 5

26-A.2

22. A hummingbird's wings beat as fast as 80 beats per second. Write the inequality that represents how fast its wings can beat.

$h \le 80$

26-A.2

For questions 23–24, use the table.

p	-3	-2	-1	0	+1
q	-8	-5		+1	+4

23. What number completes the table?

-2

26-A.3

24. Write the expression, using p, that gets the value of q.

$3p + 1$ or $1 + 3p$

26-A.3

Form B • Free-Response   B253   ▶ **Stop!**

Write the correct answer.

1. Write 0.9 as a fraction.

$\frac{9}{10}$

1-A.2

2. List the integers in order from least to greatest.

4, -3, 0, 1, -5, 2

-5, -3, 0, 1, 2, 4

1-A.4

3. Use mental math to find the difference.

52 - 29

23

2-A.1

4. Estimate the sum.

5,122
9,372
+ 8,910

23,000

2-A.4

5. 12.18 ÷ 0.42

29

3-A.3

6. Why is the number 12 called a composite number?

It has factors other than itself and 1. The other factors are 2, 3, 4, and 6.

4-A.1

7. Write $6\frac{5}{8}$ as an improper fraction.

$\frac{53}{8}$

4-A.5

8. Write the difference in simplest form.

$\frac{7}{15} - \frac{2}{15}$

$\frac{1}{3}$

5-A.1

9. Find the sum in simplest form.

$4\frac{2}{3} + 3\frac{1}{12}$

$7\frac{3}{4}$

6-A.1

10. Write the product in simplest form.

$3\frac{1}{5} \times \frac{1}{8}$

$\frac{2}{5}$

7-A.1

11. Write a true statement about parallel lines.

Parallel lines never intersect.

8-A.2

12. Construct an angle congruent to the angle below.

8-A.3

Form B • Free-Response   B254   Chapters 1–26   **Go on.** ▶

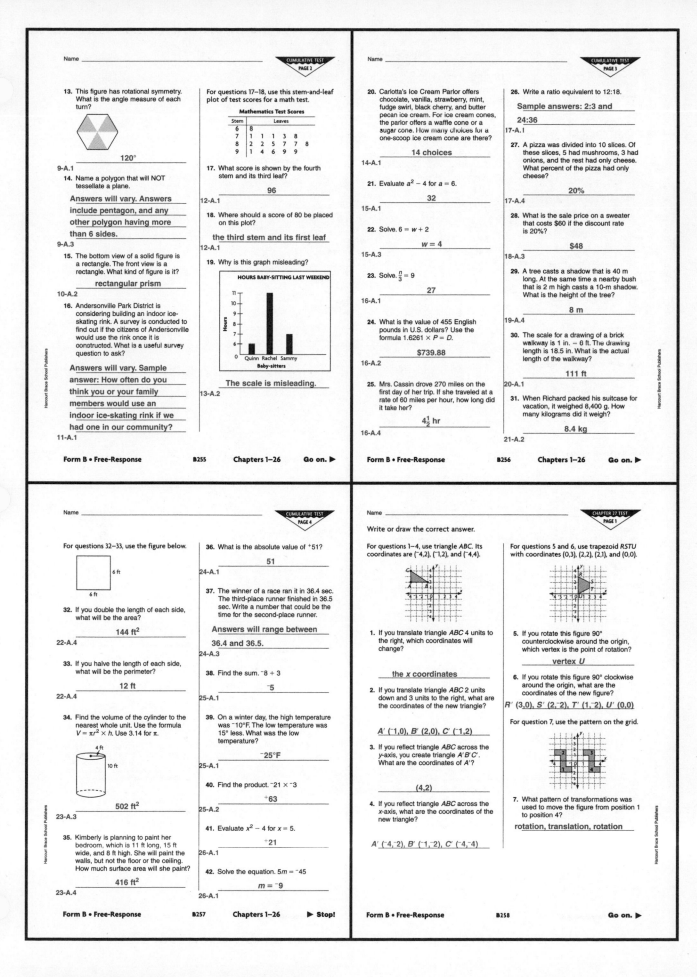

13. This figure has rotational symmetry. What is the angle measure of each turn?

120°

9-A.1

14. Name a polygon that will NOT tessellate a plane.

Answers will vary. Answers include pentagon, and any other polygon having more than 6 sides.

9-A.3

15. The bottom view of a solid figure is a rectangle. The front view is a rectangle. What kind of figure is it?

rectangular prism

10-A.2

16. Andersonville Park District is considering building an indoor ice-skating rink. A survey is conducted to find out if the citizens of Andersonville would use the rink once it is constructed. What is a useful survey question to ask?

Answers will vary. Sample answer: How often do you think you or your family members would use an indoor ice-skating rink if we had one in our community?

11-A.1

For questions 17–18, use this stem-and-leaf plot of test scores for a math test.

Mathematics Test Scores

Stem	Leaves
6	8
7	1 1 1 3 8
8	2 2 5 7 7 8
9	1 4 6 9 9

17. What score is shown by the fourth stem and its third leaf?

96

12-A.1

18. Where should a score of 80 be placed on this plot?

the third stem and its first leaf

12-A.1

19. Why is this graph misleading?

HOURS BABY-SITTING LAST WEEKEND

Hours / Baby-sitters (Quinn, Rachel, Sammy)

The scale is misleading.

13-A.2

Form B • Free-Response　　B255　　**Chapters 1–26**　　**Go on.** ▶

---

20. Carlotta's Ice Cream Parlor offers chocolate, vanilla, strawberry, mint, fudge swirl, black cherry, and butter pecan ice cream. For ice cream cones, the parlor offers a waffle cone or a sugar cone. How many choices for a one-scoop ice cream cone are there?

14 choices

14-A.1

21. Evaluate $a^2 - 4$ for $a = 6$.

32

15-A.1

22. Solve. $6 = w + 2$

$w = 4$

15-A.3

23. Solve. $\frac{n}{3} = 9$

27

16-A.1

24. What is the value of 455 English pounds in U.S. dollars? Use the formula $1.6261 \times P = D$.

$739.88

16-A.2

25. Mrs. Cassin drove 270 miles on the first day of her trip. If she traveled at a rate of 60 miles per hour, how long did it take her?

$4\frac{1}{2}$ **hr**

16-A.4

26. Write a ratio equivalent to 12:18.

Sample answers: 2:3 and 24:36

17-A.1

27. A pizza was divided into 10 slices. Of these slices, 5 had mushrooms, 3 had onions, and the rest had only cheese. What percent of the pizza had only cheese?

20%

17-A.4

28. What is the sale price on a sweater that costs $60 if the discount rate is 20%?

$48

18-A.3

29. A tree casts a shadow that is 40 m long. At the same time a nearby bush that is 2 m high casts a 10-m shadow. What is the height of the tree?

8 m

19-A.4

30. The scale for a drawing of a brick walkway is 1 in. = 6 ft. The drawing length is 18.5 in. What is the actual length of the walkway?

111 ft

20-A.1

31. When Richard packed his suitcase for vacation, it weighed 8,400 g. How many kilograms did it weigh?

8.4 kg

21-A.2

Form B • Free-Response　　B256　　**Chapters 1–26**　　**Go on.** ▶

For questions 32–33, use the figure below.

6 ft / 6 ft

32. If you double the length of each side, what will be the area?

144 ft²

22-A.4

33. If you halve the length of each side, what will be the perimeter?

12 ft

22-A.4

34. Find the volume of the cylinder to the nearest whole unit. Use the formula $V = \pi r^2 \times h$. Use 3.14 for π.

4 ft / 10 ft

502 ft²

23-A.3

35. Kimberly is planning to paint her bedroom, which is 11 ft long, 15 ft wide, and 8 ft high. She will paint the walls, but not the floor or the ceiling. How much surface area will she paint?

416 ft²

23-A.4

36. What is the absolute value of $^+51$?

51

24-A.1

37. The winner of a race ran it in 36.4 sec. The third-place runner finished in 36.5 sec. Write a number that could be the time for the second-place runner.

Answers will range between 36.4 and 36.5.

24-A.3

38. Find the sum. $^-8 + 3$

$^-5$

25-A.1

39. On a winter day, the high temperature was $^-10°F$. The low temperature was 15° less. What was the low temperature?

$^-25°F$

25-A.1

40. Find the product. $^-21 \times ^-3$

$^+63$

25-A.1

41. Evaluate $x^2 - 4$ for $x = 5$.

$^+21$

26-A.1

42. Solve the equation. $5m = ^-45$

$m = ^-9$

26-A.1

Form B • Free-Response　　B257　　**Chapters 1–26**　　▶ **Stop!**

Write or draw the correct answer.

For questions 1–4, use triangle ABC. Its coordinates are $(^-4,2)$, $(^-1,2)$, and $(^-4,4)$.

1. If you translate triangle ABC 4 units to the right, which coordinates will change?

the x coordinates

2. If you translate triangle ABC 2 units down and 3 units to the right, what are the coordinates of the new triangle?

A' $(^-1,0)$, B' $(2,0)$, C' $(^-1,2)$

3. If you reflect triangle ABC across the y-axis, you create triangle $A'B'C'$. What are the coordinates of A'?

(4,2)

4. If you reflect triangle ABC across the x-axis, what are the coordinates of the new triangle?

A' $(^-4,^-2)$, B' $(^-1,^-2)$, C' $(^-4,^-4)$

For questions 5 and 6, use trapezoid $RSTU$ with coordinates (0,3), (2,2), (2,1), and (0,0).

5. If you rotate this figure 90° counterclockwise around the origin, which vertex is the point of rotation?

vertex U

6. If you rotate this figure 90° clockwise around the origin, what are the coordinates of the new figure?

R' $(3,0)$, S' $(2,^-2)$, T' $(1,^-2)$, U' $(0,0)$

For question 7, use the pattern on the grid.

7. What pattern of transformations was used to move the figure from position 1 to position 4?

rotation, translation, rotation

Form B • Free-Response　　B258　　**Go on.** ▶

Free-Response Format • Test Answers　　　　**295**

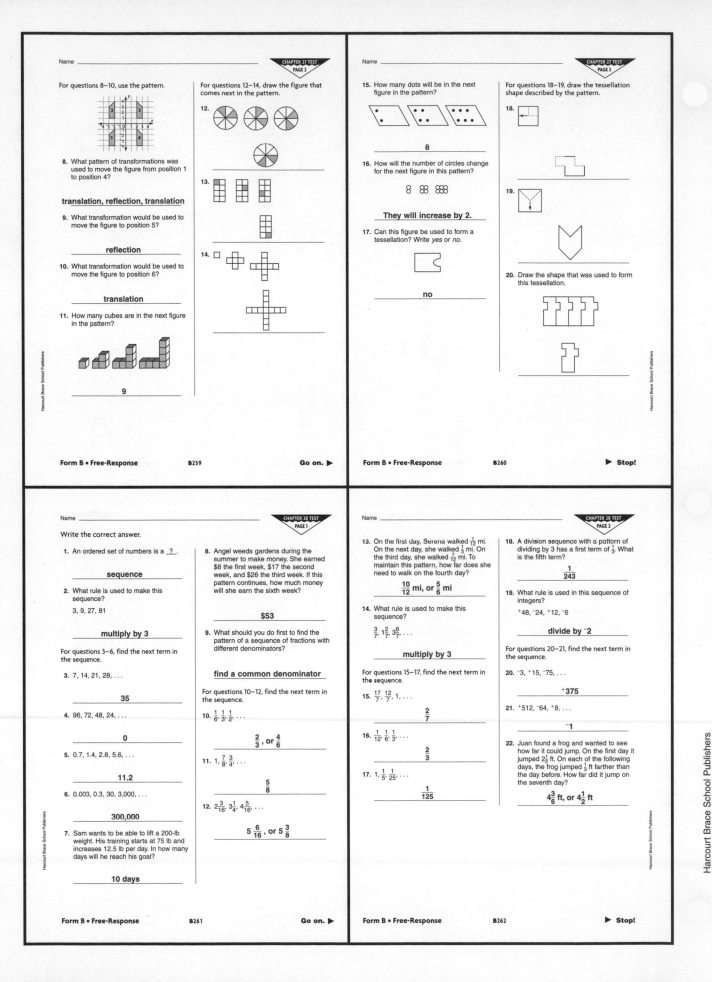

For questions 8–10, use the pattern.

8. What pattern of transformations was used to move the figure from position 1 to position 4?

translation, reflection, translation

9. What transformation would be used to move the figure to position 5?

reflection

10. What transformation would be used to move the figure to position 6?

translation

11. How many cubes are in the next figure in the pattern?

9

For questions 12–14, draw the figure that comes next in the pattern.

12.

13.

14.

15. How many dots will be in the next figure in the pattern?

8

16. How will the number of circles change for the next figure in this pattern?

They will increase by 2.

17. Can this figure be used to form a tessellation? Write *yes* or *no*.

no

For questions 18–19, draw the tessellation shape described by the pattern.

18.

19.

20. Draw the shape that was used to form this tessellation.

Write the correct answer.

1. An ordered set of numbers is a ? .

sequence

2. What rule is used to make this sequence?

3, 9, 27, 81

multiply by 3

For questions 3–6, find the next term in the sequence.

3. 7, 14, 21, 28, . . .

35

4. 96, 72, 48, 24, . . .

0

5. 0.7, 1.4, 2.8, 5.6, . . .

11.2

6. 0.003, 0.3, 30, 3,000, . . .

300,000

7. Sam wants to be able to lift a 200-lb weight. His training starts at 75 lb and increases 12.5 lb per day. In how many days will he reach his goal?

10 days

8. Angel weeds gardens during the summer to make money. She earned $8 the first week, $17 the second week, and $26 the third week. If this pattern continues, how much money will she earn the sixth week?

$53

9. What should you do first to find the pattern of a sequence of fractions with different denominators?

find a common denominator

For questions 10–12, find the next term in the sequence.

10. $\frac{1}{6}$, $\frac{1}{3}$, $\frac{1}{2}$, . . .

$\frac{2}{3}$, or $\frac{4}{6}$

11. 1, $\frac{7}{8}$, $\frac{3}{4}$, . . .

$\frac{5}{8}$

12. $2\frac{3}{16}$, $3\frac{1}{4}$, $4\frac{5}{16}$, . . .

$5\frac{6}{16}$, or $5\frac{3}{8}$

13. On the first day, Serena walked $\frac{1}{12}$ mi. On the next day, she walked $\frac{1}{3}$ mi. On the third day, she walked $\frac{7}{12}$ mi. To maintain this pattern, how far does she need to walk on the fourth day?

$\frac{10}{12}$ mi, or $\frac{5}{6}$ mi

14. What rule is used to make this sequence?

$\frac{3}{7}$, $1\frac{2}{7}$, $3\frac{6}{7}$, . . .

multiply by 3

For questions 15–17, find the next term in the sequence.

15. $\frac{17}{7}$, $\frac{12}{7}$, 1, . . .

$\frac{2}{7}$

16. $\frac{1}{12}$, $\frac{1}{6}$, $\frac{1}{3}$, . . .

$\frac{2}{3}$

17. 1, $\frac{1}{5}$, $\frac{1}{25}$, . . .

$\frac{1}{125}$

18. A division sequence with a pattern of dividing by 3 has a first term of $\frac{1}{3}$. What is the fifth term?

$\frac{1}{243}$

19. What rule is used in this sequence of integers?

$^+48$, $^-24$, $^+12$, $^-6$

divide by $^-2$

For questions 20–21, find the next term in the sequence.

20. $^-3$, $^+15$, $^-75$, . . .

$^+375$

21. $^+512$, $^-64$, $^+8$, . . .

$^-1$

22. Juan found a frog and wanted to see how far it could jump. On the first day it jumped $2\frac{1}{2}$ ft. On each of the following days, the frog jumped $\frac{1}{3}$ ft farther than the day before. How far did it jump on the seventh day?

$4\frac{3}{6}$ ft, or $4\frac{1}{2}$ ft

Free-Response Format • Test Answers

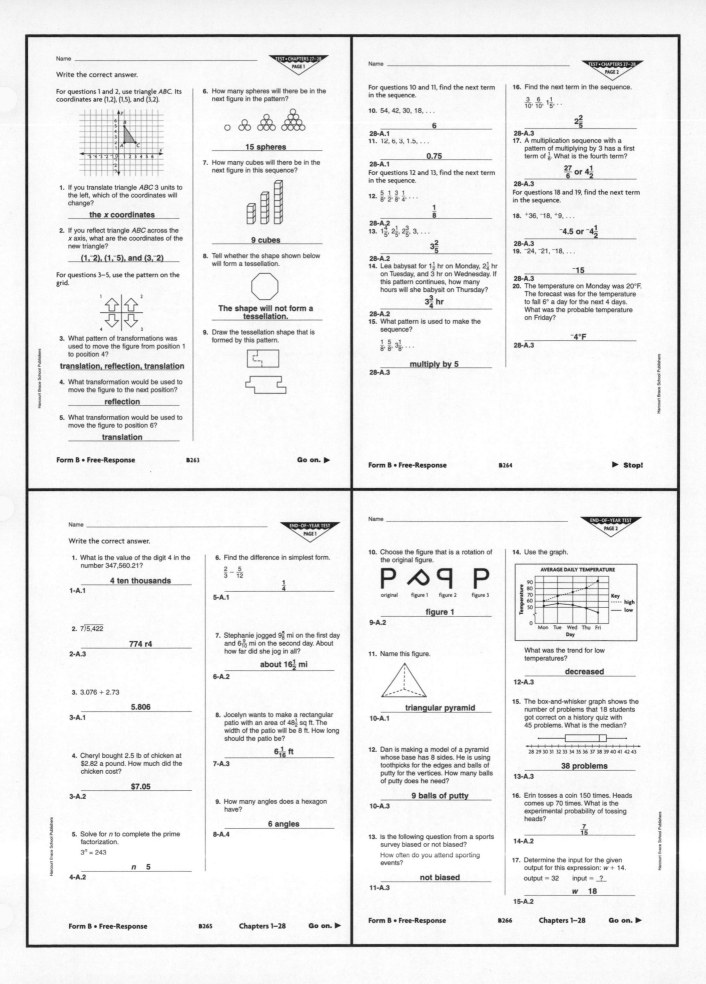

Name _____

Write the correct answer.

For questions 1 and 2, use triangle *ABC*. Its coordinates are (1,2), (1,5), and (3,2).

1. If you translate triangle *ABC* 3 units to the left, which of the coordinates will change?

the *x* coordinates

2. If you reflect triangle *ABC* across the *x* axis, what are the coordinates of the new triangle?

(1,⁻2), (1,⁻5), and (3,⁻2)

For questions 3–5, use the pattern on the grid.

3. What pattern of transformations was used to move the figure from position 1 to position 4?

translation, reflection, translation

4. What transformation would be used to move the figure to the next position?

reflection

5. What transformation would be used to move the figure to position 6?

translation

6. How many spheres will there be in the next figure in the pattern?

15 spheres

7. How many cubes will there be in the next figure in this sequence?

9 cubes

8. Tell whether the shape shown below will form a tessellation.

The shape will not form a tessellation.

9. Draw the tessellation shape that is formed by this pattern.

Form B • Free-Response   B263   **Go on. ▶**

Name _____

For questions 10 and 11, find the next term in the sequence.

10. 54, 42, 30, 18, . . .

6

28-A.1

11. 12, 6, 3, 1.5, . . .

0.75

28-A.1

For questions 12 and 13, find the next term in the sequence.

12. $\frac{5}{8}, \frac{1}{2}, \frac{3}{8}, \frac{1}{4}, \ldots$

$\frac{1}{8}$

28-A.2

13. $1\frac{4}{5}, 2\frac{1}{5}, 2\frac{3}{5}, 3, \ldots$

$3\frac{2}{5}$

28-A.2

14. Lea babysat for $1\frac{1}{2}$ hr on Monday, $2\frac{1}{4}$ hr on Tuesday, and 3 hr on Wednesday. If this pattern continues, how many hours will she babysit on Thursday?

$3\frac{3}{4}$ hr

28-A.2

15. What pattern is used to make the sequence?

$\frac{1}{8}, \frac{5}{8}, 3\frac{1}{8}, \ldots$

multiply by 5

28-A.3

16. Find the next term in the sequence.

$\frac{3}{10}, \frac{6}{10}, 1\frac{1}{5}, \ldots$

$2\frac{2}{5}$

28-A.3

17. A multiplication sequence with a pattern of multiplying by 3 has a first term of $\frac{1}{6}$. What is the fourth term?

$\frac{27}{6}$ or $4\frac{1}{2}$

28-A.3

For questions 18 and 19, find the next term in the sequence.

18. ⁺36, ⁻18, ⁺9, . . .

⁻4.5 or ⁻$4\frac{1}{2}$

28-A.3

19. ⁻24, ⁻21, ⁻18, . . .

⁻15

28-A.3

20. The temperature on Monday was 20°F. The forecast was for the temperature to fall 6° a day for the next 4 days. What was the probable temperature on Friday?

⁻4°F

28-A.3

Form B • Free-Response   B264   **▶ Stop!**

Name _____

Write the correct answer.

1. What is the value of the digit 4 in the number 347,560.21?

4 ten thousands

1-A.1

2. 7)5,422

774 r4

2-A.3

3. 3.076 + 2.73

5.806

3-A.1

4. Cheryl bought 2.5 lb of chicken at $2.82 a pound. How much did the chicken cost?

$7.05

3-A.2

5. Solve for *n* to complete the prime factorization.

$3^n = 243$

***n*   5**

4-A.2

6. Find the difference in simplest form.

$\frac{2}{3} - \frac{5}{12}$

$\frac{1}{4}$

5-A.1

7. Stephanie jogged $9\frac{5}{8}$ mi on the first day and $6\frac{7}{10}$ mi on the second day. About how far did she jog in all?

about $16\frac{1}{2}$ mi

6-A.2

8. Jocelyn wants to make a rectangular patio with an area of $48\frac{1}{2}$ sq ft. The width of the patio will be 8 ft. How long should the patio be?

$6\frac{1}{16}$ ft

7-A.3

9. How many angles does a hexagon have?

6 angles

8-A.4

Form B • Free-Response   B265   Chapters 1–28   **Go on. ▶**

Name _____

10. Choose the figure that is a rotation of the original figure.

original   figure 1   figure 2   figure 3

figure 1

9-A.2

11. Name this figure.

triangular pyramid

10-A.1

12. Dan is making a model of a pyramid whose base has 8 sides. He is using toothpicks for the edges and balls of putty for the vertices. How many balls of putty does he need?

9 balls of putty

10-A.3

13. Is the following question from a sports survey biased or not biased?

How often do you attend sporting events?

not biased

11-A.3

14. Use the graph.

AVERAGE DAILY TEMPERATURE

Key
---- high
— low

What was the trend for low temperatures?

decreased

12-A.3

15. The box-and-whisker graph shows the number of problems that 18 students got correct on a history quiz with 45 problems. What is the median?

28 29 30 31 32 33 34 35 36 37 38 39 40 41 42 43

38 problems

13-A.3

16. Erin tosses a coin 150 times. Heads comes up 70 times. What is the experimental probability of tossing heads?

$\frac{7}{15}$

14-A.2

17. Determine the input for the given output for this expression: $w + 14$.

output = 32   input = _?_

***w*   18**

15-A.2

Form B • Free-Response   B266   Chapters 1–28   **Go on. ▶**

Free-Response Format • Test Answers

Harcourt Brace School Publishers

18. Solve for c. c − 7 = 8

c = 15

15-A.3

19. Solve for m. 4m = 52

m = 13

16-A.1

20. What is 18°C converted to degrees Fahrenheit? Use the formula $F = (\frac{9}{5} \times C) + 32$. Round to the nearest degree.

64°F

16-A.3

21. Barbara is in a 30-mi bike race. How long is this ride in kilometers? (1 mi = 1.609 km)

48.27 km

16-A.5

22. Keri answered 28 of the 40 problems on her science test correctly. What percent did she answer correctly?

70%

17-A.3

23. What is 20% of 90?

18

18-A.1

24. Barry had $100 that earned 6% simple interest a year in a bank. After 3 years, he withdrew his money. How much did he withdraw?

$118

18-A.5

25. Find n in this pair of similar triangles.

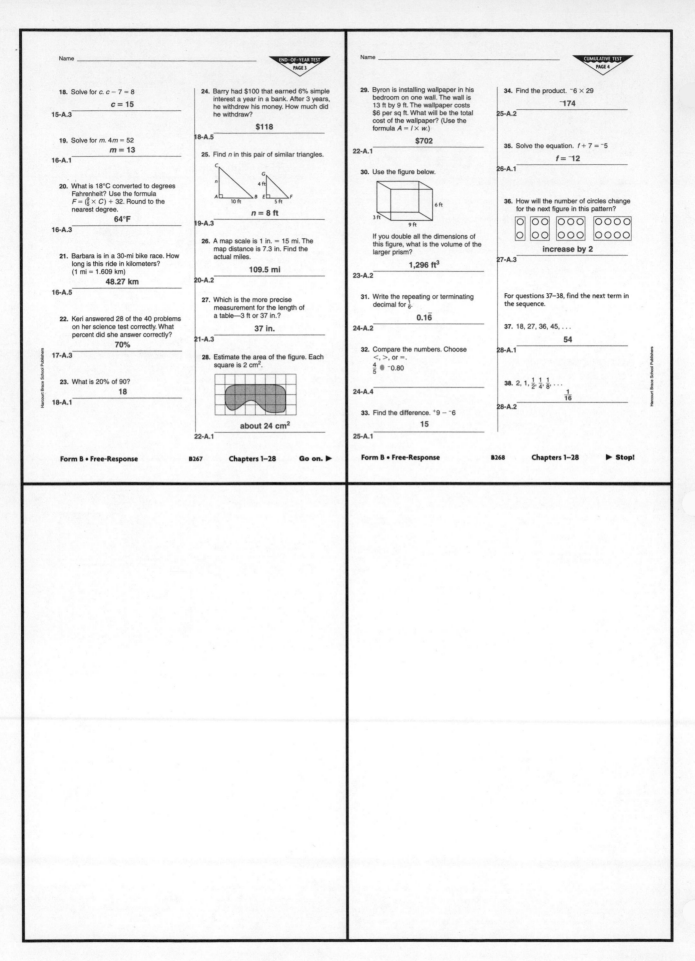

n = 8 ft

19-A.3

26. A map scale is 1 in. = 15 mi. The map distance is 7.3 in. Find the actual miles.

109.5 mi

20-A.2

27. Which is the more precise measurement for the length of a table—3 ft or 37 in.?

37 in.

21-A.3

28. Estimate the area of the figure. Each square is 2 cm².

about 24 cm²

22-A.1

Form B • Free-Response   B267   **Chapters 1–28**   **Go on. ▶**

---

29. Byron is installing wallpaper in his bedroom on one wall. The wall is 13 ft by 9 ft. The wallpaper costs $6 per sq ft. What will be the total cost of the wallpaper? (Use the formula A = l × w.)

$702

22-A.1

30. Use the figure below.

If you double all the dimensions of this figure, what is the volume of the larger prism?

1,296 ft³

23-A.2

31. Write the repeating or terminating decimal for $\frac{1}{6}$.

0.1̄6̄

24-A.2

32. Compare the numbers. Choose <, >, or =.

$\frac{4}{5}$ ● ⁻0.80

24-A.4

33. Find the difference. ⁺9 − ⁻6

15

25-A.1

34. Find the product. ⁻6 × 29

⁻174

25-A.2

35. Solve the equation. f + 7 = ⁻5

f = ⁻12

26-A.1

36. How will the number of circles change for the next figure in this pattern?

increase by 2

27-A.3

For questions 37–38, find the next term in the sequence.

37. 18, 27, 36, 45, . . .

54

28-A.1

38. 2, 1, $\frac{1}{2}$, $\frac{1}{4}$, $\frac{1}{8}$, . . .

$\frac{1}{16}$

28-A.2

Form B • Free-Response   B268   **Chapters 1–28**   **▶ Stop!**

Free-Response Format • Test Answers

Management Forms

Test Answer Sheet

This copying master is an individual recording sheet for up to 50 items on the multiple-choice (standardized) format tests.

Grading Made Easy

This percent converter can be used for all quizzes and tests. The percents given are based on all problems having equal value. Percents are rounded to the nearest whole percent giving the benefit of 0.5 percent.

Individual Record Form

One copying master for each content cluster of chapters is provided. Criterion scores for each learning goal are given for the chapter test. The student's total scores are recorded at the top of the page for chapter tests, the multi-chapter test and the cumulative test. The scores for each learning goal can also be recorded. You can use the Review Options that are listed on the form to assign additional review for the student unable to pass the test.

Formal Assessment Class Record Form

The scores for all the tests can be recorded for your class on these record forms. The Criterion Score for each test is given.

Learning Goals

The learning goals for the entire grade level are provided. These goals are referenced throughout the program. Each test item is referenced to a learning goal. You may wish to use these pages to cross-reference the Math Advantage Learning Goals with local, district, or statewide benchmarks.

Test Answer Sheet

MATH ADVANTAGE

Test Title _____

1. (A) (B) (C) (D)		26. (A) (B) (C) (D)
2. (A) (B) (C) (D)		27. (A) (B) (C) (D)
3. (A) (B) (C) (D)		28. (A) (B) (C) (D)
4. (A) (B) (C) (D)		29. (A) (B) (C) (D)
5. (A) (B) (C) (D)		30. (A) (B) (C) (D)
6. (A) (B) (C) (D)		31. (A) (B) (C) (D)
7. (A) (B) (C) (D)		32. (A) (B) (C) (D)
8. (A) (B) (C) (D)		33. (A) (B) (C) (D)
9. (A) (B) (C) (D)		34. (A) (B) (C) (D)
10. (A) (B) (C) (D)		35. (A) (B) (C) (D)
11. (A) (B) (C) (D)		36. (A) (B) (C) (D)
12. (A) (B) (C) (D)		37. (A) (B) (C) (D)
13. (A) (B) (C) (D)		38. (A) (B) (C) (D)
14. (A) (B) (C) (D)		39. (A) (B) (C) (D)
15. (A) (B) (C) (D)		40. (A) (B) (C) (D)
16. (A) (B) (C) (D)		41. (A) (B) (C) (D)
17. (A) (B) (C) (D)		42. (A) (B) (C) (D)
18. (A) (B) (C) (D)		43. (A) (B) (C) (D)
19. (A) (B) (C) (D)		44. (A) (B) (C) (D)
20. (A) (B) (C) (D)		45. (A) (B) (C) (D)
21. (A) (B) (C) (D)		46. (A) (B) (C) (D)
22. (A) (B) (C) (D)		47. (A) (B) (C) (D)
23. (A) (B) (C) (D)		48. (A) (B) (C) (D)
24. (A) (B) (C) (D)		49. (A) (B) (C) (D)
25. (A) (B) (C) (D)		50. (A) (B) (C) (D)

Total Number of Test Items

Number of Test Items Wrong (row labels)

	4	5	6	7	8	9	10	11	12	13	14	15	16	17	18	19	20	21	22	23	24	25	26	27	28	29	30	32	50
1	75	80	83	86	88	89	90	91	92	92	93	93	94	94	94	95	95	95	95	96	96	96	96	96	96	97	97	97	98
2	50	60	67	71	75	78	80	82	83	85	86	87	88	88	89	89	90	90	91	91	92	92	92	93	93	93	93	94	96
3	25	40	50	57	63	67	70	73	75	77	79	80	81	82	83	84	85	86	86	87	88	88	88	89	89	90	90	91	94
4	0	20	33	43	50	56	60	64	67	69	71	73	75	76	78	79	80	81	82	83	83	84	85	85	86	86	87	88	92
5		0	17	29	38	44	50	55	58	62	64	67	69	71	72	74	75	76	77	78	79	80	81	81	82	83	83	84	90
6			0	14	25	33	40	45	50	54	57	60	63	65	67	68	70	71	73	74	75	76	77	78	79	79	80	81	88
7				0	13	22	30	36	42	46	50	53	56	59	61	63	65	67	68	70	71	72	73	74	75	76	77	78	86
8					0	11	20	27	33	38	43	47	50	53	56	58	60	62	64	65	67	68	69	70	71	72	73	75	84
9						0	10	18	25	31	36	40	44	47	50	53	55	57	59	61	63	64	65	67	68	69	70	72	82
10							0	9	17	23	29	33	38	41	44	47	50	52	55	57	58	60	62	63	64	66	67	69	80
11								0	8	15	21	27	31	35	39	42	45	48	50	52	54	56	58	59	61	62	63	66	78
12									0	8	14	20	25	29	33	37	40	43	45	48	50	52	54	56	57	59	60	63	76
13										0	7	13	19	24	28	32	35	38	41	43	46	48	50	52	54	55	57	59	74
14											0	7	13	18	22	26	30	33	36	39	42	44	46	48	50	52	53	56	72
15												0	6	12	17	21	25	29	32	35	38	40	42	44	46	48	50	53	70
16													0	6	11	16	20	24	27	30	33	36	38	41	43	45	47	50	68
17														0	6	11	15	19	23	26	29	32	35	37	39	41	43	47	66
18															0	5	10	14	18	22	25	28	31	33	36	38	40	44	64
19																0	5	10	14	17	21	24	27	30	32	34	37	41	62
20																	0	5	9	13	17	20	23	26	29	31	33	38	60
21																		0	5	9	13	16	19	22	25	28	30	34	58
22																			0	4	8	12	15	19	21	24	27	31	56
23																				0	4	8	12	15	18	21	23	28	54
24																					0	4	8	11	14	17	20	25	52
25																						0	4	7	11	14	17	22	50
26																							0	4	7	10	13	19	48
27																								0	4	7	10	16	46
28																									0	3	7	13	44
29																										0	3	9	42
30																											0	6	40
31																												3	38
32																												0	36

MATH ADVANTAGE

Individual Record Form

GRADE 6 • Chapters 1-3

Student Name _____

Test	Chapter 1	Chapter 2	Chapter 3	Chapters 1-3	Cum Chapters 1-3
Date					
Score					

LEARNING GOALS

Goal #	Learning Goal	Form A CHAPTER TEST — Concept	Test Items — Skills	Test Items — PSolv	Criterion Scores	Lesson page #	PE	TE	Workbooks P	R	E
1-A.1	To use place value to express and compare whole numbers and decimals	1-2	3-6 7-8		7/10	16-17 18-19	MP-H42	KS-H10	1.1 1.2	1.1 1.2	1.1 1.2
1-A.2	To write a decimal as a fraction and a fraction as a decimal	11-12	13-14	15-16	4/6	20-23	MP-H42	KS-H19	1.3	1.3	1.3
1-A.3	To use exponents to represent numbers	17-18	19-20		3/4	24-25	MP-H43	TAA-20	1.4	1.4	1.4
1-A.4	To order integers and identify opposite integers	21	22-24		3/4	28-29	MP-H43	PA-3A	1.5	1.5	1.5
2-A.1	To use properties and mental math to find sums and differences		1-4		3/4	34-35	MP-H43	KS-H7	2.1	2.1	2.1
2-A.2	To solve problems by using the *guess and check* strategy			5-8	3/4	36-37	MP-H44		2.2	2.2	2.2
2-A.3	To multiply and divide whole numbers	9 13-14	10-12 15-18	19-20	9/12	38-39 40-43	MP-H44	KS-H8	2.3 2.4	2.3 2.4	2.3 2.4
2-A.4	To use estimation to find sums, differences, products, and quotients		21-22	23-24	3/4	46-49	MP-H45	PA-5A	2.5	2.5	2.5
3-A.1	To add and subtract decimals		1-4 7-10	5-6 11-12	9/12	54-55 56-57	KS-H12	PA-11A	3.1 3.2	3.1 3.2	3.1 3.2
3-A.2	To multiply decimals	13-14	15-18	19-20	6/8	58-61	MP-H46	PA-10A	3.3	3.3	3.3
3-A.3	To divide decimals	21	22-24		3/4	64-67	MP-H46	PA-11A	3.4	3.4	3.4

REVIEW OPTIONS

KEY: I–Intervention **IF**–Idea File **KS**–Key Skills **MP**–More Practice **PA**–Prac. Activ. **TA**–Tech. Amaz. Ang. **TAA**–Tech. Astro Alg.
TDG–Tech. Dr. Gee **TDL**–Tech. Data Tool Kit **TFF**–Tech. Frac. Fireworks **TG**–Tech. Geoboard **TGA**–Tech. Geo Acad. **TP**–Tech. Prob.

Individual Record Form

GRADE 6 • Chapters 4-7

Student Name _____

Test	Chapter 4	Chapter 5	Chapter 6	Chapter 7	Chapters 4-7	Cum Chapters 1-7
Date						
Score						

LEARNING GOALS

Goal #	Learning Goal	Form A CHAPTER TEST — Test Items Concept	Skills	PSolv	Criterion Scores	REVIEW OPTIONS — Lesson page #	PE	TE	Workbooks P	R	E
4-A.1	To identify factors and multiples of a number and tell whether a number is prime or composite		1-4	5-6	4/6	76-77	MP-H46	PA-13A	4.1	4.1	4.1
4-A.2	To write a composite number as the product of prime numbers	7-8	9-10		3/4	78-79	MP-H47	KS-H4	4.2	4.2	4.2
4-A.3	To find the least common multiple and greatest common factor	11-12	13-15	16	4/6	80-83	MP-H47	KS-H5	4.3	4.3	4.3
4-A.4	To write fractions in simplest form		17-20		3/4	86-87	MP-H47	I-96A,96B	4.4	4.4	4.4
4-A.5	To write fractions as mixed numbers and mixed numbers as fractions	21	22-24		3/4	88-89	MP-H48	PA-18A	4.5	4.5	4.5
5-A.1	To add and subtract like fractions	1	2-3	4	3/4	94-95	MP-H48	PA-20A	5.1	5.1	5.1
5-A.2	To add and subtract unlike fractions	5-6 / 9 / 10	7-8 / 11-12 / 15-16	13-14 / 17-18	10/14	98-99 / 100-101 / 102-103	MP-H49	PA-20A	5.2 5.3 5.4	5.2 5.3 5.4	5.2 5.3 5.4
5-A.3	To estimate sums and differences of fractions	19	20-22		3/4	104-107	MP-H49	PA-20A	5.5	5.5	5.5
6-A.1	To add and subtract mixed numbers	1-2 / 5-6	3-4 / 7-8 / 9-10	11-14	10/14	112-113 / 116-117 / 118-121	MP-H50	PA-21A	6.1 6.2 6.3	6.1 6.2 6.3	6.1 6.2 6.3
6-A.2	To estimate sums and differences of mixed numbers	15-16	17-18	19-20	4/6	122-123	MP-H51	KS-H19	6.4	6.4	6.4
7-A.1	To simplify factors and multiply fractions and mixed numbers	1-2 / 7 / 11	3-6 / 8-10 / 12-14	15-16	12/16	128-131 / 132-133 / 134-135	MP-H52	TFF-X	7.1 7.2 7.3	7.1 7.2 7.3	7.1 7.2 7.3
7-A.2	To divide fractions	17-18	19-20		3/4	138-139	MP-H52	PA-20A	7.4	7.4	7.4
7-A.3	To solve problems by working backward			21-24	3/4	140-141	MP-H52		7.5	7.5	7.5

KEY: I–Intervention **IF**–Idea File **KS**–Key Skills **MP**–More Practice **PA**–Prac. Activ. **TA**–Tech. Amaz. Ang. **TAA**–Tech. Astro Alg.
TDG–Tech. Dr. Gee **TDL**–Tech. Data Tool Kit **TFF**–Tech. Frac. Fireworks **TG**–Tech. Geoboard **TGA**–Tech. Geo Acad. **TP**–Tech. Prob.

Individual Record Form

GRADE 6 • Chapters 8-10

Student Name _____

Test	Chapter 8	Chapter 9	Chapter 10	Chapters 8-10	Cum Chapters 1-10
Date					
Score					

LEARNING GOALS

Form A CHAPTER TEST

REVIEW OPTIONS

Goal #	Learning Goal	Test Items Concept	Test Items Skills	Test Items PSolv	Criterion Scores	Lesson page #	PE	TE	Workbooks P	Workbooks R	Workbooks E
8-A.1	To identify and describe points, lines, and planes		1-4		3/4	150-151	MP-H53		8.1	8.1	8.1
8-A.2	To classify lines and angles and measure angles		5-8 9-12		6/8	152-153 154-155	MP-H53	TG-B	8.2 8.3	8.2 8.3	8.2 8.3
8-A.3	To construct congruent line segments and angles	13-14	15-16		3/4	156-159	MP-H54	TG-L	8.4	8.4	8.4
8-A.4	To identify polygons by the number of sides and angles		17-20		3/4	162-163	MP-H54	TGA-D	8.5	8.5	8.5
9-A.1	To identify line symmetry and rotational symmetry	1-2	3-6		4/6	168-171	MP-H54	TGA-O	9.1	9.1	9.1
9-A.2	To identify and use transformations of geometric shapes	7-8	9-12		4/6	174-177	KS-H20	TGA-N	9.2	9.2	9.2
9-A.3	To use polygons to make tessellations		13-16		3/4	178-179	MP-H55	TGA-N	9.3	9.3	9.3
9-A.4	To use a model to solve a problem			17-20	3/4	180-181	MP-H55		9.4	9.4	9.4
10-A.1	To identify solid figures and their parts	1-2	3-5 6-8	9-10	7/10	186-189 190-191	KS-H23	KS-H22	10.1 10.2	10.1 10.2	10.1 10.2
10-A.2	To identify nets for solid figures and different points of view	11-14 15-18			6/8	192-193 196-197	MP-H57	TDG-C	10.3 10.4	10.3 10.4	10.3 10.4
10-A.3	To solve problems by using the strategy solving a simpler problem			19-20	2/2	198-199	MP-H57		10.5	10.5	10.5

KEY: I–Intervention **IF**–Idea File **KS**–Key Skills **MP**–More Practice **PA**–Prac. Activ. **TA**–Tech. Amaz. Ang. **TAA**–Tech. Astro Alg.
TDG–Tech. Dr. Gee **TDL**–Tech. Data Tool Kit **TFF**–Tech. Frac. Fireworks **TG**–Tech. Geoboard **TGA**–Tech. Geo Acad. **TP**–Tech. Prob.

Individual Record Form

GRADE 6 • Chapters 11-14

Student Name _____

Test	Chapter 11	Chapter 12	Chapter 13	Chapter 14	Chapters 11-14	Cum Chapters 1-14
Date						
Score						

LEARNING GOALS

		Form A CHAPTER TEST			Criterion	REVIEW OPTIONS			Workbooks		
		Test Items				Lesson					
Goal #	Learning Goal	Concept	Skills	PSolv	Scores	page #	PE	TE	P	R	E
11-A.1	To identify information needed to make decisions	1-4			3/4	208-209	MP-H57		11.1	11.1	11.1
11-A.2	To identify sample sizes and types of samples when conducting a survey		5-6	7-10	4/6	210-211	MP-H58		11.2	11.2	11.2
11-A.3	To determine whether a sample or question in a survey is biased	11-12		13-14	3/4	212-213	MP-H58		11.3	11.3	11.3
11-A.4	To use and organize data from a survey		15-16	17-18	3/4	216-219	MP-H58	TDL	11.4	11.4	11.4
12-A.1	To display data in a bar graph, a line graph, and a stem-and-leaf plot	1-2	3-6		4/6	224-227	MP-H59	TDL	12.1	12.1	12.1
12-A.2	To make histograms and circle graphs	7-8 17-18	9-10 19-20		7/10	228-229 234-235	MP-H60	TDL	12.2 12.4	12.2 12.4	12.2 12.4
12-A.3	To graph two or more sets of data	11	12-14	15-16	4/6	230-231	MP-H59	TDL	12.3	12.3	12.3
13-A.1	To analyze graphs and make predictions from graphs		1-5 10-11	12-13 20-24	10/14	240-241 244-245 252-253	MP-H61	TDL	13.1 13.3 13.5	13.1 13.3 13.5	13.1 13.3 13.5
13-A.2	To identify misleading graphs		6-9		3/4	242-243	MP-H60		13.2	13.2	13.2
13-A.3	To find the mean, median, and mode		14-17	18-19	4/6	246-249	KS-H26		13.4	13.4	13.4
14-A.1	To use the strategy account for all possibilities to solve problems			1-4	3/4	258-259	MP-H62		14.1	14.1	14.1
14-A.2	To find the probability of events	5 11	6-8 12-15	9-10 16-17	9/13	260-263 264-265	MP-H62	TP-E	14.2 14.3	14.2 14.3	14.2 14.3
14-A.3	To find the experimental probability of an event	18-20		21-22	3/5	268-269	MP-H63	TP-B	14.4	14.4	14.4

KEY: I–Intervention **IF**–Idea File **KS**–Key Skills **MP**–More Practice **PA**–Prac. Activ. **TA**–Tech. Amaz. Ang. **TAA**–Tech. Astro Alg.
TDG–Tech. Dr. Gee **TDL**–Tech. Data Tool Kit **TFF**–Tech. Frac. Fireworks **TG**–Tech. Geoboard **TGA**–Tech. Geo Acad. **TP**–Tech. Prob.

Individual Record Form

GRADE 6 • Chapters 15-16

Student Name _____

Test	Chapter 15	Chapter 16	Chapters 15-16	Cum Chapters 1-16
Date				
Score				

LEARNING GOALS

		Form A CHAPTER TEST				Criterion	REVIEW OPTIONS				Workbooks		
			Test Items				Lesson						
Goal #	Learning Goal	Concept	Skills	PSolv		Scores	page #	PE	TE	P	R	E
15-A.1	To write, interpret, and evaluate numerical and algebraic expressions		1-4 7-10	5-6 11-12		9/12	278-279 280-281	MP-H63	TAA-5	15.1 15.2	15.1 15.2	15.1 15.2
15-A.2	To use input/output tables to evaluate algebraic expressions		13-16			3/4	282-283	MP-H64	TAA-41	15.3	15.3	15.3
15-A.3	To solve addition and subtraction equations		17-20	21-24		6/8	286-289	MP-H64	TAA-24	15.4	15.4	15.4
16-A.1	To solve multiplication and division equations	1-2	3-6			4/6	296-299	MP-H64	TAA-66	16.1	16.1	16.1
16-A.2	To use equations to show money relationships		7-10	11-12		4/6	300-301	MP-H65	IF-292C	16.2	16.2	16.2
16-A.3	To convert temperatures between the Fahrenheit and Celsius scales		13-14	15-16		3/4	302-303	MP-H65	IF-292C	16.3	16.3	16.3
16-A.4	To calculate distance, rate, or time by solving an equation		17-18	19-20		3/4	304-305	MP-H65	IF-292C	16.4	16.4	16.4
16-A.5	To use the strategy *make a table* to solve problems			21-24		3/4	306-307	MP-H66		16.5	16.5	16.5

KEY: I–Intervention   **IF**–Idea File   **KS**–Key Skills   **MP**–More Practice   **PA**–Prac. Activ.   **TA**–Tech. Amaz. Ang.   **TAA**–Tech. Astro Alg.
TDG–Tech. Dr. Gee   **TDL**–Tech. Data Tool Kit   **TFF**–Tech. Frac. Fireworks   **TG**–Tech. Geoboard   **TGA**–Tech. Geo Acad.   **TP**–Tech. Prob.

MATH ADVANTAGE

Individual Record Form

GRADE 6 • Chapters 17-20

Student Name _____

Test	Chapter 17	Chapter 18	Chapter 19	Chapter 20	Chapters 17-20	Cum Chapters 1-20
Date						
Score						

LEARNING GOALS

		Form A CHAPTER TEST				REVIEW OPTIONS					
		Test Items			Criterion	Lesson			Workbooks		
Goal #	Learning Goal	Concept	Skills	PSolv	Scores	page #	PE	TE	P	R	E
17-A.1	To write a ratio to compare two objects	1-2	3-4		3/4	316-317	MP-H66	PA-22A	17.1	17.1	17.1
17-A.2	To find rates and unit rates		5-6	7-8	3/4	318-319	MP-H66		17.2	17.2	17.2
17-A.3	To write ratios and decimals as percents and write percents as decimals and ratios	9-10	11-14	15-16	6/8	320-324	KS-H28	PA-25A	17.3	17.3	17.3
17-A.4	To express parts of a whole as percents		17-18	19-20	3/4	324-325	KS-H28	PA-25A	17.4	17.4	17.4
17-A.5	To write a proportion to solve a problem			21-24	3/4	328-329	MP-H67	TAA-47	17.5	17.5	17.5
18-A.1	To find the percent of a number	5	6-9	1-4	6/9	334-335 336-339	MP-H68	TAA-45	18.1 18.2	18.1 18.2	18.1 18.2
18-A.2	To use percents to make a circle graph and interpret circle graphs that use percent		10-13		3/4	340-341	MP-H68	TDL	18.3	18.3	18.3
18-A.3	To find the amount of discount and the sale price of an item if given the price and the discount rate		14-17	18	3/5	342-343	MP-H69	IF-332	18.4	18.4	18.4
18-A.4	To find simple interest		19-20	21-22	3/4	344-345	MP-H69		18.5	18.5	18.5
19-A.1	To identify similar and congruent figures		1-4		3/4	354-355	KS-H23	TGA-M	19.1	19.1	19.1
19-A.2	To use ratios to identify similar figures	5	6-9	10-11	5/7	356-359	MP-H70	TAA-47	19.2	19.2	19.2
19-A.3	To use similar figures to find the unknown length of a side	12	13-14	15	3/4	360-361	MP-H70	TA-I	19.3	19.3	19.3
19-A.4	To use proportions to measure indirectly	16	17-18	19-20	3/5	362-363	MP-H70		19.4	19.4	19.4

KEY: I–Intervention **IF**–Idea File **KS**–Key Skills **MP**–More Practice **PA**–Prac. Activ. **TA**–Tech. Amaz. Ang. **TAA**–Tech. Astro Alg.
TDG–Tech. Dr. Gee **TDL**–Tech. Data Tool Kit **TFF**–Tech. Frac. Fireworks **TG**–Tech. Geoboard **TGA**–Tech. Geo Acad. **TP**–Tech. Prob.

Individual Record Form

Harcourt Brace School Publishers

MATH ADVANTAGE

Individual Record Form

GRADE 6 • Chapters 17–20 (continued)

Student Name _____

LEARNING GOALS

Goal #	Learning Goal	Form A CHAPTER TEST			Criterion	REVIEW OPTIONS			Workbooks		
		Test Items				Lesson					
		Concept	Skills	PSolv	Scores	page #	PE	TE	P	R	E
20-A.1	To use scale to find dimensions of drawing or actual length	1-2	3-5	6-7	5/7	368-371	MP-H71	TAA-50	20.1	20.1	20.1
20-A.2	To read and use scales on a map	8-9	10-12	13-14	5/7	374-375	MP-H71		20.2	20.2	20.2
20-A.3	To draw a diagram to show directions			15-18	3/4	376-377	MP-H71		20.3	20.3	20.3
20-A.4	To use ratios to determine if similar rectangles are Golden Rectangles		19-22		3/4	378-379	MP-H72		20.4	20.4	20.4

KEY: I–Intervention **IF**–Idea File **KS**–Key Skills **MP**–More Practice **PA**–Prac. Activ. **TA**–Tech. Amaz. Ang. **TAA**–Tech. Astro Alg.
TDG–Tech. Dr. Gee **TDL**–Tech. Data Tool Kit **TFF**–Tech. Frac. Fireworks **TG**–Tech. Geoboard **TGA**–Tech. Geo Acad. **TP**–Tech. Prob.

Individual Record Form

GRADE 6 • Chapters 21-23

Student Name _____

Test	Chapter 21	Chapter 22	Chapter 23	Chapters 21-23	Cum Chapters 1-23
Date					
Score					

LEARNING GOALS

		Form A CHAPTER TEST				REVIEW OPTIONS				Workbooks		
		Test Items			Criterion	Lesson						
Goal #	Learning Goal	Concept	Skills	PSolv	Scores	page #	PE	TE	P	R	E
21-A.1	To change one customary unit of measurement to another	1	2-3	4-5	3/5	388-389	KS-H24	I-392A,B	21.1	21.1	21.1
21-A.2	To change one metric unit of measurement to another	6	7-8	9-10	3/5	390-391	KS-H24		21.2	21.2	21.2
21-A.3	To measure length by using precise measurements		11-14		3/4	392-393	MP-H73		21.3	21.3	21.3
21-A.4	To use a network to find the distance from one place to another		15-16	17-18	3/4	394-395	MP-H73		21.4	21.4	21.4
21-A.5	To find the perimeters of polygons		19-22		3/4	396-397	MP-H73	TG-G	21.5	21.5	21.5
22-A.1	To estimate the area of irregular figures		1-4		3/4	404-405	MP-H74	TG-O	22.1	22.1	22.1
22-A.2	To use a formula to solve problems			5-8	3/4	406-407	MP-H74		22.2	22.2	22.2
22-A.3	To find the area of triangles and parallelograms	9	10-12		3/4	408-411	MP-H74	TG-W	22.3	22.3	22.3
22-A.4	To double the dimensions of a polygon and determine the effects on its perimeter and area		13-16	17-18	4/6	412-413	MP-H75	TG-W	22.4	22.4	22.4
22-A.5	To find the area of a circle		19-20	21-22	3/4	416-417	MP-H75	TA-H	22.5	22.5	22.5
23-A.1	To estimate and find the volume of rectangular and triangular prisms	1-2	3-4	5-6	4/6	422-425	MP-H75	TGA-L	23.1	23.1	23.1
23-A.2	To determine how the volume of a rectangular prism changes when the dimensions change	7-8	9-12		4/6	426-429	MP-H76	TGA-L	23.2	23.2	23.2
23-A.3	To find the volume of a cylinder		13-16	17-18	4/6	432-433	MP-H76	TGA-L	23.3	23.3	23.3
23-A.4	To find the surface area of a rectangular prism		19-22	23-24	4/6	434-435	MP-H76	TGA-L	23.4	23.4	23.4

KEY: I–Intervention   **IF**–Idea File   **KS**–Key Skills   **MP**–More Practice   **PA**–Prac. Activ.   **TA**–Tech. Amaz. Ang.   **TAA**–Tech. Astro Alg.
TDG–Tech. Dr. Gee   **TDL**–Tech. Data Tool Kit   **TFF**–Tech. Frac. Fireworks   **TG**–Tech. Geoboard   **TGA**–Tech. Geo Acad.   **TP**–Tech. Prob.

Individual Record Form

GRADE 6 • Chapters 24-26

Student Name _____

Test	Chapter 24	Chapter 25	Chapter 26	Chapters 24-26	Cum Chapters 1-26
Date					
Score					

LEARNING GOALS

		Form A CHAPTER TEST				REVIEW OPTIONS			Workbooks		
		Test Items			Criterion	Lesson					
Goal #	Learning Goal	Concept	Skills	PSolv	Scores	page #	PE	TE	P	R	E
24-A.1	To classify and compare sets of numbers	5-6	1-4 7-8		6/8	446-447 448-449	MP-H77	I-456A,B	24.1 24.2	24.1 24.2	24.1 24.2
24-A.2	To write fractions as terminating and repeating decimals		9-12		3/4	450-453	MP-H77	I-520A,B	24.3	24.3	24.3
24-A.3	To find a rational number between two rational numbers		13-16	17-18	4/6	454-455	MP-H78		24.4	24.4	24.4
24-A.4	To compare and order rational numbers		19-22	23-24	4/6	456-457	MP-H78	I-24	24.5	24.5	24.5
25-A.1	To add and subtract integers	1 7	2-4 8-10	5-6 11-12	9/12	464-465 468-469	MP-H79	TAA-6	25.1 25.2	25.1 25.2	25.1 25.2
25-A.2	To multiply and divide integers	13 19	14-16 20-22	17-18 23-24	9/12	470-471 472-473	MP-H79	TAA-13	25.3 25.4	25.3 25.4	25.3 25.4
26-A.1	To evaluate numerical and algebraic expressions involving integers		1-4		3/4	478-479	MP-H80	TAA-27	26.1	26.1	26.1
26-A.2	To solve one-step equations and inequalities involving integers	11	5-8 12-14	9-10 15-16	9/12	480-481 484-485	MP-H80	TAA-65	26.2 26.3	26.2 26.3	26.2 26.3
26-A.3	To locate points and graph relations on a coordinate plane		17-20 21-24		6/8	486-489 490-491	MP-H81	TAA-53	26.4 26.5	26.4 26.5	26.4 26.5

KEY: I–Intervention   **IF**–Idea File   **KS**–Key Skills   **MP**–More Practice   **PA**–Prac. Activ.   **TA**–Tech. Amaz. Ang.   **TAA**–Tech. Astro Alg.
TDG–Tech. Dr. Gee   **TDL**–Tech. Data Tool Kit   **TFF**–Tech. Frac. Fireworks   **TG**–Tech. Geoboard   **TGA**–Tech. Geo Acad.   **TP**–Tech. Prob.

Individual Record Form

GRADE 6 • Chapters 27-28

Student Name _____

Test	Chapter 27	Chapter 28	Chapters 27-28	Cum Chapters 1-28
Date				
Score				

LEARNING GOALS / Form A CHAPTER TEST / REVIEW OPTIONS

Goal #	Learning Goal	Test Items Concept	Test Items Skills	Test Items PSolv	Criterion Scores	Lesson page #	PE	TE	Workbooks P	Workbooks R	Workbooks E
27-A.1	To transform figures on a coordinate plane		1-6		4/6	500-503	MP-H82	TGA-I	27.1	27.1	27.1
27-A.2	To find a pattern to solve problems that involve transformations on the coordinate plane			7-10	3/4	504-505	MP-H82	TGA-I	27.2	27.2	27.2
27-A.3	To identify the next two- or three-dimensional figures in a geometric pattern		11-16		4/6	506-507	MP-H82	TA-P	27.3	27.3	27.3
27-A.4	To make shapes for tessellations		17-20		3/4	508-509	MP-H83	TA-P	27.4	27.4	27.4
28-A.1	To identify, extend, and make number patterns with whole numbers and decimals	1-2	3-6	7-8	6/8	516-519	MP-H83		28.1	28.1	28.1
28-A.2	To identify, extend, and make number patterns with fractions	9 14	10-12 15-17	13 18	7/10	522-523 524-525	MP-H83		28.2 28.3	28.2 28.3	28.2 28.3
28-A.3	To identify, extend, and make sequences of integers	19	20-21	22	3/4	526-527	MP-H84		28.4	28.4	28.4

KEY: I–Intervention **IF**–Idea File **KS**–Key Skills **MP**–More Practice **PA**–Prac. Activ. **TA**–Tech. Amaz. Ang. **TAA**–Tech. Astro Alg. **TDG**–Tech. Dr. Gee **TDL**–Tech. Data Tool Kit **TFF**–Tech. Frac. Fireworks **TG**–Tech. Geoboard **TGA**–Tech. Geo Acad. **TP**–Tech. Prob.

Formal Assessment
Class Record Form

School / Teacher	Inventory	Chapter 1	Chapter 2	Chapter 3	Chapters 1-3	Cumulatives 1-3	Chapter 4	Chapter 5	Chapter 6	Chapter 7	Chapters 4-7	Cumulatives 1-7
Criterion Score	26/38	16/24	16/24	16/24	16/24	33/48	16/24	15/22	14/20	16/24	15/22	29/42
NAMES Date												

Formal Assessment
Class Record Form

School / Teacher	Chapter 8	Chapter 9	Chapter 10	Chapters 8-10	Cumulatives 1-10	Chapter 11	Chapter 12	Chapter 13	Chapter 14	Chapters 11-14	Cumulatives 1-14	Chapter 15
Criterion Score	14/20	14/20	14/20	14/20	28/40	12/18	15/22	16/24	15/22	12/18	28/40	16/24
NAMES **Date**												

Formal Assessment
Class Record Form

School	Chapter 16	Chapters 15-16	Cumulatives 1-16	Chapter 17	Chapter 18	Chapter 19	Chapter 20	Chapters 17-20	Cumulatives 1-20	Chapter 21	Chapter 22	Chapter 23
Teacher												
Criterion Score	16/24	15/22	32/46	16/24	15/22	14/20	15/22	14/20	30/44	15/22	15/22	16/24
NAMES Date												

Formal Assessment

Class Record Form

School / Teacher	Chapters 21-23	Cumulatives 1-23	Chapter 24	Chapter 25	Chapter 26	Chapters 24-26	Cumulatives 1-26	Chapter 27	Chapter 28	Chapters 27-28	Cumulatives 1-28
Criterion Score	14/20	28/40	16/24	16/24	16/24	16/24	29/42	14/20	15/22	14/20	26/38
NAMES Date											

Harcourt Brace School Publishers